"The anonymous obituarists who provide the readers of this newspaper with a regular diet of instructive entertainment have a talent for the arresting opening sentence. Here is a perfect example: 'Charles Horace Jones, the South Wales street-corner poet who has died aged 92, stood beside a lamp-post in the High Street at Merthyr Tydfil, Glamorgan, for 45 years with a knuckleduster in his pocket as protection against the Welsh whom his poems had attacked' ... It seems a pity that this diverting and informative series has to come to an end, but the five volumes will continue to give this reader, at least, a peculiar pleasure."

Paul Bailey, *Daily Telegraph*

"Marvellously durable bedside books ... Like some Dantean vision of the great spirits of the age, they wander before us in Massingberd's pages – Red Indian princesses, generals, dons, playboys, all being riotously themselves ... This great soul harvest."

Literary Review

Shortlisted for the inaugural Bollinger Everyman Wodehouse Prize for Comic Writing, 2000.

The Daily Telegraph

FIFTH BOOK OF OBITUARIES

Hugh Massingberd has written or edited some 40 books, including works of genealogical reference, studies of royalty and social history and a series of illustrated volumes on palaces, grand hotels and country houses, great and small. His previous collections of obituaries, *The Daily Telegraph Book of Obituaries: A Celebration of Eccentric Lives*, *The Daily Telegraph Second Book of Obituaries: Heroes and Adventurers*, *The Daily Telegraph Third Book of Obituaries: Entertainers* and *The Daily Telegraph Fourth Book of Obituaries: Rogues*, were all bestsellers and are now available as Pan paperbacks.

Also in this series

The Daily Telegraph
BOOK OF OBITUARIES
A Celebration of Eccentric Lives

The Daily Telegraph
SECOND BOOK OF OBITUARIES
Heroes and Adventurers

The Daily Telegraph
THIRD BOOK OF OBITUARIES
Entertainers

The Daily Telegraph
FOURTH BOOK OF OBITUARIES
Rogues

The Daily Telegraph

FIFTH BOOK OF
OBITUARIES

20th-Century Lives

Edited by
HUGH MASSINGBERD

PAN BOOKS

First published 1999 by Macmillan

This edition published 2000 by Pan Books
an imprint of Macmillan Publishers Ltd
25 Eccleston Place, London SW1W 9NF
Basingstoke and Oxford
Associated companies throughout the world
www.macmillan.co.uk

ISBN 0 330 37111 8

1 3 5 7 9 8 6 4 2

A CIP catalogue record for this book is available from
the British Library.

Typeset by SetSystems Ltd, Saffron Walden, Essex
Printed and bound in Great Britain by
Mackays of Chatham plc, Chatham, Kent

For friends and colleagues
on the Telegraph *obituaries desk*
past and present

Aurea Carpenter	*Adam McEwen*
Will Cohu	*John McEwen*
Claudia FitzHerbert	*Martine Onoh*
Robert Gray	*James Owen*
Diana Heffer	*Katherine Ramsey*
George Ireland	*David Twiston Davies*

The Daily Telegraph

FIFTH BOOK OF OBITUARIES

INTRODUCTION

"I HAVE ridden a yak in the snows of Central Asia," Lieutenant-Colonel the 19th Lord Dunsany, a veteran of the Raj and of Ascendancy Ireland (who died in 1999, aged 92) used to say, "and flown in Concorde at 1,400 miles an hour." The existence of Concorde was made possible by the engineering genius of the Jet Age pioneer Sir Frank Whittle (who died in 1996, aged 89), whose interest in aircraft grew during the First World War. The last surviving consort of the "Big Four" belligerent monarchs in that tragic conflict, Empress Zita of Austria, who shared the historic throne of the Holy Roman Empire, lived on until 1989. And the Great War's last surviving poet, the hitherto underrated Geoffrey Dearmer, died in 1996, aged 103.

These remarkable characters are just a handful of the hundred lives gathered together in this fifth (and final) volume of biographical short stories chosen from what we must now rejoice in calling the Obituaries *page* of *The Daily Telegraph*. (It was only a couple of columns, as I recall, when we started the ball rolling in September 1986.) It would, perhaps, be tempting to indulge in portentous Millennial-speak and suggest that these assorted lives, artfully assembled to form a multi-layered mosaic (no, let's make that *rich tapestry*) of 20th-century experience, reflect the extent of the extraordinary changes that have taken place in the course of a single lifetime – beginning in a pastoral age before motor cars, wireless and kinematography, taking in two World Wars and the eclipse of Empires and ending in the modern era of interplanetary travel and global mass-media. *Et cetera, et cetera* . . .

Yes, well, we can take all that as read, or more unlikely unread. Any artistry in the pages that follow is accidental, or rather attributable – especially in the curious juxtapositions that Fate has thrown up – to a "Greater Power", which is, lest we forget, what the Millennium is really about. For this does not pretend to be a work of history or demography; it is merely a ragbag of individual human diversity, with all its flesh and blood foibles, oddities and bizarre behaviour related in the usual deadpan style. The sub-title, *20th-Century Lives*, is a gesture of homage to the role model I mentioned in my introduction to the first volume in this series, John Aubrey's *Brief Lives*, described by his biographer, Anthony Powell (whose tribute to his Eton contemporary Harold Acton adorns this volume) as "that extraordinary jumble of biography from which later histories have plundered so much of their picturesque detail".

When working on the Obits desk at the *Telegraph* I generally felt too stressed-out (*"We've reached a deadline/A press headline . . ."* as Noël Coward wrote in *Twentieth-Century Blues*) to appreciate that we were working, so to speak Millennially again, at the coalface of history. Yet on re-reading the 12,000 or so obituaries published in the *Telegraph* since 1986, I was struck by how often some reference would be made to the deceased's place in the 20th-century scheme of things. Thus the occasional claim that So-and-So may have been the best, or worst, something or other "of the century" is not a neat bit of editorial hindsight for the purposes of this book.

On the whole, though, I have tried to ignore obvious

"great" players and overfamiliar celebrities and sought to string together an unpredictable medley of colourful, larger-than-life characters whose often unsung contribution to the 20th century – whether for good or, as in the case of James Watts, the American neurosurgeon who popularised the pre-frontal lobotomy, ill – seemed to deserve to be recorded between hard covers. Preferring an oblique approach, I have tended to the view that the marginal spectatorial figures can sometimes see more of the game. Similarly, we can learn more from the ostensibly trivial than from the would-be profound. Hence we shall find more dowagers than dictators, boffins than bureaucrats, popinjays than philosophers – though an exception was made for Michael Oakeshott, who held that life is "a predicament not a journey".

Far from the "Big Picture", this selection might only lay claim to be an idiosyncratic study in miniature, were not "selection" and "study" rather too heavy words to describe the subjective hotch-potch that follows. For it would be absurd to pretend that this is anything remotely approaching a representative cross-section of 20th-century life. None the less, certain categories do seem, however unwittingly, to have formed.

Royalty, for instance, finds itself represented by, apart from Empress Zita, the unassuming Lady May Abel Smith (formerly Princess May of Teck), the last surviving great-great-grandchild of King George III, and by Princess Paul of Yugoslavia, widow of the Regent of that troubled country overthrown in 1941 and sister of Princess Marina, Duchess of Kent. ("Quite nice, my niece-in-law, sometimes," Princess Paul remarked of Princess Michael of Kent, "but I can't bear seeing darling Marina's tiara wrapped up in those *dreadful* sausage rolls.") Princess

Brown Thrush, a leader of the Matinnecock Indian nation
(otherwise a school luncheon server called Lila Harding),
carried high the torch of Native American rights in New
York, where she laid claim – unsuccessfully, alas – to old
hunting-grounds now filled with highways, corner delicatessens and Chinese take-aways.

Among the Aristocracy to appear are the Dowager
Marchioness of Cholmondeley (the former Sybil Sassoon,
an Edwardian beauty painted by Sargent) and Lady
Lindsay of Dowhill, who looked back on her 90th
birthday to a helter-skelter life that had included being
a Bright Young Thing and the third wife of "Bendor",
the 2nd Duke of Westminster: "Rich as Croesus, then
not a penny ... that was all very exciting, I must
say ..." Those mourning the disappearance of the hereditary element in the "People's" House of Lords may
well look back with nostalgia at such Wodehousian
ornaments of the Peerage as the 13th Viscount Massereene and 6th Viscount Ferrard (who pointed out during
a debate on the Brixton Riots of the early 1980s that he
was "the only member who has spoken today who has
had agricultural estates in Jamaica"), the 8th Earl of
Clancarty (editor of *The Flying Saucer Review* and founder
of the Lords UFO Study Group) and the 2nd Lord
Milford, a Communist whose telephone in the Cotswolds
was bugged during the Second World War. "Oh, come
on Constable," he would remonstrate, get off the line!"
A voice would reply: "Sorry, Sir".

Flying the flag for the Empire, we find "the last of
the great imperial statesmen", Sir Roy Welensky, who,
when asked by John Freeman on television's *Face to Face*
whether he knew much about the ordinary African,
retorted: "Considering that when I was a lad I swam

bare-arsed in the Makabusi with many piccaninnies . . . I think I can say I know something of the Africans." Representing the Raj are the Kiplingesque Philip Mason (himself a *Telegraph* obituarist); Countess Wavell, the last surviving Vicereine; and Lady Alexandra Metcalfe, daughter of Lord Curzon and widow of Major "Fruity" Metcalfe of Skinner's Horse.

Fresh Heroes and Adventurers not featured in the earlier volume of that name in the series now include "Mad Mike" Calvert of the Chindits ("one of the finest fighting soldiers produced by the British Army in the Second World War"); Odette Hallowes, GC, of Special Operations Executive; the indomitable war correspondent (and third wife of Ernest Hemingway), Martha Gellhorn; and the champion of Tito's Yugoslav Partisans, Sir Fitzroy Maclean, 1st Bt. The dashing Sir Fitzroy also dabbled in politics, though politicians – for reasons surely not necessary to spell out – receive fairly short shrift in this volume. (*Rogues* did them justice, I felt.)

Some political insights, though, emerge from the obituaries of Gleb Kerensky (who struggled for more than 60 years to force the realities of the Soviet tyranny upon the uncomprehending English mind and was enraged by the criminal complacency of visiting Socialist VIPs); Lord Brockway, the indefatigable crusader against racial discrimination; Lady Elliot of Harwood (whose father, Sir Charles Tennant, had been born in 1823), the first woman, other than the Sovereign, to speak in the House of Lords; and Rose Fitzgerald Kennedy, the formidable matriarch of the Irish-American political dynasty. Of the diplomatists, none cuts a nobler figure than Count Edward Raczynski, spirit of the exiled Poles; nor a more controversial one than the "Pocket Hercules of the Foreign Office", Sir Frank Roberts, who advised Churchill and Attlee at Yalta.

It is a relief to turn to the religious life represented by Bertha Lindsay, last Eldress of the Shakers (and author of the cookbook *Seasoned With Grace*); Lord MacLeod of Fuinary, founder of the Iona Community; the complex and controversial Bishop Mervyn Stockwood; and the beagling clubman, Monsignor Alfred Gilbey, the last Roman Catholic priest to be ordained in his own patrimony. The 20th-century substitute religion of Freudian analysis is given some healthy whacks by Dr William Sargant, while Dr Benjamin Spock was finally driven to remind readers of his *Common Sense Book of Baby and Child Care* (the world's best-selling volume after The Bible) that discipline might also have a part to play.

From the other learned professions came the head-masters Colonel E. A. Loftus (who complained, before his death aged 103, that he had never found the time to write his autobiography); "Jack" Meyer of Millfield ("the only comprehensive school that really works"); and the grammar-school champion Lord James of Rusholme ("A man who had acquired a deep knowledge and understanding of de Tocqueville, Matthew Arnold and John Stuart Mill was not to be shaken by the hortations of Mrs Shirley Williams"). On the bench we find Sir James Comyn (described by Sir John Mortimer, QC, as the only judge he had encountered who summed up fairly) and the erratic Judge Michael Argyle, who, as the obituary notes, "sometimes attracted public criticism", as when he handed a suspended sentence to a barman convicted of attempted rape. "You come from Derby," the Judge said, "which is my part of the world. Off you go, and don't come back."

Industry, in the shape of the internal combustion engine, is represented by Henry Ford II. The Rothschilds field Baron Philippe, the dynamic viticulturist, and the philanthropic "Dollie", the hitherto little-known bene-factress of the emerging Jewish state of Israel. Jack ("All out!") Dash, the Communist agitator who helped to wreck London's Docks, fails to represent the Workers in death as in life.

When the trouble-makers have departed it is the buildings, or at least some of them, that remain and to represent Architecture we are not confronted with the usual suspects of Modernism but an unknighted Goth and Classicist, Stephen Dykes Bower. There is also the architectural historian Sir John Summerson and some pillars of the Heritage movement – James Lees-Milne of the National Trust's Country House Scheme (and inci-dentally, the best diarist of the 20th century); the publisher and artist Sir Brian Batsford; Anne Countess of Rosse, a prime mover in the foundation of the Georgian Group and the Victorian Society; and the Marquess of Bath, the first Stately Home showman.

Out in the Country (where did the word "country-side" come from?) we find the foxhunter Lord Daresbury, the shooter Sir Joseph ("Partridge Joe") Nickerson, the riders Charlie Smirke and the Duke of Albuquerque, the golfer Joyce Wethered (Lady Heathcoat Amory), the model squire William Bulwer-Long and the least-known Mitford Sister, Pamela Jackson – described by her father as "the best judge of a pig's face in the South of England".

Style is probably the most lasting index of Time and two key arbiters of taste in the 20th century to feature here are Nancy Lancaster ("Paint it," she once commanded a decorator, "the colour of elephant's breath") and David Hicks. From the world of fashion came Diana Vreeland, Erté, Alexander Plunket Greene (husband and business partner of Mary Quant) and "Bunny" Roger, the bachelor dandy who claimed to have advanced through enemy lines in the Italian campaign of the Second World War with his chiffon scarf flying as he brandished a copy of *Vogue*.

As for Art, the obits begin, appropriately enough, with that authority on the transience of fame, Andy Warhol; later we encounter the cartoonists Charles Addams and Willie Rushton, the potter Dame Lucie Rie and the artists' model, Henrietta Moraes, "ever a stranger to moderation", as Christopher Gibbs puts it in a tribute. Under the Big Top in the sky is the circus impresario Dick Chipperfield, whereas above Ronnie Scott's Jazz Club the proprietor may yet still be exhorting "Let's join hands and contact the living."

On the Stage are Athene Seyler, the last surviving link with the Victorian theatre (and subject to one of Sir John Gielgud's most celebrated *gaffes*); Evelyn "Boo" Laye, who sang "I'll See You Again" in Coward's *Bitter Sweet*; and George Abbott, the Broadway musical producer, who, when asked how a new script of his was progressing, replied: "Hard to say, but it's better than most 106-year-old writers are doing."

Up on the Silver Screen there is room for such Hollywood legends as Lana ("the Sweater Girl") Turner, discovered in Schwab's drug-store on Sunset Boulevard, as well as the character players Kathleen Harrison and Michael Ward, master of the camp one-liner. The Television personalities include Lord Grade, George Burns, the wrestler "Big Daddy" and the snobbish "Annie

Walker" of *Coronation Street* (otherwise the actress Doris Speed). The wireless was the preferred medium for the contrasting voices of John Snagge of the BBC ("I don't know who's ahead – it's either Oxford or Cambridge.") and Kenny Everett. "Radio", he used to say, "is a good place to work if you are not really a jolly person, but want to appear to be one."

The range of writers encompasses "the Irish Chekhov" Sean O'Faolain and the novelist Molly Keane; the Sci-Fi supremo Isaac Asimov and the aesthete Sir Harold Acton; the poets Sir Stephen Spender and Charles Horace Jones (whose eccentricity strains credulity); the eye-opening foodie Elizabeth David; the Reverend W. Awdry, creator of *Thomas the Tank Engine*; the oral chronicler Tony Parker and the "from below" historian E. P. Thompson; and Philip O'Connor, author of one of the strangest autobiographies of modern times.

Finally, there has to be a song – preferably *not* sung by the vexatious Dorothy Squires but at least written by Irving Berlin. Berlin, who had actually outlived the copyright of his first hit, "Alexander's Ragtime Band" (1911) by the time of his death in 1989, wrote, as Philip Larkin put it, "not so much songs as bits of the 20th century".

Before calling it a day and slipping off stage, I must pay due tribute again to my successors as Obituaries Editor at the *Telegraph* after I left the chair in 1994, the dedicatees of the fourth volume, (David) Lewis Jones, Kate Summerscale and Christopher Howse. This fifth volume is dedicated to other friends and colleagues on the desk, past and present – namely, in alphabetical sequence, Aurea Carpenter, Will Cohu, Claudia Fitz-Herbert, Robert Gray, Diana Heffer, George Ireland,

Introduction

Adam McEwen, John McEwen (junior), Martine Onoh, James Owen, Katherine Ramsey and David Twiston Davies. Special thanks to them and the dedicatees of the earlier volumes, Teresa Moore, Philip Warner, Edward Bishop, John Winton, Andrew Barrow and Eric Shorter.

All of those mentioned above have been of great help in the piecing together of this volume, especially Teresa Moore, who again took on the task of photocopying and pasting up the material (in the good old way) for publication in book form. And invaluable contributions were made by, among others, Mark Bence-Jones, Adrian Berry, John Casey, Jonathan Cecil, Robert Chalmers, Sebastian Conran, Laurence Cotterell, Simon Courtauld, the Duchess of Devonshire, Philip Eade, Dave Gelly, Christopher Gibbs, Mark Girouard, Jim Godbolt, Dean Godson, Robert Golden, the Earl of Gowrie, Derek Granger, Tim Heald, the late David Holloway, the late Dr Kenneth Hutchin, Ian Irvine, John Jolliffe, Charles Kidd, Gerard Kiley, James Knox, the late James Lees-Milne, Elisabeth Luard, Major-General James Lunt, Candida Lycett Green, John McEwen (senior), the late Philip Mason, Charles Nevin, John Oaksey, Jane O'Grady, Anthony Powell, Geraldine Ranson, Bronwen Riley, John Martin Robinson, Gavin Stamp, E. W. Swanton, Nicholas Usherwood, Martin Van Der Weyer, Anna Vaux, Hugo Vickers, Captain Ronnie Wallace, Ian Waller, David Watkin, Geoffrey Wheatcroft, David Williamson and Sir Peregrine Worsthorne.

HUGH MASSINGBERD
London, March 1999

ANDY WARHOL

ANDY WARHOL, who has died aged 58, was celebrated as the inventor of "Pop Art" and for his pronouncement that "everybody will be world famous for 15 minutes".

He was born in McKeesport, Pennsylvania, on August 6 1928, the son of Czechoslovakian immigrants, and brought up in the Czech ghetto of the city. His father was away a lot on coalmining business and all Warhol remembered from that time was "babushkas and overalls on the clothes lines".

As a child he suffered three nervous breakdowns, but he was from the first outstandingly talented as an artist. He studied at the Carnegie Institute of Technology from 1945, graduating BFA in 1949.

He then went to New York City and got a job as an illustrator for *Glamour* magazine. Over the next 10 years he became one of the most successful of American commercial artists.

As a commercial artist he was famous before the public knew him, and was also a collector of art and financial supporter of artists – notably his contemporaries Jasper Jones and Robert Rauschenberg – before he was himself known as a fine artist.

But he had always wanted to be a painter. The question was how. He was respected in New York artistic circles as an intellectual prodigy, the man who knew the answer to every question he asked and it was this intelligence that seems to have held him back from committing himself as an artist in his own right for so long.

Rauschenberg summed up Warhol's dilemma when he wrote: "Andy had a kind of facility which I think drove him to develop and even invent ways to make his art so as not to be cursed by that talented head. His works are like monuments trying to free himself of his talents. Even his choice of subject matter is to get away from anything easy. Whether it's a chic decision or a disturbing decision about which object he picks, it's not my aesthetic choice. And there's strength in that."

Warhol at first concentrated on making paintings derived from strip comics and advertisements. Part of his motive was in common with other New York avant gardists of that late 1950s time to undermine the solemn artistic claims made for the prevailing fashion of abstract expressionist painting.

Abstract expressionism was widely regarded as an ultimate baring of the artistic soul, and pop art's machine-like detachment challenged such portentousness. Warhol took this to the extreme of painting multiple images of Campbéll's soup cans and Coca-Cola bottles. In a matter of months these hymns of praise to banality were adorning the walls of the smart set as the latest thing in artistic refinement.

Warhol's attitude remained dandified in its detachment. He had outdone the surrealist in making the ordinary extraordinary. He pressed home the point by producing equally detached, silk screen images of contemporary disasters – a car crash, an air crash, an electric chair scene – which no less quickly, and ironically, became pieces of fashionable decoration.

Warhol produced these paintings using a team of

helpers at his studio, which he called "the Factory" in emphasis. If there was an ironic side to this machine-like method, there was also a no less disturbingly honest simplicity in the way it rejoiced in the latest techniques and attitudes brought about by technology.

His popularisation of the screen print method revolutionised Western graphics, as did his use of commercial subject matter. "The reason I am painting this way is because I want to be a machine," he said. "Whatever I do and do machine-like, is because it is what I want to do. I think it would be terrific if everybody was alike."

Warhol treated success with no less detachment. He began to record everything in his life with the aid of the new cassette recorders and videos.

He made his most publicised statement – "In the future everybody will be world famous for 15 minutes" – and realised the truth of it for a succession of unknowns through his underground films. He even got shot himself by one of his "superstars" and almost died, but characteristically viewed this appalling event with a detachment that allowed the photographer Richard Avedon to make a glamorous record of the stitched wound.

He opened a nightclub called the Exploding Plastic Inevitable, which had a famous house band called The Exploding Galaxy. The band became one of the most influential in the history of rock music.

In these various ways, including the publication of a less influential magazine called *Interview*, Warhol manipulated society itself providing an endless source of ideas, from helium balloons for children to the "gender-bender" fashions of the 1970s and every aspect of commercial design. He himself continued to be as seemingly detached as always, his hair dyed a more ghost-like white, his face more of a mask, his position more paradoxical with every year that past.

Andy Warhol may reasonably be considered the most influential artist of his time, the most intelligent witness to the post-industrial world of ever increasing technological change, and at the same time perhaps a presager of our death by the machine.

"I still care about people", he said, "but it would be so much easier not to care . . . It's too hard to care . . . I don't like to touch things . . . That's why my work is so different from myself. If you want to know all about Andy Warhol, just look at the surface of my paintings and films and me, and there I am. There's nothing behind it."

February 22 1987

COLONEL E. A. LOFTUS

COLONEL E. A. LOFTUS who has died in Harare, aged 103, was an energetic schoolmaster with a place in *Guinness Book of Records* as the oldest teacher and longest-serving civil servant in the world.

He began teaching at York in 1901 and finally retired in Zambia after being "a pedagogue for 74 years", according to his entry in *Who's Who*. In that time he was headmaster of one of the country's first co-educational grammar schools, a local councillor and an inveterate committee joiner who served in both World Wars and wrote several books and numerous articles.

Ernest Achey Loftus was born in Hull in 1884, the son of a master mariner sailing tea clippers to Australia. He was a chorister at Beverley Minster before going on to Archbishop Holgate's School, York, where he began his teaching career at 17.

Five years later, he became a geography master at Palmer's School in Gray's, Essex, where he joined the Cadet Corps and began his long association with the Territorial Army on being commissioned in the Essex Regiment in 1913. After the outbreak of war in 1914 he was sent first to Gallipoli and then to Egypt from both of which he was invalided home. In 1916, he became Adjutant of an NCOs' School at Halton, Wendover, then helped the Derby Yeomanry to convert infantry before becoming a staff education officer for the 67th Division.

For the next year, he was involved in organising the non-military education of 10,000 young recruits until he was passed fit for active service again in July 1918 and posted with his old regiment to the Arras area. After the Armistice he commanded one of the first contingents – 1,000 miners and a few schoolmasters – to be demobilised.

Apart from a few months in 1921 when he was remobilised as a temporary major to deal with trouble which never materialised during a coal strike, he remained a Territorial, commanding the 6th Essex Regiment from 1925 to 1929. On retirement he was appointed OBE, and a Deputy Lieutenant of Essex.

On returning to Palmer's School in 1918 he earned an external degree at Trinity College, Dublin, and went on to become head of Southend-on-Sea's Junior School and the town's Assistant Director of Education before taking over as the first Headmaster of Barking Abbey School in 1922.

Not fully stretched by the care of a new school, a young family and Territorial duties, Loftus threw himself into a host of additional activities.

He was the founding secretary of the Essex Playing Fields Association, a governor of several other schools and president of the Barking Rotarians. He also wrote a history of Barking Abbey and contributed scenes to local pageants.

In the early 1930s he attracted widespread attention with a series of vigorous articles in the *Daily Express* attacking the tyranny of universities through the school certificate syllabus, which, he said, crammed children with useless information. Even examination fees of 7s 6d per pupil amounted to a waste of £150,000 a year, he thundered.

More to the point, he emphasised the importance of children appreciating the value of good health. Coining the phrase "Health Science" he called for specially trained physical education instructors, for whose training course he was later to draw up the first syllabus.

In his book *Education and the Citizen* (1935), he unveiled a rosy future with an anomaly-free state school system. By the year 2,000 there would be a new England where people would "happily and beautifully" live after studying "civics", he predicted.

Thirty-five years later, however, his enthusiasm had been moderated by the reduction of Barking Abbey to a comprehensive and, in his last years, he saw Mrs Thatcher as the one person to rekindle a sense of discipline in Britain.

Despite his activity in forming cadet corps and raising regiments for a new war, Loftus was considered too old for active service in 1939. But he still managed to get to France where he commanded No. 13 group of Pioneer Corps, a motley group of anti-Mussolini Italians and others, whom he eventually had to abandon in the Dunkirk evacuation. He escaped from Rouen, disguised as a Breton onion-seller.

Placed in command of No. 31 Group, he was active in London during the Blitz and was responsible for the creation of smoke screens at Derby which successfully prevented the Rolls-Royce factory from being bombed.

Loftus returned to Barking Abbey until reluctantly retiring at 65, when he found himself in greater need than ever of things to do. He became a vice-president of Thurrock Council, a controller of local defence and also did some part-time teaching. But the experience of having his pension halted if he did too much paid work led him in 1953 to become English master at the élite Prince of Wales School in Nairobi, where one of his two sons lived.

Three years later, he moved to Nyasaland and then briefly to Uganda before going to the newly independent Zambia where his ultra-traditional methods achieved a remarkable number of passes at O- and A-level for many who are now the country's leaders. In 1975 he retired after 12 years and was appointed CBE.

The work in Africa was easier than at home, he explained, beause there were no discipline problems. His pupils in Zambia, aged 18 to 20, were keen to absorb all they could. Teaching could never be enough for Loftus, of course, and he edited several textbooks and wrote *A Visual History of Africa* which is still used in schools more than 30 years later.

He also continued to be a periodic contributor to the Letters column of *The Daily Telegraph*, usually on the subjects of discipline or English grammar. And, on finally moving with his son to Rhodesia, he began to study for another degree by correspondence but had to give up after breaking his wrists in a car crash. To overcome the resulting problems he taught a nurse to read and write so she could act as his secretary at the Nazareth House Home run by Roman Catholic nuns where he lived.

Loftus still managed to return home, becoming a Freeman of Hull in 1968 and making his last trip at 98, when he said he would never live in England again because the climate would kill him.

A well-built man of 5ft 10ins who continued to play tennis in his 80s, Col. Loftus was a heavy smoker in his younger days and liked to drink, though never to excess. He made a point of going for a walk every day. Among his many other accomplishments was keeping a diary – a crisp account of each day's activities – throughout his life.

Although his endless activities led him to become estranged from his wife Elsie, whom he married in 1916 and who died in 1979, Loftus wrote an account of her ancestors, *A History of a Branch of the Cole Family*. He did the research for a companion volume on the Loftus family but, as with his proposed autobiography, never found the time to write it.

July 14 1987

HENRY FORD II

HENRY FORD II, who has died aged 70, was for 34 years the absolute ruler of the Ford Motor Company, which was founded by his grandfather, the first Henry Ford, and through its phenomenally successful Model-T had a key role in the development of mass consumerism.

When he became its president in 1945, at the age of 28 and after a two-year power struggle with the Rasputin-like figure of Harry Bennett – a former prize-fighter and a favourite of his grandfather – Ford found himself in command of a dying giant. The company was losing $1 million a day; but he rescued it from the brink of disaster and built it up to become the world's fourth largest multinational corporation.

An impression of the man, and of the importance to him of those early years at the helm, may be derived from his table talk. "Would you rather have Aids or a Third World War?" he enquired of a neighbour at dinner shortly before his death. "I'm not sure," replied the lady, "Aids, I suppose." Ford disagreed: "Oh, I'd rather have another war. I had a good war last time round. I enjoyed that war."

If he felt happy when he woke up in the morning he would look at himself in the shaving mirror and say: "I am the king, and the king can do no wrong." Certainly he lived and ran his company in regal style, but not everyone thought him infallible.

Lee Iacocca, for example, who was credited with much of the company's success in the 1960s and 1970s – notably the Mustang car, which broke all sales records

9

— was bitterly critical of Ford after being forced to resign by him in 1978, on the grounds that "sometimes you just don't like somebody".

Henry Ford II was born at Detroit in 1917, the elder son of Edsel Ford, who was dominated by his father (the first Henry) and did not assert himself during his time as president of the company; the family was of Irish Protestant stock. He was educated at the Detroit University School, at Hotchkiss School, Connecticut, and at Yale University.

At Yale he began to read engineering in preparation for his expected role at Ford but gave it up after a year. Unlike his grandfather he had no mechanical understanding of motor cars: he would later say that while the first Henry was an expert in motor engineering, the second's skill was in "human engineering". His next subject, accordingly, was sociology; but he failed to graduate when it was discovered that he had paid someone else to write his thesis.

This early ignominy always rankled with Ford, and in 1972 he was delighted when his second wife persuaded the actress Merle Oberon to charm Kingman Brewster, at that time president of Yale, into giving him an honorary doctorate of law.

Ford had been made a director of the family firm in 1938, when he was still a student, and on leaving Yale he went to work at its River Rouge plant in Michigan, supposedly to learn about the business from the bottom up. His interest was at best desultory, however, and in 1941, when it seemed he was about to be called up, he volunteered for the Navy, spending two years on shore duty and rising to the rank of lieutenant.

When Edsel Ford died in 1943 the American

Government (which had a contract with Ford Motor Company for thousands of aeroplanes) released Henry to return to his company, where he was elected vice-president in charge of sales and promotion. Two years later he became president, after a frightening struggle with Bennett and his henchmen during which he always took a pistol with him to the office.

Bennett's succession was finally blocked by Ford's mother, who threatened her octogenarian father-in-law with the sale of her large block of shares if her son were not preferred; and Henry Ford II's succession was urged by President Roosevelt, who feared for the company's future under Henry Ford I (who died two years later).

Ford made his company a success by divesting it of the many sidelines instituted by his father; by cultivating good relations with the unions, and by recruiting a new generation of managers – a group of ex-Air Force officers, including Robert McNamara (later Defence Secretary to Presidents Kennedy and Johnson and president of the World Bank), who wanted to continue working together in civilian life and who were known as the "whiz kids".

Within four years the company was selling more than a million cars a year, and by 1953 it had overtaken Chrysler to stand second only to General Motors, a position it has held ever since. At the same time as he was building up his firm Ford was attracting attention outside the motor industry with his lectures at universities on social, industrial and environmental problems. In 1970 he published a collection of such lectures in a book called *The Human Environment and Business*.

In various areas he put his theories into practice – in

that of pollution, for example, by insisting that oil companies increase their production of unleaded petrol; and at Ford by hiring illiterate blacks from the ghettoes, "to give people who have been held back by prejudice and poverty a chance to earn a decent life". He was greatly disturbed by the Detroit riots of 1967, which he thought "the most serious domestic crisis since the Civil War". He did much philanthropic work, in Detroit and farther afield, largely through the Ford Foundation, of which he was a trustee from 1943 to 1976.

In 1960 the company acquired its first plant in Britain, at Dagenham, Essex, at a cost of £120 million. Its experiences here were not always happy. After strikes at Halewood in 1972 Ford declared; "Everything that comes out of Britain is junk. I won't put another cent in there."

He changed his mind, however, when the Government gave him a grant of £150 million; and in due course the British operation became the most profitable in the Ford empire, saving the parent company more than once. In 1978 Ford was able to beat the Labour Government on its pay policy sanctions.

The end of Ford's career was marred not only by the rancorous feud with Lee Iacocca but also by allegations, which he contrived to shrug off, that he had received $2 million cash in bribes from Imelda Marcos. He also caused annoyance in the company by his lavish personal expenses, his arbitrary decision-making and various minor scandals involving alcohol and sex.

When he was arrested in California for being drunk in charge of a car he complimented his jailers on their newly built prison: "A nice-looking place – I'd like to buy it." His passenger was Kathleen DuRoss, a blonde model some decades his junior who later became his third wife. In the words of the journalist Nicholas Von Hoffman, Ford seemed to be "a 60-year-old adolescent". He resigned control of the company in 1979 and retired in 1982.

Ford lived at Palm Beach, Florida, and had estates at Grosse Point Farms (a suburb of Detroit) and at Henley-on-Thames. His favourite pastime was golf, but he was also a keen art collector, concentrating on Impressionist nudes.

He was married three times – to Anne McDonnell (divorced 1964), Cristina Austin (divorced 1976) and Kathleen DuRoss – and is survived by his wife, two daughters and a son, Edsel Bryant Ford II.

September 30 1987

COUNTESS WAVELL

COUNTESS WAVELL, who has died a few days after her 100th birthday, was the last surviving Vicereine of India and the last non-royal member of the Imperial Order of the Crown of India.

Her late husband, Field Marshal Earl Wavell, the Second World War commander in the Middle East, India and the South-West Pacific, was the penultimate Viceroy of India, serving from 1943 until 1947 when he was succeeded by Lord Mountbatten.

Lady Wavell, a large, humorous, motherly woman of Irish descent who was called "Queenie" by her husband, always followed the drum like a good soldier's wife, creating a comfortable domestic atmosphere wherever she went. She worked with vigour and a refreshing common sense for the welfare of troops under her husband's command and continued to show the same qualities as Vicereine when she became president of the Indian Red Cross and chairman for India of the Women's Voluntary Service.

Before giving Churchill a definite answer when he was offered the Viceroyalty, Wavell asked leave to consult his wife and thought of how "she would obviously make an excellent Vicereine". In his journal, the Viceroy frequently referred with admiration to his wife's gifts as a hostess.

The Wavells clearly adored one another, though according to Wavell's somewhat unlikely friend, the aesthete and social butterfly "Chips" Channon, he "rarely listened to what she said".

As Vicereine, Lady Wavell came well up to her husband's expectations, except that, being rather vague, she was inclined to be unpunctual. "The Japanese could almost be in the suburbs of Calcutta, but she still seldom surfaced before eleven," recalled one ADC.

"D'you realise you're keeping half a *sub-continent* waiting?" Wavell once bellowed at her as she came late aboard the Viceregal Dakota in which they were about to take off for Calcutta. Her response to her husband's occasional outbursts was to exclaim in a manner at once plaintive and admonitory: "*Archie!*"

Eugenie Marie Quirk was born in 1887, the year of Queen Victoria's Golden Jubilee, the only child of Colonel John Owen Quirk, who commanded the 1st Battalion of the Welch Regiment in the mid-1890s.

She married in 1915 Major Archibald Wavell of the Black Watch, while he was on leave from the Ypres

Salient. The following year she braved the War Office, the Foreign Office and the Central Powers to join her husband in Tiflis, travelling by Norway, Sweden, Finland and St Petersburg where she heard at the Opera the announcement that the Tsar had abdicated.

Between the wars she was a keen rider to hounds, side-saddle, and, having excellent hands, could be trusted on difficult mounts. When her husband was Commander-in-Chief in the Middle East it was typical of Lady Wavell to do anonymous stints serving up meals at the Other Ranks Club at Gezira. She was active in several Army welfare schemes, such as leave camps for young soldiers on leave with nowhere to go.

In India she used her considerable charms to persuade maharajahs and business tycoons to contribute funds to The Wavell open air theatre for the troops' entertainment by ENSA. Peter Coats, an effete aide (known as "Petticoats") who worked closely with Lady Wavell on these projects, said: "She was loyal, funny and knew how to get her own way when the cause was worthwhile. A very feminine, sometimes maddening, always enchanting, woman."

Another ADC, Lord Euston (the present Duke of Grafton) received encouragement in his painting at Lady Wavell's art classes in the basement of the Viceroy's house. To all the many opportunities for charitable work which fell to her position she added personal touches of kindness, such as housing on the Viceregal estate young officers posted to Delhi.

Back in Britain after leaving India she continued her charitable work as a vice-president of the Soldiers', Sailors' and Airmen's Families Association. She took an active interest in arrangements for an official biography of her husband, who died in 1950, and her comments on some of the candidates proposed were individual and perceptive.

On Christmas Eve, 1953, Lady Wavell suffered a personal tragedy when her only son, Archie John, the 2nd (and last) Earl Wavell, was killed during the Mau Mau campaign in Kenya. She founded the Wavell Memorial Prizes for outstanding Army boys in memory of her son who, though he lost a hand with the Chindits in Burma, remained an enthusiast for outdoor pursuits especially moutaineering.

She is survived by three daughters.

October 14 1987

BARON PHILIPPE DE ROTHSCHILD

BARON PHILIPPE DE ROTHSCHILD, who has died in Paris aged 85, was not only one of the great viticulturists of the century, but also a man of wider cultivation – a poet, scholar and sportsman.

In 1973, having dedicated 65 years of his life to his Château Mouton in Bordeaux – for most of which he was obliged, first by a wartime vow and then by his health, to remain teetotal – he achieved for his wine the coveted rank of *premier grand cru*. In 1982 he attempted to raise it still further when he requested a change in its status from a wine to a work of art, so as to avoid paying President Mitterrand's increased capital gains tax.

Such a gesture – an entirely appropriate one for

oenophiles – was typical of Rothschild's flamboyant arrogance, and of his supremely aesthetic approach to life. In 1979, for example, he argued the superiority of a Channel Bridge over a Tunnel on purely artistic grounds, as "one of those inspiring follies that leave the prosaic and the reasonable gaping".

In the field of literature Rothschild was best known for his admirable translations from the English. His bilingual anthology of Elizabethan poetry published in 1969 was awarded a special prize from the Académie Française and became a university textbook; and he translated Marlowe's *Doctor Faustus* and *Tamburlaine*. He also translated plays by Christopher Fry, two of which were successfully staged in Paris: *The Dark is Light Enough* and *The Lady's Not for Burning*. In 1978 he published a book of his own poems, *Le Pressoir Perdu*, and in 1981 an autobiographical history of Mouton, *Vive La Vigne*.

In his youth he was responsible with his father for building the Theatre Pigalle, of which he was the sole director between 1928 and 1931, during which time he put on many successful plays by Sacha Guitry, Jules Romains, Giraudoux and others. He was also active in the foundation of the famous repertory group Cartel des Quatre.

He worked in music, too, providing in 1950 the lyrics for the *Ballet Vendange*, which had music by Darius Milhaud and was first performed at the Nice Opera during a festival celebrating the composer's 80th birthday; and in the cinema, producing in 1932 *Lac Aux Dames*, one of the first French "talkies", directed by Marc Allégret and based on a story by Colette.

Rothschild's other great love was sport, particularly

motor racing. He was a frequent competitor in the Grand Prix of Monaco and won the Grand Prix of Saint-Sebastian, Germany, and the 24-hour Le Mans race; and he twice managed to bring back the Coupe de France sailing trophy. He also leaves his mark in the field of medicine, for he was a leading light in the foundation of the Curie (Radium) Institute in Paris, which has for many years been in the forefront of cancer research.

Philippe Georges de Rothschild was born at Paris in 1902, the son of Baron Henri de Rothschild and Mathilde de Weisweiller, and educated at the Lycée Condorcet and the Faculty of Science at the University.

When Rothschild took over the Pauillac estate of Château Mouton Rothschild in 1922, at the age of 20, he had been sent there as much because his family were unsure what to do with the young playboy as because he had any great interest in wine. But Rothschild had fallen in love with the place as a boy aged 16, when he fled there to escape the threat of the Germans, and now found himself with an estate that was neglected but had great potential.

In the great 1855 classification of Bordeaux wines, Château Mouton had been described as the first of the second growths. To Rothschild the rightful place for Mouton was with the first growths. The case was made worse because Château Lafite, owned by a rival branch of the Rothschild clan, was one of the four favoured firsts.

It took Rothschild more than 50 years to right that wrong, when in 1973 Jacques Chirac, then Minister of Agriculture, announced that Château Mouton Rothschild would join the élite of first growths. It was the only change ever made to the 1855 classification, and could never have been made without Rothschild's persistence.

He had to prove the wine all the time. From the start he took the defiant motto: "First I cannot be, second I scorn to be, I am Mouton." His wine was going to be different. The first change he made to the running of the estate was to institute château bottling, which is now almost universal.

Another innovation was to invite famous artists to create different labels for each vintage of his wine, a practice he introduced in 1924, though the next design was not until 1945, one of the finest claret years of the century. Since then the artists he has employed have included Dali, Picasso and Warhol (*qv*).

From the original estate of Mouton, Rothschild increased his domain many times. He bought what is now Château Mouton Baronne Philippe in 1933, and in 1970 the estate of Château Clerc-Milon. But his biggest expansion was after a run of disastrous vintages in 1930, 1931 and 1932, when Mouton Cadet was born – the junior wine of the estate.

He also created at Mouton one of the finest wine museums in the world, which includes antiquities from Egypt and ancient China as well as a superb collection of wine silver and some small wine associated paintings. The whole is displayed with the immense taste and style so characteristic of Rothschild – apart, perhaps, from *Milady Vine*, the dubious memoirs written jointly with his mistress, Joan Littlewood, the theatrical director.

In 1942 he fled from occupied France to join General de Gaulle (whom he did not like) in London, and later landed in Normandy as Liaison Officer with the Free French Forces. At the end of the war he was stationed in Germany, where he was in charge of liberating prisoners from the German camps.

His first marriage was to the Countess Elisabeth Pelletier de Chambure, who was deported to the Nazi extermination camp of Ravensbrück in June 1944 and died there less than a year later. In 1954 he married Pauline Fairfax-Potter, an American socialite. He is survived by his wife and his daughter.

January 21 1988

DICK CHIPPERFIELD

DICK CHIPPERFIELD, who has died aged 83, was the patriarch of the travelling circus and menagerie dynasty whose business dates back to the reign of Charles II.

One of the world's most experienced animal men – who in his time trained such beasts as bulls, camels, llamas, zebras, hippos, giraffes, ostriches, sea lions and chimpanzees, as well as lions, tigers, leopards, polar, black and brown bears – Chipperfield established the family circus as one of "the Big Three" after the Second World War alongside Bertram Mills's and Billy Smart's.

Chipperfield was particularly proud of his record in breeding wild animals and in helping to maintain stocks of endangered species. In the 1940s he managed to bring 20 elephants to England from Ceylon – the biggest group of pachyderms ever seen in this country.

With his showman's boots, commodious fur coat and barking tones, Chipperfield cut a formidable figure. He had no time for the "busybodies" who claimed that cruelty was synonymous with the Big Top; even as a boy, he would recall, he had been badgered by "white-haired old biddies telling me how wicked circuses were".

Richard Chipperfield was born in 1904, the eldest of five children of his namesake, an equally famous circus and menagerie operator in the first three decades of this century. Young Dick's brother Jimmy was to leave the family circus in the mid-1950s and carve out a new career in "drive-through safari parks" at Longleat (for the Marquess of Bath – *qv*) and elsewhere.

At the age of five Dick Chipperfield was performing as a clown in his father's fairground variety show which he took out on the road alongside that latest Edwardian entertainment rage, the bioscope – forerunner of the modern cinema. But the Chipperfields, whose ancestors toured with puppies, monkeys and seals in the 17th century, were soon back in the traditional circus and menagerie business, joining forces with the Purchase Menagerie.

In the early 1930s, having already trained ponies and elephants, Dick Chipperfield began working with wild animals and rescued Tom Purchase from a severe mauling in the big cage although the victim died of his wounds a fortnight later. Chipperfield graduated to showing the menagerie's wild animals, including a group of bears, wolves and hyenas, and in 1938, together with his siblings, took over the running of the family circus on the retirement of his father.

After the Second World War the Chipperfield show extended its circuit to include Ireland; settled in South Africa for three years; and, more recently, enjoyed several successful seasons in the Far East. Along the way there were various alarums and excursions – in 1955 Dick Chipperfield had to make a hasty departure from the BBC Television commentary box in the big top at Dagenham to restore order after a young lioness suddenly took exception to her trainer. In 1960 an 18-year-old trapeze girl fell 40 feet to her death in the ring at Slough but the show went on. "If a soldier is killed in battle the war does not stop," said Dick Chipperfield. "It is the same with the circus."

In 1961 the 23-stone comedian Fred Emney, who had been engaged by Chipperfield as a ringmaster – "that's me and that's the hippopotamus," he said on being shown the circus newspaper in court – sued the company for damages after breaking his ankle when he fell out of a caravan. During the case it emerged that Chipperfield had arranged for Emney to be provided with a wooden pedestal for his entrances and exits which was normally used by the camels. Another guest ring-master hired by Chipperfield, "Mr Pastry" (Richard Hearne) also sued the circus when he was bitten by Charlie the chimpanzee.

Although in recent years Chipperfield left the day-to-day running of the show to his son Dick junior, he retained a lively interest in the circus business and was still training animals in his eighties. "I own five houses," he said, "and I never sleep in any of them", preferring to bed down in his trailer in the circus's winter quarters near Chipping Norton, Oxon.

In 1963 he published his memoirs, *My Friends the Animals*. He is survived by his wife Myrtle and their three children, all carrying on the circus tradition.

March 5 1988

LORD BROCKWAY

LORD BROCKWAY, who has died aged 99, spent his long life crusading against poverty, injustice and racialism at home and abroad.

Fenner Brockway, as he was always known, was the last of those who pioneered the Labour party at the turn of the century. A saintly man – in the mould of Gandhi, whom he revered – he eschewed violence or venom however passionately he felt; he lived with the barest of material necessities and gave all he earned above the national average wage to causes he supported.

He used to tell a story concerning Margaret Thatcher that said much about both their temperaments. As a young MP she often gave him a lift to his home in Finchley after late sittings. "One night she asked what I had wanted to be. I replied 'I've never thought about it, I only wanted to do'. 'But to do, you must be,' she protested."

He celebrated his 99th birthday by speaking in the House of Lords on African affairs and, although somewhat infirm in the last few years, remained a powerful and moving orator. His tenacity was nowhere better demonstrated than in campaigning against racial discrimination in Britain: he introduced bills outlawing it for nine successive years before the Government agreed to introduce one in 1964.

Brockway never lost the energy of the Socialist convictions he learned at the feet of Keir Hardie – "I went to him as a young Liberal and left him a young Socialist" – and from Bernard Shaw. H. G. Wells was his mentor in world politics.

Brockway was a man of the Left but a democrat who fervently opposed doctrinaire Marxism or violence as an instrument of change. He was an ardent supporter of Gandhi's Freedom for India campaign and founder of the postwar Movement for Colonial Freedom. In the 1930s he was in the forefront of the anti-fascist movements, taking part in the last demonstration in Germany against the rise of the Nazi movement in 1932 and was regularly in Spain during the Civil War. He led the famous Cable Street counter-demonstration to Sir Oswald Mosley's blackshirt march through the East End of London in 1936 and his influence was credited with containing the violence it provoked.

The range and strength of Brockway's radical convictions inevitably brought him into conflict with authority. He supported the pre-1914 Suffragettes until their resort to arson changed his mind about their methods if not their aims.

The Boer War made him pacifist and he was prosecuted nine times in the First World War as a conscientious objector, spending nearly three years in prison. He was always a prolific writer and, while inside, tried to maintain his output by producing pamphlets written on toilet paper.

Brockway could often be justly accused of naivety stemming from his belief in man's innate goodness and he inevitably attracted hostility and cheap jibes. But he never bore malice and even those most bitterly opposed to his views – he often clashed with his own party as well as political opponents – recognised his selfless sincerity.

For someone on the political scene for so long,

Brockway was in the Commons for a comparatively short time, first as Labour MP for East Leyton from 1929 to 1931 and then for Eton and Slough from 1950 to 1964. There he was nicknamed "Member for Eton and Africa" and claimed to enjoy a surprising amount of support from masters and boys at the College.

His lack of a Commons seat was due to his insistence on remaining committed to the Independent Labour party long after its decline as a political force. He had become its organising secretary in 1922 and was either chairman or general secretary throughout the 1930s.

He unsuccessfully fought four elections between 1934 and 1942 until finally joining the Labour Party in 1946. After losing Eton and Slough in 1964 by a mere 11 votes, Brockway was, at the age of 76, offered a life peerage by Harold Wilson. He accepted after much heart-searching about joining a bastion of privilege, persuaded that it would give him a continuing public forum which, indeed, it did.

Archibald Fenner Brockway was born at Calcutta in 1888, the son of missionary parents, and educated at the School for Sons of Missionaries, now Eltham College. This upbringing profoundly influenced him and his manner was always that of the missionary rather than a rabble-rouser. Although he never formally embraced the Christian faith, he accepted its tenets and once said he sought to put socialism in place of Christianity.

He began work as a journalist on the *Examiner* in 1907 and then moved to the *Christian Commonwealth*. By way of recreation he played in the three-quarter line for Blackheath Rugby Football Club. Brockway attributed his longevity to a life of vegetarianism but was a companionable man who liked a smoke and a glass of whisky.

His long involvement with anti-colonialism began in 1919 as joint secretary of the British Committee of the Indian National Congress and editor of their journal, *India*. From then until independence in 1947 he worked closely with Congress party leaders. Once in the Commons he donned headgear similar to that worn by Gandhi in protest against a ban on its use in India.

Even in his very late years Brockway's interests were legion: human rights, the African nations, the Sahara peoples, Afghanistan, oil problems and the international control of space. He was a member of various peace missions, including the British Campaign for Peace in Vietnam in 1970.

In 1979 he and Lord Noel-Baker founded the World Disarmament Campaign, which helped to bring together the peace movements of the world and to marshal public opinion against the arms race. He addressed a World Peace Assembly in Czechoslovakia in 1983 on efforts to ban the bomb.

Brockway was a foundation member of the National Union of Journalists and a prolific writer. Among his 40-odd books were *English Prisons Today* (1921), *The Indian Crisis* (1930), *Hungry England* (1932), *The Bloody Traffic* (1933), *Death Pays a Dividend* (1944), *African Journeys* (1955), *Commonwealth Immigrants* (1965) and *The Colonial Revolution* (1973). He wrote a couple of novels and three autobiographical studies, the last whimsically entitled *98 Not Out*.

His first marriage in 1914 to Lilla Harvey-Smith was dissolved; and in 1946 he married Edith Violet King.

There are four daughters of the first marriage and a son of the second who declined, with some vehemence, to use the courtesy title of "Honourable".

April 30 1988

DR WILLIAM SARGANT

DR WILLIAM SARGANT, the celebrated television psychiatrist who has died aged 81, was a world authority on brainwashing and in 1975 flew to California to examine Patricia Hearst at the request of the kidnapped heiress's parents.

He talked to Miss Hearst on five occasions while she was in jail awaiting trial for offences committed with the "Symbionese Liberation Army" and he remained convinced that she was "forcibly converted". But, in the event, he was not called as an expert witness, attributing this to his insistence that a simple Pavlov-dog-style solution should be used to explain to the jury what had happened – "rather than using the metaphysical and doubtful work of Freud and other such philosophical theorists".

Sargant was indeed the most effective spokesman for the influential psychiatric school which emerged in Britain between the wars, partly as a reaction against Freud. Its main expectation was that physical cures would be found for most forms of mental illness; and this led to the adoption of electroconvulsive therapy, brain surgery and extensive use of drugs.

He was prepared to express his belief in them on radio and television at a time when it was by no means safe to do so, on account of the General Medical Council's rules about self-advertisement – and perhaps still more on account of the ill-disguised envy of some colleagues. He was never to receive the honours his work in retrospect deserved.

Sargant's great success as a clinician at St Thomas's Hospital was held against him. Any type of treatment he tried worked wonders, which was one of the reasons why he was so powerful an advocate.

Psychiatrists at other hospitals, using the same techniques, could not match his results. There was no question of his fudging them; and gradually it began to become clear why, reluctant though he remained to admit it. It was his faith in his methods, transmitting itself to his patients.

Sargant's interest in the similarity between the results of drug-abreaction, brainwashing techniques and the methods used by some evangelists to win converts – described in his book *Battle for the Mind* (1957) – led him to explore the phenomenon of "possession", as displayed in tribal communities and charismatic cults all over the world. He became convinced of what he described as their "tremendous importance".

It helped to explain so much that has been mystifying in history – as he pointed out in his remarkable book *The Mind Possessed* (1973) – shamanism, mass hysteria, religious ecstasies, even orgasm. His inherent scepticism melted through personal experience of the beneficial effects of rituals in which trance states were induced by rhythm and dancing.

He was repeatedly impressed by the evident mental balance which so many of the participants showed – even in voodoo, which he had assumed to be sinister and evil, but which, he asserted, gave to many of its practitioners increased dignity, relief from fear, and something to live for. Sargant was careful to insist that beneficial though these shamanic methods were, ECT or drugs are more effective and more reliable. Ironically, though, neither they nor brain surgery have lived up to his expectations; the results he obtained with patients have never been matched.

William Walters Sargant – younger brother of the founder of Justice, Tom Sargant – was born in 1907 and educated at Leys School, St John's College, Cambridge, and St Mary's Hospital. A formidable performer on the rugby field, he captained Middlesex and played for the Barbarians.

During the Second World War as assistant clinical director of Sutton Emergency Hospital he treated shell-shocked soldiers rescued from Dunkirk. In 1948 Sargant was appointed Physician-in-charge of the Department of Psychological Medicine at St Thomas's, retiring in 1972.

The numerous cases in which he was involved included the trial in 1964 of Detective Sergeant Harold Challenor (accused of planting pieces of brick on demonstrators) who was found unfit to plead. Sargant told the subsequent inquiry that although Challenor was medically "as mad as a hatter" he was completely sane and responsible in law.

In the same year he upset the Special Branch and CID by suggesting in a lecture that the methods by which British police questioned witnesses could bring about a false confession. Three years later he played a key role in the Government's controversial decision to hand over the Russian physicist Vladimir Tkachenko to the Soviet Embassy.

Sargant's autobiography, *The Unquiet Mind* (1967), presents a gentler picture than he conveyed on television, where, though courteous, he was always a little awe-inspiring; it is also an interesting apologia for his work as a psychiatrist. But it was in *The Mind Possessed*, where he was free from his medical preconceptions – and from the inhibitions which the absurdities of structuralism were imposing on anthropologists – that he really came into his own.

He married, in 1940, Peggy Glen who survives him.

August 31 1988

CHARLES ADDAMS

CHARLES ADDAMS, the American cartoonist and demonic *doyen* of the *New Yorker*, who has died aged 76, gave his name to the ghoulish characters inhabiting a spooky Gothic-suburban pile in the popular 1960s television show, *The Addams Family*.

The amiably macabre Addamses – from Morticia, the black-gowned matriarch with the heart of pure embalming fluid, and the grotesque Uncle Fester to Lurch, the giant butler, and Thing, a hand that popped out of a box – were directly inspired by Addams's cartoons which had been one of the most distinctive features of the *New Yorker* for the previous 30 years.

A similar show, *The Munsters*, was also derived from Addams's characters, though without the artist's blessing. But when the cult grew into an international sensation, the *New Yorker*'s long-serving editor, William Shawn, feeling that the television exposure had "vulgarised" the characters, barred the Family from the magazine. Recently, however, the new editor, Robert Gottlieb, had reinstated them after nearly 20 years of dormancy and Addams also resumed drawing covers for the magazine.

Addams's most reproduced cartoons included the seasonal scene in which the Family prepare to pour boiling oil from the roof of their creepy, gabled residence on to the carol singers below; and the classic study of the lady skier whose downhill tracks lead to a tree and then, mystifyingly, continue in perfectly parallel lines on either side of the tree. First published in the *New Yorker* in 1940, the lady skier was syndicated around the world. Addams was pleased to hear that a lunatic asylum in Nebraska used this drawing to test the mental level of its patients, though he characteristically confessed that he never quite understood the original himself.

Charles Samuel Addams, the son of a manager of a piano company, was born at Westfield, New Jersey, in 1912. As a boy, he recalled, he broke into a deserted house where he "drew skeletons all over the walls". He also used to jump out of a dumb waiter and "scare the wits" out of his grandmother.

His first cartoons were published in the Westfield High School magazine and, when he was studying architecture at Pennsylvania University, he submitted a drawing to the *New Yorker* of a man in his stockinged feet standing on ice and saying "I forgot my skates". Addams admitted that it was "not very funny and I don't know why they ever bought it".

He took a job as a re-touch man on a detective

magazine, making photographs of murder victims look less grisly. Addams recalled that he always felt they were "kind of interesting the way they were".

Soon he went freelance, selling drawings to *Life*, *Collier's*, *Cosmopolitan* and other magazines, but it was the sophisticated and irreverent tone of the *New Yorker* that perfectly suited the Addams style. In its pages his sardonic black humour won him an instant following.

While it could be said that Addams drew his inspiration from a restricted range of subjects, his repertoire of oddly lovable ghouls, monsters and depraved humans was an innovation in situation jokes. Within a sinister framework of evil-turreted mansions and Munch-faced châtelaines, Addams set the commonplace incidents of everyday life, thus investing them with total absurdity. The lady of the house looks startled as the door creaks open: "Ah, it's only you," she says in relief as the horrific, swaying Boris Karloff figure of a manservant looms on the threshold.

The Family fastened on to the American consciousness like domesticated vampire bats. Addams's name became part of the American idiom; an "Addams house" nicely described any gloomy, cobwebby Victorian structure. He came to be regarded as the funniest spokesman for all the repressed violence that lurks in "normal" people.

During the Second World War Addams served as a private in the United States Army in a Signal Corps detachment where he was assigned to animating films about "syphilis or prosthetic devices".

Addams published 10 collections of his cartoons including *Drawn and Quartered*, *Addams and Evil*, *Monster Rally*, *Dear Dead Days*, *The Chas Addams Mother Goose* and *Favourite Haunts*. In 1971 one volume, *My Crowd*, was launched in the Chamber of Horrors at Madame Tussaud's.

A tall, gentle, whimsical man – with a face described as a cross between Lyndon Johnson and Walter Matthau – Addams lived in appropriately Gothic style in a tower apartment in Manhattan adorned with such objects as a headsman's axe, a guillotine, articulated skeletons, an old embalming block serving as a coffee table and a piece of tombstone doing duty as a paperweight.

He was thrice married, the third marriage taking place in a pets' cemetery with Addams's dog, Alice B. Cur, as the only attendant. The bride wore black.

October 1 1988

DOROTHY DE ROTHSCHILD

DOROTHY DE ROTHSCHILD, who has died aged 93, was the matriarch of the leading family in world Jewry and, as head of the Rothschild charities in Israel, played an active role in major developments in the Jewish state.

She was also a munificent benefactress at home in Britain where she was the châtelaine of the great treasure-house of Waddesdon Manor, near Aylesbury, and occupied a distinguished place in the public life of Buckinghamshire.

Born Dorothy Pinto in London in 1895, she received her education at home and in private classes. "Dollie" (as she was known) always recalled her childhood as having been wonderfully carefree. Her father, Eugene Pinto, was bilingual and transmitted to her his own fluency in French. This became a valuable asset when in 1913, at the age of 17, she married James Armand de Rothschild, then 35, the son of Baron Edmond de Rothschild, the head of the French House of Rothschild.

She was immediately hurled into the hectic life of her large new family and her husband's numerous pursuits. He was much involved in the Zionist movement, in British politics (later as Liberal MP for the Isle of Ely) and on the Turf.

Not all the Rothschilds supported Zionism from the beginning. But the imagination of Baron Edmond was fired by the ideal of the revival of Jewish nationhood and he took up the cause with vast enthusiasm.

So great was his contribution that he has become known as the "Father of the Jewish State". James was inspired by his father and by Dr Chaim Weizmann, the charismatic Zionist leader and subsequently the first President of the State of Israel. When James de Rothschild went to France in 1914 to serve in the Army, his wife became the line of communication between Dr Weizmann and the two Rothschilds in France as the Balfour Declaration evolved.

She modestly described her function as a "post office" but it is evident from Dr Weizmann's own letters that she was much more. Not yet 20, she learned to exercise her own judgement and made a personal contribution.

Dorothy de Rothschild remained a committed Zionist for the whole of her long life. No Zionist and later no Israeli leader would visit London without a call on Mrs de Rothschild at her house in St James's Place.

After the death of her husband in 1957 she assumed

his responsibilities in Israel and at home. In the Jewish state it was as President of the Hanadiv Foundation that she provided the means for the building of the Knesset, Israel's Parliament (*Hanadiv*, the Benefactor, was the name by which her father-in-law was known among the Jews of Palestine). In the same capacity, she provided for a new Supreme Court, in which she took a detailed interest. Sadly, she did not live to see it completed.

After the establishment of the state of Israel, the Rothschild properties in Palestine were all given to the Government. James de Rothschild, and later his widow, then directed their resources to a variety of philanthropic projects. The Open University, one of their contributions, now has an enrolment of 12,000 students.

The Foundation introduced educational television, a prestigious Rothschild prize for research, regional libraries, the Jerusalem Music Centre and a host of other benefactions. In 1982, when Dorothy de Rothschild was prevailed upon to receive the Freedom of Jerusalem, the President of Israel — in a reference to her humility — described her as the "unknown benefactress" of his country.

In Britain she pursued an active life as an MP's wife carrying an extra burden because her husband was in poor health for most of his adult life. She was an alderman of Buckinghamshire County Council, a working magistrate for almost 40 years (she sat every week) and eventually became vice-chairman of the local bench.

Running such a vast establishment as Waddesdon was itself, almost a full-time occupation. After the death of her husband (there were no children of the marriage), the estate was given, with an endowment to the National Trust. But she continued her interest as the vigorous chairman of the management committee until her death. She had also inspired the compilation of a sumptuous catalogue of *The Waddesdon Collection*, of which 11 volumes have so far been published.

Dollie de Rothschild shunned publicity, believing that the really decent individual only appeared in the newspapers on two occasions – birth and death.

She was gentle in disposition, unassuming in manner and ever-sensitive to the needs of others. Her work with the disadvantaged in the East End of London occupied her thoughts throughout her life and her generosity reached out to the most humble. She gave of herself as well as of her means and the quality of her personality brightened the lives of all who knew her.

December 12 1988

EMPRESS ZITA
OF AUSTRIA

EMPRESS ZITA OF AUSTRIA, who has died aged 96, had a unique claim in the contemporary world to the phrase "living history". As the Consort of Karl, the last Hapsburg Emperor, she shared the throne of an Empire that ceased to exist 70 years ago, consisting of Austria, Hungary and what is now known as Czechoslovakia, together with parts of present-day Italy, Yugoslavia, Romania, Poland and Russia.

She shared the historic throne of the Holy Roman Empire; she was crowned Queen of Hungary in Budapest with her husband beside her wearing St Stephen's Crown as Apostolic King. In the First World War, she was at the very centre of affairs, as consort of one of the "Big Four" among the belligerent monarchs – of the other three consorts, Alexandra of Russia was murdered in 1918 and Augusta Victoria of Germany died in 1921; while Queen Mary, the only one of the three to approach the Empress Zita in longevity, died in 1953.

The distinction frequently attributed to the Empress Zita of being the last European Empress belongs, however, to Queen Elizabeth The Queen Mother, one-time Empress of India.

Princess Zita of Bourbon-Parma was born in 1892, fifth of the 12 children whom Duke Robert I of Parma had by his second wife, the Infanta Maria-Antonia of Portugal, having already had 12 children by his first wife. Her links with European history through her parentage were as remarkable as those of her own life.

Her father reigned as Duke of Parma from 1854 to 1859 when his Duchy was still an independent state, before the unification of Italy. Her maternal grandfather, Dom Miguel, usurped the Portuguese throne in 1828, causing the conflict known as the Miguelite War or "the War of the Brothers" – in which he had the sympathy of the British Prime Minister, the Duke of Wellington, who had seen him out with the Buckhounds, when staying with George IV at Windsor, taking "his fences like anyone else".

Princess Zita's aunt, Dona Maria das Neves, was married to one of the Carlist pretenders to the Spanish throne and fought in the Second Carlist War. Her eldest half-sister, Princess Maria Luisa, was the first wife of "Foxy Ferdy" of Bulgaria.

The other consort of a reigning sovereign among her

siblings belongs to much more recent history: her younger brother Prince Félix, who married the Grand Duchess Charlotte of Luxembourg.

Princess Zita had a happy childhood and girlhood at her father's castle in Austria and his villa in Italy; the family moved from one to the other in a special train with 15 or 16 coaches to hold the children, the servants, the horses and the baggage, not to mention the scholarly Duke Robert's books. She grew up to be a Princess of exceptional beauty and intelligence; it came as no surprise when, in 1911, at the age of 19, she married Europe's greatest Catholic royal *parti*, the 24-year-old Archduke Karl, second in line of succession to the throne of his great-uncle, the Emperor Franz Joseph.

It was a love match; in falling in love with an eligible Princess, Karl differed from most Hapsburg Archdukes of the previous generation. They had either made loveless dynastic marriages, as his father the Archduke Otto and his cousin the ill-fated Crown Prince Rudolf (of Mayerling notoriety) had done, or else, like his uncle the Archduke Franz Ferdinand, found happiness in *mésalliances*.

And unlike the Emperor Franz Joseph's marriage to the Empress Elisabeth, which turned out unhappy even though he had married her for love and never ceased to love her, the marriage of Karl and Zita was an enduring success, blessed with five sons and three daughters. In this, as in other respects, the eventual heir to the throne was eminently satisfactory; he had been diligent in his studies, he was conscientious in his duties; he was a young man of exceptionally sweet nature though he knew his own mind; he inspired affection in everyone he met.

For the first three years of their marriage, the young Archduke and Archduchess lived mostly away from the limelight while he soldiered. Though it was almost certain that Karl would one day be Emperor (the son of Franz Ferdinand, the immediate heir, being excluded from the succession on account of his morganatic marriage) that day seemed a long way off. Franz Ferdinand was in the prime of life.

But in 1914 Franz Ferdinand and his morganatic wife fell victims to the bullets of Sarajevo; making Karl the immediate heir to the throne. It was to Karl and to the Archduchess Zita that Franz Joseph, after hearing the news, made his famous remark: "I am spared nothing."

On that same occasion, the Emperor said to Karl: "At least I can rely on you." And indeed, for the two years that remained of his reign, he worked far closer with his great-nephew than he had ever done with his nephew; at his request the couple and their children moved into Schönbrunn.

Karl's initiation into affairs of state was interrupted by frequent visits to the front; he was, after all, a soldier and the Empire was fighting a war. However much that war may be blamed on Austria–Hungary, the young Archduke was in no way responsible for its making; he loathed the war and on succeeding as Emperor in November 1916 lost no time in trying to bring it to an end.

The Emperor Karl's peace attempt of 1917, in which the Empress Zita's brother, Prince Sixte of Bourbon-Parma, acted as intermediary, was the only serious effort to end the war made by the leader of any of the belligerent powers. It failed, but only just; he had the enthusiastic support of the British Prime Minister, Lloyd George.

Had it succeeded, millions of lives would have been saved and the subsequent history of Europe would have been very much happier. At the same time as he worked for peace, the Emperor Karl set about reconstructing his heterogeneous Empire on federal lines so that he came to be known both as the "Peace Emperor" and the "Emperor of the People".

In these the two objects which, as Emperor, he put before all others, Karl had the full support of the Empress, with whom he constantly discussed them. Happily married to a highly intelligent wife, who was dedicated to her husband and his subjects, it was natural that he should have initiated her into the secrets of state and sometimes taken her advice. There were those who accused the Empress of influencing her husband, but as he and she were so much at one in their views her influence did no more than strengthen his own convictions.

Because of the lack of space in the house which the Emperor occupied when he was at Army Headquarters, the Empress was sometimes present in the room when he held audiences; but she always avoided joining in. In April 1918, however, while the Emperor was laid up with a minor heart attack, she had a confrontation with Count Ottokar Czernin, the brilliant but unreliable Foreign Minister, who had caused a crisis by allowing the Emperor's secret peace overtures of the previous year to be leaked out.

This drew Austria–Hungary closer to Germany, which had a fatal effect on the attitude of the Entente powers; having intended to preserve the Hapsburg Empire, they now wished to see it dismembered. So with the defeat of the Austrian forces in the autumn of 1918, Karl's Empire collapsed around him.

For a brief while, as the outlying states of the Empire fell away in an orgy of self-determination, it seemed that Karl might at least have kept the throne of Austria; but the fall of the German monarchies brought down the monarchy in Austria as well. The Emperor, who refused to abdicate, which he felt would be to renounce a responsibility given to him by God, agreed to withdraw from all affairs of state, while remaining in Austria.

A few months later when Austria was on the verge of a Communist takeover, and there was a real danger that the Emperor and Empress and their children might suffer a fate similar to that of the Tsar and his family, they were prevailed upon to go into exile in Switzerland. In 1920, after the collapse of a short-lived Communist regime, Hungary was declared a monarchy once again, under the Regency of Admiral Horthy.

Horthy had told the Emperor that he would not rest until he had restored him to his throne in Budapest and Vienna; but having become Regent of Karl's Hungarian kingdom, he showed himself to be in no hurry to bring Karl back as King. So in 1921 Karl made two attempts to regain his Hungarian throne, by going to Hungary himself; but each time he was foiled by Horthy, who on the second occasion used force against him and the Empress.

For the second attempt, the Emperor and Empress flew from Switzerland to Hungary in a rickety mono-plane. "I've never liked flying," the Empress remarked more than 60 years later, having travelled to Rome by jet.

As a result of Karl's second restoration bid, which was very nearly successful, he and his family were banished to Madeira. Here, in a damp and primitive villa which was the best they could afford, the Emperor died of pneumonia early the following year aged 34.

Two months later, the Empress gave birth to their youngest child, the Archduchess Elisabeth. She and her children were then living in Spain, where they had been offered hospitality by King Alfonso XIII. Later, the Empress and her family settled in Belgium; she moved to the United States during the Second World War and then, after a period in Mexico, returned to Switzerland.

She spent her long widowhood in retirement, devoting herself to her family and to the memory of her husband, who is so widely acknowledged to have been a saint that the cause for his canonisation has been opened. She travelled frequently; towards the end of her life she paid her first visit to Austria since the fall of the monarchy and was given a tumultuous reception.

She also paid two visits to Rome, being on cordial terms with Pope John Paul II, whose father had not only been a subject of the Emperor's but had been commissioned by him in the Kaiserlich und Königlich Army. Those fortunate enough to be received by the Empress in her extreme old age found someone to whom the adjective "old" could hardly be applied.

She is survived by all her children, except for her eldest daughter, Archduchess Adelheid, who died in 1971. Her eldest son, the Archduke Otto, who prefers to be known as Dr Otto von Hapsburg, is a distinguished member of the European Parliament and author of many books on political science, history and world affairs.

March 15 1989

JACK DASH

JACK DASH, the colourful former unofficial leader of London's dockers who has died aged 82, made a familiar progression in the national consciousness from dangerous firebrand to treasured old "character".

The legendary Communist agitator, whose cry of "All out!" would plunge the docks into crippling inactivity, ended up as an amiable London tourist guide, dabbling in painting and poetry, giving talks to the boys at Eton and campaigning for his fellow old-age pensioners. But behind the folksy *persona* of the mellowed Dash was a man who had made a major contribution to the rapid decline of the Port of London after the Second World War. In less than a quarter of a century he and his fellow Communists appeared to destroy a whole industry through systematic disruption along textbook lines.

Thanks to the loquacious Dash – a shrewd operator who knew how to dominate a committee and to sway a crowd with his rhetoric – the "docker-on-strike" became a music-hall joke. Demarcation disputes seemed to stretch out like cascading dominoes.

Dash – nicknamed "the Red Napoleon" or, on account of his habit of working stripped to the waist, "Nature Boy" – first came to public notice in 1949 during a 25-day stoppage at the docks involving some

16,000 strikers. It was an offshoot of the Canadian seamen's strike which was regarded, and not only by those obsessed with "reds-under-the-bed", as a worldwide conspiracy at the height of the Cold War. Eventually, when 96 ships were idle in the Port of London, including 27 with food cargoes, the Attlee administration sent in the troops.

Dash and the other agitators defied the Government, the National Dock Labour Board and officers of the Transport and General Workers' Union. Three were expelled from the union, and Dash and four others were debarred from holding union office for two years.

When the strike finally collapsed, its committee was reconstituted, and eventually became the unofficial London Port Workers' Liaison Committee, with Dash in the chair. It was better known in Poplar and Canning Town as "Jack Dash and his Merry Men".

Having won the confidence of 8,000 dockers he claimed to represent, Dash became the spearhead of unofficial strike action in the London docks. Figures of working days lost through strikes in the Port of London illustrate the ravages: 1949, 240,000; 1955, 192,000; 1957, 81,000; 1958, 339,000; 1967, 252,000 and 1970 (the year he retired), 221,000.

Striking and Dash were to become synonymous: time after time dockers would stream out of the gates in their thousands to a meeting in some local park without always knowing why. Importers, sick of seeing their ships regularly queuing for handling, abandoned London in numbers which only the most short-sighted union member could ignore.

When it was suggested that his members might follow the example of their continental counterparts and organise a night shift to accelerate turn-round, Dash is supposed to have replied: "The British docker is not a nocturnal animal."

In the 1960s Dash vigorously resisted the plans of the Devlin committee aimed at improving efficiency and ending restrictive practices; Frank Cousins, the general secretary of the Transport and General Workers' Union, appeared unwilling to intervene. Dash was labelled a wrecker by the committee. He hotly denied the allegations, saying his task in life was to make life better for dockers. That came first, he claimed. His membership and allegiance to the Communists came second.

A true Cockney, Jack Dash was born in the East End on April 23 1907. After the death of his mother when he was a boy, the family broke up and he was sent to a Poor Law School.

He would recall that he became politically conscious during the General Strike of 1926 and gained his education from books such as Jack London's *The Iron Heel* and Robert Tressell's *The Ragged-Trousered Philanthropists*. He soon switched his allegiance from the Labour party to the Stepney branch of the Communist party.

During a stint as a hod carrier in the building trade he became active in trade unionism and while out of work, as he frequently was in the 1930s, he was an enthusiastic participant in the National Unemployed Workers Movement. On one occasion he and his colleagues invaded the Ritz Hotel (where Barbara Cartland was among those in the Palm Court); on another he donned funerary garb to process with a symbolic coffin towards St Paul's.

During the Second World War Dash served with the Fire Brigade and afterwards he managed to get taken on in the Royal Docks. In later life he would reminisce about the gruelling conditions: "We casual workers, dockers and stevedores – 'Beef', they called us – would hitch lifts on lorries from one dock to another and hang around for three or four hours hoping for work. In the Royal Docks you'd have 600 to 800 men 'on the stones'. They'd be fighting and kicking to be picked, like seagulls battling over scraps. Accidents were frequent. On average, dockers needed medical attention four times a year." Once Dash fell 50 feet from the top of a ship to the bottom, but survived.

"When we did get work," he said, "it was 10 hours a day, seven days a week. There were often times when everything pawnable was pawned. Food got very sparse and the local pigeons often ended up feeding people via the saucepan. Families were big and mothers always ate last. My wife's meals were half the size of the ones she gave the rest of us."

He described the constant industrial battles as his "university education", saying: "I studied an 'ology' all right – dockology". In retirement Dash was much in demand as a lecturer and he published an autobiography, *Good Morning Brothers* (1972), as well as various poems. He also trained as a guide with the London Tourist Board.

A keen student of architecture and history, he brought an individual approach to his conducted tours of St Paul's Cathedral: "Even in those days," he would say, "they had cuts in wages to speed up building. They cut Christopher Wren's salary by half."

Wren's celebrated epitaph, *Si monumentum requiris, circumspice* ("If you would see his monument, look around"), could equally have been applied to Dash if it had been carved amid the ruins of Docklands during the

1970s. After his retirement the power of the liaison committee waned; as containerisation increased, privately owned ports like Felixstowe flourished and ships moved away from the once great Port of London.

Today only Tilbury and some wharfage survives; where once many thousands of dockers teemed, loading and unloading scores of ships, is now the mushrooming Isle of Dogs and other development areas.

This recent regeneration left Dash unimpressed: "Apart from the improvement in housing for some of the people who've always lived there, the only benefits locals are going to get out of it are a few temporary gardeners' jobs on the landscaping schemes."

Latterly Jack Dash had passed into the historical mythology of the Left, though his death occurred at a time when dock labour troubles were once again in the news.

June 9 1989

DIANA VREELAND

DIANA VREELAND, the high priestess of American fashion who has died in New York in her eighties – "dates bore me," she once said, though she apparently had two birth certificates – was the formidable editor-in-chief of *Vogue* from 1963 to 1972.

Before that she was fashion editor of *Harper's Bazaar* for 28 years; and after she was sacked from *Vogue* she became special consultant at the Metropolitan Museum, where she was responsible for a series of dazzling annual exhibitions.

Mrs Vreeland was one of New York's "sacred monsters." She looked like a glorified Red Indian, her pronounced nose and high rouged cheekbones made more prominent by her drawn back, black lacquered hair, and the appearance completed by large earrings and necklaces.

Her looks inspired her friends to avian similes: Cecil Beaton compared her to "an authoritative crane"; while Truman Capote thought she resembled "some extraordinary parrot – a wild thing that's flung itself out of the jungle." Nothing about her was conventional. Her diminutive stature and slim figure filled any room she entered, and she dominated the assembled company with her pyrotechnical conversations and monologues – original, outrageous and contradictory.

She was born Diana Dalziel, probably in 1903, probably in Paris – "I'm sure I chose to be born in Paris" – and claimed an infant acquaintance with such luminaries as Diaghilev and Nijinsky. Her parents moved to New York in 1914, where Diana received no formal education – though she was taught how to ride by Colonel William "Buffalo Bill" Cody in Wyoming.

In 1924 she married the banker T. Reed Vreeland, and she liked to tell the story that her mother was named co-respondent in a blazing divorce suit on the eve of the wedding: "She was often involved with somebody. She travelled with a very good-looking Turk."

The Vreelands went to live in London, where Reed was employed by the Guaranty Trust Company of New York. The couple did not occupy a prominent social position, though Diana was sketched by Beaton at the beginning of a career that ran side by side with hers.

She first achieved a certain social notoriety in the

1930s, when she and her husband moved back to New York and she began to contribute a column to *Harper's Bazaar* under the heading "Why Don't You?" Such questions as "Why don't you wash your blond child's hair in dead champagne?" exercised an exotic fascination at the height of the Depression, and she was paid $18,000 a year.

At *Harper's* – and later at *Vogue* – Mrs Vreeland gave readers the full benefit of her rich and bizarre imagination. Sometimes she outraged the public, as when she published a close-up photograph of one of Lauren Hutton's breasts.

Nor was she easy to work with, arriving at the office in the early afternoon and keeping her youthful staff working late into the night. She was by no means universally liked. "What is the name of that designer who hates me so?" she once asked a colleague: "Legion," came the answer. But *Vogue* was never better than under her guidance.

Mrs Vreeland was an energetic promoter of new talent and ideas. She would recall with glee the arrival of the young Cockney photographer David Bailey in her office. He had come from the rain outside with a bedraggled model (Jean Shrimpton). He looked, she said, "just like a Shetland pony". Both were instantly employed.

Her approach to her readers was to show them things they had never imagined. She was inspired to introduce the thonged sandal, for example, after inspecting a pornographic mural at Pompeii. In all matters, especially visual ones, she was a perfectionist.

Dismissed by *Vogue* after 10 years in the editorial chair, Mrs Vreeland rose like the phoenix and accepted a new post overseeing the Costume Institute at the Metropolitan Museum. Her exhibitions there, which appeared in a blaze of publicity each December, comprised such subjects as *The 18th-Century Woman*, *Man and the Horse* and the Indian exhibition *A Second Paradise*.

Meanwhile she herself, having moved in the world of the Windsors, Schiaparelli, Cole Porter and Chanel, was now to be seen with Truman Capote, Andy Warhol (*qv*) and a younger, equally admiring set. She liked to entertain small groups in the blood-red L-shaped room which represented "a garden in Hell". Incense burned in the corner, Bérards and Beatons adorned the walls, neat Russian vodka was drunk and exotic food was served.

Mrs Vreeland was celebrated for a variety of eccentric aphorisms – "Pink is the navy blue of India" – and the fashion editor in the musical *Funny Face* was directly inspired by her. She also produced two books: *Allure* (1980), a lavish volume in which she discussed her favourite visual images; and *D V*, a best-seller in America in 1984. In the latter she drew her reader into her world with such lines as: "Do you notice any scent on me now? Don't come any closer – if you have to sniff like a hound, it's not enough."

Reed Vreeland died in 1966, and Diana Vreeland is survived by two sons.

August 24 1989

IRVING BERLIN

IRVING BERLIN, who has died in New York aged 101, was the longest-lived and most prolific of all popular song composers, with a genius for combining perfectly straightforward words and original melody.

His greatest hits included such "standards" as "White Christmas"; "Easter Parade"; "Isn't This A Lovely Day?"; "A Pretty Girl Is Like A Melody"; "Cheek to Cheek"; "Top Hat, White Tie and Tails"; "Puttin' On the Ritz"; "Let's Face the Music and Dance"; "Blue Skies"; "Always"; "What'll I Do?"; "Couple of Swells"; and "There's No Business Like Show Business".

Berlin managed perhaps better than anybody else this century the most difficult task in popular art: writing from the heart for money. He had no pretensions: his tunes were simple, his lyrics easy. Their universal popularity made him a multi-millionaire.

Not for him the musical questing and lyrical trickery of the Gershwin brothers, Jerome Kern or Lorenz Hart. Berlin came from the people, understood the people and composed for the people.

As Kern himself said: "Irving Berlin has no *place* in American music. He *is* American music." The Broadway lyricist Howard Dietz wrote of Berlin: "He does not care to be considered witty or brilliant or artistic. He wants to be a hit."

George Gershwin described him as "the greatest American song composer. He has vitality which never seems to lose its freshness. His songs are exquisite cameos of perfection. Each one is as beautiful as its neighbours. Irving Berlin is America's Franz Schubert."

Cole Porter paid his tribute in song:

> *You're the top, you're a Waldorf salad*
> *You're the top, you're a Berlin ballad.*

Nobody knows how many songs Berlin wrote: perhaps as many as 5,000, some a lot less good than others, some to be borrowed from at a later date, some never published. He wrote both the lyrics and the music though he never learned to read music or to play the piano properly (he once spent two days taking lessons, but "realised I could have written two songs and made myself some money in that time"). He knew little about harmony and fingered the piano only on the black keys in the somewhat eccentric key of F sharp.

A piano was specially made for him with a lever for transposing his melodies from that key into any other he desired. It is now exhibited in the Smithsonian Institution in Washington.

His first big success was "Alexander's Ragtime Band" in 1911, which has been called "the overture to the jazz age". At 74 he was still happily in tune with the age, composing, for example, "The Secret Service Makes Me Nervous".

A small, introspective, modest man, genial and generous, though always careful in business matters, Berlin lived a quiet life in New York with a retreat in the Catskill Mountains. He considered song-writing to be a business and to meet deadlines at short notice often worked until four or five in the morning; "Cheek to Cheek", for example, was written overnight.

He disliked fuss about himself, but many have agonised over his facility to write potently evocative songs which, in the words of Philip Larkin, are "not so much songs as bits of the 20th century". Berlin himself seemed wary of analysing his ability and was less than good at judging his own output.

Recalling the success of "White Christmas", originally composed as a nostalgic song for soldiers and featured in the film *Holiday Inn* (1942), he said: "I didn't think it would be a hit. But [Bing] Crosby saw something there. Of course, he's not the one to throw his arms around and get excited. When he read the song he just took his pipe out of his mouth and said to me: 'You don't have to worry about this one, Irving'."

It duly won Berlin an Oscar and sold 100 million records and 140 million copies of the sheet music.

Berlin also wanted to scrap "There's No Business Like Show Business" because he thought the producer of *Annie Get Your Gun* – his most successful musical – did not like it. The up-tempo song became a veritable showbiz anthem.

"Everyone has one good tune in his head," he said in 1936. "When you're shaving or something you may start to hum it. A songwriter just has more than one. That's the only difference."

He thought of studying formal composition but decided against. When Cole Porter told him he did not like one of his own songs, Berlin told him: "Listen, kid. Take my advice. Never hate a song that has sold half a million copies."

The Berlin watchword was "the mob is always right." He did, however, once define the themes a successful songwriter should concentrate on: 1) home; 2) love; 3) self-pity; and 4) happiness. But what that leaves out is the simple, unsophisticated sincerity of Berlin's music, the sheer Americanism of it, the energy, the guileless, open sentiment, whether it be happy or sad.

Nowhere in his songs is there a trace of envy or sneer, just all-American independence, optimism and can-do. In "Always" and "What'll I Do?" Berlin touched people with unembarrassed, unembarrassing sentiment in a way that the sophistication of a Porter never achieved.

Berlin was never afraid to be corny, as in songs such as "God Bless America". This classic was sometimes mocked but it is more fruitful to consider the belief, emotion and pride that have sustained its popularity.

Berlin once said: "A guy born in Russia who comes to America and winds up being Irving Berlin should be very grateful." Indeed, the story of his life encapsulates much of the traditional "American Dream".

He was born Israel Baline on May 11 1888 at Temun in Siberia. His earliest memory was of the Cossacks burning his home and village in a pogrom against the Jews.

When he was four his family emigrated to America. His father tried to maintain the family in New York's poverty-stricken immigrant area on the East Side by combining duties as a synagogue cantor with work in a slaughterhouse but overtaxed himself after four years and died.

Young Izzy left school at eight to help the family by selling newspapers. One of his early jobs was as a guide for "Blind Sol", a singing tramp from the Bowery.

His own singing career began in occasional audience participation in music-halls; then he began busking in the streets and at 16 became a "singing waiter" in a Chinatown saloon known as "Nigger Mike's". Judging by the few early recordings that have survived Berlin did not have much of a voice; "To hear him," it was said, "you have to hug him."

He began to work out his own tunes on Nigger Mike's piano after hours and at 19 wrote his first song, "Marie From Sunny Italy". His new name, "I. Berlin" appeared on the cover through a printer's error. (George M. Cohan later referred to the composer as "a Jewboy who named himself after an English actor and a German city.")

"Marie From Sunny Italy" made only 37 cents but at the age of 21 another of his songs interested a music publisher who gave him a job as a lyric writer. He wrote some humorous songs, including "Sadie Salome, Go Home", which sold up to 300,000 copies.

This put him on the road to success, and through hits such as "Oh, That Beautiful Rag", he obtained a partnership. In 1910 he made his first Broadway appearance as a singer in *Up and Down Broadway*.

The next year he wrote the immortal "Alexander's Ragtime Band" about a young bandleader and his clarinet, which has been played ever since in thousands of arrangements. It was followed by "Everybody's Doing It", written for a revue of that name by George Grossmith and C. H. Bovill at the Empire, London, in 1912; and by "That Mysterious Rag" and the enticing "When the Midnight Choo-Choo Leaves for Alabam'". Into these tunes Berlin injected a new vitality, with overtones of the latent jazz of the future.

His early songs were humorous but the death of his first wife, Dorothy Goetz, in 1913, only five months after their wedding, made him turn, with "When I Lost You", to the personal ballads that were in the next two decades among his greatest successes.

Berlin's first complete musical show, *Watch Your Step*, was a hit at London's Empire Theatre with Lupino Lane during the First World War. It was followed in 1916 by *Follow the Crowd*, also at the Empire.

In 1917, when America entered the war, Berlin served as a sergeant at Camp Upton, New York, and there wrote the songs for a show about army life, appearing on the stage to sing "Oh, How I Hate to Get Up in the Morning", which soon acquired folksong status.

After the First World War he composed songs for the Ziegfeld Follies and for several years produced his own revues at the Music Box Theatre, New York, which he built with a partner. *The Music Box Revue of 1924* introduced "What'll I Do?", one of his most haunting songs of the nascent jazz era.

His finest waltz ballads, such as "All Alone", "Remember" and "Always" appeared in the mid-1920s. "Always" was a tribute to his second wife, Ellin Mackay, the heiress to a considerable fortune made by her grandfather, a Nevada pioneer. Her father, Clarence Mackay, who was head of America's Postal Telegraph Company, told Berlin: "The day you marry my daughter I'll disinherit her."

Berlin countered: "The day I marry your daughter I'll settle two million dollars on her." (He was already his own publisher and proving rather good with money.) The Berlins eloped in 1926 but eight years later Clarence Mackay was reconciled to his daughter's marriage which lasted until Mrs Berlin's death in 1988.

In the late 1920s the composer diversified into various business interests but the 1929 slump caused their collapse and he returned to song-writing. In the 1930s he wrote the music for the New York musicals *Face the Music*, *As Thousands Cheer* and *Louisiana Purchase*, as well as the lyrics and the music of several films.

In 1935 he wrote the score for *Top Hat*, setting the standard and creating the most popular and best-loved of the Fred Astaire and Ginger Rogers film musicals. *The Daily Telegraph* observed: "Its success is the more remarkable because Mr Berlin, the first and greatest of the jazz composers, has for some time been regarded as an old master of Tin Pan Alley, a little out of touch, perhaps, with the tastes of the 1935 public."

He was also responsible for *Follow the Fleet, On the Avenue, Carefree* and *Second Fiddle*. Among Berlin's most celebrated songs of this period were "Soft Lights and Sweet Music", "Puttin' on the Ritz", and "Isn't This A Lovely Day?"

"God Bless America" was first performed on Armistice Day in 1938 by Kate Smith on a radio broadcast. The stirring song, embracing patriotism and religious faith, soon became an unofficial national anthem – and has indeed been proposed more than once as a replacement for the official one, "The Star-Spangled Banner".

During the Second World War Berlin returned to Camp Upton to write another successful soldiers' revue, *This Is the Army*. He toured with it for three years and it played at the Palladium in 1943 – the proceeds going to army relief funds and British charities.

In that year he was invited to lunch with Winston Churchill at 10 Downing Street. The story goes that Mr Churchill was under the impression that he was Isaiah Berlin, the noted philosopher, then at the Washington Embassy. The Prime Minister plied Berlin for a while with questions about the American elections, war production and economics and the modest composer did his best to cope. But it became apparent that the conversation was missing more than a beat until at last, misunderstandings overcome, they settled down to a friendly compromise in the exchange of ideas.

Mrs Berlin said afterwards: "If after listening to you

for two hours Mr Churchill really thought you were an economist then I'm worried about the war."

After the war came his best musical, *Annie Get Your Gun*, full of hit tunes such as "Anything You Can Do", "Doin' What Comes Naturally", "You Can't Get a Man with a Gun", "They Say It's Wonderful", and "There's No Business Like Show Business". The show came to the Coliseum in London and was later filmed.

Among his other musical comedies were *Miss Liberty* (1949) and *Call Me Madam* (produced in London at the Coliseum in 1952). His films included *Blue Skies* (1946), *Easter Parade* (1948) and *White Christmas* (1954).

Berlin's last musical was *Mr President* (1961), which was panned by the critics. He retreated into seclusion – sometimes promising the one last big hit that never came – and devoted himself to painting, fishing and litigation.

Well into his tenth decade he continued to walk about New York for exercise – defying the threat of muggers – and to pay occasional visits to his own music publishing office in Times Square, where royalties poured in from all over the world. In 1986 he outlived the copyright on "Alexander's Ragtime Band".

His 100th birthday was celebrated in 1988 with a serenade of his songs outside his Manhattan residence and a gala concert at Carnegie Hall, featuring Frank Sinatra, Leonard Bernstein and Ray Charles, which he did not attend.

In 1945 President Truman awarded Berlin a medal of merit for "extraordinary service in building up army morale". President Eisenhower gave him a gold medal for "God Bless America" (the royalties of which Berlin had assigned to the Girl Scouts and Boy Scouts of America); and in 1977 he received the United States Medal for Freedom. He was also admitted to the French Legion of Honour.

Berlin's only son died in infancy; he is survived by three daughters.

September 25 1989

A. J. SYLVESTER

A. J. SYLVESTER, who has died aged 99, was Private Secretary to Lloyd George for 23 years and a man of extraordinary intellectual and physical energy; at the age of 86, he qualified for the *Guinness Book of Records* as the world's oldest competitive ballroom dancer.

Sylvester was no stranger to unusual records. As a young man he was among the world's fastest shorthand writers and typists, a skill that in 1914 led to his appointment to work for Colonel (later Lord) Hankey, the Secretary to the Committee of Imperial Defence and then the War Cabinet. The job took Sylvester to the heart of government, albeit as an observer, and so into the ambit of Lloyd George.

After that prime minister's downfall in 1922, Sylvester stayed at Downing Street as Private Secretary to Bonar Law and Baldwin. But he was not happy in the new political climate, and in 1923 accepted Lloyd George's offer to head his private office in opposition. He insisted on the title of "Principal Private Secretary", to establish his authority over that other power in the household – Frances Stevenson, Lloyd George's private secretary and, until their marriage in 1943, for 30 years his mistress.

One of the demands on Sylvester's diplomacy was to soothe the domestic tensions this relationship created, particularly on Mrs Lloyd George's rare visits to London. On one of these, Miss Stevenson had to be slipped out of the back of Number 10.

"AJ", as everyone knew him, was a familiar figure at Westminster as Lloyd George's right-hand man, almost as his *alter ego*. He acted as his press officer, handled a voluminous correspondence and a staff of as many as 20 and, as Lloyd George's visits to Westminster became more irregular, acted as his ears, with his own seat in the officials' box under the Gallery.

The son of a tenant farmer who had lost his livelihood in the agricultural depression and become a brewery worker, Albert James Sylvester was born at Harlaston, Staffs, on November 24 1889. Obliged to leave Guild Street School, Burton-on-Trent, at the age of 14, he became a clerk in a brewery, where he perfected his shorthand and typing.

At 20 Sylvester sought his fortune in London, where he did a variety of jobs. In both 1910 and 1911 he was chosen for the British "speedwriting" team, which competed at the Business Efficiency Exhibition at Olympia. His first job in the official world was to assist a Royal Commission in India.

In 1947 he published a book, sensationally entitled *The Real Lloyd George*, which turned out to be a fairly innocuous collection of trivia. The picture that emerged of the great man came as a surprise to many at the time.

Far from being a great organiser, by Sylvester's account Lloyd George was a muddler, constantly losing letters and changing his mind, scarcely able to dress himself without knocking things over and losing his clothes.

One point of historical interest was Sylvester's account of Lloyd George's meeting with Hitler at Berchtesgaden in 1936: "He was frankly spellbound by the man and declared Germany had a leader who could bring about complete understanding and friendship between Britain and Germany . . . For Germany Hitler is the resurrection and life."

This greatly embarrassed Lloyd George's admirers, particularly in the light of the doubts there had been after 1940 of his confidence in victory. Sylvester's account was angrily denied by Lloyd George's widow, who received a characteristically blunt reply: "My account was written from day to day in Germany and is accurate."

After Lloyd George's death Sylvester considered entering Parliament and was on the short list for his former master's constituency, but not being Welsh counted against him. He joined Beaverbrook's staff for three years, and then worked for a year as an unpaid assistant to the then party leader, Clement Davies.

In 1975 he published *Life With Lloyd George*, which was based on his diaries; like his earlier book, it gave a flavour of the times but was not particularly revealing.

An indefatigable worker, a model of discretion, charm and shrewdness, Sylvester retired in 1949 to a farm he had bought in Wiltshire, where he continued to run a smallholding and to ride and hunt into his nineties. He bequeathed his notes and papers – more than a million words – to the National Library of Wales, where they will provide historians with a unique record of his times.

His wife, the former Evelyn Welman, died in 1962, and he is survived by their daughter.

October 30 1989

THE DOWAGER MARCHIONESS OF CHOLMONDELEY

THE DOWAGER MARCHIONESS OF CHOLMONDE-LEY, who has died aged 95, was a legendary survivor from *la belle époque*, retaining an aura of pre-1914 luxury into the last years of the 20th century as the redoubtable châtelaine of Houghton in Norfolk, and as the last private resident of Kensington Palace Gardens – commonly known as "Millionaires' Row".

As Sybil Sassoon she was an exotic beauty of the Edwardian era; her striking dark features were captured by John Singer Sargent. Like her brother, the politician and socialite Sir Philip Sassoon, owner of Trent Park and Port Lympne, she had an eye and a taste for beautiful things and she could afford to collect and conserve.

An admirable conversationalist – quick, witty, never malicious, but invariably interested in other people's views – her devoted friends included Winston and Clementine Churchill. Together with Lady Violet Bonham Carter and Sylvia Henley, she formed part of what

Mary Soames has described as "an unofficial committee, who would in turn come to dine with Winston, while Clementine had a 'night off' ".

Lady Cholmondeley worked hard but most unostentatiously for a number of causes. In the First World War she was an assistant principal in the WRNS, and during the Second World War she rose to become Superintendent.

At first the Wrens were a bit nervous of her but she proved herself a hard worker, not minding that there was no desk for her in the "Big Room" and perching where she could. She became staff officer to the *doyenne* of the WRNS, Dame Vera Laughton Mathews, and one of her duties was to organise royal visits and other ceremonies.

She won Dame Vera's respect by only contributing to committee meetings when she had something of value to say. Dame Vera wrote: "She has the most silver tongue of anyone I have met. She can talk to anyone and of anything, and whether driving through falling bombs or skidding sideways through the world's worst traffic, and one is never tired of it because she is so entertaining and witty and sympathetic."

Sybil Rachel Betty Cecilie Sassoon was born on January 30 1894, the only daughter of Sir Edward Sassoon, 2nd Bt, and his wife Aline, daughter of Baron Gustave de Rothschild. The Sassoons, originally banking sheikhs in Baghdad, had been naturalised in Bombay at the end of the 18th century.

Miss Sassoon was orphaned when she was 18 and then lived with her brother, whom she helped in his political endeavours. After the First World War she acted as the bachelor Sir Philip's hostess at several important international conferences held at Port Lympne

– notably the occasion in May 1920 when the question of reparations was discussed by Lloyd George and the French.

In 1913 she married Lord Rocksavage, elder son and heir of the 4th Marquess of Cholmondeley and widely regarded as the best-looking man of his generation – "I think he's probably Apollo," observed the actress Maxine Elliott. "Rock", who succeeded to the marquessate in 1923, was a polo player and a fine calligrapher who founded the handwriting prize at Eton. His italic Elizabethan signature adorned the tickets admitting guests to the State Opening of Parliament during his time as the Lord Great Chamberlain.

According to the 5th Marquess of Salisbury, Rock Cholmondeley belonged to "a past world, a world on which it is too often the habit of younger people to pour scorn. He was indeed an aristocrat in the best sense of that much abused word, and, with Lady Cholmondeley, he added immeasurably to the grace and beauty of life."

Although the Cholmondeley family had a part share in the office of state of Lord Great Chamberlain and owned the seats of Houghton and Cholmondeley Castle, Cheshire, they had been feeling the pinch financially for some time. Indeed in the 19th century the Palladian palace of Houghton, inherited through marriage into the Walpole family, was offered for sale to both the Duke of Wellington and the Royal Family.

The Sassoon dowry brought about a remarkable transformation in the family fortunes. In 1918 the Rocksavages bought 12 Kensington Palace Gardens, where she was to entertain lavishly, indulging her passion for bridge. Though to her sorrow Winston Churchill did not play the game, Lady Cholmondeley was perfectly happy to play bezique with him, especially when he was old.

The Cholmondeleys also built a house at Golfe-Juan in the South of France to the designs of the ingenious architect Barry Dierks. Appropriately called Villa Le Roc, it was rented by the Prince of Wales — to whom, as King Edward VIII, Lord Cholmondeley was to act as Lord Great Chamberlain — for a holiday with Mrs Simpson in 1935.

But Lady Cholmondeley's outstanding contribution was the rebuilding of the splendid double staircase which rises in front of the basement to the *piano nobile* on the west front of Houghton, the great house built for Sir Robert Walpole, the first "Prime Minister". The staircase was replaced in 1973 as a memorial to her husband, the 5th Marquess of Cholmondeley, who had died in 1968.

A celebrated figure in Society, Lady Cholmondeley features in numerous 20th-century memoirs and diaries. Cecil Beaton, for example, revelled in her "sophisticated refreshing company".

In 1984 President Mitterrand paid a special visit to Houghton at the end of his State Visit to Britain in order to invest Lady Cholmondeley with the *Légion d'Honneur*. One of her many services to France was to persuade René Massigli to move his embassy from Albert Gate to be her neighbour in Kensington Palace Gardens. She finally gave up her house on "Millionaires' Row" in 1978.

In 1984 she celebrated her 90th birthday at Houghton in the presence of almost the entire Royal Family. She was appointed CBE in 1946.

She had two sons and a daughter, who became a probation officer. The elder, and only surviving, son became the 6th Marquess of Cholmondeley and Lord Great Chamberlain.

December 28 1989

LORD DARESBURY

THE 2ND LORD DARESBURY who has died aged 87, was a celebrated rider to hounds, earning widespread affection and respect as Master of both the Belvoir and the Co Limerick.

An immaculate figure in top hat and swallow-tailcoat, "Toby" Daresbury's appearance suggested a Corinthian of the last century. He lost two wives in the hunting field, and survived many falls in an adventurous career which gave rise to a legion of anecdotes.

There was the time he cured a "thruster" in a hard-riding Field with the injunction: "Turn round and jump it again!" And in the 1930s Mr Greenall (as he then was) became involved in a celebrated argument with the Master of a neighbouring hunt, Captain Filmer-Sankey.

As related by a London evening paper of the time, "something was said which caused Greenall to challenge Filmer-Sankey to a 'knuckle' fight in the good old English style". Early one morning the two met by appointment beside a fox covert called Blackberry Hill, situated on the border of the two hunting countries. "Filmer-Sankey wore a low-neck jersey, flannel trousers and tennis shoes," noted the diarist. "But Greenall contemptuously retained his collar and tie. They set to it with a will. Weight and experience were in Greenall's favour, and he looked to be winning, when Filmer-

Sankey landed a punch between 'wind and water' straight in the *Derby Kelly*. Though Mr Greenall's heart was willing, previous digestive trouble had made his stomach weak. The fight was ended."

A member of the Cheshire brewing family, Edward Greenall was born on October 12 1902, the younger son of Sir Gilbert Greenall, 2nd Bt, Master of the Belvoir and director of the Royal Show, who was created Baron Daresbury in 1927.

Young Toby was educated at Eton and commissioned into the Life Guards, with whom he served during the Second World War. He succeeded to the peerage in 1938 on the death of his father; his elder brother had been killed in a motoring accident.

Daresbury was Joint Master of the Belvoir from 1934 until 1947 when he proceeded to transform the Co Limerick, where the sport and the fun became fast and furious. A practical man, Daresbury installed an asphalt floor when he moved from Clonshire House to Altavilla so that it could be swilled down.

Daresbury also took a close interest in the family brewery Greenall Whitley and in freemasonry. He was appointed a JP for Cheshire in 1945.

He married first, in 1925, Madeline Sheriffe, who died of injuries sustained when out with the Quorn the next year; and secondly, in 1927, Josephine, youngest daughter of Brig-Gen Sir Joseph Laycock, who died in 1958.

He married thirdly, in 1966, Lady Helena ("Boodley"), formerly wife of Major "Chatty" Hilton-Green and fourth daughter of the 7th Earl Fitzwilliam.

Lady Daresbury was killed out cub-hunting in 1970. Lord Daresbury is survived by a son of the second marriage, Edward Gilbert Greenall, born 1928, who succeeds to the peerage. The eldest grandson, Peter Greenall, is a former champion amateur rider under National Hunt rules.

Captain Ronnie Wallace writes: Toby Daresbury was one of the famous foxhunters of the 20th century. He liked to give an impression of an unorthodox approach which concealed deep knowledge and ability.

Toby's early influences were his parents – his father ensured all that was best for the Duke of Rutland's hounds and staff, and his mother was a devoted fox preserver – and then a rugged character from Cumberland, "Doggie" Robinson, who persuaded him of the significance of earths and terriers.

The wonderful combination of a Master of Hounds and his Huntsman was seen at its best with Toby and George Tongue, DCM, at the Belvoir. Toby was running the brewery at Warrington with skill but also organised the hunting and nightlife on the high Leicestershire side of the country.

Toby's horsemanship was in a class of its own, mounted on horses which he schooled himself – people still talk with awe of two thoroughbreds, Big Exeter and Little Exeter. Enthusiasts for hunter judging also recall his performance at one Royal Show when the scheduled judge was taken ill and Toby was pressed into service. He rode all those strong, ring-crafty horses in his Homburg hat and a pair of chaps over his suit without ever touching their mouths.

He paid much attention to the fox coverts in his country with the assistance of the family 'keeper from Cheshire. One spring they were contemplating a woodland together at Daresbury, with little sign of pheasants. "They're nesting," said Toby. "Aye," was the reply, "in the fox's stomach."

When war came, and Toby was called to the colours, he somehow managed to keep a representative pack. In the last year of the war George broke his leg and Toby carried the horn.

Inspired by this and his knowledge of Co Limerick from pre-war days, he transferred his allegiance to that pack. At a time of struggle to restore English hunting to its rightful place, his departure was a major loss; but he was able to leave the Belvoir Hounds in good hands and established a regime at Clonshire which can never be forgotten.

He persuaded Boodley Hilton-Green, a legendary figure in her own right, to come over "for the season" – in fact 23 of them until her death – to organise the stables. Then there was Merry Atkinson, of point-to-pointing fame and also bred in a medical family, to look after the whelping bitches. This suited Toby, who was a born chemist.

The atmosphere, with an element of hubbub, was unique. Priceless pictures adorned the walls, delicious food emanated from a none-too-sanitary kitchen, retainers dashed in all directions, grooms, too, and top-class horses emerged from every cubby-hole. Toby had a delightful kennel huntsman, Paddy Reagan, but worked in the kennel and walked hounds himself, with long hours of exercise in the summer months.

I remember one breakfast the second morning after a Hunt Ball, when Boodley had failed to negotiate the bridge over a big river when coming home, and Toby, peering over his spectacles, said: "Darling, I haven't seen the Mercedes the last two days."

"To tell you the honest truth, it's in the Maigue."

"Indeed," commented Toby.

No great lover of white hounds and certainly not black ones, he was faithful to the strains from Belvoir and Quorn and the surplus puppies from those establishments were flown over in incubator boxes to establish the Limerick pack.

What fun they had in that wild and varied hunting country, with many like-minded friends settling out there too, and ever a welcome for the stream of guests. Boodley seemed to know of every young horse in Ireland; she was tireless in suiting them to her friends.

Toby established a marvellous rockery outside the sitting-room window by his own hand and crowbar, and some slightly reluctant help from his assistant "Simo", another character. In that category too we must remember Steer, his batman, and Dan the butler.

Sadly, even the best does not last for ever, and Boodley's death in 1970 was a mortal blow. Toby carried on most gallantly, gradually handing over the kennels when Hugh Robards came as Huntsman.

In 1977 Toby left the hounds in the capable hands of his great friends Lord Harrington and Lady Melissa Brooke, though he continued to ride the country in a style of his own, accompanied by the faithful Gerry, until his last illness.

We do not know whether he fulfilled his promise to ask at the Pearly Gates, "Why wind?" but foxhunters and countrymen must be grateful for all Toby Daresbury did to promote the true place of hunting in rural affairs, for great kindnesses and much laughter.

February 19 1990

SIR JOSEPH NICKERSON

SIR JOSEPH NICKERSON, the Lincolnshire agriculturalist who has died at Palm Beach, Florida, aged 75, was a distinguished plant breeder and pioneering experimental farmer, producing some of the world's top yielding cereals.

From the early 1940s he introduced improved varieties of cereals, potatoes and forage crops to Britain from the Continent and, having set up his own plant breeding operation in the 1950s, he became a major force in the move to introduce plant breeders' legislation in the early 1960s. But for all his remarkable achievements in agrogenetics, the bluff, outspoken "Joe" Nickerson was perhaps most widely known as a shooting man – whether dispatching pheasants on his Rothwell estate in Lincolnshire; grouse at Middleton-in-Teesdale, Co Durham, and in Scotland; partridges in Spain or wildfowl on British coasts and marshes. The Duke of Edinburgh and the Prince of Wales were among his shooting guests.

Nickerson first came to prominence as a shot in 1952 when he set the official British record of the largest partridge bag on a single day. Between 9 a.m. and 6 p.m. he and five other guns on his Lincolnshire estate accounted for 1,059½ brace.

Sir Joseph liked to compare himself with the 2nd Marquess of Ripon, who died in 1923 having killed a total of 187,763 birds in his last 24 seasons; Sir Joseph's total for a similar period was 188,172 – an average of 7,841 a year.

Although Nickerson came under fire from critics

who deplored large bags he argued strongly that his own conservationist record was unimpeachable. He pointed out that he reared far more birds than he shot.

He undoubtedly made a significant contribution to the welfare of the red grouse – his favourite quarry – by establishing the Heather Improvement Foundation, which has achieved much in promoting heather as a valuable crop – producing both grouse and sheep on the same land without detriment to conservation.

If the bags were big, the number of guns was comparatively small. Sir Joseph believed that "seven is the maximum number of Guns that should be accommodated at any shoot in Britain".

A staunch advocate of traditional sporting values and a stickler for etiquette, Sir Joseph roundly condemned the excesses of commercial shooting. It was a theme which pervaded his characteristically forthright book, *A Shooting Man's Creed* (1989).

"To me," he wrote, "shooting has long been something of a religion. As all religions do, it requires discipline, reverence, ritual and, above all, love. My reverence is for the wild surroundings which make challenging shooting possible and for the splendid quarry, which is something non-shooters find hard to understand."

The chapter on "Behaviour in the Field" contains such diverting observations as how to read the palm of a gamekeeper's hand: "I can generally tell what sort of day is in prospect when I shake hands with the 'keeper. A calloused hand, good day. Soft hand, poor day. This I find is a sure indication."

As for safety, he remarked: "Of course, the most dangerous act is to swing through the line when following a low bird. This happens most frequently on grouse moors and at partridge shoots."

Sir Joseph was to have first-hand experience of the dangers of shooting in 1984 when Viscount Whitelaw, then Deputy Prime Minister, slipped in the butts and peppered both his host and his gamekeeper. A statement, emanating from 10 Downing Street, announced that "Lord Whitelaw is naturally deeply upset but is relieved that no lasting damage was done either to Sir Joseph or to Mr Waddell."

There were no hard feelings and indeed Willie Whitelaw contributed a generous encomium to the book (which made no mention of the unfortunate accident) stating that Sir Joseph was a knowledgeable naturalist and enthusiastic conservationist.

Joseph Nickerson was born on April 19 1914, the son of a Lincolnshire farmer who encouraged him to immerse himself in a particular subject. The boy opted for partridges, eventually earning the sobriquet "Partridge Joe".

"I began thinking like a partridge," he recalled, "and imagined myself as a male hatched on 20 June on the Lincolnshire Wolds with 12 brothers and sisters . . . My parents were extraordinarily attentive and when weasels or predatory birds were about they clucked us up, ushered us into cover and protected us."

Although he received no scientific training Nickerson developed a special interest in plant breeding – the "Cinderella of sciences". He founded Rothwell Plant Breeders, Britain's largest independent research station, which produced many high yielding world varieties of barley and wheat.

The Nickerson Seed Co went on to operate in more

than 60 countries. He also founded the Nickerson Group of Companies which includes Cherry Valley Farms (formed in 1959 to pioneer scientific duckling breeding and production) and the Cotswold Pig Development Co, which produces minimal-disease breeding stock.

Sir Joseph was also chairman of Concord Farms of North Carolina, honorary president of Track Marshall and honorary chairman of North American Plant Breeders. He was a founder member of the World Wildlife Fund and from 1947 he owned and managed an island in the Humber Estuary as a nature reserve.

He instituted the annual Joseph Nickerson Husbandry Award to identify farmers using advanced farming methods, and he was a co-founder of the Agricultural Forum. Sir Joseph was proud of the family farms' high standard of amenity and environmental management, claiming that they demonstrated how modern commercial farming and wildlife conservation could prosper together.

His numerous appointments included the chairmanship of the Caistor rural district council and the presidency of the Lincolnshire Agricultural Society and the Lincolnshire Playing Fields Association.

Always something of a controversial character – there was an unfortunate incident with a postman, who complained of being kicked – Joe Nickerson had a slightly forbidding appearance and a reputation for having a short fuse. But his friends and staff maintained that *au fond* he was a kindly and generous man.

Sir Joseph enjoyed sharing his thoughts on the shooting scene with readers of the correspondence columns of *The Daily Telegraph*. In August 1988, for example, he expressed his concern about the effect of gunfire on gundogs' hearing and called for the invention of an aural protector "that would not irritate the dog while it sat waiting and could easily be removed before the dog was sent off to retrieve".

Another reader responded by suggesting that dogs, like humans, feign deafness when they get older, to avoid obeying orders.

Nickerson was knighted in 1983 and was an Officer of the Order of Leopold II of Belgium as well as holding the European Medal for Excellence.

He is survived by his wife, Eugenie, two sons and four daughters.

March 6 1990

ERTÉ

ERTÉ, the exuberant Russian-born fashion and stage *styliste* who has died aged 97, enchanted the international art and theatre worlds with his boundlessly inventive designs and was one of the last links with the Paris of the 1920s.

Besides clothes and sets, he designed accessories, fabrics, shop-window displays, jewellery, furniture, playing cards and domestic interiors; but it was only relatively recently – through a series of international retrospective exhibitions in the 1960s and 1970s – that he was acclaimed as a key figure in the development of art deco style (a categorisation he disliked).

He first made his mark as a fashion illustrator on

Harper's Bazaar, in which he defined the look of 20th-century woman, creating a fantasy world of sinuous, sophisticated temptresses swathed in velvet and fur.

Erté's fanciful extravagance appealed to the Parisian high society which had greeted Bakst and Diaghilev's Ballet Russe with such enthusiasm; and it was not long before his success as a fashion artist led to commissions for costumes and sets for music hall revues, ballets and operas on both sides of the Atlantic.

His theatrical innovations included "living curtains" of elaborately costumed showgirls, usually dripping with jewels and plumes, and *costumes collectifs* – immense, single costumes shared by a group of performers. Even more spectacular, though, were his *tableaux vivants*, such as *L'Or* in the 1923 version of the *Ziegfeld Follies*, which, according to the designer, required six and a half miles of gold lamé.

Repelled by such mainstays as "the ubiquitous little black dress" and Coco Chanel's "dreary uniform", Erté delighted in defying convention and was not concerned with following "the trend of fashion". He also revelled in the limelight, and never lost an opportunity for display. In the 1920s he caused a memorable sensation when he arrived at a *Grand Prix* Ball adorned from head to foot in clinging silver lamé.

With his luxuriant white hair, twinkling blue eyes and "elfin, turned-up nose", Erté apparently resembled nothing so much as "a small, animated doll". He had been an advocate of unisex designs since the mid-1920s and was always impeccably dressed, usually in clothes of his own design.

"I firmly believe that every human being has a duty to make himself as attractive as possible," he wrote in his autobiography, *Things I Remember* (1975). "Not many of us are born beautiful; that is why I have always attached so much importance to clothes. Clothes are a kind of alchemy: they can transform human beings into things of beauty or ugliness."

Erté was born Romain de Tirtoff on November 23 1892, the only son of Piotr Ivanovich de Tirtoff, an Admiral of the Imperial Fleet and a descendant of a long line of Tartars.

As a boy, Romain often accompanied his mother and sister on shopping expeditions to the elegant retail and dressmaking establishments on the Nevsky Prospekt, and would spend hours looking at his mother's fashion magazines. At the age of five, he sketched a design for a silk evening dress which so delighted Madame de Tirtoff that she had the gown made.

Two years later, after seeing his first ballet, *The Humpbacked Horse*, he persuaded his parents to let him attend dancing classes. He also staged imaginary ballets of his own, representing the dancers with empty scent bottles trimmed with scraps of chiffon and lace.

During most of his childhood, Romain was educated at home, but when he was 12, his father sent him to Kronstadt College, a private boys' school in St Petersburg. Accustomed to wearing Little Lord Fauntleroy velvet suits or dashing Tcherkess costumes, the boy was repelled by the severe student uniforms and the rowdy behaviour of his classmates.

But he was an excellent student, and was able to pursue his artistic bent outside the classroom. Mme de Tirtoff recognised her son's talent and arranged for him to take lessons with Ilya Repin, the portrait painter; his father was at first vehemently opposed to his son's desire for a career in the arts, but when he graduated with honours in 1911, he rewarded him with a passport and passage to Paris.

When he arrived in Paris in 1912, Romain broke his promise to train as an architect at the Ecole des Beaux Arts and enrolled instead in a painting class at the Académie Julian. Refusing his parents' offers for financial assistance, he subsisted on a meagre income, selling drawings of contemporary French fashions to the Russian magazine *Damsky Mir* (*Woman's World*).

In January 1913 he went as a designer to the House of Poiret, where he later carried out his first designs for the stage, including one for a then unknown performer who used the name Mata Hari.

It was at this time that he adopted the professional name Erté – derived from the French pronunciation of his initials – and began his 22-year association with *Harper's Bazaar*.

In 1915 Erté was commissioned to design the costumes for *Revue de Saint-Cyr*, a new theatrical presentation by Rip, the best-known stage satirist of his time. And over the next 15 years – the heyday of the revue – he was in his element, working at first for the Folies Bergère and then for Paul Sandrini at the Bal Tabarin.

International fame came quickly as many of his costumes and stage sets were copyrighted and recreated for productions all over the world, including seven editions of *George White's Scandals* and two productions of Irving Berlin's (*qv*) *Music Box Revue* in New York.

After a brief flirtation with cinema design in Hollywood in 1926, Erté stopped contributing fashion drawings and began to concentrate on his covers for *Harper's*

Bazaar – which were increasingly influenced by Cubism – and on his illustrations of serialised novels and short stories for such publications as *Cosmopolitan* and *The Illustrated London News*.

In 1944 he created his first opera sets for the Riga Opera's production of Donizetti's *Don Pasquale* and soon afterwards began to work on ballets. His surrealistic designs for the Opéra-Comique's *Les Mamelles de Tirésias*, in 1947, and for the Paris Opéra's *La Traviata*, in 1951, won him critical acclaim; but he scored one of his greatest successes with the romantic sets and costumes he devised for the Glyndebourne Festival Opera production of *Der Rosenkavalier*, in 1980.

In 1964, he added a new phase to his multi-faceted career with an exhibition in Paris of the painted metal and wood sculptures that he called *formes picturales*.

The many retrospective shows that followed this were initiated by Jacques Damase, a French writer, and by Damase's friend Eric Estorick, the owner of the Grosvenor Gallery in London; and thereafter, Estorick and his wife, whom Erté called his "new family", became his exclusive agents.

It was they who, in an effort to reach a wider audience, encouraged Erté to try lithography, which unleashed another stream of creative energy and gave rise to his celebrated sets of lithographs *Les Quatres Saisons* (1970) and *Alphabet* (1977). During this period he also illustrated Alan Aldridge's *The Beatles Illustrated* (1969) and Lytton Strachey's saucy frolic *Ermyntrude and Esmerelda* (1969).

In his later years Erté divided his time between his Paris home and the Bahamas. He remained spry and extraordinarily industrious to the end: "My work has been my mother, my wife, my friend, my mistress and my children," he said recently. "It has been my life."

April 23 1990

ALEXANDER PLUNKET GREENE

ALEXANDER PLUNKET GREENE, who has died aged 57, was the husband and vital business support of Mary Quant, the originator and high priestess of Britain's "Swinging Sixties" fashion revolution.

With their friend Archie McNair – who until a split in 1987 was the financial brain behind the Quant empire – they formed a brilliant triumvirate in which Plunket Greene was the promotion and marketing wizard, gaining worldwide recognition for his wife's talent.

From the early days Plunket Greene skilfully managed to keep Quant in the public eye. He would organise trips to the Paris fashion shows; not so much to get ideas (she never claimed, incidentally, to have invented the mini-skirt and hated the stodginess of *haute couture*) but to be seen by the American press, then largely ignorant of London fashion.

It was Plunket Greene who organised the subsequent deals to market the Quant range in America, and he was the guiding light in the huge mass of licensing franchises – for lingerie, hosiery, sunglasses, shoes, interior design, perfume and, above all, cosmetics – that were to prove so lucrative and make her a global household name.

It all began in 1955, when the Plunket Greenes opened a boutique called Bazaar on the ground floor of their house on the corner of the King's Road and Markham Square in Chelsea. Bazaar was the first shop to produce fashion exclusively for the young in a relaxed atmosphere.

The Plunket Greenes would often open up after hours for friends dining at their basement restaurant, Alexander's; and at weekends the queue would stretch around the corner into Markham Square. The Sixties could be said to have begun here.

Certainly the Plunket Greenes came to epitomise the period. While Quant represented one aspect of the so-called "classless" New Aristocracy, Plunket Greene, with his raffish Bohemian charm and devil-may-care manner, personified the authentic aristocratic flip-side which was just as much part of the Sixties ethos.

As the *ne plus ultra* of the swinging élite they were guyed in *Private Eye*, where he was known as "Mr Alexander Plonk-It-In". The *bourgeoisie* reacted in a satisfyingly shocked manner to Quant's defiant pronouncement that "good taste is death", or to such titillating items as the topiary of her pubic hair, cut into a heart shape to complement her Vidal Sassoon-trimmed geometric hairstyle.

Although such things were not supposed to matter in the Sixties, Plunket Greene's ancestry proved of considerable interest to the genealogists and the gossip columnists: on his father's side he descended from a line of eminent Irish Ascendancy lawyers; on his mother's from the Russells, Dukes of Bedford. More specifically, his father, Richard Plunket Greene, was a fellow private school master of Evelyn Waugh, and his aunt Olivia, an early love of the novelist, was both a prominent "Bright Young Thing" and supposedly a model for "the Honourable Agatha Runcible" in *Vile Bodies*.

Alexander's grandfather, Harry Plunket Greene, was a well-known Edwardian singer who married the daughter of the composer Sir Hubert Parry who was also a niece of Baron von Hügel, the theologian.

Alexander Plunket Greene was born on June 17 1932 and educated at Bryanston and Goldsmiths' College of Art in London, where he met Mary Quant at a fancy dress ball. He went as Oscar Wilde and, while flirting with Quant, found himself the object of tiresome attention from a young man decked out as Lord Alfred Douglas.

Plunket Greene and Quant soon became inseparable and eventually married in 1957. Although she failed her finals and he never even attempted his, love and bright ideas triumphed.

Sustained by temporary jobs selling fabric at Selfridges, trying to be a photographer and playing a mean jazz trumpet, Plunket Greene expounded grandiloquent plans for changing what he called "the depressing and stultifying life young Londoners then led".

On inheriting a legacy of £5,000, Plunket Greene suggested to McNair that they and Quant should open a dress shop. The premises in the King's Road became a magnet for London's young innovators, attracted as much by the convivial Plunket Greene as by Quant's creativity.

In fact Quant was originally the buyer, but when she failed to find the iconoclastic clothes she wanted she proceeded to design them herself. In later years Plunket Greene recalled that initially they were so unbusinesslike that they kept the takings from the shop in a drawer and went to the bank only when the drawer was full. None the less, in 1957 a second Bazaar shop, designed by Terence Conran, opened in Knightsbridge; and in 1967 a third in Bond Street.

Sir Terence has recalled that Plunket Greene "loved food, drink, flirting and teasing"; and that in Bazaar he would urge "young girls to wear mini-skirts and enjoy themselves".

In the late 1950s the Plunket Greenes dipped their toes into the international market by showing their collection to an ecstatic audience at the Palace Hotel in St Moritz. Encouraged by this success, Plunket Greene decided that they should go to New York.

As *Women's Wear Daily* gushed at the time: "These Britishers have a massive onslaught of talent, charm and mint-new ideas. English chic is fiercely NOW . . . by the young . . . for the young."

The Plunket Greenes were widely feted and photographed together running down an empty Fifth Avenue. This led to the signing of a contract in 1962 with J. C. Penney, which at that time owned 1,700 stores right across America, for Quant to design a collection to be made in America.

Emboldened by this venture, the next year the Plunket Greenes produced their own wholesale collection, called Ginger Group. In 1964 a further American contract with the Puritan Group led the couple to set off on a three-week promotion across the United States. Their progress was charted by 50 television stations, and millions saw their fashion shows.

By 1966 Mary Quant was producing 22 collections every year. Though she and her husband shared an extraordinarily symbiotic relationship, the hectic pace of their lives was beginning to tell. They consulted a psychiatrist who taught them to deal with stress and in later years observed a routine of not communicating with each other in the early morning.

The Puritan contract made the couple paper dollar millionaires in 1964; and in 1968 the sale of 40 per cent of the Mary Quant company to Thomas Jourdan allowed them to enjoy the fruits of their hard work.

After the birth of their son, Orlando, in 1970, the Plunket Greenes decided to move to the country near Guildford, Surrey, into his great-aunt's large house, decorated with Quant's co-ordinated fabric and wallpaper designs. They also bought a house in the hills behind Nice in the South of France.

Today the Mary Quant company has an annual turnover of £100 million at retail level, of which more than 80 per cent is earned abroad. Asked the secret of the continuing success of the company, Alexander Plunket Greene replied: "integrity". He never allowed the Mary Quant label to be attached to a product that they had not improved with good design.

He is survived by his wife and their son.

Sebastian Conran writes: When I was a child, Alexander was my favourite adult.

One of my father's old school chums, he was tall, witty and wonderfully generous in kind and in spirit, with an ability to relate to us children as adults, often by sharing tales of his past naughtinesses. A trip to the shops could sound like some amazingly glamorous adventure when described *à la* Plunket Greene.

He seemed so carefree compared to other grown-ups, constantly entertaining everyone with anything from spirited jazz renditions on his shining trumpet to a bit of impromptu revolver practice from hotel bedrooms.

Appointed as my brother Jasper's godfather, he always acted like mine too, honouring me in turn by appointing me as his treasured son Orlando's godfather when he was born and I was 15 and just beginning to understand the uniqueness of this elegant, eloquent Peter Pan.

Although apparently totally different characters, Mary and Alexander were inseparable. Both highly charismatic, Mary is quiet and appreciative while Alexander was the exuberant gentleman. Only once in 34 years did I see Mary without Alexander and was shocked by my surprise.

He encouraged me creatively as a boy with his spontaneous draughtsmanship on anything from napkins to the garden wall, illustrating his shocking fairy stories. Even my first suit was a replica of his elegant, tailored houndstooth ones.

I will think of him with love and every time I see the miniature Jacobean rocking chair he and Mary gave me when I was born.

May 9 1990

ATHENE SEYLER

ATHENE SEYLER, the actress who has died aged 101, was a brilliant exponent of comedy and the last surviving link with the world of Victorian theatre.

Her mother had lived next door to Henry Irving and in 1905 Athene was taken to Drury Lane to see the great man in his swansong as Becket. He did not notably impress her as an actor, but she did recognise the force of his personality: "you felt you were in touch with something".

Athene Seyler's own professional debut was in 1909, when she appeared as Pamela Grey in *The Truants* at the Kingsway Theatre, and for the next 60 years she was hardly ever out of a job. She specialised in queens, dames, dowagers and duchesses, with their wreathed smiles, their clucking and fluttering, their nods, becks, quips and cranks. She wore a tiara as to the manner born.

Given the right part she was the equal of any of her contemporaries; indeed James Agate remarked that when it came to clowning she could act any other English actress off the stage. If, in her own estimation, she never became a great star, that was partly because she cared little for the trappings of success. In particular she remained cavalier about what she was paid, an attitude which, she claimed, sharply distinguished her from Dame Edith Evans, who possessed a "Christian Science sense of money".

Athene Seyler held that the standard of acting had vastly improved in her lifetime; the trouble with today's theatre, she held, was that the plays were so bad. Harold Pinter's *No Man's Land*, "with Ralph and John", finally put her off the theatre. "I couldn't follow a word of it, so when one of the characters yawned I said 'Oh, I do *so* agree' rather too loudly, and people turned and stared at me."

The improvements in acting may be ascribed to the advent of the director, a development which Miss Seyler did not regard with wholehearted approval. "Nowadays directors try to tell you even how to move your hands; I don't care for that. [Tyrone] Guthrie was one of the early troublemakers."

Miss Seyler refused to study any of her characters until rehearsals had begun. When she first started working in the theatre, the author would read his play – "usually quite badly" – at the first rehearsal, after which matters were left in the hands of the leading actor.

Miss Seyler remembered a brush with Beerbohm Tree. She had taken the trouble to learn Portuguese for a part, and Tree was rash enough to suggest that her accent did not sound very convincing. "So I said perhaps he'd like to demonstrate for me how a Portuguese accent should sound, and after that he was extremely nice to me."

She also played with Ellen Terry, whom she pronounced "adorable", and with Mrs Patrick Campbell, whom she regarded with very much less favour. In the script the dazzling Mrs Campbell was required to exclaim "Oh, isn't she *beautiful*!", of the character whom Athene Seyler was playing. Pulchritude was never Athene Seyler's strongest suit and the audience duly guffawed.

Mrs Campbell wantonly repeated the line, but when she ventured a third repetition Miss Seyler made the ugliest face that she possibly could and won the audience to her side.

The anecdote reflects the way that Athene Seyler's strong and determined character combined with her talent to overcome all obstacles – most particularly her striking lack of conventional allure. She claimed to have lived her life by four inalienable principles: "I have never cut my hair, never had a car, never worn trousers, and never said 'okay' ".

Athene Seyler was born on May 31 1889, the seventh child of Clarence Seyler, who worked for a Greek millionaire – hence her Christian name. By her own account she was early classified as an Unmitigated Nuisance, but at eight, she appeared in a children's play at the Conway Hall, in which she danced a hornpipe. When, to universal merriment, her drawers fell off she knew that she had found her métier.

She was educated at Coombe Hill School, Westerham, and at an early co-educational establishment at East Grinstead, where she appeared in *As You Like It*, playing her first Rosalind. In the teeth of family disapproval she forced her way onto the stage by simulating a very Victorian "decline", the symptoms of which instantly disappeared when she was allowed to go to RADA.

She had previously helped with school dancing lessons in order to save up for the fees; and once at RADA (Pinero was among those who auditioned her) she won enough prizes to cover her dues, as well as picking up the Academy's Gold Medal.

By the end of the First World War Miss Seyler had played over a score of West End roles, steadily developing her talent and technique. In 1920 she again played Rosalind, this time at the Lyric Hammersmith, and next year appeared as Mrs Frail in Congreve's *Love for Love*. Other successful parts included Lady Pidget in Wycherley's *The Country Wife*, and Beatrice in *Much Ado About Nothing*.

In 1924 her needle-sharp Hermia faced Edith Evans's haughty Helena in Basil Dean's production of *A Midsummer Night's Dream*; both actresses showed once and for all that these parts are in their essence comic, not romantic.

Yet despite Miss Seyler's talent and vitality she often found herself relegated to secondary parts in drawing-room comedy. She held the fashionable West End theatre of the interwar years in contempt, and considered that the cinema had benefited the drama by disturbing its complacency.

The problem was exacerbated because Miss Seyler, an intelligent woman sharply aware of her limits, would not touch anything to which she felt her talents were unsuited. She hardly ever played tragedy, except in roles which allowed some scope for her sense of mockery – the Nurse in *Romeo and Juliet*, Emilia in *Othello*.

In her favourite roles she never failed to give a memorable performance. James Agate, writing of her Mme Ranevsky in Chekhov's *The Cherry Orchard*, called her "an artist of intense perception", who played the part "not in the manner of a great actress showing off, but of the honest craftswoman giving us what her author wrote".

And of her Lady Bracknell: "Miss Seyler, who normally looks like some magnanimous mouse, swelled to Wagnerian size and gave a performance of such bite and gusto that every line was in danger of being lost through being drowned in the laughter greeting the one before. But Miss Seyler knows what she is about and did not throw away a comma."

Her understanding of comedy was exhibited not only in her acting but in an influential albeit slim volume,

The Craft of Comedy (1944). The text took the form of an exchange of letters between herself and Stephen Haggard, a promising young actor.

The book explored matters of style and technique. Miss Seyler's experience, theatrical taste and scholarship combined with Haggard's intelligence and sensibility to produce a minor classic. Haggard, tragically, died in 1943.

Miss Seyler, however, went from strength to strength. After playing Fanny Farrelli in *Watch on the Rhine* in 1942 she was in great demand in the West End, stealing the show as Veta Simmons in *Harvey* and later, in 1954, as Miss Holroyd in *Bell, Book and Candle* – when she played opposite Rex Harrison and Lilli Palmer.

Her Mrs Malaprop in *The Rivals* (1955), and her Mrs Caution in Wycherley's *The Dancing Master* (1961) also showed her at the height of her powers.

In 1966 Athene Seyler appeared in a famous revival of *Arsenic and Old Lace*, in which she and Sybil Thorndike played the Brewster sisters. The play had dated (one critic crudely complained of "Lace-Knick and Old Arse"), but the performances brought the house down.

One evening the two actresses, who were the fastest of friends, were talking so animatedly in the wings that they missed their cue, and poor Richard Briers, who had discovered a dead body on stage, was left mouthing expressions of horror – "ooh, *aah*, AARGH!!" – for far longer than the allotted time.

At the reopening of the Lyric Hammersmith in 1979 Athene Seyler recited one of Rosalind's speeches from *As You Like It* – the part she had played in the same theatre 59 years previously. In 1986 she presented an Olivier

Award to Albert Finney; she showed that her voice retained all its old calibre.

She had given both Peggy Ashcroft and Laurence Olivier their diplomas at Central School, and she always prided herself on her eye for talent. When, decades ago, RADA asked her to select the student of the year she chose John Gielgud: "I said to the administrator, 'You see that boy there, he has just given a very bad performance, but he is the one to watch'. I think that was very clever of me."

Miss Seyler later struck up a friendship with Johnny Gielgud and she enjoyed telling how she once heard the legendarily *gaffe*-prone performer moaning about being cast opposite old actresses – "They're such bores. . . . Gladys, Sybil, Athene . . . of course I don't mean *you*, Athene."

Her acting was not confined to the stage. Her films included *Dear Octopus* (1943), *Nicholas Nickleby* (1947), *The Pickwick Papers* (1952), *Doctor at Large* (1957), *The Inn of the Sixth Happiness* (1958), and *Two and Two Make Six* (1961).

Miss Seyler's executive abilities were widely recognised. In 1950 she became the first former pupil of RADA to be elected its president; and she was also president of the Theatrical Ladies' Guild, the honorary treasurer of Equity, and a member of the Arts Council.

She married, first, J. B. Sterndale-Bennett, a newspaper editor, by whom she had a daughter; and secondly, after nearly 40 years' cohabitation – necessitated by his Catholic wife's refusal either to die or to grant a divorce – the actor Nicholas "Bo" Hannen, with whom she was supremely happy. Hannen died in 1972.

September 13 1990

ELDRESS BERTHA LINDSAY

BERTHA LINDSAY, who has died aged 93, was the last Eldress of the Shakers, the American millenarian sect that espoused communal living, equality of the sexes, celibacy and pacifism, but is best remembered for its production of plain wooden furniture and handicrafts.

The sect was founded in Manchester, Lancashire, in the 1770s by "Mother" Ann Lee, who moved to New York with eight followers in 1774. Formally known as the United Society of Believers in Christ's Second Appearing, its congregation was nicknamed the "Shaking Quakers" – and later simply the "Shakers" – for the members' habit of trembling with fervour during church services.

When they received mystical "gifts from on high" the Shakers shook from head to toe in a bizarre ritualistic dance, which variously amused and repelled their visitors – who included Charles Dickens. The celibacy rule was instituted by Mother Lee herself, who, having lost several babies in childbirth, had had a vision of Adam and Eve entwined in carnal union, which convinced her that sexual intercourse was the root of all evil.

The Shakers were thus able to expand only by taking in orphans and converts, but the movement soon took root, and by the mid-19th century numbered some 6,000 members, who lived in a score of communal villages in New England, New York, Ohio, Indiana and Kentucky. Life in the communities was strictly regulated, with different parts of the day set aside for work, study and prayer. Traditional sexual roles were maintained – the women would cook, spin and weave, while the men worked the land and managed the workshops. But men and women were considered spiritual equals, and the leadership was shared between Elders and Eldresses.

Living together as "brothers and sisters", they slept in separate dormitories under the same roof. Couples suspected of forming attachments were segregated, expelled from the community or allowed to return of their own volition to the World.

Eldress Bertha was one of two surviving Shakers at the Canterbury Shaker Village, New Hampshire – where Sister Ethel Hudson, 94, survives her – and one of fewer than 10 remaining in the whole of America.

She joined the community at Canterbury in 1905, when the Shakers were already in sharp decline, and the Elders and Eldresses had begun to encourage cultural assimilation. This culminated in 1965, when they formally closed the sect to new members.

As the Shakers' enthusiasm for converting the "World's People" waned, so their material legacy to the world grew. Pioneers in several aspects of furniture manufacture, they were among the first to machine wood; and they invented an astonishing selection of tools, including rotary harrows, water turbines, screw propellers, mechanical threshers, automatic pea shellers, palm-leaf bonnet looms, revolving ovens and contraptions for peeling and coring apples.

Genuine old Shaker pieces – especially ladderback chairs, chests and boxers – now fetch thousands of dollars at auctions at Sotheby's, Christie's and elsewhere; and even Shaker brooms, farm implements and clothes-pegs are much sought after by collectors. The Shakers themselves, however, shunned all thought of making money from their craft. They regarded patents as immoral, and deemed it wrong to appropriate the "gifts of the spirit" for worldly gain.

When asked if she was sad about the Shakers' demise, Eldress Bertha would recall the prophecy of Mother Lee: "When the Shakers diminished to as many as a child could count on one hand, there would be a revival of the spirit."

She was quick to clarify, though, that they would not be called Shakers. "They wouldn't live in communities. But it would be felt and known worldwide. And we think that is coming to pass."

Bertha Lindsay was born on July 28 1897 at Braintree, Massachusetts, and as an infant moved with her family to Laconia, New Hampshire. Orphaned at the age of four, young Bertha lived for three years with an older sister, but was then placed with the Canterbury Shakers according to the wishes of their parents, who had attended services there.

One of Eldress Bertha's favourite anecdotes told of how as a frightened young girl she was comforted by the love and acceptance of the Shaker sisters. She would recall the day after her arrival, when she joined them in an apple celebration, and how she was touched by the beauty and perfume of the orchard in bloom.

She shared the chores, was educated at the community school and on her 21st birthday, having chosen to remain in the community, signed the covenant and donned the white starched bonnet of the Shaker sister. "I felt that I could give as much here as I could anywhere else in the world," she said, "and could have more friends, both men and women. If I had gone into the world and married, I wouldn't have had that."

Bertha Lindsay soon distinguished herself during her shifts in the kitchen and was put in charge of catering to the business leaders of the community and their guests. She also managed the community's fancywork trade – mainly small handkerchiefs and sewing-boxes – from 1944 to 1958.

In the course of the next decade, having watched as other Shaker communities were sold off, she was instrumental in establishing a museum which later evolved into Shaker Village Inc, a non-profit-making educational corporation which now preserves the Canterbury community as an historic site and museum.

In 1967 she was elected second Eldress of the Canterbury Shaker community and on the death of Eldress Marguerite Frost in 1970, she became Canterbury Eldress.

Her final years brought a brief period of limelight from the outside world which her forefathers had eschewed so vehemently. When not planning and overseeing the production of meals, she greeted visitors and gave interviews to schoolchildren, scholars, television and the press. In 1987 she published her cookbook, *Seasoned With Grace*, in which each chapter of recipes is preceded by stories of her life as a Shaker.

Despite appearing to some as old-fashioned, Eldress Bertha was not mired in the 19th century. She loved television, and faithfully followed the news and programmes such as *Jeopardy* and *The Bill Cosby Show*.

Eldress Bertha once said that she wanted to be remembered simply as someone who lived a true Shaker life. She lost her sight after her 90th birthday and then began recording her memoirs on a cassette recorder: "I want people to know we did have fun, and plenty of it."

October 11 1990

GLEB KERENSKY

GLEB KERENSKY, who has died at Warwick aged 83, was the son of Alexander Kerensky, the Prime Minister of Russia from July to October 1917, and all his life he remained fiercely dedicated to the defence of his father's reputation and to the exposure of the satanic nature of those who destroyed him.

Kerensky *père* has always been recognised in the West as a brilliant orator, but he has usually been portrayed as a man who lacked at once the perspicacity to identify Lenin as his most dangerous opponent, and the will to combat the savage power-hunger of the Bolsheviks. These charges were absolutely denied by Gleb Kerensky, who stressed that his father, "a true democrat", had never been anything but intensely hostile to Bolshevism, and indeed had succeeded in repressing it by force of arms in July 1917, only to fail in the autumn for want of loyal troops.

As an exile in England, Kerensky *fils* struggled for more than 60 years to force the realities of the Soviet tyranny upon the uncomprehending English mind. He was enraged by the criminal complacency with which power-worshipping Socialists like Bernard Shaw and the Webbs, whose vanity was flattered by VIP treatment on visits to Russia, regarded the atrocities of the regime.

Kerensky never accepted that Stalinism was a perversion of the original pure stream of the Revolution. Leninism, he insisted, was essentially a method by which hoodlums captured the machinery of state and refashioned it in their own image. Not that Kerensky in any degree underrated the horrors of Stalin, whose iniquity he found more rebarbative than Hitler's.

"At least Hitler does not pretend to be the leader of anti-militarist and anti-imperialist forces throughout the world," he wrote in 1939, as the Russians threw themselves upon Finland.

Kerensky also crusaded against the Western delusion that the designs of the Communists were merely a continuation of Tsarist ambitions: "No Russian Tsar has yet been seriously accused of wishing to make the whole world his domain."

Such views were continually set forth in letters to the newspapers, including many to *The Daily Telegraph*. Kerensky detested the "pseudo-Christian forbearance" that so often characterised English attitudes towards Russia. There was nothing that the Communists despised and detested more, he urged, than "sloppy" enemies.

Gleb Alexandrov Kerensky was born in St Petersburg on December 7 1907, and at the age of nine found himself living at the heart of some of the most dramatic events of the 20th century. But when his father, having failed to mobilise reinforcements against the Bolsheviks, slipped away from St Petersburg early in November 1917, young Gleb was left behind in the capital with his mother and his brother Oleg. Kerensky senior eventually escaped from Russia with the help of Robert Bruce Lockhart, a British agent.

In 1918 the abandoned mother and children were arrested and sent by train to Moscow. The Tartar guards threatened to kill them, but Mrs Kerensky managed to persuade them that the family might be valuable as hostages.

In Moscow the Kerenskys were committed to the Lubianka prison, where they were put into a cell with some 50 women who completely covered the floor. "There was no room for us to stand or sleep," Gleb remembered.

After a fortnight, though, the family was mysteriously released. Gleb always believed that this unforeseen mercy might have had something to do with the fact that he and his brother had been at school with Trotsky's sons.

At the end of 1918 the Kerenskys returned to St Petersburg, where the boys were boarded out at school while Mrs Kerensky went to live with her mother through a winter of freezing and starving misery. Rescue came in 1920 when a friendly revolutionary arranged false travel papers. A girl at the police station recognised Mrs Kerensky, but kindly slipped the documents into the middle of a pile so that they were signed unnoticed.

Thus the family escaped to Sweden, and shortly afterwards to England. Gleb was still only 12, and enfeebled by dysentery and anaemia; on the other hand, as he remarked, "when you live in the midst of a revolution you grow up very quickly".

His father was also in England at this time, although he later lived in America, and died in New York in 1970, at the age of 89. Mrs Kerensky established herself with her sons at Southport; she died there in 1975, aged 91.

The two boys qualified as engineers, Oleg went on to play an important part in the design and construction of the Severn and Humber bridges. Gleb joined the English Electric Co at Rugby, where he lived for the rest of his life.

The emergence of Mr Gorbachev and the breakdown of the Soviet system put this arch anti-Communist in something of a quandary. In 1987 he warned that Gorbachev was simply changing course a little, trying to get all he could out of the West. "He wants to be a better Leninist than any of his predecessors, and one must remember that, having brought the country to chaos and desolation, Lenin himself introduced 'The New Economic Policy' – i.e. a small dose of private enterprise."

But by the beginning of 1990 he was paying tribute to Gorbachev's courage. He argued that if the Russian people should be tempted to a bloody revenge after suffering so terribly at Communist hands, they should be careful at least that they did not destroy their liberator – "though we must remember that he was once a top official in the KGB".

Kerensky regretted that his father had not lived to see the recent changes. As for himself, he would never contemplate a return to his native land until Leningrad was once more called St Petersburg.

He is survived by his wife Mary, a son and two daughters.

December 19 1990

MICHAEL OAKESHOTT

MICHAEL OAKSHOTT, who has died aged 89, was the greatest political philosopher in the Anglo-Saxon tradition since Mill — or even Burke. He held that human life "is a predicament, not a journey"; that experience, truth and reality are inseparable; and that there is no reality outside experience.

A Fellow of Gonville and Caius College, Cambridge, he was a guru to the largely Cambridge-led New Right; and in 1951 his appointment to succeed the Socialist Harold Laski at the London School of Economics caused some consternation on the Left.

At his inaugural lecture Oakeshott declared that true political education would teach that political activity had no starting point or appointed destination — or even a detectable strand of progress. What had to be learnt was a concrete, coherent manner of living.

He maintained that a philosophical ethic was no less a contradiction than a philosophical science or a philosophical history; and his specific endeavour was to disentangle the confusion into which the language of politics had fallen. He dismissed the currency of most political talk as ambiguous clichés.

Politics, he once said, was the art of knowing how to provide against the new tyrannies that in societies threatened abuse of power; he held that the main purpose of political activity was to keep the State afloat rather than to provide wealth and well-being. Rationalism, according to Oakeshott, had placed too high hopes on political achievements. And its greedy disciples were "sold a pup" in Marxism, which he called a "crib" for the instruction of a politically under-educated class.

Oakeshott was attacking not only Socialism but the whole post-Enlightenment style of thought, according to which everything can be understood quasi-scientifically, and reduced to a set of clear-cut "problems" to which there must exist equally clear-cut "solutions".

He was certainly a conservative, though he regarded such expressions as "conservative political philosopher" as solecisms, and thought philosophy a quite different activity from the affirmation of political doctrines. "I am a member of no political party," he once said, "I vote – if I have to vote – for the party which is likely to do the least harm. To that extent, I am a Tory."

In print he was a sceptical idealist, and his work developed without any serious break from *Experience and its Modes* (1933). In character he was a romantic, for whom life was an end and a value in itself, and – like his own thought – a glorious adventure.

His dislike of public recognition and his disinclination to establish a school of disciples, made him academically a somewhat remote figure. Oakeshott seldom attended conferences and was much more at home in conversation with friends than in seminars.

He was quite indifferent to worldly success, and even to creature comforts; but he was by no means a hermit, and there was something irrepressibly boyish and Bohemian about him. A keen follower of the Turf, in 1936 he published, with another don, a book about how to pick a Derby winner; its title, *A Guide to the Classics*, greatly confused those schoolmasters who recommended it to sixth-formers learning Latin and Greek.

The amused irony with which he regarded human

life masked an extremely punctilious performance of his academic duties, and a great affection for his students. The bewitching style of his utterance, no less than his thoroughness and profundity, will make him an increasingly significant figure in political philosophy.

Michael Joseph Oakeshott was born on December 11 1901 and educated at St George's School, Harpenden. He later wrote of his cloudless provincial schooldays: "And when with inky fingers a schoolboy unpacked his satchel to do his homework he unpacked three thousand years of the fortunes and misfortunes of human intellectual adventure."

Cambridge, to which he went up just after the First World War, seemed to young Michael a magical place: "Almost overnight, a world of ungracious fact had melted into infinite possibility; we who belonged to no 'leisured class' had been freed for a moment from the curse of Adam, the burdensome distinction between work and play. What opened before us was not a road but a boundless sea; it was enough to stretch one's sails to the wind. The distracting urgency of an immediate destination was absent, duty no longer oppressed, boredom and disappointment were words without meaning; death was unthinkable."

He became a Fellow of Caius in 1925, and there passed his early years in an idyll of scholarship. "Some people say the world's the thing," he later remarked in a speech, "and the rare glimpses of it I have had suggest that they might be right. I too have dabbled in it from time to time. But, on the whole, I have found it overrated."

When the Second World War began, though – shortly after the publication of his book *Social and*

Michael Oakeshott

Political Doctrines of Contemporary Europe – Oakeshott was extremely quick to enlist. He ended up in "Phantom", a special unit whose purpose was to report from close to the Front the effect of artillery fire.

In 1945 he returned to Cambridge, where he wrote his famous introduction to the Blackwell edition of Thomas Hobbes's *Leviathan*. Oakeshott later wrote a book, *Hobbes on Civil Association* (1975), in which he came close to formulating his own political credo: "Our predicament is not the difficulty of attaining happiness, but the difficulty of avoiding the misery to which the pursuit of happiness exposes us. Government has a qualified but important part to play in extricating us from this predicament: its role is not to civilise but to maintain that peace and order without which civilisation is impossible."

His main activity in the early postwar years was editing and writing for the *Cambridge Journal*, an influential counterblast to the emerging consensus of the Attlee government. Some of these essays were published in *Rationalism in Politics* (1962), an example of Oakeshott at his polemical best.

The collection also included one of his treatments of the myth of the Tower of Babel, which always seemed to him the key to the character of modern life. With typical inadvertence, Oakeshott left several notable essays out of this book – and an expanded *Rationalism in Politics* was published in America in 1991.

In a later essay, *The Voice of Poetry in a Conversation of Mankind* (1959), he posited the notion of the philosopher as the contemplator of innumerably disparate voices.

Oakeshott's final achievement is to be found in his book, *On Human Conduct* (1975), in which he elaborated the distinction between enterprise associations (which are devoted to some specific purpose) and civil associations (which share only a common set of rules). An association of speakers of the same language illustrates this latter type of association; and – however much it was subverted by enthusiasts for one enterprise or another – Oakeshott believed that this was the model by which a modern European state should be understood.

Although Oakeshott was always the lone scholar, much of his work may be aligned with the linguistic analysis of such contemporaries as Gilbert Ryle and John Austin. It was held by some that Oakeshott was eager to dispel the illusions of others without ultimately seeming to stand for anything very much.

Such critics were perhaps answered by his last book, *The Voice of Liberal Learning* (1989), of which Ferdinand Mount, writing in *The Sunday Telegraph*, observed: "What does Oakeshott teach us then? Well, I think that as a general rule there are no general rules, and therefore that we should pay close attention to the particular rules of the game we happen to be playing."

In 1949 Oakeshott spent a year at Nuffield College, Oxford. Four years later he was a Muirhead lecturer at Birmingham University, and in 1957 he spent a term as Professor at Harvard.

At the LSE he turned out to be a brilliant administrator of the Government Department, orchestrating its affairs with a stream of notes in his precise and stylish handwriting, and spreading a spirit of collegiality. He rather detested the one-year Masters degrees which were set up in the early 1960s, but responded by creating one such course in the history of political ideas which became a magnet for scholars from all over the world.

Michael Oakeshott

He devoted the energies of this seminar to working out with immense thoroughness the character of historical understanding, work later to be published in *On History and Other Essays* (1983).

Oakeshott retired from the School in 1969, to live in a tiny, Spartan cottage in Dorset, heated only by an open fire and packed from floor to ceiling with books. There he pottered about in a fisherman's cap, grubby macintosh and scuffed trainers – a far cry from the "Tory dandy".

He enjoyed the company of women and was often in love. He enjoyed wine, too, and remained an unrepentant chain-smoker.

He was a sceptic only in accepting the necessity to endure "uncertainties, mysteries, doubts", and religious in the sense that he felt obliged to do penance for his sins, and to reconcile himself to "the unavoidable dissonancies of the human condition".

"It's dogged as does it." The sermon preached by Trollope's old brick-maker was Oakeshott's abiding conviction. In the last few weeks, when he was extremely uncomfortable, he kept saying, "It will pass."

Peregrine Worsthorne writes: As a man Michael Oakeshott was about as unsuitable a guru of the New Right as it is possible to imagine. On the whole, the New Right is somewhat earnest and humourless – not unlike the Old Left.

Michael was neither. He loved the company of free spirits, devil-may-care young bloods who lived life to the full without a care for the morrow. Victorian values were not for him.

Possibly his happiest years were during the war when he was Adjutant to B Squadron of Phantom, an intelligence unit which included a rum assortment of officers ranging from David Niven, at the height of his Hollywood fame, to me, still up at Cambridge.

Michael did not let on he was already a well-known Cambridge political philosopher. So far as his fellow officers were concerned, he was just marvellous company, always game for the most unsuitable of escapades.

On returning to Cambridge after the war I went to a lecture by its famous M. J. Oakeshott, not having the slightest idea that the man mounting the podium was my old comrade-in-arms of every kind.

When, years later, he was appointed to succeed Harold Laski at the LSE he lodged with my wife and me at Cardinal's Wharf, on the other side of the river from St Paul's. The house, reputed to be where Christopher Wren had lived while building the Cathedral, was infested with rats. Michael gave not a damn. He thought the rats a great joke and persuaded my wife – no mean feat – to think likewise.

My only regret about Michael as a lodger was that I could never get him to talk about "Conservatism", in which I was supposed to be interested. "Leave talking about politics to the Left," he used to say. "They have nothing better to do."

Yet in a way he was a guru. No piece of writing has ever influenced me as much as his famous essay *Rationalism in Politics*. By comparison, all the other political writers of the time – Laski, Cole, Bertrand Russell, not to say Marx – seemed vulgar and commonplace, not to say stuffy and pretentious.

Oakeshott's style was enchanting. Here was a man who taught my generation how Conservatism could be combined with Bohemianism, convention with eccentricity, orderliness with wild abandon, pleasure with responsibility.

Michael was the least worldly of men. To the end of his life he lived simply. No public recognition came his way.

Unlike a number of other leaders of the New Right, whose dislike of state handouts does not preclude them from accepting honours, he despised such baubles. Laughter and the love of friends – these were what he cherished and never lacked.

John Casey writes: In his late eighties Michael Oakeshott became the guiding spirit of a dining and discussion society in Caius College. He would sit until the small hours drinking with the young men. Michael's conversation had a curiously innocent, child-like quality, often exceedingly funny, but never self-regardingly witty.

For Michael, the "conversation of mankind" was the most enduring symbol of human life. Conversation is what distinguishes the civilised man from the barbarian. His talk must have had something of the sinuous charm which was always attributed to Newman.

The young who were so enchanted by his words were, whether they knew it or not, being introduced to philosophy. It always seemed to me that Michael took the greatest pleasure in the company of those of the young who would be men of the world rather than intellectuals.

He was by conviction a Romantic. His lifelong opposition to the managerial State was also a positive sense of life's adventure.

I think he deplored any political philosophy which aims to reduce the element of adventure – and hence the need for courage – in human life. Oakeshott celebrated "younger sons making their way in a world that has little place for them, footloose adventurers who left the land to take to trade".

His heroes included the intellectually audacious: Abelard, Benvenuto Cellini, St John of the Cross, and, above all, Montaigne.

Although he was a man of superlative intellectual distinction, Michael was not an academic grandee. He never featured as one of the great and the good. I doubt if he ever sat on a committee.

Quite simply, the intellectually most memorable evenings of my life were spent in Oakeshott's company, and I cannot expect to find anything in the future that will compare with them.

December 21 1990

SIR BRIAN BATSFORD

SIR BRIAN BATSFORD, who has died aged 80, was a politician, publisher and above all a painter, whose signal contribution to the heritage movement in Britain has tended to be undervalued.

The urbane and worldly-wise Batsford was an improbable combination of aesthete, conservationist and, from 1964 to 1967, deputy Opposition Chief Whip – though he relied on charm rather than strong-arm tactics to chivvy his flock into the division lobbies.

As an assistant Government Whip Batsford played an important part in the events that led to the choice of

Sir Alec Douglas-Home as party leader and Prime Minister in 1963.

Batsford's principal role in Parliament, however, was concerned with the history of the Palace of Westminster. He was chairman of the Commons Library Committee and of the Commons advisory committee on the preservation of its works of art.

For many years he was the National Trust's tenant at Lamb House in Rye, though with characteristic modesty he used to claim that – in the wake of such previous occupants as Henry James and E. F. Benson – he was rather letting the side down as a publisher. But Sir Brian was certainly no ordinary publisher. During his nigh on 50-year association with the family publishing house, the name of Batsford became synonymous with well-produced books on heritage subjects.

Indeed, the pioneering multi-volumed Batsford "British Heritage" publications of the 1930s played a significant part in opening people's eyes to the manifold riches of the land in which they lived. The books were adorned with an entirely new form of coloured wrap-around jacket. The limitations of the printing process, which allowed only the use of brilliant primary colours, helped to give the Batsford jackets their distinction.

Until recently little was known about the artist of these gloriously evocative covers, with their sympathetic sense of place and excellent draughtsmanship – one Brian Cook. Nothing had been heard of him since the 1940s.

In fact, the artist was none other than Sir Brian Batsford himself: in 1946 he had changed his name from his patronymic of Cook to his mother's maiden name of Batsford.

Brian Caldwell Cook was born on December 18 1910 and educated at Repton and the Central School of Arts and Crafts. Besides designing more than 200 book jackets and contributing numerous pen-and-ink illustrations to Batsford publications, he exhibited in Paris and designed posters for Thomas Cook, the London & North Eastern Railway and the British Travel and Holidays Association.

During the Second World War he served with the RAF in Bomber Command Intelligence and afterwards contested Chelmsford for the National Government. He was finally elected to the Commons in 1958 for Ealing South.

The management of the publishing house and his political career left him little time for painting. But Batsford did not lay aside his brush.

At his holiday house in north Cornwall he produced canvases that delighted, among others, his old friend and neighbour Sir John Betjeman, whose Cornish poems Batsford illustrated.

Then, in the mid-1980s, "Brian Cook" was suddenly rediscovered, revealed as Sir Brian Batsford and accorded a cult status among illustrators. "I am the artist who came in from the cold," he said.

Batsford reverted to signing his work under his earlier name and was in demand for commissions ranging from Christmas catalogue covers for the National Trust to the labels of Harrods' biscuit tins. In 1987 he published a handsome collection, *The Britain of Brian Cook*, and the Michael Parkin Gallery in London put on a retrospective exhibition.

He served the Arts and Recreation Committee of the

Greater London Council and was also chairman of the Royal Society of Arts, president of the London Appreciation Society and of the conservation society in Rye — where his tall, benevolent, Panama-hatted figure was a familiar sight in the cobbled streets.

He was knighted in 1974 on retirement from the House of Commons and from the chairmanship of Batsford. Latterly he simply described himself in *Who's Who* as a "painter".

He married, in 1945, Wendy Cunliffe; they had two daughters.

March 6 1991

R. J. O. 'JACK' MEYER

R. J. O. "JACK" MEYER, who has died aged 85, was the most remarkable and arguably the most successful headmaster in Britain in the years after the Second World War.

His foundation, Millfield in Somerset, began with a sprinkling of Indian princes in 1935, and grew into an outstanding public school. In particular it gained a reputation for sending forth a stream of first-class athletes.

"Jack" Meyer himself had been a formidable all-round games player, and his school reflected his versatility. There were Olympic gold-medallists such as David Hemery and Mary Bignal Rand, a lorry driver's daughter who was obliged to leave the school owing to an infatuation with a Siamese prince; tennis players such as

111

Mike Sangster; golfers such as Brian Barnes; the swimmer Duncan Goodhew; and, most illustrious of all, the great Welsh scrum-half Gareth Edwards.

But Millfield was, and remains, far more than a sporting nursery. The school also produced an annual clutch of Oxbridge scholarships, occasionally achieved by candidates who had come to the school after failing the 11-plus.

For it was Meyer's credo that, no matter how indifferent the material, there was always talent to be elicited. He liked to call Millfield "the only comprehensive school that really works" – the kind of phrase that never failed to irritate the zealots of Left-wing educational theory.

It was true, though, that there was no entrance examination to Millfield. If Meyer liked a boy or girl he took him or her in and with no regard to rank, riches or class.

He never scrupled to demand outrageous fees – and even "entrance" charges of, say, £10,000 – from those who could afford them, a policy which allowed him to educate children of the poor for nothing. "I don't mind taking money off the rich," he explained. "If I didn't have it they'd only spend it on drink or motor cars or something."

The story goes that a Duke once approached Meyer, a shade diffidently, to take his son into the school. The boy had failed to gain entrance to Eton, despite the fact that generations of his ancestors had graced the school. Meyer explained the peculiar character of his school to the Duke; that it had girls as well as boys, that it was not exclusive to the rich and that he made a point of taking talented children from the local town.

The Duke looked doubtful. "One has to think carefully about this," he said. "What if my son were to meet and get attached to a chimney-sweep's daughter? What would I do then?"

"What makes you think a chimney-sweep's daughter would *want* to get involved with a boy who had failed entrance to Eton?" Meyer returned. The Duke sent his son to Millfield.

The school's success certainly could not be explained in terms of the physical environment. For years its buildings were lamentable: Nissen huts, with pupils in their overcoats huddled round a stove, and "chicken runs" as they were called, no better than wooden sheds.

From the start, though, Meyer grasped the overwhelming importance of good teachers – both David Cornwell (John Le Carré) and Robert Bolt served on his staff. He made a point of seeking out and recruiting mature staff – whether ex-Servicemen or outstanding public schoolmasters (such as the ebullient Charles Lillingston of Harrow) who were on the point of retirement, men who still had 10 years or more of good teaching in them, not least as coaches for Oxbridge.

Meyer also insisted on small classes, with a teacher-pupil ratio never greater than one to eight. Much of the teaching was one-to-one, and not simply for scholarship preparation: Meyer made a speciality of taking in dyslexic children and other public school rejects.

"A backward boy is like a broken-down lorry," he explained. "You can push him up the hill by brute force – that's cramming. Or you can try and get his engine started, and that's what we do at Millfield."

But Meyer was not a sentimentalist; he resisted any

idea of disguising from children that some were less able than others. Life was a battlefield, and all must be taught to fight for their place in the sun.

It was important to turn the attention of backward children towards other activities – be it bird-watching, climbing, photography, gardening, or whatever. The confidence thus gained would bear fruit in their academic studies – or, in the case of Tony Blackburn, in an ability to jabber between gramophone records.

But Millfield's conspicuous success did not earn it much support from other public schools. Meyer was never invited to join the prestigious Head Masters Conference (HMC).

And when the school governors tried to join the Governing Bodies Association they were told that the school was "not up to our standards". Yet in that same year Millfield received a glowing report from Her Majesty's Inspectors – "the best school we have seen in years".

Meyer believed that the hostility was based on deliberate prejudice against him because of the unconventional nature of his school. He also thought there was a great deal of jealousy because his school attracted an impressive array of celebrities' offspring – Hailie Selassie's grandson, Dame Margot Fonteyn's stepson, the 1st Earl Attlee's son ("I am sending him to your school because of my Socialist principles," the Labour statesman told Meyer) – and many others.

Elizabeth Taylor sent her children by Michael Wilding to Millfield. But Richard Burton, when he met Meyer, professed that he found him "disappointing . . . I had imagined a much wiser, more authoritative man. This man was tall, thin, very English, nervous in gesture and a compulsive talker. One white liar recognises another and I found some of his stories too highly polished . . . still, he's obviously good at his job."

Meyer's own memories of meeting Richard Burton were that the actor was so drunk that the headwaiter was obliged to put a screen round their table. And his relations with Miss Taylor declined sharply when he insisted that she should herself deliver her son to Millfield.

Meyer's views on education were by no means uniformly progressive. With his conviction of the moral and educative function of games, he expressed outrage that the standard of public school cricket should be sacrificed to the quest for marginally higher standards at "A" Level.

Known in the school as "Boss", he was a stout defender of the cane, believing that it was necessary to resist the natural tendency of children to probe for the weak spots in authority. "The young should be made to realise that behind the work of reproof is something hard that hurts."

Meyer worked for the school day and night, claiming in 1968 to have gone 17 months without going to bed. But his headmastership ended unhappily.

In 1953 he had made the school over to an educational trust, which meant that his own position became dependent on the continued support of the governors. He had always had a weakness for the gaming tables, and in 1970 the governors were obliged to demand if he had been playing the casinos from fees which parents had paid.

"Of course," Meyer replied; and the school had gained handsomely from his speculations. The answer was not deemed satisfactory and the headmaster was demoted to the office of Warden, being succeeded by another Somerset cricket captain of more ascetic bent, Colin Atkinson.

A canon's son, Rollo John Oliver Meyer was born in Bedfordshire on March 15 1905, and educated at Haileybury before reading History and English at Pembroke College, Cambridge.

On the games field Meyer was at once brilliant and unpredictable. When he opened the bowling against Oxford at Lord's he sent down a lemon first ball and professed himself most satisfied with the amount of swing obtained.

After Cambridge he thought of becoming a schoolmaster, but finding himself in the embarrassing position of having accepted offers from Eton and Harrow simultaneously escaped to India as a cotton broker. When this first career was ended by the stockmarket crash of 1929, Meyer turned to tutoring Indian princes.

In 1935 he returned to England and took a house at Millfield to prepare six Indian princes and three English boys for various kinds of further education – Sandhurst, the Civil Service and Oxbridge entrance.

"I didn't mean to found a school," he later reflected, "it was all a mistake." But once Millfield was launched Meyer never doubted that he would succeed, despite numerous difficulties with the bank; today there are more than 1,200 pupils.

Even in retirement Jack Meyer remained irrepressible. After toying with a scheme to found a new Millfield on Francis Noel-Baker's estate on Euboea, in 1973 he became president of the Campion International School in Athens and spoke highly of the help he received from the Greek military junta – "the Colonels have helped in every way".

Meyer appointed a sociologist as headmaster – "I told him straight that hogwash was not one of my subjects." In two years the school was thriving, but when the governors sacked a woman teacher without consulting him he resigned.

He said that he would like his ashes to be spread on the Millfield wicket: "It's a pretty fast pitch as it is . . . and a few ashes should make it even faster."

Meyer was appointed OBE in 1967. He married, in 1931, Joyce Symons; they had two daughters, one of whom predeceased him.

E. W. Swanton writes: The personality, imagination and energy which had enabled him to found Millfield were reflected in Meyer the sportsman. He was a rackets Blue and on coming down from Cambridge became a good enough golfer to be made a member of the Oxford and Cambridge Golfing Society. But it was as a cricketer that his qualities found special scope.

An outstanding bowler and captain at Haileybury, he played all his three years in the strong Cambridge sides of 1924–26, in his last year shaking the Australians by taking six of their wickets for 65 with a versatile mixture of swing and spin. Following 10 years of first-class cricket in India, he returned in 1936 as a fully-fledged all-rounder for Somerset.

With a remarkable 202 not out in 3¾ hours at Taunton he deprived Lancashire of victory. Two years later, for the Gentlemen against the Australians, he had five, including Don Bradman's wicket, for 66 runs. He was very much a man for the occasion.

Meyer could only be an intermittent player for Somerset except in 1947 when, aged 42, he took on the captaincy. He had to battle courageously through the summer with back trouble while the solid professional core of the side could not always keep up with his theories.

His admiring contemporary R. C. Robertson-Glasgow, recounting how Meyer experimented with every variety of slow bowling including the occasional, enormously high leg-break known as the "Spedigue Dropper", quotes him lamenting that he really needed 12 or 13 fielders. " 'It works,' he said in his philosophical way, 'but like the earlier models of the motor-cycle it needs a lot of attention.' "

Undoubtedly Meyer's most valuable contribution to cricket was the beckoning finger he extended throughout his long headmastership of Millfield to potential cricketers, including many whose parents had to have generous help with the school fees. No one expressed better the "*mens sana*" ideal.

March 11 1991

SEAN O'FAOLAIN

SEAN O'FAOLAIN, the Irish writer who has died aged 91, was the author of more than 20 volumes, including four novels, five biographies, collections of essays and a play.

He said, though, that if his name was to live he hoped it would be for his short stories, even if only for a handful of them. V. S. Pritchett has called O'Faolain the greatest short story writer of the 20th century, and he was also known as "the Irish Chekhov".

Tall, slim and carefully groomed, O'Faolain did not look like the traditional idea of an Irish writer. Highly self-disciplined and costive of his art, he wrote every day with great deliberation, aiming at 500 words.

His manner was cautious, sometimes ruefully genial, and his life was full of contradictions. A policeman's son, he joined the IRA when he was in his teens; a bitterly anti-clerical polemicist, he was also a devout Roman Catholic; an exile, he embraced his home country in middle age.

O'Faolain conducted a long and deeply felt battle against censorship in Ireland. His fiction posed awkward questions about the conflict and confluence of religion and nationalism, and he maintained that this was the true reason for its being banned, though the Catholic clergy argued that it was because his work was "in general tendency indecent".

"You will not always find legs or breasts or beds in these books," O'Faolain wrote. "What our censors consider to be dangerous, evil or imponderable questions are those about God and love and sin and the devil, and it is this that they like most of all to ban."

He conducted his campaign in a literary journal, *The Bell*, which he founded from a garden shed in 1940, and in which he also attacked Ireland's new "peasant government". Twenty years earlier he had worshipped the architect of this, Eamon de Valera, but subsequently decided that de Valera was "not a great man but merely a great Irishman", there being a world of difference between permissive Irish criteria and universal standards of greatness. In Dublin, he said, "objectivity is as rare as anonymity".

Although he lived in Dublin for 30 years, O'Faolain never rubbed shoulders with the tiny literary coterie of the Palace and Pearl Bars, sharing Cyril Connolly's view that this bitterly jealous enclave was "an alligator tank".

The youngest of three sons, he was born in Cork on February 22 1900, and christened John Whelan; his later adoption of the Gaelic form was symptomatic of a breach with his father over loyalty to the Crown.

His father was a constable in the Royal Irish Constabulary, and the family lived almost next door to the Cork Opera House. In his autobiography, *Vive Moi*, O'Faolain gives a faithful account of what life was like at the time for people such as his parents, whose ambition for their children was at odds with their income and social background.

After primary school, young John went to the Christian Brothers' secondary school in Cork, where he disliked the severe and restricted atmosphere, although he was always a conscientious scholar. The Easter Rebellion of 1916 shocked him at first – as it did his father – but he soon became involved in the Republican movement led by Tom Barry in the county. He took lessons in Irish, and became a fluent speaker before he entered University College, Cork, in 1918.

O'Faolain had made an influential friendship before this with a younger boy who was to change his name from Michael O'Donovan to Frank O'Connor. Both of them were taken up and encouraged by Daniel Corkery, a Gaelic enthusiast and a variously gifted autodidact.

O'Faolain joined the IRA in 1920 and played a

minor role in skirmishes during the sacking of Cork by British Auxiliaries. He later fictionalised this distinctly unheroic episode, describing it as "seven months spent wandering on wet mountainsides".

In the Civil War that followed the Anglo-Irish Treaty of 1921 he worked as a propagandist for the Republican cause and also tried his hand at bomb-making, meanwhile earning a meagre living as a commercial traveller for educational books.

He and O'Connor had become Republicans because they envisioned a state such as Wolfe Tone and the revolutionaries of 1798 had dreamed of, with intellectual liberty to the fore; but they were disillusioned by the narrow Jansenist and provincial atmosphere in the new state.

O'Faolain's disappointment was particularly keen. In an essay he wrote at that time about the short story he warned against the use of the word "dawn" in prose, and this may have been less a piece of technical advice than a pointer to his own disillusion.

In 1928 he managed to escape to America, where "AE" (George Russell) had sponsored him for a Commonwealth Fellowship at Harvard. "I couldn't have been happy in the Ireland I had left behind," he said. "The bullying and spying that followed the revolution was too much, as well as the exploitation and conservatism."

The next year he moved across the Charles River to teach English at Boston College, and then found a job at a Roman Catholic teacher training college at Strawberry Hill in Middlesex, where he remained until 1933.

O'Faolain had been writing stories in America and sent one to Richard Garnett, who acted as adviser to Jonathan Cape and had an exceptional eye for spotting talent; when he read the story he encouraged O'Faolain to write enough to make up a book. (He was also to be encouraged by Evelyn Waugh.) The result was *Midsummer Night Madness* (1932). O'Connor's *Guests of the Nation* appeared at much the same time, and the chorus of critical praise was a landmark in Irish literary history, though O'Faolain's book was banned by the Irish clergy.

Cape gave him £200 a year for three years to return to Ireland and concentrate on writing. O'Faolain published his first novel, *A Nest of Simple Folk*, in 1934, which he followed with *Bird Alone* (1936).

O'Faolain produced another collection of stories, *A Field of Coppers*, in 1937; a third novel, *Come Back to Erin* (1940), a play, *She Had to Do Something*, which was performed at the Abbey Theatre in 1937, and biographies of Constance Markievicz, Daniel O'Connell and de Valera.

He left Ireland again in 1946, this time for Italy. His mischievous spirit delighted in finding there the same moral duality as in Ireland, where the "medley of venery and sanctity" and the mixture of corruption and superficial respectability were not, he felt, the hideous dishonesty seen by Calvinist historians but an *esuberante* of emotion, imagination and human sympathy.

O'Faolain's travel books, *A Summer in Italy* (1949) and *South to Sicily* (1953), are celebrations of Italian temperament and character. "The large numbers of Italians who believe in the miraculous", he wrote, "will never surprise an Irishman."

O'Faolain returned to Ireland again in 1956, and after the fall of de Valera's government the new coalition administration provided him with an income by appointing him director of the Arts Council for a five-year term.

This was no sinecure, however, and he happily abandoned it after three years when he was appointed a Fellow of Princeton University.

His other works included a fourth novel, *And Again* (1979), as well as eight more collections of stories.

The Italian government honoured him with the Star of Solidarity, but O'Faolain remained unhonoured in Ireland until quite recently. In 1986 he became the first writer since Samuel Beckett to be elected to the position of *Saoi* (senior), by the Aosdana, the Irish arts academy, and also received the Freedom of Cork – though he declined to attend either of these ceremonies.

O'Faolain married Eileen Gould, the writer of children's stories and compiler of Irish sagas and folk tales; she died in 1988. They had a son and a daughter, the novelist Julia O'Faolain.

April 22 1991

THE VERY REVEREND LORD MACLEOD OF FUINARY

THE VERY REVEREND LORD MACLEOD OF FUINARY, a former Moderator of the Church of Scotland, who has died aged 96, was a preacher given to burning jeremiads in the manner of an Old Testament prophet; but the central achievement of his life was the creation of a community on Iona to be a spiritual forcing-house amid the religious indifference of the modern world.

MacLeod claimed that St Columba's purpose in founding the original monastery on Iona in the 6th century had been "ecstatically active". If the brotherhood had occasionally been found in retreat on the island, this was only so that they might sally forth refreshed for their essential missionary purpose.

A similar philosophy lay behind the community MacLeod founded there in 1938. "We have had enough books to declare the superiority of the Kingdom of God over Fascism and Communism," he declared. "What men begin to want is a little more evidence that we believe in the efficacy of that Kingdom with something of the forthright intensity that these lesser creeds might seem able to command."

MacLeod's experiences among the unemployed in 1930s Glasgow had made him sharply aware that the Church of Scotland was in crisis, quite out of touch with the new industrialised society. The first aim of the Iona Community was to recruit ministers for pastoral work in the new housing estates of Scotland.

The original scheme provided for 20 probationer-ministers to visit Iona during the summer months; they would then work in the crowded industrial cities for the remainder of their two-year contract. The summer community also included unemployed masons, carpenters and other craftsmen from the mainland, who helped restore the ruined Benedictine monastery.

MacLeod hoped that on Iona the ministers should be "corporately separate" from the 20th century; but he also intended that they might learn, through the experience of living with the craftsmen, how removed they were from their flocks.

This was the core of the community. But every year pilgrims came from all over the world to make retreats on the island, and hundreds of young people arrived to join in the work of the community, and so the project took on the character of an ecumenical movement within the Church.

MacLeod himself was far from being a blinkered Presbyterian. When he was elected as Moderator of the General Assembly in 1957 an objector expressed his disgust at the new Moderator's "episcopal emphasis".

Indeed, though the mere mention of "bishop" smacked of popery among his co-religionists, MacLeod did favour some reconciliation of the episcopal, presbyterian and congregational principles of ecclesiastical organisation.

His political views, though, were much more dogmatic; nor did he hesitate to identify them with true Christianity. Proud to declare himself a Socialist, he showed himself fiercely opposed to those who believed that religion was simply a matter between a man and his Maker, independent of any social obligation.

Those who thought of religion only in terms of worship, MacLeod argued, were unlikely to hear the voice of God. Equally, "whether we are to go to hell or heaven is dependent on what we do about people's bodies, not their spiritual welfare".

MacLeod regarded well-intentioned capitalists in the same way as Tolstoy did: "I sit on a man's back, choking him and making him carry me, and yet assure myself and others that I am sorry for him and wish to lighten his load by all possible means – *except by getting off his back*."

When he published the Cunningham lectures he had given at Edinburgh University in 1954 he chose the significant title *Only One Way Left*.

A preacher in the great Scottish tradition, whose impassioned eloquence swept through the congregation like a rushing mighty wind, MacLeod never hesitated to denounce the evils of this world. His later utterances were haunted by the apocalyptic nightmare of racial war; and he feared that the time might come when one would pray to be delivered from being born white.

As for the power of international finance: "This new Moloch devours our young," he thundered. And Mac-Leod was sure that God would regard the Common Market beef and butter mountains as "sin".

Another target was "the gross impurities of secular science", a phrase which chiefly related to research on chemical warfare. Notably valiant as a soldier in the First World War, MacLeod afterwards became a dedicated pacifist, in contrast to the vast majority of Christians, whom he dubbed "passivist: they have neither the gumption to be pacifist nor the guts to be participant."

By the 1950s MacLeod believed that the British people had learned the lesson of interdependence, that the Welfare State was an application of Christianity to society, and that Christian Socialism would alone save humanity. The coming of Mrs Thatcher, far from undermining this faith, left him all the more convinced that it was securely founded.

George Fielden MacLeod was born on June 17 1895 into a family which had already given notable service to the Church of Scotland – both his great-grandfather and grandfather had been Moderators of the General Assembly. His father, John MacLeod, an accountant, was

Conservative MP first for the Central, and then for the Kelvingrove division of Glasgow, and was created a Baronet in 1924.

Young George was educated at Winchester and Oriel College, Oxford. In the First World War he served in Salonika and France, mostly with the Argyll and Sutherland Highlanders, of which he was adjutant for three years; his gallantry was recognised by the award of a Military Cross and the *Croix de Guerre* with palms.

Upon his return from the war he took his degree at Oxford, and passed through the Divinity Hall at Edinburgh. In 1921 he obtained the Scottish nomination to the Union Theological Seminary in New York, and then undertook missionary work at the Arrow Lakes Lumber Camps in British Columbia.

Those who take to the straight and narrow path in adulthood are inclined to dwell somewhat exaggeratedly upon the sins of their youth; certainly before he "surrendered his life to Christ" MacLeod had been given to drinking and gambling and had smoked 50 cigarettes a day. In the early days of ministry, when he was an assistant at St Giles's, Edinburgh, he would arrive dashingly at the cathedral door in an open-topped sports car, before proceeding to stir the consciences of the rich and the hearts of the women in the congregation. The genteel church-goers of Edinburgh decided that here, indeed, was a preacher for the Jazz Age.

Already, though, a transformation was bubbling up through the yeast of his spirit – born partly, perhaps, of his experiences in the trenches, and partly of a steadily growing rage for social justice. In the mid-1920s he was ordained as chaplain to Toc H in Glasgow.

From 1926 to 1930 MacLeod was Collegiate Minister at St Cuthbert's in Edinburgh, where he won golden opinions for his work among the young, "for whom he seemed to have a magnetic attraction"; and then from 1930 to 1938 he was minister of Govan Parish Church in the depressed shipyards of Glasgow.

In the Second World War MacLeod appeared on Hitler's list for liquidation – the Nazi "roll of honour" as Humphrey Bogart described it in *Casablanca*. At the same time, thanks to his pacifism, the British would not allow him to broadcast.

In 1963 MacLeod was made president and chairman of the Council of International Fellowship of Reconciliation, and in 1989 he received the Templeton Prize for progress in religion. His books included *We Shall Rebuild* (1944), in which he outlined the principles of the Iona community.

MacLeod inherited the family baronetcy from his nephew in 1944, and in 1967 was created a life peer as Baron MacLeod of Fuinary. He married, in 1948, Lorna, daughter of the Reverend Donald MacLeod, who died in 1984; they had two sons and a daughter.

The elder son, John Maxwell Norman MacLeod, born in 1952, now succeeds to the baronetcy.

June 28 1991

SIR ROY WELENSKY

SIR ROY WELENSKY, Prime Minister of the ill-starred and short-lived Central African Federation, who has died aged 84, was the last of the great imperial statesmen.

A Rhodesian train driver, trade union leader and heavyweight boxing champion, Roy Welensky used to boast of being 50 per cent Lithuanian, 50 per cent Jewish, yet 100 per cent British. He promised to create a multiracial dominion that would help the Mother Country to recover from the Second World War.

But Welensky succeeded to power in November 1956, just as the Suez crisis started. The subsequent haemorrhage of British self-confidence went with an increasingly vocal demand for a public show of racial equality that struck at the heart of the white-led Federation – which envisaged majority black rule only in a distant and unspecified future.

The Central African Federation began its decade of life in 1953 – the year of the Queen's Coronation and centenary of Cecil Rhodes's birth – with the slightly hesitant motto *Magni esse mereamur* ("Let us deserve to be great").

Greeted as a bulwark between the emerging independent black autocracies to the north and South Africa's apartheid society to the south, it promised considerable economic advantages in bringing together the more developed Southern Rhodesia, the copper-rich Northern Rhodesia and Nyasaland with its potentially large black workforce.

A steady, if unspectacular, flow of white immigrants from Britain responded to the call. They became Welensky's electoral backbone and political millstone as he attempted to steer the Federation slowly towards a multiracial society.

As the Federation's principal architect and driving force, he commanded wondering admiration from the Tories in Britain with his abrasive talk of imperial leadership. Nevertheless, they also saw in him the representative of a feather-bedded white working-class minority.

The Socialists, who should have been his natural allies, recoiled at his belief that blacks would remain the junior partners until they achieved an undefined standard of civilisation and, instead, backed those Africans who were demanding independence. Welensky pleaded, threatened, blustered, while Harold Macmillan – sometimes with tears in his eyes – swore the undying support of his government in London. But the story was one of steady retreat before the slightest blast from Kenneth Kaunda and Dr Hastings Banda, the future rulers of the economically stagnant Zambia and Malawi (as Northern Rhodesia and Nyasaland respectively became).

When the experiment was finally wound up in 1963, it represented not just Welensky's failure, but Britain's abdication as an imperial power. Macmillan later attempted to justify the decision with the reflection that the problems involving three such diverse states made it like trying to unite East and West Germany under a single system.

Raphael Welensky was born in Salisbury, Southern Rhodesia, on January 20 1907, the 13th child of a Lithuanian Jew and his Boer wife who had trekked from South Africa by ox-wagon and ended up running a boarding house. Roy (as he was always known) left school at 14 to work as a barman, butcher, clerk and store-keeper.

From 1926 to 1928 he was heavyweight boxing champion of the two Rhodesias. As a fighter he probably owed his success more to his burly 6ft frame than to sound knowledge of ringcraft – an advantage, it was later remarked, that did him no good in political life for all his pugilistic talk of straight punching, corners and knockouts.

His first piece of luck was in marrying Elizabeth Harrison, a waitress, who bore him a son and a daughter and encouraged him to channel his ambitions.

Welensky settled down to join the white artisan élite by becoming an engine-driver, a job that turned him into a keen trade unionist and enabled him to use long hours on the footplate reading widely in biography, politics and history.

After exciting railway company ire during a bitter strike at Wankie, Southern Rhodesia, he was moved to Broken Hill, in the North, where he revived the local branch of the Railway Workers Union. His rapid success as a negotiator was due to the fact that he remained carefully within the bounds dictated by the rulebook; but he did not hesitate to resort to his fists when, in his first taste of politics, he found his engine was daubed with anti-Semitic and anti-masonic slogans.

Welensky's reputation as the "Railwaymen's KC" led him to be elected to the Northern Rhodesia legislature in 1938. He was firmly committed to preventing settlers' rights from being downgraded in favour of cheap black labour and also to improving the rights of the "unofficial" members of Legco, who formed the informal opposition to the Whitehall-appointed governor and his civil servants.

In 1941 Welensky formed a Labour Party but the same year he was brought within the government for the duration of the war. After taking part in an inquiry into a strike he was appointed the colony's director of manpower, in which capacity he did not hesitate to send back to Britain one particularly troublesome union official.

With the end of hostilities Welensky devoted his energies to waging a campaign to claim part of the royalties from mineral resources, which the British South Africa Company had retained when it gave up responsibility for the government of Northern Rhodesia in 1918, and to pressing for amalgamation of the two Rhodesias. He ultimately proved successful with the first, but the second was out of the question, as he discovered on a visit to London when he saw both the Labour and Tory spokesmen on colonial affairs.

Afterwards, however, he called on Sir Godfrey Huggins, the long-serving Southern Rhodesian Prime Minister, who was staying at the Hyde Park Hotel. He persuaded Huggins to seek a federation of the two Rhodesias and Nyasaland.

The inclusion of the latter, a largely undeveloped agricultural economy – often dismissed as an "imperial slum" – was the price Britain put on the chance to be rid of an embarrassing responsibility.

Welensky took the leading part in pushing through the plan for the Central African Federation; at one point he employed the White Russian Prince Yurka Galitzine as a public relations consultant in London to counter the activities of the already significant lobby which was championing opposition from the territories' Africans.

The resulting constitution was so complicated as to be incomprehensible to all but a small minority of whites. It had to accommodate both the settler-dominated administration of Southern Rhodesia, which had enjoyed a large measure of independence since 1923, and the London-ruled territories. The latter's suspicious Colonial Office masters justified their lack of encouragement for industrial development on the grounds that they were only acting as trustees until their charges were ready for independence.

In all, the four governments in the Federation had to deal with five Whitehall departments. This was not an insuperable problem for the shrewd Huggins, who knew Whitehall's ways and was to retire with a seat in the House of Lords as Viscount Malvern.

On resigning the Southern Rhodesian premiership, Huggins became the Federation's first Prime Minister and acknowledged Welensky's right to the succession by making him Minister of Transport and Posts. This appointment ended the engine-driver's career on the footplate with the compensation of having overall responsibility for the entire railway network.

After three years of comparative peace and consolidation – although the soft bubble of African dissent, which had always existed, continued to grow – Welensky succeeded to the prime ministership in 1956 just as the honeymoon period was ending.

A decline in copper prices was on the horizon, although provision had been made for this. The consumer boom in Britain ensured that the flow of immigrants was not going to reach the half-million figure for which Welensky had hoped.

The Mau Mau emergency in Kenya, the abandonment of the French empire and the granting of independence to Ghana all fuelled British unease. Britain became all the more vulnerable when the precipitate abandonment of the Congo by the Belgians proved so chaotic that United Nations representatives were brought in.

Welensky's sympathies lay with the breakaway Katanga province, whose borders were contiguous with the Federation. But Macmillan would not permit him to intervene; it would have led to an outright clash with the UN, which nursed suspicions following the death of Dag Hammarskjöld in a plane crash within the Federation's borders.

The return home of Dr Banda, a former north London doctor, prompted an outbreak of violence in Nyasaland. This was dealt with firmly by the Territorial governor; but its importance was blown out of all proportion, first by opposition at Westminster and then by Lord Devlin's inflammatory critical report which Macmillan had to reject. Macmillan next resorted to the well-tried device of a Royal Commission to look at the Federation's future.

Welensky fought back, winning considerable sympathy and admiration for his pluck, not least in braving a new form of political torture, the television interview. Asked by John Freeman on *Face to Face* if he knew much about the ordinary African, he retorted: "Considering that when I was a lad I swam bare-arsed in the Makabusi with many piccaninnies ... I think I can say I know something of the Africans."

But as he continued his progress up the honours ladder, with his appointment as KCMG in 1959 and his membership of the Privy Council in 1960 (having been appointed CMG in 1946 and knighted in 1953), Welensky's suspicions became more marked.

He won a promise from Macmillan that the Monckton Commission inquiry into the future of the Federation would not consider the possibility of secession. Macmillan, however, could only enlist Lord Shawcross as its lone Labour member by agreeing in private that secession would not be excluded from the agenda.

Welensky's troubles with London grew worse, first with the appointment in 1959 of Iain Macleod as a Colonial Secretary who believed his duty was to speed up the pace of independence in Africa. Then there was Macmillan's "Wind of Change" speech, delivered to the Cape Town Parliament, in which the British leader confirmed the new era – despite an assurance to Welensky that an earlier remark about Northern Rhodesia and Nyasaland being offered a chance to decide their future had been misquoted.

A regular pattern developed, of British assurances and demands for further concessions, then pleas by Macmillan that Welensky would not rock the boat, followed by further promises that would be quickly broken. Eventually Macmillan appointed R. A. Butler as Africa Secretary, a post which Welensky had been demanding for years. The final obsequies of the Federation were said, with Northern Rhodesia and Nyasaland being waved off along the path towards one-party states. Ominously, Southern Rhodesia was refused any further independence.

When the Federation ended in 1963 Welensky announced his intention to stay on and start a market garden. He turned down the offer of a peerage by Butler, which he later regretted, and also refused a GCMG. Ultimately he accepted only an inscribed cigarette box from the Queen at a private lunch, although he was a non-smoker.

While there was no place for him in Southern

Rhodesia politics, Welensky had strong support on the right wing of the Tory party, which led to his being offered five British seats.

Instead, Welensky decided to get in his side of the story first, for once. His book *Welensky's 4,000 Days* (1964) had a tone of bitter exasperation, matched by some extremely sharp remarks about his opponents – such as that Macmillan's mind was "the most complicated that I have encountered in my political life" and that Macleod was "a mixture of cold calculation, sudden gushes of emotion and ignorance of Africa".

The outrage on publication, however, concerned a passage which revealed that a conversation in jail between Banda and the Labour MP Dingle Foot, QC, had been taped at the order of Sir Edgar Whitehead, the Southern Rhodesian premier. No hint of the bugging of Welensky's suite at the Savoy by the British Government leaked out, however.

Back in Rhodesia, Ian Smith's government was seriously contemplating the option of rebellion, a move Welensky himself had once contemplated but which he now launched a new party to fight. The government called a special by-election in which Smith's minister Clifford Dupont won a signal victory over Welensky.

Welensky abandoned his party and from then on remained a voice of reason on the sidelines. He deplored the unilateral declaration of independence in 1965 and spoke out, with the octogenarian Lord Malvern, against the decision to declare the rebel state a republic four years later.

At the same time, Welensky's private life took a tragic turn when his wife, Elizabeth, died in 1969. However, three years later, on a visit to London, he met and married Valerie Scott, a Conservative party worker in London and Westminster who was 30 years his junior.

They settled in Salisbury, Rhodesia, and had two daughters, for the birth of whom Lady Welensky travelled home so that they could be born British.

Shortly after the Smith regime collapsed Welensky announced that his health necessitated that he move to Britain. He became a regular attender at the big heavyweight boxing fights and devoted his leisure to gardening and watching his young family growing up.

In his last years, the by now physically frail Welensky surprised visitors by his tolerant attitude towards his old political enemies, black and white, although he remained deeply hurt by Britain's duplicity. "A prime minister, like a general, has to have luck," he would say. "My share of luck was on the thin side."

He particularly enjoyed showing off an African bust in the corner of his untidy sitting-room which had been given him by a fellow freemason, the Nigerian Prime Minister Sir Abubakar Tafawa Balewa.

Welensky's only expression of public irritation was against the virulence of the local insect population at his home at Blandford Forum in Dorset; in a letter to *The Daily Telegraph* in 1990 he complained that they were more vicious than African tsetse flies.

Welensky's last political gesture had come in 1980, just as the dictatorial Robert Mugabe took power in Zimbabwe. Acknowledging that Britain's Central African colonies had been no more lasting than the Middle East Crusader kingdoms, he gave his papers to the Bodleian Library at Oxford, Rhodes's own university.

December 6 1991

PRINCESS BROWN THRUSH

PRINCESS BROWN THRUSH, a leader of the Matinnecock Indian nation, who has died at Flushing, New York, aged 79, dedicated her life to the territorial and cultural rejuvenation of the last native American tribe organised within the New York metropolitan area.

The Matinnecocks were part of the once-mighty Algonquin family which held most of the country east of the Mississippi, from Virginia in the south to Hudson Bay in the north. Before the arrival of the *Wissunkies* ("white men"), the Matinnecocks were one of 13 tribes that roamed Long Island: their lands extended around Oyster Bay and modern-day Queens, where they subsisted, *inter alia*, on beached whales.

Their totem was the wild turkey. "We are the Turkey People," said Princess Brown Thrush's sister, Sun Tama, "famous for manufacturing wampum and loghouses, and for the beautiful singing voices of our women."

Partly on account of the small size of the tribe – but also because of their extensive intermarriage with the local black population – the Matinnecocks were little noticed by the white authorities. One United States government survey early this century stated that the tribe had disappeared altogether in the 1860s.

While the formal tribal structure had disintegrated, Matinnecock families none the less remained in contact with one another. They claimed the survey had been designed to cover up a land grab, for which they had received no compensation.

But from the 1950s onwards a series of dynamic leaders – Chief Wild Pigeon, the 102-year-old Chief John Standing Waters and Princess Brown Thrush's siblings, Princess Sun Tama and Chief Bald Eagle – reorganised the tribe, which was formally reconstituted at Douglaston, Long Island, in 1958.

In attendance were Indian chiefs from the Four Corners of Mother Earth, including Chief One Arrow of the North American Council of Indians and that body's formidable medicine man, Chief Flying Squirrel. At the ceremony, Princess Brown Thrush – who hitherto had been known as Lila Elizabeth Harding – was installed as keeper of the wampum (or treasurer).

She had been born in Flushing, New York, on June 5 1912 and educated at the local high school. For much of her life she worked for the New York Board of Education, serving school luncheons.

Along with her colleagues on the 14-member tribal council – who included, among others, Chief Little Moose as Junior Chief, Chief Thunderbolt as Serjeant at Arms and Princess Heatherflower as Keeper of the Long Count, or secretary – Princess Brown Thrush carried high the torch of Indian rights at a time of passivity and inactivity among Native Americans. Although their cause has since become fashionable, when Princess Brown Thrush began her campaign it had a rarity value on the East coast (Indian issues having endured in the public consciousness mainly in the western states).

Princess Brown Thrush met both Governor Averell Harriman and his successor, Nelson Rockefeller, to press the land claims: after one meeting at a fairground in

Queens, Rockefeller graciously gave orders that Princess Brown Thrush should be conveyed to her home in the gubernatorial limousine. But the Princess was not seduced by the attentions of the establishment, and in 1964 she and other members of the tribe protested vigorously when the town of North Hempstead sought to expand a hospital in Manhasset, next to a sacred tribal burial ground.

"Desecration!" cried Princess Sun Tama at a town meeting, with Princess Brown Thrush at her side. "We want you to know you are dealing with the landlord!" As a direct result of their efforts, the construction project was abandoned, as were many subsequent ones.

Foremost among Princess Brown Thrush's duties was the maintenance of the tribal longhouse, or gathering place. She spoke fluent Algonquin, and devoted much time to teaching ritual dancing, cooking (especially the medicinal "bone set" tea) and tribal law to the younger generation.

When Princess Sun Tama died in 1969, Princess Brown Thrush became chairman or spokesman of the tribe: she was also regarded as *sachem* (or medicine man) and as an Earth Mother, had the task of ensuring harmony in the tribe.

Emboldened by the successful land claims of other Native Americans, Princess Brown Thrush again went "on the warpath" in the 1970s and 1980s. In an attempt to create a semi-autonomous society, she and other members of the tribe claimed ownership of as much as one per cent of Suffolk County and 25 per cent of Queens County. This covered some of the choicest real estate in America, including Oyster Bay, Flushing

Meadow Park, the National Tennis Stadium and the New York Mets' Shea Stadium.

As an interim measure, however, Princess Brown Thrush and the tribal leadership were prepared to accept a small reservation on the old Flushing Meadow World Fair Ground, which she hoped would be transformed into a centre for Indian crafts.

It appeared that some of the Matinnecocks' claims might be acknowledged, because of New York State's violations of the Indian Non-Intercourse Act of 1789. This was the first piece of legislation passed under George Washington's presidency, and stipulated that no Indian lands could be alienated without the consent of the federal government. But their efforts have not enjoyed much success.

This is partly because the tribe – which still totals only 250 families – does not have the resources required to launch a suit; but also because the prerequisite of a successful action is federal recognition, which the Matinnecocks do not currently possess, and which would be costly to obtain.

However, Princess Brown Thrush could claim to have played a large part in combating the massive urbanisation of Long Island.

To the moment when she "left this world", Princess Brown Thrush, who was unmarried, remained true to Matinnecock tradition. She was buried upon sprigs of pine needles, in a red satin dress specifically made for her passage by Chief Little Fox, while the choir of her local episcopal church (of which she had been an enthusiastic member) sang "What a Friend We Have in Jesus".

Although their old hunting grounds are now filled

with highways, corner delicatessens and Chinese take-aways, the recent validation of Mohawk land claims in upstate New York and the continuing work of her successor, Chief Osceola Townsend, offer some hope.

March 11 1992

ISAAC ASIMOV

ISAAC ASIMOV, who has died in New York aged 72, was best known for his works of science fiction, a genre in which he reigned supreme, but he could also claim to have written more books about more subjects than any other author.

Of his 467 works, many were non-fiction. They included a two-volume guide to Shakespeare's plays; an investigation into the authorship of the *Book of Genesis*; a commentary on the poems of Kipling and Byron; a biographical encyclopaedia of all the scientists who have ever lived; musings on music and humour; and a series of informative books with titles beginning *How Did We Find Out About. . . .?* on subjects ranging from black holes and life in the deep sea to number theory.

"I write as a result of some inner compulsion," he once remarked, "and I'm not always in control of it."

A bearish, messianic figure with mutton-chop whiskers, frequently clad in cowboy boots and "bolo" tie, Asimov was stoically resigned to his own eccentricity. He liked to attribute his success to a "lucky break in the genetic-sweepstakes". Asked if he had been a child prodigy, he would answer: "Yes I was – and I still am."

Isaac Asimov was born at Petrovichi, Russia, on January 2 1920, the son of a Rabbi who brought him to America at the age of three. The family ran a candy store in Brooklyn, where little Isaac had access to the science-fiction magazines which proliferated in the 1920s.

Asimov taught himself to read English at five, and began writing soon afterwards. His first short story, *Marooned off Vesta*, was published when he was 18, and his next work, *Nightfall*, appeared three years later.

As a student at Columbia University, New York – where he took a degree and a doctorate – and subsequently as a teacher of biochemistry at Boston University, he continued to write in his spare time. By the mid-1950s his growing reputation enabled him to concentrate on a literary career.

For the next 35 years, almost without a break, Asimov produced 90 words a minute, eight hours a day, seven days a week, first on a typewriter and later on a word processor, and he invariably wrote three books at once. His only respite was in travel. Curiously, for a man who wrote so much about spaceships, he detested flying, and went everywhere on cruise liners, usually paying his way by giving popular science lectures to the passengers.

A master of spontaneous oratory, Asimov could hold forth on almost any subject with brilliant lucidity – as in his much-cited off-the-cuff description of how human life depends on the Sun: "All of us are living in the light and warmth of a huge hydrogen bomb, 860,000 miles across and 93 million miles away, which is in a state of continuous explosion."

His most celebrated science fiction work was *The Foundation Trilogy*, published in instalments in the early

1950s. It sold millions of copies and in 1966 won a special Hugo Award as the best science-fiction series ever.

Set far in the future, it told of the fall of a mighty Galactic Empire, and of the efforts of Hari Seldon, a great social scientist, to build a new and better empire out of the ruins of the old. Few novelists have created a character as cunningly idealistic as Seldon, who used the science of "psychohistory", a combination of history, mathematics, sociology and psychology, to predict and control the future. Although the hero met his death within the first 30 pages of the trilogy, the vast and mysterious intricacies of his "Seldon Plan" still amazed the reader after 700. Just before his own death Asimov completed *Forward the Foundation*, a new novel about Seldon's last years.

In spite of his success, Asimov steered clear of literary pomposity. When asked about the "meaning" of his *Foundation* cycle, he was apt to burst into a song which he had adapted from the Gilbert and Sullivan opera, *Patience*:

> *Success is not a mystery, just brush up on your history,*
> *and borrow day by day*
> *Take an Empire that was Roman, and you'll find it is*
> *at home in*
> *All the starry Milky Way.*

Asimov advised aspiring writers to take their models from history and the classics. Too much invention, he argued, resulted in gratuitously enigmatic plots.

In one short story, *In a Good Cause* (1951), he explored the idea that political strength could lie not in unity but in disunity. The plot centred on mankind's confrontation with a Galactic enemy called the Diaboli. While the enemy were creatures of absolute mental conformity, the human protagonists were in perpetual conflict. When it came to war the humans won overwhelmingly – because their internal fights had given them plenty of military experience, while their enemies, although more formidable on paper, had had none. Asimov took the idea from the tales of the feuding Greeks' victories over the united Persians who so vastly outnumbered them.

Yet for all protestations at being a plain old wordsmith, and a plagiarist at that, Asimov displayed one of the most dynamic imaginations in the sci-fi business. Long before the advent of robots and personal computers, he invented a race of super-intelligent robots. Many of these machines were indistinguishable in appearance from human beings, but not all – one of his stories described a race of intelligent motor-cars which, once parked for the night, would zoom away to sex orgies.

Besides the *Foundation* stories, Asimov's best known book was probably his second, *I, Robot* (1950), in which he promulgated three unalterable "Laws of Robotics" – first, that a robot may not harm a human being, or, through inaction, allow a human being to come to harm; secondly, that a robot must obey the orders of a human being, except when this would conflict with the first law; and thirdly, that a robot must protect itself, except when this would conflict with the first and second laws.

Asimov's kindly robots succeeded in transforming the image of the conscienceless marauders which had long dominated the pages of pulp sci-fi.

Robots and the Galactic Empire remained the pivotal themes of Asimov's novels. Taken together, they offered a picture of humanity in millennia to come – spread across the galaxy, with Earth but a distant memory – yet in thrall to its sublunary nature.

Asimov also thought deeply about time. One of his most striking novels was *The End of Eternity* (1955), about how time travel could threaten freedom.

In a classic portrait of a "nanny state", a group of initially well-meaning bureaucrats has the task of manipulating "Eternity" to maximise human happiness. But because this ruled out all danger or adventure, Eternity became destructive to the spirit, and the bureaucrats had themselves to be destroyed.

This plot gave expression to one of Asimov's pet hates, "pseudo-science", which he saw as a threat to liberty. "Some people", he said, "say they have 'absolute proof' that alien beings have landed on Earth. I've never found a way to convince them otherwise . . . It turns out they read it in sensational newspapers at the supermarket checkout counter."

One of the hallmarks of Asimov's fiction was that its science, though sometimes mindboggling, was nonetheless convincing. Indeed, as a leading member of the Committee for the Scientific Investigation of Claims of the Paranormal, he conceived it his duty to draw attention to any person or event which might bring science into disrepute.

Most notably, he co-wrote a scathing attack on the gullibility of the Reagans, after it was learned that the First Lady consulted an astrologer.

Asimov's extraordinary output of 10 books a year did not let up, even after he suffered a heart attack in 1977 and triple bypass surgery two years later. But the operation marked a turning-point.

Formerly he had been prone to pessimism, full of gloomy prognoses about overpopulation and wars, which would prevent mankind from ever fulfilling its dream of colonising other planets. After the surgery, told to lose 50 pounds, he duly transformed himself into a jogging optimist. "If I can pull myself up by my own bootstraps," he declared, "then so can the human race."

In contrast to his fiction, Asimov took nine months to write his autobiography, which was considerably longer than *War and Peace*. "I wanted it to be unanalytical, without wisdom," he explained. "I wanted to show the reader what it was like *to be me*. A genius, maybe, but also a schmuck. It's a big effort for me to behave like other people."

Asimov is survived by his second wife, Janet, and by two children from his first marriage.

April 7 1992

LORD JAMES OF RUSHOLME

THE LORD JAMES OF RUSHOLME, the former High Master of Manchester Grammar School and the first Vice-Chancellor of York University, who has died aged 83, stood out unflinchingly for academic standards – and in particular for grammar schools – against the meretricious educational nostrums peddled with such disastrous results in the postwar years.

His period at Manchester Grammar School between 1945 and 1962 must be counted one of the most notable headmasterships of this century, comparable in terms of contemporary prestige and achievement – if never in style or ideology – with that of Arnold at Rugby in the 19th century. The abiding misfortune for Britain was that, whereas Arnold's muscular Christianity permeated the English governing classes for several generations, James's devotion to the cause of intellectual excellence made little appeal to the educational theorists of the 1960s.

Eric James was caricatured as reactionary and undemocratic when in fact he was by background, temperament and conviction a Fabian Socialist who believed passionately in equality of opportunity. Nonetheless he made a sharp distinction between equality of opportunity and uniformity of treatment.

To him it was axiomatic that able children are a nation's most precious asset, and equally self-evident that the academically gifted, no less than great athletes or musicians, will best develop their talents in company with their peers. In the 1950s and 1960s it required considerable moral courage to stand out against the dominant educational opinion, which had settled dogmatically upon scrapping grammar schools in favour of the supposedly more egalitarian comprehensive system.

James, however, had established his position on firm foundations. A man who had acquired a deep knowledge and understanding of de Tocqueville, Matthew Arnold and John Stuart Mill was not to be shaken by the hortations of Mrs Shirley Williams.

Above all, James responded eagerly to Plato's ideal of an aristocracy of talent. The educational system, he believed, had an essential role to play in ensuring that the brightest and the best became the Guardians of contemporary England.

James advocated a pure meritocracy. Selection at Manchester Grammar School was by competitive examination, with no marks added for wealth or family connections. It was the essence of his philosophy that grammar schools should serve as ladders, giving all levels of society access to the highest places in the land.

His High Mastership bore splendid witness to this ambition. In the mid-1950s Manchester Grammar School was attaining up to 45 scholarships every year at Oxford and Cambridge.

This success, however, only confirmed the antipathy of those who judged the system of selection by its ability to be divisive. Eventually Manchester Grammar would be obliged to become a private fee-paying school rather than submit to the comprehensive principle.

James, by that time, had long since ceased to be High Master, but his prolonged championship of grammar schools, although doomed to failure in his lifetime, looked for ultimate vindication in the spirit of his beloved Matthew Arnold:

> *Let the victors, when they come,*
> *When the forts of folly fall,*
> *Find thy body by the wall!*

At York, happily, James was able to build a more enduring monument, for the university has always been one of the more successful of the foundations created in the wake of the Robbins Report. James took up office as Vice-Chancellor in 1962, and was involved with every detail of the university's development. He described his work with the architects as one of the most exciting times of his life; a particular satisfaction was the creation of the lake, described as "a balancing reservoir" in order to mollify the accountants.

Although James never intended, in his own words, "to set down a pale imitation of Oxford in the Yorkshire meadows", the new foundation followed the Oxford tradition in several respects. James stressed that at least half the students should live on the campus; he housed them in separate colleges which were conceived not simply as halls of residence, but as the centres of the university's social and academic life.

To create the closest possible relationship between teacher and taught, tutors as well as students were given rooms in the colleges; and the tutorial became the basic form of instruction. Rather less in tune with Oxford – at least in the early 1960s – half of the undergraduates were women.

James's prescription for running a university was deceptively simple: "First, get extremely good men on your staff. Secondly, create the kind of place where schools will want to send their best people. Thirdly, look after the students when you have got them."

He proved more successful than many of his peers in dealing with the student troubles of the 1960s. As he was always available for discussion with anybody, it could never be claimed that he was out of touch; when he retired in 1973 the president of the student union admitted to the respect and admiration which the Vice-Chancellor had earned.

James left a university which contained nearly 3,000 students; and, in higher education at least, he could be pleased with the advance of his meritocratic ideals. Jude (the Obscure), he wrote, "need no longer look despairingly at the towers and spires of an inaccessible university, provided he has three good A-level passes, can satisfy one of a multiplicity of entrance requirements, and is prepared, if necessary, to do without spires."

In 1970 Mrs Thatcher, then the Secretary of State for Education and Science, asked him to be chairman of an inquiry into teacher training. James developed a lively admiration for Mrs Thatcher; indeed one of his own pronouncements, in 1973, strikingly anticipated Mrs Thatcher's outburst about "caring" in the 1987 election campaign.

"Most people give the impression that I don't care about ordinary people," James said. "I do, only one can't say it, I can't go round bleating 'I care'."

In one respect James was an odd choice to head a committee dealing with teacher training because the essence of his position was that teachers should be *educated* rather than *trained*. He wanted teachers who could inspire children; beside this great principle, *what* or *how* they should teach were questions of lesser import.

James held that a single subject, well taught, might form the basis of a true education; equally that an apparently alluring spread of studies, badly taught, would simply become a drab routine.

The James Report on Teacher Training, which appeared in 1972, envisaged the colleges of education as mini-universities where students would follow a two-year, purely academic, course leading to a Diploma of Higher Education, before engaging specifically with teaching. Only after the DipHE, the committee recommended, should fledgling teachers undertake a further two-year course addressed to the theory and practice of work in the classroom. It was also proposed that teachers should attend an in-service course for not less than one term every seven years.

Despite opposition from the National Union of Teachers, both the Government and the preponderance of opinion supported the recommendations of the James committee, whose chairman went into retirement with the satisfaction of having established the basis for a better educated teaching profession.

Eric John Francis James was born at Derby on April 13 1909, into a Nonconformist background; his family were Congregationalists. His father, a commercial traveller, was devoted to literature, an enthusiasm which the boy absorbed with a will from infancy.

Young Eric's early schooling was at Brighton; then, at 13, he went to Taunton's School at Southampton, from where he won an exhibition to Queen's College, Oxford. He gained a first in chemistry and represented the university at chess; a steady player, he concluded a draw with his Cambridge opponent.

His earliest ambition had been to become a doctor, but since a medical training was scarcely feasible at that time without private resources, his decision settled upon a teaching career. In 1933 the University Appointments Board offered him a temporary appointment at Winchester, where he soon secured a permanent place on the staff. Besides teaching chemistry, he became a "div don" – a master who teaches his form a range of subjects – of high repute.

James remained at Winchester until 1945, and the experience was crucial in the development of his educational ideas. In particular he was influenced by Spencer Leeson, the headmaster. James did not share his mentor's

Christianity – for which reason he felt himself disquali-
fied from a public school headmastership – but he did
imbibe Leeson's conception of the headmaster as *primus
inter pares*.

"You must not become a distant, inaccessible figure
in office," Leeson wrote to him when he was appointed
to the High Mastership of Manchester Grammar School.
"Insist on doing a substantial amount of teaching.
Encourage all possible contacts with parents. Get to
know your staff as intimately as you can."

These precepts, however difficult to apply in a school
of some 1,450 boys, were at the root of James's success
at Manchester. Full of energy, and adept at the brisk
discharge of routine business, as High Master he found
time for everyone, until all the school's activities became
imbued with the aspiration of excellence.

James possessed an infectious enthusiasm which conveyed that scholarship was not just a grind to be endured
for the sake of exams, but an enduring source of satisfaction. His own intellectual range was exceptionally broad;
always open to new ideas, he was both eager and
formidably equipped to debate any issue – and more
than willing to concede the point if he found himself
bettered in argument.

The High Master never pulled rank. No style of
leadership could have been further removed from the
traditional conception of the headmaster as a distant
authority figure; James's talisman was his own personality. "To some of us he was almost too good to be true,"
a member of the staff, O. R. Corbett, has written. "By
merely being about the place he brought a vigour to the
school which amounted in the course of time to a kind
of revolution."

James always maintained that clever boys were not pale little swots, but were *more*, not less, likely to be good at other things as well. The school had a good games record, and, as the High Master put it, was one of the foremost in "Outward Boundery". Art, music and drama were encouraged: the actors Ben Kingsley and Robert Powell were both at Manchester Grammar during James's time.

The High Master also proved an effective fund raiser, and there were many physical improvements in the school, including a new physics block.

Neither at Manchester nor at York, however, were James's energies entirely absorbed by the task in hand. He was a member of the University Grants Committee, an experience that left him quite content that the government should inspect university accounts.

In 1953–54 he was chairman of the Headmasters' Conference. As a member of the Central Advisory Council on Education he made his influence felt in the Crowther report on secondary education, published in 1959; in particular he supported two of the recommendations – for the raising of the school leaving age to 16, and for specialised studies in sixth forms.

James was also a member of the Standing Commission on Museums and Art Galleries and of the Press Council. After his retirement from York in 1973 he served on the Social Science Research Council and was chairman of the Personal Social Services Council and of the Royal Fine Art Commission.

He broadcast in both the radio and television versions of *The Brains Trust*. He campaigned vigorously, however, against popular television, which he considered had a "diseducative" effect on the young.

James set forth some of his educational ideas in two books, *An Essay on the Content of Education* (1949) and *Education and Leadership* (1951). His *Elements of Physical Chemistry*, written in collaboration with another master during his Winchester period, became a standard school textbook.

James was knighted in 1956 and created a life peer as Baron James of Rusholme in 1959.

He married, in 1939, Cordelia, only daughter of Major-General Fitzgerald Wintour, and sister of Charles Wintour, formerly editor of the *Evening Standard*. Their son, Oliver, is a consultant and professor of medicine at Newcastle.

May 18 1992

ELIZABETH DAVID

ELIZABETH DAVID, the *grande dame* of the kitchen, who has died aged 78, wrote a remarkable sequence of books in which she transformed previous conceptions of cookery writing in Britain and America.

Her writing was distinguished by its ease and grace, its blend of profound scholarship with practical advice, and a rare ability to convey an unaffected delight in matters of the table. Even today her books of the 1950s seem wonderfully evocative; to the reader still fettered by the constraints of 10 years of food rationing they provided a window on a larger and an almost magical world, shaping the attitudes and aspirations of a generation.

The publication in 1950 of Mrs David's first work,

A Book of Mediterranean Food (revised 1988), was greeted
with the joyous enthusiasm accorded to those who touch
a tender nerve in the national consciousness. That the
ingredients in her recipes – eggs, butter, fine seafood,
meat, poultry and game, tomatoes, pimentos, almonds,
figs, melons – were often difficult, or impossible, to
obtain at the time, augmented rather than diminished
her impact.

Her recipes for herb and garlic-scented stews, flavou-
red with olive oil and wine, sent ripples of nostalgic
delight through austerity-ridden Britain. Suddenly,
through Mrs David's enlightened eye, beleaguered Brit-
ons were shown the sunshine at the end of the tunnel;
how, with the gates of Europe once more open, they
might eat and live.

Mrs David's cookery books have earned their place
on kitchen shelves from the Outer Hebrides to Tasmania.
They had immediate universal appeal, both as kitchen
manuals that became thumbed and sauce-spattered with
use, and for their incisive prose.

Of Sussex landed stock, she was born Elizabeth
Gwynne on Boxing Day 1913. Her father, Rupert
Gwynne, was a barrister, MP for Eastbourne and briefly
a junior minister at the War Office; her mother, Stella,
was the second daughter of the 1st Viscount Ridley, the
late-Victorian Home Secretary.

Her early upbringing might have seemed to presage
for Mrs David a conventional English upper-class life,
but her time at the Sorbonne as a student of history and
literature altered her destiny. In Paris during the 1930s
she lived with a family "of which every member appeared
to be exceptionally food-conscious".

When she returned to England, "forgotten were the

Sorbonne professors and the yards of Racine learnt by heart . . . what had stuck was the taste for a kind of food quite ideally unlike anything I had known before. Ever since I have been trying to catch up with those lost days when perhaps I should have been profitably employed watching Léontine in her kitchen."

The food which she resolved to learn to recreate for herself was that "which constitutes the core of genuine French cookery, but which to us seems so remarkable because it implies that excellent ingredients and high standards are taken for granted day by day, whereas in our own kitchens the best efforts tend to be made only for parties and special occasions".

She brought a vivid intelligence and the habit of scholarship to her study of the literature of the table, and to her collection of recipes and cooking methods; and an informed judgement to her analysis of the resultant dishes.

During the Second World War she served with the Admiralty and the Ministry of Information. In 1944 she married Lieutenant Colonel I. A. ("Tony") David of the Indian Army (the union was dissolved in 1960).

Her life gave her the experience of keeping house in France, Italy, Greece, Egypt and India. She fixed her curiosity upon the dishes and culinary traditions of each country and upon their relation to a wider culture.

On her return to England after the war, she began to write articles and then, in 1950, published *A Book of Mediterranean Food*. Four more Mediterranean-based books appeared in the next decade.

She described *French Country Cooking* (1951, revised 1987), with characteristic self-effacement, as "no more than an indication of the immense diversity and range of

French regional cookery". It included a poignant chapter on stuffed cabbage dishes, "to show what can be done with a cabbage apart from the one and only, and far too notorious, way common to railway dining-cars, boarding-schools and hospitals". It could equally be "an acceptable main-course dish, inexpensive, but abounding in the rich aromas of slow and careful preparation".

Her pioneering *Italian Food* (1954), the fruit of a year's officially funded research in the kitchens of Italy from Sicily to Milan, was hailed by Evelyn Waugh as the book that had given him most enjoyment that year. It revolutionised attitudes to what had previously been regarded in Britain as nursery fare.

Summer Cooking (1955, revised 1988) was an eclectic and entertaining collection of seasonal dishes relying on fresh ingredients and fresh herbs. And then, in 1960, Mrs David published her undoubted masterpiece, *French Provincial Cooking*, a book that may be read as literature, as a work of reference, and as a splendid and representative collection of recipes. Readers were plunged, through the passion and skill of her writing, deep into the sights and scents of the markets and kitchens of rural France.

As the novelist Angela Carter observed: "Elizabeth David's books are full of the essence of place." They also penetrate to the essence of good food. Britain's young postwar housewives found the delicious traditional dishes of the French *bourgeoisie* entirely to their taste.

Mrs David, galvanised into action by unpalatable English provincial catering, then turned her attention to the culinary habits of her native land. Having suffered a stroke, and temporarily lost her sense of taste (happily later regained, although she came to find the smell of her beloved onions offensive), she decided, by way of a restorative, to open a kitchen shop in Pimlico in 1965.

This immensely influential establishment was stocked with the handsome fish-kettles, earthenware cooking-pots, copper saucepans and those indispensable little kitchen gadgets which French housewives accept as their birthright but which were so hard to obtain in London. Soon Mrs David's disciples were opening kitchen shops all over the Anglophone world.

Then followed the first of what was intended to be a trilogy entitled *English Cookery, Ancient and Modern*. In the first volume, *Spices, Salt and Aromatics in the English Kitchen* (1970), Mrs David explored the influence of Empire on the English store-cupboard, and revived recipes for home-pickled meats such as brawn, brisket and spiced beef, potted shrimps and fish pastes.

The book's publication fuelled a national revival of interest in traditional English dishes, the influence of which is still being felt today. *English Bread and Yeast Cookery* followed in 1977.

An essentially private – and apparently prickly – person, Mrs David never wrote an autobiography, although much of her life and philosophy can be found in her collected journalism, *An Omelette and a Glass of Wine* (1984). This became an immediate best-seller – a tribute to her phenomenal reputation in a decade when mass recognition comes easily only to television cooks.

These pieces, laced with Mrs David's laconic wit, include few recipes. They were chosen principally from her contributions to the *Sunday Times* from 1955 to 1960 (where Mrs David had a less than happy relationship with the late Ernestine Carter, for whose busy editorial shears she had harsh words), and from articles published during her "joyous years" under Katharine Whitehorn at the *Spectator*.

Under Mrs David's benevolent patronage *Petits Propos Culinaires*, Alan Davidson's idiosyncratic culinary publication, was launched in 1979. It was under this magazine's auspices that, two years later, the first international Oxford Symposium on Food was held in St Antony's College.

She was appointed OBE in 1976, CBE in 1986 and elected a Fellow of the Royal Society of Literature in 1982. In 1977 she was appointed a Chevalier du Mérite Agricole of France.

Her pen did not merely inspire a thousand cooks. It is largely to Mrs David that Britain owes its growing appreciation of good food.

"Whoever", wrote her friend Norman Douglas, "has helped us to a larger understanding is entitled to our gratitude for all time." These words might serve as Elizabeth David's epitaph.

May 23 1992

THE MARQUESS OF BATH

THE 6TH MARQUESS OF BATH, the founding father of the "stately home industry" who has died aged 87, was the first owner of a great country house to open it to the public on a full-blown commercial basis after the Second World War – and he did so with a panache seldom equalled by those who followed him.

Deeply though he loved Longleat, the Thynne family's magnificent seat in Wiltshire, Lord Bath had no desire to live there under the conditions prevailing when he inherited in 1946. Faced with a bill of £750,000 in death duties, which forced him to sell off 9,000 acres, Henry Bath was much attracted by modern ideas, and had little time for the dead pre-war world and what he saw as its stuffiness.

So in 1949 he threw Longleat open to the public and entered enthusiastically into the novel role of titled showman. By August 1957 he was able to welcome, with a characteristic flourish, the millionth visitor.

It was in the 1960s that the Longleat venture really took off, when Jimmy Chipperfield, the circus impresario, suggested introducing game to roam the estate. Led by the celebrated lions, it grew into a safari park of worldwide fame, with Bengal tigers, baboons, chimpanzees, giraffes, zebras, hippos and sea-lions soon following. Latterly he added two rare white tigers to the menagerie, which became the finest in Wiltshire – even outdoing the collection formed by the 5th Earl of Pembroke at Wilton in the 1650s.

Bath deployed every tourist magnet conceivable: a funfair, pedal boats on the mile-long lake, a putting green and tea-rooms. To the disapproval of his fellow peers he even allowed the estate to be used for staging pop concerts – a practice which has now been copied by other great houses.

Bath spoke vigorously against crippling death duties and taxation, and was occasionally forced to sell heirlooms to cover the unrelenting maintenance bills for Longleat. To avoid further penal tax at his death he made over most of his remaining estate of 10,000 acres to his eldest son, Viscount Weymouth. But he gave the

70-acre Cley Hill – an 800ft high landmark on his estate – to the nation.

A useful source of income remained from the Cheddar Caves, which the family owned in Somerset. But he always maintained that he was a "tenant for life" of Longleat rather than a multimillionaire.

"My chief claim to fame", he once said, "is that I am chairman of the Football Pools Panel." He deserves, however, to be remembered for more than merely introducing the lions at Longleat.

Bath sat for a portrait by Graham Sutherland, commissioned furniture by John Makepeace and added many hundreds of books to the libraries at Longleat. But like many book collectors, he spent little time reading them.

He was also an inveterate collector of memorabilia, assembling exhibitions of Churchilliana, Hitleriana (Bath found the Führer's watercolours of particular interest) and Thatcheriana, which included "Maggie" toilet-paper rolls, *Spitting Image* puppets and mugs.

Yet despite all his efforts Bath pointed out that when the net takings from the tripper attractions of Longleat were set against the costs of daily maintenance and repair of the great Elizabethan house, the operation still ran at a loss.

Henry Frederick Thynne was born on January 26 1905, the youngest of the five children of the 5th Marquess of Bath. The founder of the family fortunes, Sir John Thynne, acquired the old Augustinian priory of Longleat for £55 and built the Elizabethan mansion from 1567 onwards. Thynne himself collaborated on the "lantern" design with the architects Robert Smythson and Allen Maynard. The stone was dragged across from Thynne's own quarry at Box.

Although there have been few alterations to the exterior down the centuries, the interior of Longleat was largely done over in the 19th century by Sir Jeffry Wyatville and John Crace.

In 1916 the elder son of the 5th Marquess was killed in action and henceforth young Henry was styled Viscount Weymouth.

He was educated at Harrow (Eton, he used to recall, turned him down as "a moron") and then went up to Christ Church, Oxford – where, he recalled, "I was a playboy, but not a very rich one." In 1927 Lord Weymouth married, in secret, Daphne Vivian, elder daughter of the 4th Lord Vivian, before setting off alone for America. A year later they were married again in public, but the marriage ended after the war.

In their day they were a fashionable and much photographed couple, and Lady Weymouth went on to write some amusing books, including *Mercury Presides*, which gave an evocative picture of life at Longleat.

From 1931 to 1935 Lord Weymouth sat in the House of Commons as Conservative MP for Frome – "under orders", as he put it, from his father, who had also represented Frome in his youth. Lord Weymouth served on the Council of the Duchy of Cornwall from 1933 to 1936, and by this time was playing a part in running the then extensive Longleat estate, and in modernising and lighting the Cheddar Caves.

With the help of the landscape gardener Russell Page, he began a planting scheme in the park at Longleat which has proved a worthy sequel to the earlier work there of "Capability" Brown.

Lord Weymouth joined the Wiltshire Yeomanry and served with them in the Second World War. He saw action in the Western Desert and was wounded in the neck. Later he also served with distinction as a liaison officer with the Americans.

On his succession to the Marquessate of Bath and to the estate in 1946, he threw himself with gusto into the business of making Longleat attractive to the public.

He also had considerable success in the field of forestry and was a keen conserver of the family treasures – although he greatly disturbed his more old-fashioned neighbours with a plan to buy the "Skylon" (a metal tower more than 200ft high, left over from the 1951 Festival of Britain) and erect it at the top of the park, from where it would have been visible for many miles around. Fortunately the plan came to nothing.

After turning over the estate to his son, Bath lived modestly in a converted mill in a village near Longleat. Strolling around his lands, he was habitually attired in a vigorously patterned tweed jacket with red polka-dot tie and handkerchief – a touch he attributed to childhood memories of tramps' knotted kerchiefs. He enjoyed being mistaken for the gardener. "If you're the Marquess of Bath," one woman told him, "I'm Diana Dors."

As well as being a fine shot, for many years Bath enjoyed coursing, and owned a number of greyhounds in partnership with his neighbour and great friend Lord Stavordale. For purposes of identification their names all began with their owners' initials, and Silly Billy, Sweaty Betty, Stink Bomb and Soda Brandy all competed, with varying success, in the Waterloo Cup.

Perhaps the most striking aspect of Henry Bath's character was a candour which could startle and even shock; his observations on Hitler once reduced Bernard

Levin to a stunned silence on the television programme *That Was The Week That Was*.

He claimed to be able to talk to anyone of any class, but caused an aristocratic stir by attending the Coronation in 1953 in his massive state coach, even though the police had asked him not to.

At the age of 85 he disarmingly described his temperament as that of "an immature 70-year-old", and it was this total lack of pretension that was an important part of his considerable charm. Bath's eccentricities stretched from organising a teddy bears picnic in the grounds of Longleat to ancient pagan fertility rites, and he was for a time a disciple of Bhagwan Shree Rajneesh.

When he and his second wife, Virginia (daughter of Alan Parsons and Viola Tree, and previously married to David Tennant, proprietor of the Gargoyle Club), were finding it difficult to conceive, they climbed a Dorset hillside to call on the help of the chalk giant of Cerne Abbas. Their exertions duly resulted in the birth of a daughter, Lady Silvy Cerne Thynne.

By his first marriage Lord Bath had four sons – of whom the eldest died as an infant, and the youngest predeceased him – and a daughter, the Duchess of Beaufort.

The heir to the marquessate is the elder surviving son, Alexander George Thynn (*sic*), Viscount Weymouth, born 1932.

July 1 1992

ANNE COUNTESS OF ROSSE

ANNE COUNTESS OF ROSSE, who has died aged 90, was sister of the designer Oliver Messel, wife of the barrister Ronald Armstrong-Jones and of the 6th Earl of Rosse, mother of the Earl of Snowdon – and a considerable personality in her own right.

A celebrated beauty between the wars, she went on to become a leading figure in the worlds of gardening (she was a noted hybridiser) and of conservation. She was to the fore in the founding of the Georgian Group and the Victorian Society, sat on several National Trust committees and, above all, was largely instrumental in preserving for posterity both Linley Sambourne House in Kensington (a remarkable Victorian time capsule featured in the film *A Room With A View*) and the outstanding gardens at Nymans in Sussex.

The Nymans estate was bought in 1890 by her grandfather, Ludwig Messel, a stockbroker from a Darmstadt banking family, who settled in England.

Anne Messel was born in 1902, the only daughter of Lieutenant Colonel Leonard Messel and his wife, Maud, who was, in turn, the only daughter of Linley Sambourne, the *Punch* cartoonist and artist. Young Anne was brought up at Nymans together with her brothers, Linley and "Darling Angel Oliver" (as she called him), the stage designer.

She recalled her horticultural training at the hands of the Nymans plantsman, James Coomber – "a terrifying Mr MacGregor, ready to pounce on anyone not doing his utmost" – and the rural idyll of the Sussex Weald in the early 1900s. She also spent some of her childhood in London and was educated by a governess, in order to avoid the bullying that might have been inflicted on a schoolgirl of German ancestry during the First World War.

She recalled visits to see her grandfather Linley Sambourne at Stafford Terrace, with its "heavy scent of rich Havana cigars" and "the sounds of the ticking of innumerable clocks, the trickle of the landing water-fountain and, from the drawing-room, strains of Schumann on the piano".

In 1922 Miss Messel was presented at Court. Three years later – in a ceremony at St Margaret's Westminster artfully rendered Arcadian by the flourishes of her brother Oliver – she married Ronald Armstrong-Jones, only son of the surgeon Sir Robert Armstrong-Jones of Plas Dinas, Caernarvonshire. They had a son, Antony, and a daughter, Susan (who later married the 6th Viscount De Vesci, and died in 1986).

Mrs Armstrong-Jones – much photographed by Cecil Beaton, Mme Yevonde and others – threw herself enthusiastically into the elaborate English social life of the time. In the "Great Pageant of Lovers" of 1927, she was Ariadne beside Tallulah Bankhead's Cleopatra.

Such occasions caused one diarist to describe her as "pretty as a picture" and the Duke of Kent to exclaim that "She's the best-looking girl in the room."

Her marriage to Armstrong-Jones was dissolved in 1934. The next year she married the 6th Earl of Rosse, an Irish peer seated at Birr Castle in Offaly. They had two sons. Her period as châtelaine of Birr has passed into Irish folklore. She herself would recall "sneaking off in the deep countryside of the Midlands of Ireland to take part in 'Dancing at the Cross Road'" or being "allowed to take part in an Irish wake in our beloved Birr".

One story has the Countess sweeping into a humble cabin on the estate and brushing aside the occupant's apologies for its rude simplicity: "My dear, don't change a *thing*!"

Yet while some teased Lady Rosse for what they saw as her affectation (she was variously nicknamed "Tugboat Annie" and "Lady Roscommon"), others, such as James Lees-Milne (*qv*), were "much impressed by Anne's intelligence and use of words". "With Anne Rosse", Lees-Milne wrote in his diary, "I am always happy. She giggles, makes the most wicked innuendoes, and giggles again. The noise she makes is like an extremely lyrical burn rushing over pebbles, and her witticisms have to be caught on the wing. Her merriment is infectious, and it is laced with just a dash of arsenic."

In 1946 her bachelor uncle Roy Sambourne, who had kept 18 Stafford Terrace as an untouched Victorian survival, died. That this extraordinary period piece was not then dispersed – at a time when everything Victorian was anathema save to a few luminaries like her great friend John Betjeman – reflects immense credit on Lady Rosse. The house is now opened to the public by the Victorian Society.

Lady Rosse's other signal contribution to the heritage came about when her father died in 1953 and Nymans passed to the National Trust. She took on the directorship of one of the great gardens of England, with its rare and beautiful plants, shrubs and trees from all over the world.

Lady Rosse, in conjunction with the Trust, carried out a programme of replanting as well as adding a delightful rose garden, planted with old-fashioned roses in the 1960s. She won awards from the Royal Horticultural Society for various rhododendra, magnolias, camellias and her *eucryphia x nymansensis*.

While taking justifiable pride in the gardens, Lady Rosse enjoyed telling the story of how Mr Bunyard the gardener had likened her giganteum lilies to "very beautiful women, utterly ruined by thick ankles".

Lady Rosse was an inspiring influence in National Trust committees. She did not hesitate to criticise the "museumisation" of Trust properties and in a stirring tirade in the *National Trust Magazine* in 1983 warned that the Trust might be "losing some of the ideals we set out to preserve" and that there was a danger of becoming an "immense supermarket".

"'Good Taste'", she observed, "has banished Aunt Jessica's sunshade and gumboots from the hall . . . Uncle Elmo's panama hat with its I Zingari ribbon – the croquet mallets, the elephant foot umbrella stand . . . and gone is the distant bark of a labrador – in fact life is no longer going on. But life is a value, part of the 'show biz'."

In 1960 Lady Rosse became a household name when her son by her first marriage, Tony Armstrong-Jones, by now a well-known photographer, married Princess Margaret. At the ceremony in Westminster Abbey, Lady Rosse cut a memorably elegant figure at the last occasion when ladies wore long day-dresses and coats, but with hats. Always exquisitely dressed, she carried it off with characteristic panache.

In old age, Lady Rosse possessed a rare serenity. She eschewed the vulgarity and harshness of the modern world to live in a rarefied atmosphere of her own.

Lord Rosse died in 1979. She is survived by her son from her first marriage and by two sons of her second marriage.

Mark Girouard writes: I find it hard to think of Anne Rosse apart from her houses and her husband. She and Michael Rosse must have been dazzling to look at when they married. In the 1950s, when I first got to know them, Michael was a little portly but still extremely handsome, Anne vivacious and very pretty. They brought a flavour of the Thirties into the postwar world, summed up for me by the memory of Michael shaking cocktails in the library at Birr, as if performing a religious act.

It was easy to laugh at Anne: she was full of gush and had a strain of "it's-only-little-me-ishness", which Michael, who doted on her, never seemed to tire of. I remember her taking me round the ruins of Leap Castle, famous for its ghost, with many pretty little shrieks and clutches.

But she was not someone one could dismiss for, under the affectation, there was competence, humour, knowledge and ambition. She had a gift for parties and for setting the scene.

She was fortunate in acquiring by marriage or inheritance two houses admirably suited to her talents, both with a stage-set or film-set quality: 18 Stafford Terrace in London, which was redolent of the Aesthetic Age and the 1890s, and Birr Castle in Ireland, which was, and is, like a house in a novel – indeed it is said to have inspired Kinalty in Henry Green's *Loving*.

Its plaster-vaulted Gothick drawing-room, and the wild cream-and-gold Gothick furnishings in her bedroom both looked like sets designed by her brother Oliver Messel, but were in fact genuine products of the early 19th century. Anne had the sensibility to see their point, and arrange, light and set them off with brilliance, instead of redecorating them with contemporary good taste, as others would have done.

The houses exuded luxury and enjoyment especially at party time. "Thank God for a week of the flesh-pots," I remember my father writing to me, when he briefly left postwar austerity to sink into the comfort of Birr, where there were footmen in bottle-green liveries with brass buttons to run one's bath for one, flowers banked in profusion everywhere, and long delicious meals in the dark Victorian dining room ("It's just a shabby old Irish house", Anne used to say).

Evening parties at Stafford Terrace were something one looked forward to with a relish that was never disappointed – not only for the guests (I remember John Betjeman, Compton Mackenzie, Harold Acton (*qv*) and Princess Margaret, among others), but for the visual delight of the dim rich lighting shining on pictures and bronze in the double drawing-room, the violets arranged in the de Lamerie silver, and the stimulus of Anne's own enjoyment and laughter. It was in this room that she assembled the group of enthusiasts who joined to found the Victorian Society in 1958.

Her other houses were Nymans, fake manorial Gothic built for her stockbroker grandfather – another stage-set, the drama of which was accentuated by its having been half-gutted by fire – and Womersley in Yorkshire, which she shared with Michael's mother, not altogether happily, for she was not cut out to be either a daughter-in-law or a mother-in-law.

Nymans, like Birr, had a wonderful garden, in part her creation, for she and Michael were gifted and dedicated gardeners. Do I remember her correctly pruning roses at Birr with extreme competence, but wearing diamonds? Perhaps I am wrong, but that is the kind of person she was.

July 6 1992

SIR JOHN SUMMERSON

SIR JOHN SUMMERSON, who has died aged 87, was the most distinguished British architectural historian of his generation and one of the very few, along with Sir Nikolaus Pevsner, ever to have received the Royal Gold Medal for Architecture.

Summerson was the eighth and longest-serving Curator of Sir John Soane's Museum in London's Lincoln's Inn Fields. His writings on architecture were conspicuous for their elegance and economy, as well as a certain ironic detachment.

Having trained as an architect, Summerson wrote about architecture with an authority which has since become rare owing to the divorce between the profession and history. He was most often associated with John Nash and the Georgian period, yet he wrote on a wide variety of subjects and was firmly committed to the

Modern Movement. This was one of many apparent paradoxes in his long career.

In the 1930s Summerson sometimes used the pseudonym "Coolmore" for his articles, derived from the seat of his mother's family in Ireland. His great friend John Betjeman ever afterwards addressed him by this name, which seemed to convey Summerson's apparently cool, unemotional character.

A man who preserved his handsome appearance into old age, Summerson seemed, from the beginning, the austere patrician. When his book on Nash was published in 1935 – the first full biography of an historical architect other than Wren to be written in English – one reviewer complained that with his "deliberate under-statements . . . Mr Summerson has stressed nothing".

But, although he was a founder of the Georgian Group (established in 1937 in an attempt to check the destruction of London's Georgian buildings), Summerson was never a committed conservationist. In the 1950s he recommended that only some of Nash's Regent's Park terraces be preserved. And in the 1970s, to the dismay of a younger generation, he declined to use his consider-able influence to save buildings by Cockerell.

Summerson's attitude to historic buildings was partly that of the fastidious expert, one only concerned with significant masterpieces. It also reflected his deter-minist attitude to history, believing that individual artists must be interpreted in wider social terms and that change is irresistible.

But it might also have been a consequence of his work during the Second World War when he helped to set up the National Buildings Record. Out of his efforts as its deputy director from 1941 to 1945 came not only this invaluable national archive but also the preparation of lists of historic buildings at risk from bombing. These formed the basis for the first systematic protection established by the 1944 Town & Country Planning Act.

Many of the early photographs in the collection were Summerson's own. At the beginning of the Blitz, as he said, "it seemed now a good deal more important to record buildings than to write about them".

Seeing buildings by Wren and Hawksmoor in flames may well have impressed upon Summerson the essential futility of individual human endeavour and the frailty of man's artistic creations. His detachment may have been pessimism. But Summerson's disdain for enthusiasm also reflected a certain vanity which was manifested in his essential perversity and determination not to conform.

Always one jump ahead of younger historians in exploring new areas of study, Summerson characteristically took up the Modern Movement when it was promoted by an avant-garde minority and ceased to write about modern architecture once it had become commonplace.

The most notorious example of Summerson's delight in being shocking and different was the occasion when, having been invited by the Irish Georgian Society to help in the desperate struggle to save Georgian Dublin, he observed that one threatened terrace was "just one damned house after another".

Both Summerson's manner and appearance reinforced an impression of Olympian detachment, of his being the last of the Whigs. Yet this was entirely belied by his background.

His grandfather had begun life as a navvy, quarrying stone sleepers for Britain's first public railway, the Stockton & Darlington, and ended as the director of a steel foundry.

John Newenham Summerson was born on November 25 1904; his father died when he was three. He was educated at Harrow and the Bartlett School of Architecture, London University, where he studied under Professor Albert Richardson.

Summerson's interest in architecture had been stimulated both by his experience of preparatory school at Riber near Matlock ("a castellated mansion of prodigious size and wild aspect") and by his admiration for the Anglican Cathedral in Liverpool, then rising. As a result, the young Summerson imagined its architect, Sir Giles Scott, to be a romantic hero and he confessed to being disappointed when Scott turned out to look no different from a bank manager.

Even so, in 1926, he succeeded in working as an assistant to this "great and good" architect. He also worked for Scott's younger brother, Adrian, and prepared all the working drawings for the octagonal tower added to the Church of the Holy Name in Manchester.

By 1930 Summerson was beginning to realise that his talents did not lie in the actual practice of architecture and he then spent an unhappy year teaching at the school of architecture at the Edinburgh College of Art. He courted dismissal by publishing an article in the *Scotsman* which concluded with a plea for the Princes Street of the future to be "a glittering spectacle of glass, steel and concrete".

After this Summerson realised that his true vocation

was arranging words, not bricks and mortar. In 1934 he began to work for the *Architect and Building News*, as well as contributing articles to other journals.

In the 1930s Summerson combined an affection for both Georgian and modern architecture. This was not then as unlikely as it may seem in retrospect – the two causes were often allied.

In 1938 he assisted with the exhibition mounted by the MARS Group, devoted to promoting the new architecture – a show "plastered with captions and exhortations of the most vacuous pomposity (I wrote them and I know)".

He later came to feel that the British production of the 1950s was of much greater merit than the work of the 1930s. After contributing an introduction to Trevor Dannatt's *Modern Architecture in Britain* (1959), Summerson ceased to write about new buildings until he published an article on the late Sir James Stirling in 1983.

Many of the buildings illustrated in *The Bombed Buildings of Britain* which Summerson published with the late Sir James Richards (1942 and 1945) were Victorian churches. The war seemed to have encouraged Summerson's interest in the 19th century.

Summerson's stimulating essay on "William Butterfield, or the Glory of Ugliness" was published in his brilliant collection, *Heavenly Mansions* (1949). This book was remarkable not least for also containing an article on "Architecture, Painting and Le Corbusier".

Summerson's interest in contemporary art was encouraged by his marriage, in 1938, to Elizabeth Hepworth, sister of the sculptress Barbara Hepworth who was then married to Ben Nicholson. Lady Summerson, who died in 1991, followed her sister in producing triplets – all boys in this case.

In 1945 Summerson was appointed Curator of Sir John Soane's Museum. His immediate task was to reassemble the contents of the building after wartime evacuation and to reopen the museum. This was achieved in 1947, although the current restoration of the building is revealing that Summerson was unable or unwilling to carry out a full recreation of the blast-damaged structure.

Nevertheless, he did a great deal to enlarge and improve the museum while maintaining a surprisingly informal and antiquated atmosphere. Summerson established the Soane as an awesome sanctum of architectural research and one in which he was able largely to dispense with journalism and devote himself to research and scholarship. Notwithstanding, he maintained the tradition of guiding visitors around the museum himself on Saturday afternoons.

Georgian London, first published in 1945, was the happy consequence of Summerson's pre-war and wartime researches. Having gone through many editions, it remains in print.

In 1953, he published his magisterial history of *Architecture in Britain: 1530–1830* in Nikolaus Pevsner's *Pelican History of Art* Series. It remains a standard, essential work, notable for the lucidity and economy with which Summerson organised and explained his broad subject.

Cogent illumination was also achieved in his little book on *The Classical Language of Architecture*, which began as the text to BBC talks in 1963. Other important publications included a biography of *Inigo Jones* (1966), *Victorian Architecture: Four Studies in Evaluation* (1970) and a study of *The London Building World in the 1860s* (1973).

In 1975 Summerson's dry, mellifluous voice and commanding presence were memorably exploited by BBC Television in the programme he made on Soane in the *Spirit of the Age* series.

Summerson retired from the Soane Museum in 1984. His successor found that the only piece of equipment left behind in his office was a 1946 *Who's Who*. There was no typewriter, for Summerson had always dealt with his correspondence in longhand.

He was appointed CBE in 1952, elected a Fellow of the British Academy in 1954, knighted in 1958 and appointed Companion of Honour in 1987.

In 1976 he was awarded the Royal Gold Medal by the RIBA – "the most distinguished honour to which an architect or a writer on architecture can aspire".

For all his loftiness and his seeming identification with the Establishment, John Summerson was warm, companionable and drily humorous. His correspondence with John Betjeman was particularly entertaining.

The once earnest partisan of the new architecture was yet a churchwarden of his local "middle-stump" Anglican church (an impressively dull Victorian pile). Like many with a profound architectural sense, Summerson loved music.

In his last years, increasingly disabled by Parkinson's Disease and deafness, he worked on his autobiography, which he felt should not appear in his lifetime. It must be hoped that this will now be published, as it is certain not only to be entertaining but to manifest that acuity of observation and studied elegance of expression which characterised all his writings. No other writer in English has managed to convey so beautifully the essentially incommunicable qualities of architecture.

November 13 1992

VISCOUNT MASSEREENE AND FERRARD

THE 13TH VISCOUNT MASSEREENE AND 6TH VIS-COUNT FERRARD, who has died aged 78, was one of the most engagingly eccentric members of the House of Lords.

He held four Irish peerages and one in the United Kingdom which enabled him to sit in the Upper House where he was revered as an institution. His singular contribution to debate and to public life prompted the then Lord Chancellor, Lord Hailsham of Saint Marylebone, to remark in a foreword to Lord Massereene's book, *The Lords*: "One hopes that Viscount Massereene and Ferrard will never be reformed."

He was able to enliven debates on almost any subject with personal anecdote and reference to his own experience – although the question was once or twice gently raised whether "Lord Mass of Cream and Feathers" was really of this world.

In a debate on the Brixton riots in the early 1980s Massereene ventured to suggest that he was "the only member who has spoken today who has had agricultural estates in Jamaica", where the only riots he witnessed were "riots of joy, because when I arrived I always gave a big barbecue for all the people".

179

On unemployment, Massereene was once able to inform their Lordships that the situation was not as bad as they supposed, since he had been trying for months to find an under-gardener at his seat, Chilham Castle, in Kent. He also found it inexplicable that British Rail should complain of shortage of staff while there was widespread unemployment, and that prisons were over-crowded when the problem could be solved by creating jobs to build more of them.

In his preface to *The Lords*, a stirring apologia for the Upper House, Massereene reflected that: "I have witnessed the swift disintegration of everything the word 'British' once stood for and I have seen the world, in consequence, become a poorer place."

Above all he stood, in his sometimes idiosyncratic way, for an old-fashioned common sense which the modern world did not always comprehend.

Massereene was originally in favour of Britain being part of Europe, but latterly he had become distrustful of the French and was a convinced Euro-sceptic. Having broken his leg in 1991, he was looking forward to returning to the Lords and "speaking up for Britain".

He had a remarkable range of interests, most of them rooted in the country and country sports. He was never busier in the House of Lords than during the passage of the Wildlife and Countryside Bill in 1981, when he spoke on 77 occasions.

Several of his speeches were about bulls (his coat of arms includes six of them); one recalled his boyhood when he had fired a catapult at a sparrow and hit an old man taking a bath. When the Wildlife (Northern Ireland) Order came to be debated in 1984, Massereene expressed his bewilderment that curlew remained on the quarry list, since they were "filthy to eat", unless it was to give Irishmen the opportunity to shoot something other than each other. The oyster-catcher was another bird that Massereene found indigestible, having once shot one by mistake.

Massereene was responsible for introducing several measures and proposals, including the 1963 Deer Act; two Acts to regulate riding schools and give protection to horses and ponies; and the Protection of Animals (Penalties) Act in 1987.

He also twice tried unsuccessfully to restore the right of Irish peers to a seat in the House of Lords. He once proposed a tax to support the major political parties which was well received in the Lords by the Labour and Liberal parties, but it got no further.

John Clotworthy Talbot Foster Whyte-Melville Skeffington was born on October 23 1914, the only surviving son of the 12th Viscount Massereene and 5th Viscount Ferrard. He spent his early years at the family seat of Antrim Castle, first built in 1613 by Sir Hugh Clotworthy, father of the 1st Viscount Massereene, who was instrumental in the restoration of King Charles II.

The 6th Viscount (and 2nd Earl) Massereene was a great Irish eccentric. He ordered 60 dogs decked out in mourning attire to attend the funeral of his favourite hound.

In 1922, on his eighth birthday, young "Jock" witnessed the burning of the castle by Sinn Feiners. He was educated at Eton and joined the Special Reserve of the Black Watch in 1933.

A dedicated sportsman, he was a gentleman-rider

under National Hunt Rules and contributed to *The Field* from the mid-1930s onwards. A motor-racing enthusiast, he drove the leading British car at Le Mans in 1937.

During the Second World War he served with the Black Watch until invalided in 1940. Later he joined the Small Vessels Pool, Royal Navy. He succeeded to the viscountcy in 1956. In addition to his principal seat at Chilham, where he kept falcons and an imperial eagle, Massereene lived at Knock on the Isle of Mull, where he spent much time observing birds of prey in the wild, and stalking on the 70,000-acre estate.

The pursuits of this most eclectic peer ranged from opera (he presented *Countess Maritza* at the Palace Theatre) to foxhunting (he served as Master of the Ashford Valley). He also kept foxes as pets.

Massereene served as vice-president, and treasurer, of the Ashford Conservative Association and was president of the Monday Club (from which he resigned last year). He once acknowledged, however, that if he had been born in a Liverpool slum, "it might have taken me a long time to become a Conservative".

He was Commodore of the House of Lords Yacht Club for 13 years, and a member of the Worshipful Company of Shipwrights. He promoted the first scheduled air service from Glasgow to Mull; and was concerned with the development of land in Florida which afterwards became the rocket-launching site of Cape Canaveral.

Among many public services for Kent, Massereene presided over the Canterbury branch of the Royal National Lifeboat Institution, and the Kent Hotel & Restaurants Association. He was treasurer of the Kent Association of Boys Clubs for more than 20 years and served as a Deputy Lieutenant for Co Antrim.

At the time of his death, Lord Massereene was engaged on a biography of his great-grandfather, George Whyte-Melville, novelist and poet, who died in the hunting field.

He married, in 1939, Annabelle Lewis; they had a son and a daughter. The son, John David Clotworthy Whyte-Melville Foster Skeffington, born 1940, succeeds to the viscountcy.

December 29 1992

LILLIAN GISH

LILLIAN GISH, the American actress who has died aged 96, was a last link with the earliest days of the cinema.

She first appeared on the stage when she was five years old; rose to become a major star of the silent screen; survived the transition to sound, which ended so many careers – though in the 1930s she worked mainly on the stage; and was still performing, very effectively, in films and on television during the 1980s. Throughout this immensely long career Gish was an epitome of professionalism. Her private life, too, spent largely with her mother and her younger sister Dorothy, also an actress, was exceptionally free of Hollywood scandal or vanity.

She attributed her success, truly but with characteristic generosity, to her mentor, the great silent-film director, D. W. Griffith. Her acting ability in those first epics cannot be fairly judged by modern eyes, but audiences and critics at the time were much moved. Her performances in later films showed a striking ability to adapt to contemporary demands.

In her old age Lillian Gish became one of Hollywood's most revered and deserving *grandes dames*. Always modest and sensible, she possessed a durability which saw her through the whole sweep of cinematic history.

She was born Lillian de Guiche at Springfield, Ohio, on October 14 1896. At the time her father was a storekeeper but he never did anything for long, and quite soon drifted out of his family's life. Her mother, by contrast, was a proud, capable woman. To make a little money during one of her husband's protracted absences, she was persuaded to become an actress in a New York stock company. It was then suggested that Lillian, and soon afterwards Dorothy, could supplement the family income by touring as children in melodramas.

The years which followed were, on the whole, enjoyable for "Baby Lillian", as she was billed. She crisscrossed the country, sometimes playing with her mother, sometimes in separate companies. The girls did not receive much formal education, but Mrs de Guiche taught them some American history; they went regularly to church and occasionally to school; above all, they learned the importance of discipline. It was not an easy life, though, and only through the kind offices of friends were they able to evade the clutches of the Gerry Society, which was trying to prevent child employment.

The Gish sisters, as they had become, made the transition from theatre to film through some theatrical acquaintances called Smith, shortly to be known as Pickford. At the office of the Biograph Company in New York, Mary Pickford introduced the Gishes to David Wark Griffith, who immediately recruited them all to appear in a film about two frightened children trapped in a lonely house.

Lillian and Dorothy went on to play in a succession of Griffith's one- and two-reelers, some of which were made in a single day. Griffith invented the films as he went along, showing his actors what he wanted scene by scene.

In the meantime Lillian continued her stage career. When her health failed during a tour of David Belasco's production of *The Good Little Devil*, he dispatched her to join Dorothy who was then working at Griffith's winter headquarters in California. She arrived at Los Angeles in February 1914. "The city", she recalled, "smelled like a vast orange grove."

Griffith again used both girls in sentimental dramas and melodramas, while their mother kept house. His first feature-length production was a Biblical epic, *Judith of Bethulia* (1913), in which Lillian had a minor role. Then, in 1915, he unveiled his masterpiece, *Birth of a Nation*, designed to help Americans appreciate their own past.

The whole concept of Hollywood film-making was transformed: and, although Griffith had never operated a star system, Lillian, who played a Southern girl narrowly saved from being raped by a villainous mulatto, was unmistakably the heroine.

Among her later films for Griffith were *Intolerance* (1916), in which, as the "Eternal Mother", she linked episodes about ancient Babylon, persecuted Christians, massacred Huguenots and a modern labour dispute; *Broken Blossoms* (1919), a melodramatic tale from Thomas Burke's *Limehouse Nights*; *Way Down East* (1920), which had a memorable climax on the ice floes; and *Orphans of the Storm* (1921), in which she played with Dorothy, about the French Revolution.

Lillian then made her own directing debut with *Remodelling Her Husband*, in which Dorothy starred. She hired Dorothy Parker to write witty subtitles – one of which described a manicurist as "The divinity that shapes our ends". But, having learned what a complex job directing was, Lillian said she never wanted to do it again.

When Griffith could no longer meet the salary that her fame merited, Lillian worked for various other companies. By being so manifestly respectable – later she would sternly reject a suggestion from a studio that it should concoct a newsworthy scandal for her – she overcame objections from the Women's Clubs of America to a film called *The White Sister* (1923), about a girl who becomes a nun when she thinks her lover has been killed.

She also made a version of George Eliot's *Romola*. But this period ended in bitter litigation against Charles H. Duell, president of the Inspiration Company, who had abused her contract. In his defence, he claimed that she had promised to marry him – he was found guilty of perjury.

Moving to MGM, she made *La Bohème* (1926) with John Gilbert; *The Scarlet Letter* (1926), in which the role of the Puritan heroine suited her particularly well; *Annie Laurie* (1926), about Glencoe, which was a box-office disaster, and *The Wind* (1927), which has been more admired subsequently than at the time.

When talking pictures arrived, Gish's voice proved perfectly suitable, though her sound debut in *One Romantic Night*, an adaptation of Molnar's *The Swan*, failed to draw the public. Lillian Gish was out of fashion. New kinds of story, new styles of acting, new stars, prevailed.

When their mother suffered a stroke in London, she

and her sister brought her back to America; Mrs Gish never really recovered her power of speech, but they made a home for her, and kept her comfortable and happy for the next 20 years.

Lillian returned to the stage. She played in *Uncle Vanya* and *Camille* on Broadway; she was Ophelia in Gielgud's *Hamlet*; she played opposite Burgess Meredith in *The Star Maker* and toured in *Life with Father*.

A supporting role in an undistinguished film, *The Commandos Strike at Dawn*, restored her to the screen in 1942. She was struck by how much Hollywood had changed. In the old days actors were involved in every aspect of production: now films were big business, and the actors simply did what they were told.

From then on, while continuing her stage career, she played smallish parts in a number of quite good films. She was Donald O'Connor's mother in *Top Man* (1943); Lionel Barrymore's wife in *Duel in the Sun* (1946), for which she received her only Oscar nomination; and the Mother Superior of a convent school in *Portrait of Jenny* (1948).

Most notably, she played a tough spinster who protects the fleeing children in Charles Laughton's remarkable film, *The Night of the Hunter* (1955). On stage she appeared with Dorothy in *The Chalk Garden* and as the nurse in *Romeo and Juliet*; she was also in *I Never Sang for My Father*.

With the advent of television, she appeared in *Arsenic and Old Lace* with Helen Hayes, and starred in the life of *Grandma Moses*. She also achieved a long-nurtured ambition to make a film tribute to Griffith, with *Silver Glory*.

Mrs Gish died in 1948, Dorothy in 1968, but

Lillian, the stronger and more practical of the sisters, continued indomitable.

Her autobiography, *The Movies, Mr Griffith and Me* (1969), showed as much interest in Griffith's career as in her own. She lobbied successfully for a postage stamp commemorating him.

In 1970 Gish received a Special Academy Award "for superlative artistry and her distinguished contribution to the progress of motion pictures". In 1987 she appeared, movingly, as Bette Davis's sister in the *Whales of August*.

She had never married, because, as she put it, although she was constantly in and out of love, she considered marriage a 24-hour-a-day job and had always been too busy. Besides, if her mother, who was "wise and perfect", could not succeed at marriage, how could she hope to do so? "My films are my children," she said.

March 1 1993

COUNT EDWARD RACZYNSKI

COUNT EDWARD RACZYNSKI, the Polish diplomatist who has died in London aged 101, witnessed the rise and fall of Communism – but was too old to return home to the free Poland he had not seen since before the Second World War.

Nevertheless, he had a triumphant 100th birthday party at the Polish Embassy in Eaton Place, which he had not entered since the British had "derecognised" the exiles' government in favour of the Warsaw Communists in 1945. Blind and standing erect, Raczynski talked in French to the German ambassador and delivered an eloquent five-minute speech in English and Polish. He thanked Her Majesty the Queen for his honorary GBE while referring to his own "exaggerated old age". He also made a shrewd dig at the Communists by referring to the new ambassador, the former Solidarity lawyer Tadeusz de Virion, as his "successor" – thereby ignoring the dozen or so party *apparatchiks* who had filled the post in the intervening 46 years.

It was a fitting end to his long wait that Raczynski was not only the last senior participant in the spiral of events which had led to war in 1939, but had lived to witness Eastern Europe savouring a second taste of the freedom it had enjoyed after the First World War.

As Polish Ambassador to Britain from 1934 to 1945, his country's acting Foreign Minister from 1941 to 1943, and President of the Government-in-Exile from 1979 to 1986, Raczynski symbolised all that was best in his indomitable countrymen. With his tall, slim figure – impeccably groomed and sporting a monocle in his heyday – he was a survival of that aristocratic age when the chancelleries of Europe had seemed the guardians of civilised values.

Always a lucid public speaker and fluent writer of letters to newspapers, Raczynski conveyed a timeless message. He reminded the British that the Poles were their first allies to join battle in 1939, and that Poland would always have an important place at the centre of any major European drama.

When he was in his late nineties and the Polish Government-in-Exile was regarded – even by many in

Poland – as a hopeless anachronism, it was still inconceivable for a non-Communist Polish leader to visit London without making contact with the Count. Visitors from many nations and several generations made their way to his Knightsbridge flat. There they would encounter an old man, often reclining on a daybed, who would lucidly offer up-to-date and well-informed opinion, enunciated as beautiful prose in a silky French-tinged Slavic accent.

Count Edward Bernard André Maria Raczynski was born on December 19 1891. The history of his title went back to a 17th-century Holy Roman Empire creation that became extinct in the 19th, but was then revived by King Frederick William II of Prussia. His inheritance included part of central Cracow and large estates at Zawaga, central Poland.

Young Edward first visited Britain at the age of 15 when he was bored by a holiday in Aldeburgh, but ensnared by English culture – unlike most of his countrymen whose traditional allegiances lay with France. After studying at Leipzig University, he attended the London School of Economics, where, in his enthusiasm for English pursuits, he took up boxing.

On the outbreak of the Great War in 1914 Poland had not officially existed on the map of Europe since the late 18th century. Raczynski found himself called up to serve in the Austrian Army while his brother, Roger, a future Polish Ambassador to Romania, was with the Russians on the opposite side.

But he was soon rejected because of his poor eyesight, and studied law at Cracow University until the last months of hostilities, when he was drafted into a Polish officers' training camp for the German Army. As a result, when Germany surrendered, he enjoyed the satisfaction of disarming German soldiers in the streets of Warsaw.

On entering the Polish Foreign Service Raczynski was posted to Copenhagen and then London, where he began to make many of the contacts that were to be invaluable to his career.

In 1925, he married Joyous Markham, daughter of Sir Arthur Markham, 1st Bt, a Liberal MP. Lloyd George was one of the witnesses – although, significantly, in the light of his later hostility to Poland, the Welshman refused to shake hands with the bridegroom.

Raczynski was recalled to Warsaw to become head of the Foreign Ministry's Eastern Department. He was appointed delegate to the Geneva Disarmament Conference and Ambassador to the League of Nations, where he ably defended his country against increasingly bitter German onslaughts.

After the death of his first wife in 1930, he married Cesia, daughter of Edward Jaroszynski, a Polish industrialist; they had three daughters.

On appointment as Ambassador in London, one of Raczynski's first duties was to have a frock-coat made – although he only wore it once, as official court dress was abolished soon afterwards by King Edward VIII.

Fleet Street's gossip columnists delighted in reporting every aspect of the young Count's life. They wrote about his artistic and literary tastes; how he brought over pictures from his Warsaw palace for the embassy in Portland Place; and about Alphonse, the terrier always to be found at his master's feet in the ambassadorial study.

In Whitehall, Raczynski's air of cool reason and

willingness to compromise – so different from many of his countrymen – played an important part in convincing Britain that Poland was the issue on which she should make a stand.

While his prickly Foreign Minister, Colonel Beck, exasperated all he met, Raczynski was the efficient antidote. He worked smoothly to bring off the Anglo-Polish alliance, explaining why Poland could not contemplate Russian troops crossing Polish borders to engage the Germans.

Moreover, he reassured the Foreign Secretary, Lord Halifax, that the Nazi-Soviet Pact was more a formal truce than anything else. As war drew nearer he was a daily caller on the determined, if uncertain, Halifax. He gave the British Foreign Secretary reports with which to refute German allegations of Polish atrocities that were helping to shake the wobbly Chamberlain cabinet's resolve.

While a younger colleague in Paris raged at the delaying tactics of the French after the Germans invaded Poland on September 1, Raczynski publicly declared himself satisfied with the British efforts.

He was privy to the Cabinet rebellion over the Government's paralysis, and two days later watched Chamberlain tell Parliament that war had begun.

When the Polish government arrived in London after the French collapse, Raczynski found himself increasingly called upon to keep the peace between his disoriented, quarrelsome countrymen. Since few of the new cabinet spoke English he was an invaluable guide to British ways, as well as an experienced interpreter at high-level meetings.

After the resignation of several ministers over the

Polish-Russian agreement of 1941, General Sikorski also made him Foreign Minister. Raczynski's diplomatic experience gave him a clear appreciation of the Polish government's diminishing strength, but his air of seeming detachment also left him open to criticism by the hardened politicians whom he found as his colleagues.

On Sikorski's death in an air crash, Racyzynski was dropped from the Cabinet to be simply Ambassador again, charged with the task of issuing ever stronger and more hopeless protests.

The British and the Americans found it hard to believe his reports on the Nazi death camps. They refused to press the Russians on the massacre of Polish officers at Katyn. And when Churchill and Roosevelt assigned Eastern Europe to Stalin at the Yalta Conference they lost any effective say over Poland's future.

Raczynski knew Churchill well enough to realise that his rudeness at meetings with Polish ministers stemmed from an uneasy conscience. The key to this – Britain's growing weakness – was not lost on those MPs who looked up to the House's diplomatic gallery during the Yalta debate. There sat the dignified envoy of the country for whom they had originally gone to war.

Although no longer officially accepted as representing the Polish government after the transference of British recognition to the Polish regime in Warsaw in 1945, Raczynski took a leading part in the resettlement of Poles in Britain. He was the most respected Pole on the Interim Treasury Committee.

Bad conscience undoubtedly contributed to its British members' exasperation at finding how much property the Free Poles succeeded in keeping from the new Warsaw government's representatives. But they strongly rebuffed attempts by the new Communist authorities to have him dismissed.

Raczynski later sat on the Anglo-Polish Resettlement Committee and made personal contributions – as when he sold his Rembrandt to raise funds. Other posts included the chairmanship of the Polish Research Centre, which brought families cut off by the Iron Curtain together again; the post of chief Polish Adviser to the Ministry of Labour; and the chairmanship of the Polish Institute and the Sikorski Museum.

Later, when the intellectual group KOR was founded in Warsaw during the mid-1970s, he headed what became known as "Raczynski's Committee", which raised funds for it in the West.

Raczynski's lack of raw political instinct became clear again when, in 1953, he initially supported August Zaleski's decision to remain the exiles' president after completing his seven-year term – a decision that led to the greatest of all the many quarrels that festered within the community. But Raczynski later made up for this when President himself. He appointed as prime minister Kazimierz Sabbat, who ended the damaging split.

With Sabbat, he fought off an attempt to have Sikorski's body removed to Poland by the increasingly threatened Communist regime. He also signed an accord with the Free Czechs in America.

This, he hoped, pointed the way to a Polish-Czechoslovakian confederation – the subject of his letter in *The Daily Telegraph* on September 1 1989, the 50th anniversary of the invasion of Poland.

It was only when Raczynski was in his seventies that he again found time for the literary pursuits which had inspired him to begin translating Edward Fitzgerald's

Rubaiyat of Omar Khayyam into Polish before the war. His works included a volume of verses; several translations from French into Polish; and *In Allied London* (1962), which contains some perceptive insights into ordinary life in the wartime capital. But his recollections on official matters remained discreet.

After the thaw in the Communist ice age he gave a series of interviews on the period, from the Geneva disarmament conference in the early 1930s to Poland's deliverance into Soviet hands, which was published in Polish.

Raczynski's second wife died in 1962; in 1991, at the age of 99, he married thirdly, Aniela Mieczyslawska, the widow of a Polish diplomat who had looked after him for some years.

Raczynski remained mentally active thanks to a band of friends who read to him for hours on end. This enabled him to talk intelligently about the latest political developments in Eastern Europe, which he characteristically greeted with a cautious optimism.

Whatever the subject, he insisted that he always spoke first as a Pole. It was this awareness that made him retain the Warsaw palace he had not seen for more than 50 years as his address in *Who's Who*. This is now the site of a museum to which many of his works of art were freely returned after the fall of Communism. He then gave them to the Polish people.

July 31 1993

E. P. THOMPSON

E. P. THOMPSON, who has died aged 69, was an inspirational figure in the "history from below" school, which puts the governed rather than their governors at the forefront of historical study.

In *The Making of the English Working Class* (1963), his most influential work, Thompson insisted that the working class "was present at its own making", an active participant rather than a brute "it", its fate determined by external forces. He was seeking, he explained, "to rescue the poor stockinger, the Luddite cropper, the 'obsolete' hand-loom weaver, the 'utopian' artisan . . . from the enormous condescension of posterity". This populist, even quixotic approach informed all Thompson's political writings and activity.

A persistent pamphleteer, an accomplished satirist and a founder of the *New Left Review*, he was a crucial figure in the 1980s revival of the moribund "peace movement". He spoke in court in defence of the women protesters of Greenham Common and was a founder of European Nuclear Disarmament (END), which galvanised activists in both the West and the East.

Edward Thompson spent his life attempting to reconcile opposites: the intellectual and the down-to-earth; stringent theory and dynamic practice; the distinctively English and the international. But although he was far-ranging in his talents and achievements, there was an extraordinary unity to Thompson's beliefs and preoccupations, which lay in his increasingly "anti-statist" position.

Edward Palmer Thompson was born on February 3 1924; his father, a Methodist missionary in India, was involved in the Indian nationalist movement and was a friend of Nehru and of Tagore, whose poetry he translated. Edward's older brother Frank – who fought with the partisans in Bulgaria during the Second World War and was shot after declining prisoner-of-war status as a British officer – was a formative influence on his opinions and character.

Young Edward was educated at Kingswood School, Bath, and Corpus Christi College, Cambridge; he broke off his studies to fight in Italy with the 17th/21st Lancers, in which he rose to become a tank commander. Thompson took a first in history in 1946, and two years later became an extra-mural lecturer at Leeds University, where he remained until 1965.

He began his political career as a Communist, and his first book, *William Morris: Romantic to Revolutionary* (1955), attempted to place Morris within an international Communist tradition. The next year, though, he was suspended from the Party for criticising the Soviet invasion of Hungary in the *Reasoner*, the Communist magazine he helped to edit. He later commented that he only "commenced to reason in this [his] 33rd year".

In his 34th he and John Saville founded the *New Reasoner*, which two years later merged with the *Universities and Left Review* to become the *New Left Review*.

"It is only by facing opposition that I am able to define my thought at all," Thompson declared. In 1965, two years after *The Making of the English Working Class* was published to great acclaim, he wrote an article attacking Tom Nairn and Perry Anderson, who had taken over editorship of the *NLR*. Dubbing them members of the "lumpen-intelligentsia", he accused them of putting too high a value on conceptual jargon and Continental Marxism, and of underestimating the richness of working-class culture and values.

But as well as excoriating the over-theoretical, Thompson proved a formidable opponent of anti-intellectual politics, such as the Paris revolts of 1968. Such events, he argued, undermined the realistic Socialism embodied in the *Mayday Manifesto* (edited by Raymond Williams), to which he contributed.

In 1965 Thompson was offered the post of Reader in Labour History at Warwick University. He was a charismatic lecturer, and several of his students went on to work with him on such collections as *Albion's Fatal Tree* (1975).

In 1970 Thompson became involved with the students who had invaded the university offices. He propagated their discovery of the involvement of local business with the university, and of files kept on staff and students alike, and wrote about the affair in *New Society*, as well as editing a book on the subject, *Warwick University Ltd* (1971).

He resigned his Warwick post the same year, and from then on – apart from occasional visiting professorships and lecture tours, mainly in America – devoted himself to writing and to political activity. While producing *Whigs and Hunters* (1975), a brilliant exposition of the abuses of 18th-century English law, Thompson was also writing articles warning of the State's increasing presence in daily life, and the diminution of political consensus. Some of these were published as *Writing by Candlelight* (1980).

His campaign against authoritarianism was also conducted within the Left. In *The Poverty of Theory* (1978) he inveighed against Althusser's anti-humanist denial of individual agency and against the structuralist Marxism which envisaged forces of production churning out a proletariat almost as mechanically as it did textiles or steel.

In the 1980s Thompson more or less abandoned historical writing to dedicate himself to the peace activism he had begun in the 1950s.

In 1980, in his pamphlet *Protest and Survive* (written with Dan Smith), he deftly ridiculed a government leaflet entitled *Protect and Survive*, which offered pitifully inadequate instructions for defence against nuclear attack.

The same year, in an article in the *New Left Review*, he attempted to produce a left-wing position on nuclear weapons, proposing the post-Marxist concept of "exterminism". What the hand-mill was to feudalism, and the steam-mill to capitalism, said Thompson, so the nuclear weapons industry was to "exterminism".

The arms race, he argued, had become a self-sustaining system, stoked by "an internal dynamic" rather than by human malevolence, and by a "reciprocal logic" which required the mutually opposed ideologies to preserve it.

It was also in 1980, together with Bruce Kent, Mary Kaldor and others, that Thompson set up END, which added to the aims of CND what Thompson considered to be the only hope – the creation of a new internationalism which "unequivocally rejects the ideology of both blocs". Such a plan inevitably incurred the suspicion and abuse of both sides: Thompson was called a KGB agent by the British Right, and a CIA agent by Yuri Zhukov, the chairman of the Soviet Peace Committee.

Thompson abused his detractors as "only-two-sides men" and went on to produce a stream of articles and essays. An invitation to give the 1981 Dimbleby Lectures on the BBC was rescinded at the last minute, and soon afterwards the text of the proposed lectures (*Beyond the Cold War*) was issued in samizdat form in Hungary.

He became an international figure, speaking at peace gatherings around the world, at which he was renowned not only for his searing oratory but also for his striking looks and tireless energy. In 1988 he was incapacitated by serious illness, but none the less continued work on his study of William Blake.

He married, in 1948, Dorothy Towers, a fellow-academic whom he always consulted and reckoned a better historian than himself; they had two sons and a daughter.

August 30 1993

LADY LINDSAY
OF DOWHILL

LADY LINDSAY OF DOWHILL, better known as Loelia Duchess of Westminster, who has died aged 91, wrote a remarkably candid volume of memoirs, *Grace and Favour* (1961), which is a valuable record of high life between the wars.

An Edwardian by birth, Loelia Ponsonby became a leading "Bright Young Thing" in the 1920s and went on to marry the 2nd Duke of Westminster — the legendary sybarite "Bendor", whose yacht features in Noël Coward's play *Private Lives*.

Coward also wrote the foreword to the Duchess's well-received memoirs. He did so, he said, "cowed by the steely inflexibility of her tone and a look in her eye that I suspect caused the late Duke of Westminster some uneasy moments". Another friend, Ian Fleming, used her as the model for Miss Moneypenny in the James Bond books.

Loelia Mary Ponsonby was born on February 6 1902, the only daughter of the courtier Sir Frederick Ponsonby, later 1st Lord Sysonby. "Fritz" Ponsonby was assistant private secretary to Queen Victoria, King Edward VII and King George V, and wrote *Recollections of Three Reigns*.

Young Loelia once occupied the lap of Edward VII and amused His Majesty by seizing his beard and demanding: "But King, where's your crown?" Her childhood – spent variously at St James's Palace, Park House at Sandringham and Birkhall – was, as she recalled, made irksome by a succession of fierce foreign governesses. She escaped from the stiffness of her parents' world into the hedonism of "the Bright Young People".

Their pranks included treasure-hunts and impersonating reporters to obtain interviews from famous people. The older generation were duly shocked, although in her own old age Loelia Lindsay insisted that it was "just light-hearted fun".

Her own contribution was to invent the "bottle-party" in 1926, when, for economic reasons, guests were bidden to bring their own drink. The first guest was the author Michael Arlen, bearing a dozen bottles of pink champagne.

Towards the end of the 1920s Loelia met Bendor Westminster, a selfish, spoilt, twice-divorced playboy, though a generous landlord and gallant officer. The diarist "Chips" Channon summed him up as "a mixture of Henry VIII and Lorenzo Il Magnifico".

The Duke courted Miss Ponsonby in style, showering her with diamonds. A typical incident occurred one night in her sleeper *en route* for Venice when she woke with an uncomfortable lump digging into her: it was an emerald and diamond brooch.

They married in 1930 in a blaze of publicity, with Winston Churchill as best man. The new Duchess became châtelaine of the Gothic palace of Eaton in Cheshire, as well as houses in Scotland, Wales and France, to say nothing of the steam yacht and a sailing ship.

But the marriage was not a success. The Duchess found Bendor a man of changing moods – charming and generous one moment, furious and cruel the next. Their choice of friends differed considerably. James Lees-Milne (*qv*) described the Duchess's married life as "a definition of unadulterated hell".

The marriage was dissolved in 1947. By this time the Duchess had established a new life for herself, in considerably reduced circumstances, at Send Grove in Surrey, where she was a skilful hostess with impeccable taste.

She was an expert needlewoman, with a knack of incorporating beads into flowers and leaves. The epicene actor Ernest Thesiger (celebrated for his summing-up of the Western Front in the First World War: "The *noise*, my dear, and the PEOPLE!") gave her his collection of beautiful multicoloured beads and she once threaded 20 shades of mauve into a dusky rose.

A talented horticulturist, she transformed a muddy rubbish dump at Send into a magnificent garden. She would bind roses high up a tree-trunk and then allow them to tumble over, giving the impression of a floral waterfall.

In the 1950s Loelia Westminster worked as a feature editor for *House and Garden*, and covered Grace Kelly's wedding in Monte Carlo. Besides her memoirs she published an evocative album of photographs, *Cocktails and Laughter* (1983), edited by Hugo Vickers.

She found much happiness in her second marriage, in 1969, to Sir Martin Lindsay of Dowhill, 1st Bt, Arctic explorer, Gordon Highlander, Conservative MP and historian of the Baronetage. He died in 1981.

Hugo Vickers writes: Some years ago I was discussing the new style of obituary with Loelia and she fixed me with a steely eye, and announced: "Now I'm counting on you for a good spread when the time comes." I rise to the challenge.

Loelia's life was almost a classic 20th-century Cinderella story. It was, she readily admitted, one of rare privilege. Yet the contrasts were too extreme for comfort: a stern childhood, the seemingly fairy-tale marriage, the sorrow that followed – including incidents that would make some of today's court cases look tame. She told me she had consigned to paper the story of a night when the Duke of Westminster, in one of his rages, tried to strangle her.

Loelia was a mixture of two souls. On the one hand she was insecure, an inheritance from childhood. "I was most unhappy," she recalled. "I never learned a thing. And I was out of everything for a very long time because I was too shy to speak."

Her parents were so strict that they often put her in the wrong unfairly. In later life, as a defence mechanism, she sometimes wrongfooted her friends. On the other hand, she had infinite patience and imagination, and made needlework designs of great finery, even picking out the clouds in a sky with strands of her own hair. Her house at Send was full of painstaking work – a wonderful hand-woven carpet, a mirror adorned with shells hand-picked by her in Australia. Her beautiful collection has been bequeathed to the National Trust.

As a hostess she had the skill of a conductor, imperceptibly bringing the silent to life, so that everyone had their say. Nor was she lacking in confidence; I once saw an American guest reach for the decanter of wine, whereupon her restraining hand descended with some alacrity.

She lived in a world in which feuds consumed considerable energy, "cutting dead" was part of the vocabulary and the morning telephone buzzed with enjoyable gossip in her rich, melodic voice. She was celebrated, too, for such aphorisms as "Anybody seen in a 'bus over the age of 30 has been a failure in life".

By her own choice Loelia spent her last years in nursing homes, first in Surrey and latterly in Pimlico, where the matron gave an annual Christmas party at which delicious champagne flowed and the atmosphere was about as far from a geriatric establishment as you could hope to find. Though Loelia always claimed rather to dislike Margaret Argyll, another resident, they were thrown together in their last days.

Matron told me she had taken them out to tea: "The Duchess of Argyll wanted to go to the Ritz and Lady

Lindsay to Claridge's, but I took them both to the Carlton Towers and they had a wonderful time."

In her rooms Loelia re-created the atmosphere of Send in miniature, with her favourite furniture, pictures and needlework. "To think", she would say, "that at one time I used to own half London, with 50 valets, and now I am reduced to one room." She retained a youthful enjoyment of life, regularly visited by old friends "that I've known since I came out of the egg".

Some of her reminiscences were broadcast on BBC Radio 4, such as the occasion at a ball at Balmoral when all her party, as a joke, decided to kiss Queen Mary's hand on presentation. When Loelia's turn came, she found, to her lasting horror, that she had left the perfect impress of red lipstick on the white-gloved royal hand.

Looking back on her life on her 90th birthday, Loelia reflected on the contrasts of her life: "Rich as Croesus, then not a penny . . . That was all very exciting, I must say. It ended badly, but things like that do end badly. I never could have done any better. I was out of my depth the whole time. It had moments, there's no question about it. I can see how lucky I've been compared to other people."

November 4 1993

LORD MILFORD

THE 2ND LORD MILFORD, who has died aged 91, was the only professed Communist in Parliament.

Although he contested the seat of Cirencester and

Tewkesbury (later the constituency of his godson Nicholas Ridley) in the 1950 general election as a Communist candidate, the then Wogan Philipps gained only 423 votes and lost his deposit. But in 1962, on succeeding his father, the 1st Lord Milford, in the peerage, he chose to take his seat in the Lords.

In his maiden speech he called for the abolition of the Upper House. He condemned the Lords as "an undemocratic anachronism composed of the inheritors of wealth and privilege and bent on their protection, an indefensible obstacle to progressive legislation and the forward march of world socialism".

In his own case, however, he was not an "inheritor of wealth" as his father had disinherited him. The 1st Lord Milford, an ardent capitalist, had reputedly never spoken to his eldest son from the day he joined the party. In his will he avoided mentioning his heir by name; the trustees were instructed that "an avowed Communist or fellow traveller with the Communist Party" should forfeit all interest in his estate.

The new Lord Milford was heard in frosty silence by their lordships. It fell to the leader of the Labour peers, Earl Attlee, to offer the customary congratulations on a maiden speech. "There are many anomalies in this country," observed Lord Attlee. "One curious one is that the views of the Communist Party can only be heard in this House. That, of course, is an advantage of the hereditary principle."

Milford recalled that when he arrived at the House "all the people I had been with at Eton and Oxford welcomed me warmly. After my speech it never happened again and no one ever offered me a drink."

Undeterred, he continued to attend the Lords regularly. He liked to address the House on foreign affairs – American intervention in such countries as Vietnam and Nicaragua being a favourite topic – as well as social issues, education and the arts.

In one debate, when deploring the lack of interest in the arts in Britain, he shared his reminiscences of hearing a lunchtime poetry reading down a Chilean coal mine. "If you are talking in a pub here," he added, "and someone says 'What do you do mate?' and you say 'I am a poet', the conversation probably does not go on for long."

Milford hinted darkly that he gave his Lords' attendance allowance to the party funds. In reality, though, he was far from the militant firebrand some of his pronouncements might suggest; his romantic dream of a Communist utopia in Britain was very different from Stalin's brutal regime in the Soviet Union. Indeed he intensely disliked what he saw on his visits to Russia, but he blamed the application rather than the creed, and persisted in calling himself a Communist to the end.

Wogan Philipps was born on February 25 1902 into a remarkable family which produced a clutch of 20th-century peers. Several of the six sons of the Revd Sir James Philipps, 12th Bt (the head of an ancient, if impoverished, Welsh dynasty which had inherited Picton Castle in Pembrokeshire from the Wogans) became rich and influential through finance, shipping and other businesses, and three of them were made peers: Viscount St Davids, Lord Kylsant and Lord Milford. The career of Lord Kylsant, whose title died with him in 1937, ended unfortunately with a term of imprisonment which he suffered through infringing company law in what he felt to be the interests of his shareholders.

Lord Kylsant's youngest brother, Richard Philipps, chairman of the Court Line, Kia-Ora and other companies, was created a Baronet in 1919 and a peer, as Baron Milford, in 1939. He married Ethel Speke, a niece of the African explorer John Hanning Speke.

Wogan, their eldest son, was educated at Eton and Magdalen College, Oxford, and began life in a conventional enough manner. He attended debutante dances, drove lorries in the General Strike and joined the family shipping firm in the City of London.

"My family were all very rich businessmen, hunting, shooting and all that," he recalled. "They were all so tremendously anti-Semitic."

Surveying his brief career as a capitalist, he said: "I felt the resentment of the staff in the company when I joined. They must have felt 'Who's this little bugger?' During the General Strike I saw men lying about the street, down and out, and I began to wonder what it was all about."

In 1928 Philipps married the novelist Rosamond Lehmann and entered enthusiastically into bohemian life. He joined the Labour Party in the 1930s and during the Spanish Civil War served with the International Brigade as an ambulance driver. A contemporary recalled that Philipps had "no supplies and just had sponges soaked in chloroform to calm the injured".

After being badly wounded himself, when a shell hit his ambulance, Philipps helped to organise shipping supplies and to assist refugees. Among the volunteers

Philipps met out in Spain was the Communist Countess of Huntingdon (daughter of the Marchese Casati, of Palazzo Barberini, Rome), who was to become his second wife after his marriage to Rosamond Lehmann was dissolved in 1944. "We read a lot of Marxism together," he recalled. "We found we agreed on it."

Initially, however, he remained loyal to Labour and was elected to the Henley-on-Thames Rural District Council and selected as the party's prospective parliamentary candidate for the constituency in 1938.

During the Second World War Milford volunteered for service in the Merchant Navy but was rejected on medical grounds. Instead he worked as an agricultural labourer at a Government farm in Gloucestershire, and subsequently started his own small farm near Cirencester.

It was in the course of the war that Philipps joined the Communist Party. His telephone was bugged by the local police; when he remonstrated, "Oh come on, Constable, get off the line!", a voice would reply: "Sorry, Sir."

Philipps was active in building up the National Union of Agricultural Workers in the county. He served on the union's local committee and represented the union on Cheltenham Trades Council for 15 years.

In 1946 he managed to win a seat for the Communists on Cirencester Rural District Council. "They were all Tories except me," he recalled, "and in the meetings notes were passed round about me, things like 'Doesn't he stink?'"

Three years later, after a concerted Conservative campaign, Philipps lost his seat on the council by a mere 14 votes.

Between political forays he carried on farming ("I introduced artificial insemination to Gloucestershire") until settling in Hampstead.

Wogan Philipps had a great love of the arts and was himself a painter of some distinction. He exhibited his oils in London, Milan and Cheltenham, and after succeeding to the peerage delighted in showing his canvases in the annual Parliamentarians Exhibition at Westminster.

These exhibits tended to have an egalitarian flavour. One was of a Tolpuddle Martyrs rally, another a semi-abstract showing two figures thrusting their arms skywards, celebrating *The Good News of the Fall of the Greek Junta*.

After the death of his second wife in 1953 he married thirdly, in 1954, Tamara, widow of William Rust, editor of the *Daily Worker*. He had a son and a daughter by his first marriage. The daughter, Sally, who died in 1958, married the poet P. J. Kavanagh – a union described in Kavanagh's acclaimed book, *The Perfect Stranger*.

The peerage now passes to Lord Milford's son, Hugo John Laurence Philipps, born 1929, a member of Lloyd's.

December 3 1993

COMMANDANT PAUL-LOUIS WEILLER

COMMANDANT PAUL-LOUIS WEILLER, who has died in Paris aged 100, was a multi-billionaire industrialist and philanthropist with business concerns and properties throughout the world.

Unlike such other tycoons as Aristotle Onassis and Paul Getty, "The Commandant" succeeded in avoiding the limelight; indeed, he may prove to be one of the most enigmatic men of the 20th century. A celebrated aviator in the First World War, he was imprisoned in the Second. The aircraft company he owned was nationalised and is now Air France. He collected houses, furniture and works of art on a princely scale, and spent his life surrounded by celebrities of stage and screen, royalty and beautiful girls. He was also an indefatigable sportsman and patron of the arts.

As part of the bicentenary celebrations of the French Revolution in July 1989, Weiller was appointed to the Grand Cross of the Legion of Honour, France's highest honour.

Paul-Louis Weiller was born in Paris on September 29 1893, a scion of two prominent industrial families. His father, Senator Lazare Weiller, from Alsace, made a fortune discovering siliceous copper, laid down the first telephone cable between America and France, and sponsored the Wright brothers when they undertook early test flights in France in 1908. Paul-Louis's maternal family, the Javals, originally textile manufacturers, later founded railway companies in central Europe, introduced electricity into several countries and promoted Michelin.

As a boy, Paul-Louis studied in France, Germany and England. The inventor Marconi was his tutor and Paul Painlevé taught him mathematics.

Weiller was fascinated by flying from an early age.

After studying at the Ecole Centrale des Arts et Manu-
factures, he became a reconnaissance pilot in the First
World War. He was commandant of the French Grande
Reconnaissance group, which made daily flights over
enemy lines, and he invented a form of vertical aerial
photography.

He was wounded five times and on one occasion had
a brush with Baron von Richthofen, "the Red Baron".
Weiller received a host of honours and decorations,
including France's Military Medal, the British Military
Cross and the Yugoslav Order of the White Eagle. He
was appointed Chevalier of the Legion of Honour in
1915 and promoted Officer in 1918.

After the war Weiller became administrator of the
Société Gnome et Rhône, which constructed aircraft
engines. During his time at the helm the business
expanded, and was soon the second-largest builder of
aero-engines in France after Rolls-Royce. The number of
employees swiftly grew from 1,200 to 20,000 in France
alone, and by 1940 the shares had risen from 160 to
3,200 francs.

A generous and ingenious employer, he quelled a
strike within 48 hours in 1936 by sending details of his
men's pay cheques and benefits to their wives. Discrep-
ancies were soon noticed, rolling-pins applied and the
men were soon back at work.

As the head of CIDNA, he was also a pioneer of civil
aviation: he opened commercial flights from Paris to
Athens, and established air links with Turkey, Asia and
Central Africa.

The late Paul Getty described Weiller as "a highly
(and most deservedly) successful entrepreneur, at once
the shrewdest of businessmen and the kindest and most

considerate of human beings". Yet Weiller had his enemies; many contradictory stories are told of his activities.

In 1932, for instance, when he was attempting to open an aircraft line to America, he was accused of bribing a government official. The case went to law and it was discovered that Weiller's signature had been forged by an official of the Compagnie Générale Aeropostale. Weiller received the damages he asked for – one franc.

During the Second World War, along with his rival Marcel Dassault, he was arrested by the Vichy government in October 1940 and imprisoned at Pellevoisin. Weiller was stripped of his honours, but eventually escaped to Cuba and, after rallying the cause of the Free French in exile, was given the Médaille de la Résistance by General de Gaulle. Meanwhile, his mother was put to death in Auschwitz concentration camp in 1943.

Weiller's businesses were nationalised in France, so he did not return to Europe until 1947. But he succeeded in making a new fortune in the oil business in South America and in international banking. Thereafter his business enterprises expanded on all fronts. But he undertook no further business in France, other than charitable works – the founding of various hospitals and medical foundations.

The Duke and Duchess of Windsor lived for five years in his Paris mansion in the rue de la Faisanderie. For many years Weiller had been a great friend of Elsie de Wolfe (later Lady Mendl), the lesbian interior decorator. He bought her house, the Villa Trianon at Versailles, and allowed her to live there until her death in 1950.

Among his many works of restoration was the Ambassade d'Hollande in Le Marais, the scene of his more public entertaining. He also built a magnificent villa in the South of France, La Reine Jeanne at Bormes-les-Mimosas. Designed in 1930 by the American architect Barry Dierks, the house nestles in the pine trees on an extensive estate with two beaches.

Over the years the Commandant's guests included Greta Garbo, Charlie Chaplin, Douglas Fairbanks, Jean Seberg and the royal families of Denmark, Sweden and Italy. Shortly before his death Princess Michael of Kent stayed there.

As the Commandant grew older, so the guests seemed to become younger. Having been a pioneer of water-skiing, he continued to practise the art until shortly before his 95th birthday and to windsurf until shortly before his 99th. He used to delight in skiing backwards, holding the rope with one ankle while concentrating on a game of *bilboquet*. Nor did failing eyesight prevent an annual snow-skiing excursion to Courcheval.

The Commandant remained in control of all his businesses until the very end, and described himself as having been "a good money-maker – and a good money-spender".

A month after his 100th birthday, Weiller was honoured by his fellow Academicians in a ceremony at the Institut des Beaux Arts.

Weiller married, in 1922, Princess Alexandra Ghika, whose ancestors dug the first oil wells in Romania. The marriage was dissolved, and he married secondly, in 1932, Aliki Diplarakos, a Greek beauty queen who became "Miss Europe" (after their divorce she married Sir John Russell, the diplomatist).

Weiller's son by his second marriage, Paul-Annik Weiller, a director of GEC, married Princess Olympia Toronia, granddaughter of Queen Victoria Eugenie of Spain.

December 9 1993

CHARLIE SMIRKE

CHARLIE SMIRKE, who has died aged 87, was one of the finest riders of the golden age of British jockeyship between the two World Wars. In the opinion of many good judges – not least his mentor, the Australian Stanley Wootton – Smirke was the greatest of them all, Gordon Richards not excluded.

Although never champion jockey, he won 11 British Classic races (the Derby four times, the St Leger four times, the 2,000 Guineas twice and the 1,000 Guineas), nine Irish Classics and numerous major French victories.

The ebullient Smirke was one of the Turf's best-known characters. Indeed, his name entered the language: "a Charlie Smirke" is Cockney rhyming slang for Turk. He had immense confidence in his own ability and scant respect for authority. He continually flouted the Rules of Racing, whereby jockeys are forbidden to bet.

Smirke was never overawed by any sense of occasion. Whether riding in the Derby or with the knowledge that connections had backed his mount for hundreds of thousands of pounds, he was unaffected by nerves.

Had he been capable of cultivating even a semblance of deference to his employers, Charlie Smirke would have achieved even more than he did.

The son of a south London fruit and fish trader, Charles James William Smirke was born at Lambeth on September 23 1906. He began his career as an apprentice to Stanley Wootton, the outstanding coach of young riders of that era, in the Treadwell House stable at Epsom.

He rode his first winner at Derby in April 1922, and in the middle of that season was given a retainer by the diamond millionaire Solomon Joel. During the last two years of his apprenticeship, 1926 and 1927, Smirke was retained by the Aga Khan. Their association was to last intermittently for 30 years.

But Smirke came to be viewed with increasing suspicion by the Stewards of the Jockey Club, who were well aware of his heavy betting. His career suffered a heavy setback in July 1928, when he rode the hot favourite Welcome Gift at the old Gatwick course. Welcome Gift was left at the post and at the subsequent inquiry the starter alleged that no attempt had been made to put the horse in the race. Smirke was warned off *sine die*.

Deprived of his livelihood, Smirke showed in adversity the courage that characterised his riding. He was reduced to menial work and frequently found himself obliged to sleep under a tarpaulin on the beach at Brighton.

After more than five years the Jockey Club relented, and at the end of 1933 restored Smirke's licence. The next year he showed that he was as great a jockey as ever by winning the Derby on the Maharajah of Rajpipla's Windsor Lad.

On his return to the weighing-room he is said to have sat down, and said to Gordon Richards: "Pull a jockey's boots off, Moppy!"

If that story is true, it typifies his attitude to the champion. He simply could not understand the adulation given to Richards, whom he regarded as a rather ordinary rider, and resented what he saw as the favouritism shown to Richards by the starters.

When one starter asked the jockeys if they were ready, Smirke shouted: "No, sir, no, sir, Gordon isn't ready!"

"Don't be impertinent, Smirke," barked the starter.

"I beg your pardon, sir," replied Smirke. "*Mister* Richards is not ready."

It was characteristic of Charlie Smirke that after winning the Derby on Windsor Lad he should have slipped away from a party at the Savoy Hotel in order to see the Crazy Gang on stage. As Bud Flanagan introduced the victorious jockey across the footlights, Teddy Knox and Charlie Naughton, armed with scissors, snipped Smirke's braces and yanked off his trousers. Smirke's elfin features cracked in a broad grin.

In 1935 Smirke resumed riding for the Aga Khan, and won the St Leger on Bahram. The Aga's horses were trained by Frank Butters, who loathed Smirke and hardly tolerated his riding work.

When the Aga had three runners in the Derby of 1936, Butters insisted that Smirke, the owner's retained jockey, should ride the doubtful stayer, Mahmoud, and gave the mount on the strongly fancied Taj Akbar to

Richards. Riding a brilliant race, Smirke enabled Mahmoud to win in record time, beating Taj Akbar by three lengths.

During the Second World War Smirke served in the Army, mostly as a staff driver, and took part in the invasion of Sicily and other operations.

Immediately after the war Smirke took great pleasure in supplanting the Australian Edgar Britt, whom he detested, as first jockey to the Maharajah of Baroda. He won the 2,000 Guineas of 1948 on My Babu for that owner.

With the retirement of Frank Butters in 1949, the Aga Khan sent his horses to Windsor Lad's trainer Marcus Marsh, with Smirke again stable jockey. The next year Smirke rode a great race to win the 2,000 Guineas on the Aga's Palestine, husbanding the last vestige of the grey colt's stamina to such good effect that he held the powerful challenge of Prince Simon by a short head.

Then, in 1952, he won both the Derby and the St Leger for the Aga Khan on Tulyar. In the Derby he was forced to pull out all the stops to hold off Gay Time, ridden by the 16-year-old Lester Piggott (who wanted to object but the owner, Mrs J. V. Rank, forbade it). "What did I *Tulyar*?" quipped Smirke, as he returned in triumph.

In 1958 Smirke was a veteran welterweight of 51 when he won his fourth and final Derby on Sir Victor Sassoon's Hard Ridden, another doubtful stayer, whom he dashed through an opening that suddenly materialised on the rails.

Smirke finally retired in 1959. He won and lost several fortunes on the casino tables and had to sell his house in the Caribbean and a substantial property over-looking Leatherhead golf course.

He was also fond of women. "Yeah, I was married four times," he told one journalist in 1984, rolling his eyes. "Who needs 'em?"

December 21 1993

LADY ELLIOT
OF HARWOOD

THE LADY ELLIOT OF HARWOOD, who has died aged 90, was the first woman other than the Sovereign to speak in the House of Lords.

The widow of the Conservative politician Walter Elliot, "Kay" Elliot was among the first women to be created peers under the Life Peerages Act of 1958. In 1962 she became the first woman to move the Loyal Address to the Queen after the State Opening of Parliament.

Lady Elliot adorned the Second Chamber with inde-fatigable energy and great charm for 35 years. She became well known to television viewers of *Their Lord-ships' House* as the apparently somnolent figure slumped on the second row of the red benches, behind the seats traditionally occupied by former Conservative prime ministers. But her relaxed posture – so as to gain the maximum benefit from the sound system – belied a keen and vigorous mind; and from her diminutive frame there emerged a firm and audible voice.

219

Lady Elliot's death not only removes the *doyenne* of the Upper House but also severs a remarkable link with the past: her grandfather, the Glasgow scientist and chemical manufacturer Charles Tennant, was born in 1768; her father, Sir Charles Tennant, 1st Bt, MP, was born in 1823.

Sir Charles had 15 children by his two marriages. His first crop of daughters, including the incorrigible Margot (afterwards wife of H. H. Asquith, the Liberal Prime Minister), were leading spirits in the coterie known as the Souls. Around the age of 80 he sired three more – the future Ladies Wakehurst, Elliot of Harwood and Crathorne.

After the birth of the youngest daughter, the nurse carried the infant into the picture gallery at The Glen, the Tennants' Scotch Baronial seat, where Sir Charles was congratulated by a friend: "Another fine work by an Old Master."

The children were born alternately dark or fair, with either curly or straight hair. Katharine Tennant was born on January 15 1903, with fair and especially curly hair.

Although one of her early memories was of throwing her Teddy bear out of a window at 10 Downing Street at some suffragettes below, she was largely brought up in the Borders, where her heart and home remained throughout her life. She farmed at Harwood in Roxburghshire and was never happier than when riding to hounds or playing a round of golf (she was a scratch player).

In the family tradition she was originally a staunch Liberal. Her future husband, Walter Elliot, proposed to her under a gas-lamp in the street as she emerged from speaking at a Liberal meeting. Elliot had been a Socialist as an undergraduate, but evolved into an idiosyncratic Tory, serving as MP for Kelvingrove, Glasgow.

But the political alliance between the two (they married in 1934) proved unshakeable. Both could outface and outargue the rowdiest Glaswegian audience. Both loved the land and its people. Both concealed beneath a rugged exterior an undeviating kindness of thought and action.

Although he never reached the high office for which he was so often tipped, Walter Elliot was one of the most striking politicians of the time. It was thanks to his presence of mind that Westminster Hall was saved when the Houses of Parliament were bombed in the Second World War. He hacked the way through the great doors and guided firemen into the blazing building.

Kay Elliot's six decades of public service began in 1936, when she was appointed a member of King George V Jubilee Trust. Three years later she became chairman of the National Association of Mixed Clubs and Girls Clubs and joined the executive of the Carnegie Trust.

Her overriding interest lay in social policy, to which she brought humanity tempered with common sense. In 1945 she was appointed to the Department of Employment's Women's Advisory Committee, concerned with the problems of adjusting from a war to a peace economy. She then went to the Home Office Advisory Committee on the Treatment of Offenders, which she served on for 16 years. She was appointed CBE in 1946.

On Walter Elliot's death in 1958, his widow considered it her duty to fight his constituency at the ensuing by-election. She lost, but the same year was appointed DBE (a distinction she shared, uniquely, with her sister Lady Wakehurst) and then created a life peer as Baroness Elliot of Harwood.

In 1960 Lady Elliot was a member of the Barry Committee, which decisively rejected calls for the restoration of corporal punishment. For a decade she was chairman of the Advisory Committee on Child Care, Scotland, and she was president of the National Society for Autistic Children.

In 1963 she became the first chairman of the Consumers Council, where she proved a champion of the citizen's right to know that what is sold is honest value. Long after she retired from that body in 1968, Lady Elliot spoke regularly in the Lords on all aspects of consumer affairs. She strongly opposed decimalisation based on the £1 rather than 10 shillings, forecasting that it would be inflationary and debase the currency.

But her interests spread far wider. In the 1950s she was a member of the British delegation to the UN, and she was for many years president of the Ladies Committee of the European-Atlantic Group and of the British Anglo-Israeli Association.

Like her husband, who had been a friend of President Weizmann, she was a strong supporter of Israel. She also continued his pioneering support for the Anglo-German Königswinter conference, and had a wide circle of friends around the world.

She was an active director of her husband's family firm, the auctioneers Lawrie & Symington of Lanark, and an equally active member of Roxburghshire County Council from 1946 to 1975. In 1973 she published *Tennants Stalk*.

Kay Elliot was a vivacious and versatile personality. Her energy did not flag with the advancing years, despite painful lameness. Whether in the House of Lords, at her London house in Lord North Street or at her Border home, she delighted in seeing people, listening to their views and keeping up to date.

January 4 1994

THE DUKE OF ALBURQUERQUE

THE 18TH DUKE OF ALBURQUERQUE, who has died aged 74, saw a film of the Grand National on his eighth birthday, and for the next 48 years held fast to his dream of winning the steeplechase.

In Spain his position as head of the household of Don Juan de Borbón, the Count of Barcelona and pretender to the throne, gave him some part in the negotiations with Franco under which, in 1969, the *Caudillo* named the Count's son, Juan Carlos, as the future King of Spain. But in Britain the Duke of Alburquerque was known for his magnificent obsession with Aintree. "He's another Don Quixote," a rival jockey observed, "and the Grand National is his own bloody windmill."

The knight of the doleful countenance though, would have lacked the spirit to go on tilting at windmills if he had sustained more than 30 fractures: the Duke regularly started the National with his bones pinned together by metal, and ended it in Walton Hospital.

Such English as he mastered – "Ze going? Good? Thank you" – related solely to racing. But his extraordinary courage required no translation, so that his

223

appearance in the saddling enclosure invariably evoked hearty applause. It was as if one of Velázquez's subjects – for the Duke's long chin recalled the portraits of his Hapsburg ancestor Philip IV of Spain – had strayed into scenes celebrated by Rowlandson.

The Dukedom of Alburquerque dates from 1464. The 18th Duke was born Don Beltrán Alfonso Osorio y Diez de Rivera on December 15 1919, and grew up in Spain and in France; his family moved to Biarritz when Alfonso XIII went into exile in 1931.

He intended to be an engineer, but his studies were interrupted by the Spanish civil war, in which he rode with the Nationalist cavalry. By 1939 he had abandoned engineering to concentrate on racing.

Although he represented Spain in the three-day event in successive Olympic Games, and achieved steeplechase victories all over Europe, his ambition remained fixed on the Grand National. He first rode in the race in 1952 when, on Brown Jack III, he fell at the sixth fence.

It was feared that he had broken his neck; it turned out to be only two vertebrae. The Duke could only think of his horse: "Poor animal, it was past it". Eleven years passed before his next attempt.

In 1948 Franco restored titles in Spain, and the Duke formally established his succession in 1954. The style in which he lived on his estate outside Madrid became increasingly modest; by the 1970s the staff no longer wore liveried uniform and had even dispensed with their muskets. There were six brothers to be provided for, and such resources as remained to Alburquerque were taken up by racing.

In the 1963 Grand National he rode Jonjo, and

stayed with the leaders before coming to grief at the 20th fence, this time suffering nothing worse than cuts and bruises. He was not so lucky in 1965; mounted on Groomsman he fell at Valentine's Brook and broke his leg. Two years later the Duke again escaped lightly when L'Empéreur pulled up only four fences from home. In 1973 he made his first attempt on the Spanish-bred Nereo. A stirrup-leather broke at the start, and it was a tribute to his horsemanship that he kept his seat over eight fences before pulling up at the Canal Turn.

Next year, again on Nereo, Alburquerque recorded his only finish in the National – a remarkable achievement, given that he had broken his collar-bone the week before and had had 16 screws taken out of his leg a fortnight previously.

Early in 1975 the Duke suffered a fall in Seville, which put him into hospital with compound fractures of his right leg. But that December, on his 56th birthday, with his leg fortified by a metal pin, secured by seven screws, he achieved a double at Leicester on Heracles and Nereo.

In the ensuing Grand National he was going well on Nereo until the 13th, when he had one of his worst falls, and was badly trampled upon. It took him two days to regain consciousness, and he broke seven ribs and a wrist, besides fracturing his thigh.

Nevertheless the Duke was eager to return in 1977, and was only foiled by the Jockey Club's ruling that amateurs over the age of 50 must undergo a medical. But he went on racing in Spain up to his 67th year.

The Duke of Alburquerque married, in 1952, Teresa Bertrán de Lis y Pidal, who was killed in a car crash in

1969; they had a son and two daughters. He married secondly, in 1975, Christina Malcampo y San Miguel; they had two daughters.

February 22 1994

SIR HAROLD ACTON

SIR HAROLD ACTON, who has died at La Pietra near Florence aged 89, was the author of more than a score of books; they included novels, memoirs, short stories, works of autobiography and history, and essays on Chinese poetry and plays. Above all, though, he was an aesthete: "Let me glory in the name of aesthete," he once wrote, "for I am one. Let me fling it in the teeth of the Philistines."

Acton feared that he would be remembered only for his connection with his friend and contemporary Evelyn Waugh, who dedicated *Decline and Fall* to him ("In homage and affection") and drew on his personality for the characters of Anthony Blanche in *Brideshead Revisited* and Ambrose Silk in *Put Out More Flags*.

"There is an aesthetic bugger," Waugh explained, "who sometimes turns up in my novels under various names – that was two-thirds Brian [Howard], one-third Harold Acton. People think it was all Harold, who was a much sweeter and saner man."

Acton's fears of oblivion were groundless, for he produced two masterly volumes of Italian history: *The Bourbons of Naples* and *The Last Bourbons of Naples*. They did much to rehabilitate the Kingdom of the Two Sicilies which his 18th-century ancestor Sir John Acton had so ably served as Prime Minister.

In those books Sir Harold demolished the 19th-century liberal myth of "King Bomba" and showed that Naples under the Bourbons was the most prosperous, advanced and happy kingdom in Italy. It flourished from the time of Charles III – who, in Acton's words, "brought with him a salutary breeze of optimism, and intellectual freedom which was luminous in comparison with other Italian states" – through the reign of Ferdinand I, the *"Lazzarone* King" – despite that monarch's innate loutishness, which Acton made no attempt to disguise.

Deploying an enormous cast of characters, Acton related the saga of the Revolution, the setting up of the Parthenopian Republic and the reprisals carried out by Nelson. No less fascinating is his account of the Kingdom in the later period under Francis I, Ferdinand II – the much-maligned Bomba who "was never forgiven for his victory over the liberal-radicals" – and Francis II, described by Acton as a Neapolitan Hamlet.

Acton was as great a talker as a writer. His friend and Tuscan neighbour, Antony Lambton, called him "the last great conversationalist".

"He will begin by using his voice alone, speaking slowly," recalled Lambton. "The tempo increases, his right hand rises, turns slowly while moulding the precise word. He dwells on suggestive syllables, in 'Byzantium' the *zant* is lingered on, accentuated, regretfully discarded while there remains in the mind the faint suggestion of the perfumed East of our imagination."

Acton lived at La Pietra, a villa outside Florence which he inherited from his parents, and made the place his monument. Princess Margaret was a regular visitor in August, when his servants had to be recalled from holiday – "the poor dear expects a good deal," he explained – and the Prince and Princess of Wales stayed there during their tour of Italy in 1985, when the Princess was often reduced to giggles by his sallies.

Harold Mario Mitchell Acton was born at La Pietra on July 5 1904, of a distinguished Anglo-Italian family: Commodore John Acton had been Prime Minister of Naples for 30 years under Queen Maria Carolina, and Lord Acton, the Roman Catholic historian, was also a kinsman.

His father was an art dealer and his mother the daughter of a Chicago banker, and Acton grew up in a Jamesian world of rich expatriates, aristocrats and connoisseurs – Diaghilev and Bakst were among the guests at the villa. Bernard Berenson, a near neighbour of his parents, was an early influence; and at the age of six young Harold declared that his favourite painter was Botticelli.

His leadership in aesthetic taste emerged while he was still at Eton, where he was one of that celebrated generation which included Cyril Connolly, Anthony Powell, Henry Green, Robert Byron and Brian Howard. With Howard he founded the Eton Society of Arts, which introduced modernist painting, writing and composition to the school; and in 1922 Acton and Howard published a magazine of prose and poetry, *The Eton Candle*, which was well reviewed in London by Edith Sitwell.

When he went up to Christ Church, Oxford, in 1922, Acton became the undoubted leader of the university's dandy-aesthetes and was credited with the invention of "Oxford bags". He deplored the contemporary admiration for Georgian poetry – the "beer and Sussex" school of middlebrow writers – and embraced the modernism of the Sitwells and T. S. Eliot.

It was Acton who declaimed Eliot's *The Waste Land* through a megaphone over Christ Church Meadow, an incident later employed in *Brideshead Revisited* by Waugh, whom Acton compared at that time to "a young faun".

Although Acton's aestheticism initially owed a great deal to the 1890s, he repudiated the *fin-de-siècle* love of failure. His art was new, modern and vital: its touchstones were Diaghilev's Ballet Russe, the prose of Gertrude Stein, the novels of Ronald Firbank and Aldous Huxley, the work of Picasso and Gershwin's *Rhapsody In Blue*.

Acton was also a passionate advocate of Victorian art, then at its nadir of public esteem. He read papers to art societies about the painters David Wilkie, Augustus Egg and William Frith; and he planned an Early Victorian exhibition, for which Lytton Strachey was to write the catalogue introduction, but which was banned by the proctors.

In these efforts, taken up by John Betjeman and others, may be found the genesis of the current rage for "Victoriana"; and Acton's role as leader of the reactionary avant garde continued for much of his life. In 1965, for example, he noted that "abstract art is nearly done for. You can't turn your back on figurative art".

After Oxford, Acton's family wanted him to become a diplomat. He chose to devote himself to literature and published two novels and a volume of heroic verse recounting the lives of five saints; but his literary career in London did not prosper.

His novel *Humdrum* (1929), was badly received, and Acton felt that he "sank without trace"; Cyril Connolly compared it unfavourably with *Decline and Fall*, which appeared at the same time.

Discouraged, he returned to Florence and wrote a biography, *The Last Medici*, about the decadent Florentine prince Gian Castone, which was published in 1932. The same year he travelled to China and set up house in Peking, lecturing on English literature at the university.

Acton was much taken with the Chinese way of life: he studied the language and literature, particularly the classical theatre, and adopted Chinese customs and dress, even taking up opium. His previous existence in Europe appeared to him "thinly frivolous".

His scholarly investigations led to several studies and translations of Chinese poetry and drama, and it seems likely he would have settled there permanently but for the Japanese invasion of Manchuria which brought him back to Europe in 1939.

During the Second World War he was eager that his knowledge of Chinese and experience of the country should be used in the Services, but it took him 18 months to achieve acceptance into the RAF. After experience on RAF stations he was torpedoed in a troopship while on his way to routine work in India and Ceylon. Hopes of liaison work with the Chinese were disappointed, and instead Acton became an RAF press censor at Supreme Headquarters Allied Expeditionary Force.

After the war he returned to La Pietra, the magnificent 15th-century villa bought by his parents in 1904. "The house and grounds had been occupied by the Germans," wrote Acton, "but apart from chipped and broken statues and the growth of weeds and unclipped hedges the gardens had been miraculously preserved." Later he expressed himself puzzled as to why the Germans had left the statues bereft of testicles.

After his father's death in 1953, Acton undertook the preservation of his father's outstanding collection of pictures, statues, furniture, books and other *objets d'art*, which rivalled that of his great rival Bernard Berenson. The villa and its contents have been bequeathed to New York University's Institute of Fine Arts.

Acton's major work since the war was his history of the Bourbons in Naples. He also wrote two volumes of autobiography, *Memoirs of an Aesthete* (1948) and *More Memoirs of an Aesthete* (1970), and a novel, *Old Lamps for New* (1965), which he was encouraged to complete by Waugh.

Set in the art world, its central characters were a wicked old man with a huge art collection and an attractive boy associate, who sometimes curls up in bed with him. The pair plague the art Establishment with thefts and forgeries; and the novel abounds in recognisable characters, drawn with sprightly malice.

Acton was appointed CBE in 1965 and knighted in 1974 for services to Anglo-Italian relations. His kindness and hospitality to visitors were well known, notably towards undergraduates from his old university.

Few people could convey the enchantment of Italy better than Sir Harold Acton. Although the Italians have a saying, "*Inglese italianato, diavolo incarnado*" it is perhaps the Italianate Englishman who understands Italy and the Italians better than anybody else.

Sir Harold listed his recreations as *jettatura* (the Italian word for "the evil eye") and "hunting the Philistines". Asked once if he believed in the hereafter, he replied "Oh, certainly." Would there be pictures? "I very much hope so."

He was unmarried.

Anthony Powell writes: Harold Acton and his younger brother Willie were in combination an extraordinary phenomenon at Eton. They had been to some extent educated on the Continent until their arrival there, were familiar with the arts from childhood as an adjunct of everyday life. This was allied to a sophistication that was remarkable, even allowing for the flood of famous people who frequented La Pietra, their father's splendid Renaissance villa.

Harold's high forehead, eyes like black olives, a swaying carriage, dramatic enunciation, slightly impish air, made him a striking figure as a schoolboy. His appearance later perfectly fitted the conventions of the Chinese artist who painted him in Chinese robes.

He was one of the key figures in launching the Eton Society of Arts (of which I now remain the sole survivor), and that remarkable publication *The Eton Candle*. At Oxford, where Harold was a pillar of the Hypocrites Club, characteristics which inevitably had to be bottled up even at the most tolerant school burst out into a flamboyance that was a trifle undirected. Although Evelyn Waugh's characters Ambrose Silk and Anthony Blanche are only marginally modelled on Acton there was a touch of antics that were more exhibitionistic than intellectual.

No one who saw Harold Acton on television could fail to appreciate the picturesqueness of his personality, though they might not guess the extent to which the somewhat baroque manner cloaked a good deal of objective shrewdness. Harold had begun life as a poet, he wrote some books, but his true background was La Pietra and its life. No one else was quite like him, and I do not doubt that he was as unlike an Italian to an Italian as he was an Englishman to an Englishman or an American (which he was half) to an American.

Finally, a vignette. I remember Harold describing to the Eton drawing master, Mr Evans, when we were schoolboys of 13 or 14, how the Head Master, Dr Alington, had gone round the house after dining with the housemaster. In Acton's room Alington had looked at the books, pulling out a collection of Picasso's drawings.

I have seen this collection in my day. It includes a picture of Salomé dancing before Herod, which, to say the least, is uninhibited. "What did the Head Master say?" asked Mr Evans. "He smiled rather sourly," replied Acton, at his most impish.

February 28 1994

PAMELA JACKSON

PAMELA JACKSON, who has died aged 86, was the least known of the legendary Mitford sisters. Hailed by John Betjeman in the 1930s as "*gentle Pamela,/Most rural of them all*", she avoided the notoriety which dogged her sisters.

The eccentric composer Lord Berners, the original of Lord Merlin in Nancy Mitford's *The Pursuit of Love*, once declared his preference for Pam. When someone objected that she lacked the Mitford shriek, he replied: "Not at all – she has a tenor shriek."

Pam was widely admired for her startling blue eyes and for an unrivalled memory for food. Her sister the Duchess of Devonshire once introduced her with the words: "This is my sister Pam. She's just arrived from

Switzerland and she'll tell you all there was to eat in the French dining cars."

She could remember perfectly a dinner eaten decades earlier, and her descriptions of food were idiosyncratic. Another sister, Diana Mosley, records the remark: "Nard, isn't hare soup the richest, loveliest soup you ever laid hands on?"

Pamela Mitford was born on November 25 1907. She was the second daughter of Lord Redesdale and his wife, Sydney, immortalised as Uncle Matthew and Aunt Sadie in Nancy Mitford's novels.

Pamela contracted polio at the age of three but was one of the first beneficiaries of physiotherapy, and made a complete recovery. She grew up passionately fond of the country and country pursuits, and in the 1930s managed her sister Diana's farm in Wiltshire. Nancy recorded how Pam bid at a farm sale for what looked like a very fine cow, only to discover that "the brute was bagless". Their father considered Pam to be "the best judge of a pig's face in the South of England."

In 1935 Pamela visited her sister Unity in Munich. Unity introduced her to Hitler. Pamela found him "very ordinary, like an old farmer in his khaki suit".

In 1936 she married Derek Jackson, a physicist and amateur jockey. As well as being the second of six daughters Pam was the second of Jackson's six wives.

The Jacksons lived in Oxfordshire and kept long-haired dachshunds, which they both adored. On a visit to America they had a competition every morning as to which of them would wake first and sing good morning to the dogs in England.

During the Second World War Jackson joined the Royal Air Force and won a series of medals, despite infuriating his colleagues with such remarks as: "When the darling Germans have won the war I shall have my own château on the Loire."

Pamela remained in Oxfordshire with the animals and provided a home for the children of Diana Mosley while she was in prison.

After living briefly in Ireland the Jacksons separated in 1950. Pam moved to Switzerland and then back to Gloucestershire where she remained, making frequent trips to France to nurse Nancy until her death in 1973.

In her later years Pamela Jackson became well known in the poultry world for introducing into Britain a breed of chicken called the Appenzeller Spitzhaube. It has a tasteful arrangement of feathers on its head which resembles a pointed cap.

She had no children.

James Lees-Milne writes: Of the famous Mitford sisters Pamela Jackson was perhaps the least Mitfordian in some respects, yet not in others. She entirely lacked the creative urge. She was totally uncerebral, unambitious and uncomplicated. Lacking the ability to shine like her sisters in wit and repartee, she nevertheless radiated a nobility of character and an unadulterated goodness.

Her features were flawless, and comparable, as a friend once remarked, with the classical beauty of Lady Diana Cooper without the tra-la-la. She was quite unaware of her own beauty.

Pam followed closely on the heels of her gifted elder sister, Nancy, of whom in childhood she was in awe. Nancy was not always kind to her, being inclined to mock her apparent simplicity. But simple she basically was not. Practical and commonsensical she certainly was.

She developed an acute sense of humour about her own limitations which endeared her to all. It was she who principally nursed Nancy in her last illness.

Her early adult years were not all unmitigated bliss. After a peculiarly cruel jilt she spent several years as farm manager to her brother-in-law Bryan Guinness at Biddesden in Wiltshire. Then in the mid-1930s she was swept off her feet by an unlikely meteor in the person of Derek Jackson, a man of extraordinary intellectual vigour and the charm of a chameleon.

An unfathomable riddle to his friends, Derek was not exactly the conventional husband she needed. At least he provided for her solitary middle and old age. She was never heard to complain or repine.

Pam – or "Woman", as she was known to her intimates because in the eyes of the sisters she epitomised the down-to-earth qualities of her sex – remained the focus of affection for a large and devoted family. For more than 40 years she lived at Caudle Green in the Cotswolds, famed for her special soups and home-made bread.

April 16 1994

LADY MAY ABEL SMITH

LADY MAY ABEL SMITH, who has died aged 88, was a first cousin once removed of the Queen and held a unique position in the royal circle. She was a member of the Royal Family both through her mother, Princess Alice, Countess of Athlone, and her father, the Earl of Athlone, Queen Mary's brother. Lady May was the last remaining member of the Royal Family to have been born with a German style and title, and the last surviving great-great-grandchild of King George III.

A woman of great charm, May Abel Smith had an infectious sense of humour and an inquiring mind which persisted into old age. A lively raconteur, she would impersonate with glee Queen Victoria's three youngest daughters, of whom she had seen much in her youth.

Diminutive but with an unmistakable presence, Lady May came to bear a striking resemblance to her mother.

She was born Her Serene Highness Princess May Helen Emma of Teck at Claremont, Esher, on January 23 1906, the eldest child of Prince Alexander of Teck and the former Princess Alice of Albany. Her father was the youngest son of the redoubtable and immensely stout Princess Mary Adelaide of Cambridge (a granddaughter of King George III) and the 1st Duke of Teck. Her mother was a daughter of Prince Leopold, Duke of Albany (Queen Victoria's fourth son) and the former Princess Helena of Waldeck and Pyrmont.

One of young May's earliest memories was watching the funeral procession of King Edward VII from the roof of the Henry IV tower at Windsor. As the *cortège* rolled past, she exclaimed to her nanny: "What, Uncle Bertie in a *box*!"

She was educated at home by an Alsatian governess, and was proud to recall that she kept the one teacher, while some of her cousins had a habit of "going through them rather quickly". She developed a taste for travelling at an early age and by the outbreak of the First World War had accompanied her parents to many of the courts of Europe.

The war put an end to her travels and altered her style and title. In 1917, as part of King George V's wish to anglicise the Royal Family (which prompted the Kaiser's joke about "The Merry Wives of Saxe-Coburg and Gotha") her father was created Earl of Athlone with the surname of Cambridge; her mother became Princess Alice, Countess of Athlone; her brother Viscount Trematon; and she herself became Lady May Cambridge.

She was rather pleased with her new rank. She had found it a bore to be curtseyed to by contemporaries, and felt much easier as "a mere Lady".

In 1923 she was a bridesmaid to Lady Elizabeth Bowes-Lyon (the future Queen Elizabeth The Queen Mother) at her wedding to the Duke of York. The next year Lord Athlone was appointed Governor-General of South Africa, in succession to Prince Arthur of Connaught. Lady May accompanied her parents to Cape Town, where she developed a love of wide open spaces – an enchantment she would experience again years later, when her husband was appointed Governor of Queensland. In South Africa she proved an excellent shot, and her bag included some formidable specimens.

To help him to find a suitable ADC Lord Athlone had approached a niece, the Marchioness of Cambridge, to see if she could recommend a "fine young soldier", with the proviso that he must not court his daughter. Captain Henry Abel Smith of the Royal Horse Guards was duly appointed, and was soon courting Lady May.

Her parents were naturally inclined to think in terms of a royal dynastic union, and there was some opposition to the match. It is said that when the Duchess of Devonshire called on Queen Mary to apologise for her son, Lord Charles Cavendish, who had married the dancer Adele Astaire, Her Majesty replied: "Don't worry. I have a niece called Smith."

But the Athlones' objections were dropped, and the wedding took place in 1931 at a village church in Sussex. Lady May became the first royal bride to omit the word "obey" from the marriage service.

Almost every member of the Royal Family attended. Princess Elizabeth (the present Queen) was a bridesmaid for the first time; the future Princess Alice, Duchess of Gloucester, was also part of the retinue.

During the 1930s Lady May was often abroad attending family celebrations. On one occasion she accompanied her mother to Coburg for the marriage of her cousin Princess Sybilla to Prince Gustav Adolf of Sweden. At a gala opera performance she and her mother were perplexed to find the Saxe-Coburgs give the Nazi salute during the playing of the anthem.

In 1940 Lord Athlone was appointed Governor-General of Canada. Her husband, by then a major, was serving with his regiment in the Middle East, and Lady May was living at Winkfield near Windsor with their son and two daughters.

It was arranged that Lady May should join her parents in Ottawa, where she would leave the children for safety. They had an anxious voyage across the Atlantic, facing the dangers of enemy attack by torpedo or mines.

In 1941 Lady May returned to England alone and became involved with war work, particularly with the Red Cross and the St John Ambulance Corps.

After the war the Abel Smiths acquired a farm in Southern Rhodesia, which they visited each winter until Ian Smith's unilateral declaration of independence in 1965. But after the creation of Zimbabwe in the early 1980s the Abel Smiths returned. At Winkfield, meanwhile, they had become involved with breeding and rearing Arab horses and maintained a respected stud.

In 1958 Colonel Sir Henry Abel Smith, as he now was, took up his appointment as Governor of Queensland. Lady May proved a popular consort and accompanied Sir Henry on countless trips into the outback.

They would frequently travel the dry, dusty roads in great discomfort, but Lady May always arrived at their destination with a cheery smile and refreshing lack of ceremony. The Abel Smiths proved so popular that their term of office was extended.

At their ceremonial departure from Brisbane in 1966 crowds ran alongside the open-topped limousine, catching hold of the couple's hands and calling out: "Come back soon!"

Sir Henry died in 1992, by which time he was the oldest member of the Royal Family, as listed in the *Court Circular* by the Lord Chamberlain.

Lady May was an assiduous attender of royal occasions: she was present at two Coronations, two Silver Jubilees and had been a bridesmaid at the marriages of six members of the Royal Family.

Lady May Abel Smith was dedicated to a life of duty to her country as a supporting member of the Royal Family. Notwithstanding great changes in royal life, she managed to achieve her aim. With her unassuming manner, she freely adapted to a minor role without losing her place or her dignity.

May 31 1994

NANCY LANCASTER

NANCY LANCASTER, who has died aged 97, was a crucial figure in 20th-century interior design.

In the 1920s, as Nancy Tree, she was principally responsible for creating the "English country house look" – a romantic, patrician, uncluttered style which has had a profound effect on English interior design, notably through the influence of her company Colefax & Fowler.

A woman of wit, style and beauty, she looked like a Gainsborough duchess and was the star of many anecdotes – "Paint it the colour of elephant's breath," she once commanded a decorator.

All her work was notable for its sense of scale, boldness, wit and mellowness. Her houses seemed to convey the essence of all that was best in English country life.

She was totally committed to England, and at the beginning of the Second World War became a British citizen out of solidarity, but was American by birth, a survivor of the world of Henry James.

She was born Nancy Perkins in 1897, the daughter of Moncure Perkins of Richmond, Virginia. Educated in France, she first visited England before the First World War, staying with her formidable aunt Nancy Astor at Cliveden.

In 1917 Miss Perkins married Henry Field, grandson of Marshall Field, the Chicago department store magnate, but was widowed within a year. Two years later she met Ronald Tree (heir through his mother to a fortune also derived from Marshall Field), whom she married in 1920.

Ronnie Tree bought her Mirador, the beautiful house in Virginia that had belonged to her grandfather, and together they restored it. In 1926 the Trees returned to England and soon afterwards rented Kelmarsh in Northamptonshire, a house by James Gibbs, which they also refurbished.

But it was at Ditchley in Oxfordshire, which the Trees bought from Viscount Dillon in 1933, that Nancy Tree came into her own. She and her husband made of that vast Palladian pile one of the most comfortable of country houses, with central heating and *en suite* bathrooms.

Winston Churchill used to spend his weekends there during the Second World War, when the danger of bombing prevented him going to Chequers or Chartwell.

But the Trees' marriage was dissolved in 1947, and their idyll at Ditchley came to an end. The next year she married Lieutenant-Colonel Claude Lancaster, MP, the owner of Kelmarsh; they soon separated.

It was at this time that Nancy Lancaster bought from Lady Colefax her decorating business and shop in Mayfair and began her far from tranquil collaboration with John ("Folly") Fowler, with whom she worked on such houses as Grimsthorpe, Mereworth and Wilton. They spent much of their time bickering over details of taste, and Lady Astor described them as "frankly the most unhappy unmarried couple I have ever met".

In 1954 Nancy Lancaster bought Haseley Court, an 18th-century house in Oxfordshire, where she created a stylish and hospitable environment and flew the Confederate flag over the pediment. When she later sold the big house at Haseley (to Viscount Hereford), she continued to live in the former coach-house, which she converted with typical flair, and continued to tend the gardens, which were largely her own creation.

As her London base she took over Wyatville's gallery, at the back of the shop in Brook Street, which she turned into one of the most glamorous rooms in London.

She had two sons by Ronald Tree: Jeremy, the late racehorse trainer, and Michael, the painter and part-owner of Colefax & Fowler.

Deborah Devonshire writes: I had a letter from Nancy suggesting that I write what I remember of Ditchley to be included in her book of houses. I said I would try. The next day came a postcard saying "I don't want a eulogy . . ."

After over 50 years does memory play you false? Do you look back on events, people and places in a slanted sort of way, slanted to summers being fine, friends always there, jokes, laughter, pleasure and entertainments galore untouched by responsibility, living for the moment? Perhaps you do, and perhaps it is lucky that adolescent discontent and the humdrum things which occupy most days are lost or run together in a vague mist of recollection, and the special times remain, leap-frogging the rest.

When I think of Ditchley all those years ago, the profound effect it had on me and must have had on everyone who went there, it is impossible to write anything but a eulogy.

We lived at Swinbrook, 11 or 12 miles away. When I was a child I loved foxhunting above all else, and it was out hunting that I first saw Nancy. The meet of the

Heythrop hounds was near our home, the unfashionable side of what was then an unfashionable hunt. The field consisted of people who lived in the Heythrop country, enlivened in term time by wild undergraduates from Oxford. Smart folk hunted in the Shires. I can't imagine what Nancy was doing there on a Saturday.

I was trotting along on my pony when a big chestnut horse came thundering by. It was ridden on a loose rein by an elegant woman on a side saddle wearing the Heythrop green livery, faultless top hat and veil, the smartest thing imaginable.

" Who is that?" I asked our old groom.

"Mrs Tree from Ditchley on a blood 'orse." He didn't have to tell me that.

Later, when we passed the few horseboxes there were in those days, I saw her second horseman, a cockade in his top hat, something I had never seen before.

I first went to Ditchley when I was 16 or 17, having got to know Michael and Jeremy out hunting. But I had seen the house before the Trees bought it, empty and desolate, the park full of rabbits and sad white grass in the time of the agricultural depression of the early 1930s. When Nancy and Ronnie arrived it came to life, and there they created perfection.

I realise now that Ditchley taught me an invaluable lesson – to notice, to look and to try and absorb and remember what was beautiful. It was certainly the first time I became aware of such things. Whatever Nancy touched had that hard-to-pin-down but instantly recognisable gift of style.

Her genius (and that is no exaggeration) was her eye for colour, scale, objects and the dressing-up of them; the stuffs the curtains were made of, their shapes and trimmings, the china, tablecloths, knives and forks. Even the bathrooms were little works of art. Warm, panelled, carpeted, there were shelves of Chelsea china cauliflowers, cabbages, tulips and rabbits of exquisite quality. A far cry from the cracked lino and icy draughts to which I was accustomed.

I had never seen such huge, square, down pillows as she went in for, nor Porthault sheets, decorated with carnations or trailing blue flowers and scalloped edges of the same colour; and the puffed-up eiderdowns covered in pale silk with tiny bows where a stitch held the down in place. The teatables had no cloths but were painted brilliant Chinese red. Anyone could have done that, but no one else did.

The rooms and their delectable contents were only part of the story. All that beauty could have been set up, and people would have delighted in it, but the whole of Ditchley reflected the personality of Nancy herself. She was the star on the stage she created.

I can see her now, sitting bolt upright at the end of the dining-room table on one of the high-backed yellow chairs with Ronnie's initials embroidered on it, wearing something enviable with a brilliant bit of colour somewhere, debunking pomposity, making a comical mountain out of a molehill, taking over the table so that people stopped to listen and laugh.

The Trees were supported by servants no less talented at making their guests comfortable and happy than the hosts. Mr Collins, the butler, was an extremely handsome man who was as polite to a 17-year-old girl as to a head of state.

Such perfect manners continued through the housemaids, the kitchen staff, the grooms and the gamekeepers.

The last were father and sons by the name of Starling, as neat and chirpy in their buttoned gaiters as the partridges they looked after. Cheerful Sunday morning visits to the chef and the stables were a pleasurable feature of staying at Ditchley. In my mind's eye there is Mr Collins, tall and splendid in his tailcoat, piling coal on the hall fire on a Monday morning when most people in his profession would thankfully leave such a task till the next invasion of guests. But at Ditchley you were made to feel they actually regretted your going. I know two other houses where you had that feeling: Houghton with Sybil Cholmondeley (*qv*) at the helm, and my sister Diana's Temple outside Paris.

Nancy and Ronnie were also innovators in the garden. It was they who began the renaissance of old-fashioned roses, edging and designs in box and so much else which has been copied in the last 40 years and is so common now that you can be forgiven for forgetting who started it all.

After the war began and there was no petrol I used to drive over from Swinbrook in a pony-trap, fetching the pony out of the field and draping its second-hand harness over it to jog along the empty roads. On arrival the stud groom fetched it from the front door. Going home the next day the pony looked quite different, shining all over, hooves dressed with oil, harness and trap polished as never before.

When Winston Churchill used the house for weekends I was delighted by Jeremy's yawns and sighs and evident longing to go to bed when the PM started (and went on) talking till the early hours. (My own children did just the same years later when Harold Macmillan came to Chatsworth and talked till the cows came home.) At Ditchley we would have preferred to listen to Nancy.

I have no doubt that, as in every other family, you only had to scratch the surface to find worries, dramas and sorrows not far away. But such was the atmosphere created by the Trees that I found unalloyed pleasure in my visits there.

How short a time this oasis of perfection lasted. I count myself very lucky to have seen it.

In my long and spoilt life I have been to many beautiful places and met many fascinating people, but I have never seen the like of Ditchley and Nancy.

"I don't want a eulogy . . ." she said. Sorry, but how could it be otherwise?

August 20 1994

STEPHEN DYKES BOWER

STEPHEN DYKES BOWER, the church architect who has died aged 91, was the last significant upholder of the Gothic Revival and was also responsible for a number of distinguished classical designs.

Dykes Bower was a man of old-fashioned courtesy and high principle, never reticent in his criticism of shoddy or gimmicky work. An educated architect and an Anglican gentleman, he was certainly not intimidated by his ecclesiastical clients.

At Bury St Edmunds he made the former parish church of St James seem more like a cathedral by replacing the Victorian chancel with a much longer choir designed in a noble Late Gothic manner of East Anglian character. He also planned a cloister, but his full scheme for the new cathedral remains incomplete.

Dykes Bower's most important appointment was at Westminster Abbey, where he was Surveyor to the Fabric for 22 years from 1951. As well as repairs to the fabric, he was responsible for new pavements and colouring to monuments. His achievement at the Abbey was clouded, though, when he was wrongly accused by the Society for the Protection of Ancient Buildings of replacing medieval timbers in the roof.

Latterly his scholarly and conservative approach to cathedrals became increasingly unpopular with an Anglican hierarchy interested in novelty, and on several occasions he was supplanted by others – most notoriously and destructively at Chelmsford. Similarly, his staunch adherence to tradition and his rejection of the originality demanded by the Modern Movement made him a controversial and somewhat isolated figure in architectural circles.

Dykes Bower's work was not all Gothic: he restored Wren's church of St Vedast in Foster Lane, for instance. Like other architects repairing bombed City churches, he did not feel obliged to recreate what had been lost. Instead he designed a new interior in the style of Wren but collegiate in plan. Dykes Bower also designed the new Rectory for St Vedast's, an unusual and idiosyncratic essay in domestic architecture.

But his most prominent work in the City is the new *baldacchino* in St Paul's Cathedral, completed in 1958. Together with the American Memorial Chapel beyond it (both of them designed by Dykes Bower with Godfrey

Allen, Surveyor to St Paul's), it is truer to Wren's manner than its predecessor was.

"If people see in it only what looks right for St Paul's," asked Dykes Bower, "then what more should one wish for?"

Stephen Ernest Dykes Bower was born on April 18 1903, the second of four bachelor sons of Ernest Dykes Bower, a Gloucester physician; Stephen's younger brother, the late Sir John Dykes Bower, became Organist of St Paul's Cathedral. Young Stephen was educated at Cheltenham and Merton College, Oxford, where he was Organ Scholar.

He then studied architecture at the Architectural Association in London, but he was antipathetic to the new European architecture and always maintained that "the only way to learn is to teach yourself". He set up in practice in 1931.

An early commission was to adapt the rambling Bishop's Palace at Exeter, which Dykes Bower converted to create a new Cathedral library. His first new church was All Saints, Hockerill, near Bishop's Stortford, a Gothic work of 1936.

The Second World War brought Dykes Bower opportunities to demonstrate his sympathetic way with historic buildings when he was asked to restore several bomb-damaged churches. He rebuilt the gutted shell of the medieval parish church of Great Yarmouth, for which he designed fine new furnishings, and also the Church of the Holy Spirit, Southsea, a late Victorian building in which he installed fittings from St Agnes's, Kennington.

During his time at Westminster Abbey he developed increasing respect for his predecessor Sir Gilbert Scott.

Indeed, Dykes Bower saw himself in the tradition of the great Victorian Goths – Scott, Pearson, Temple Moore, Comper – whose confident interpretation of precedent he so admired.

He had a particular reverence for the refined work of G. F. Bodley, and was the only modern architect to whom Bodley's churches could safely be trusted – as he showed with his restoration of St John's, Tue Brook, in Liverpool.

Dykes Bower was rightly proud of his contribution at Lancing, where he completed the great chapel begun by R. C. Carpenter in the 19th century, designing a west end with the largest rose window created in England since those in the transepts of Westminster Abbey.

He built few new churches. His most impressive is St John's at Newbury, Berkshire, a massive building of red brick in a Romanesque style, replacing one by Butterfield destroyed in the Second World War.

One of his happiest creations was at Salford, where he added to and transformed St Paul's Church (which the Diocese of Manchester wanted to demolish). By careful craftsmanship and the use of painted decoration he made it the inspiring focus of a bleak high-rise estate.

It was a source of puzzlement and dismay to Dykes Bower's friends and admirers that his achievements were not recognised by a knighthood – an honour given so freely to many undeserving Modern architects.

He lived for many years at Quendon Court, near Saffron Walden, a Georgian house which he furnished with his fastidious collection of porcelain and needle-work. Guests would be collected from Newport station in his vintage Rolls-Royce, which he would drive like a tank through the lanes of rural Essex.

November 14 1994.

DORIS SPEED

DORIS SPEED, the actress who has died aged 95, was celebrated for her superb portrayal of Annie Walker, the disdainful landlady of the Rovers Return in Granada Television's long-running drama serial, *Coronation Street*.

Annie Walker was created specifically for Doris Speed. She was said to have based her performance on the character of her own Aunt Bessie, who used to lead the Speed family in Christmas charades and had a withering look.

With her screen husband, the long-suffering Jack (Arthur Leslie), Speed appeared in the first episode of *Coronation Street* in 1960. She dominated the Rovers Return for the next 23 years, until illness forced her to leave the series.

Annie Walker struck a chord in the national psyche, as the embodiment of the genteel social climber, an icon of the proud petit-bourgeois tidiness which was subject to such virulent cultural attack in the 1960s. If there was a distinctly music-hall aspect to her character – and "the *Street*" is a television descendant of that tradition – Speed managed to bring an embattled dignity to her role, as well as affectionate satire.

Inclined to dress like the Queen, Annie Walker was

ever mindful that she should be paid the respect she felt
her due. Ever so "refained" – she preferred to see herself
as an "Anne" – she looked down relentlessly on her
common clientele. As aficionados of the *Street* knew well
enough, though, Annie was the daughter of a mill clerk
and had begun her career as a loom operative.

Annie did condescend to converse across the bar with
the university-educated Kenneth Barlow, for whose ill-
fated Silver Jubilee pageant in 1977 she took the role of
Good Queen Bess. But she was extremely disgruntled
when the unspeakably vulgar barmaid Bet Lynch was
"highly commended" for her role as Britannia, while
Good Queen Bess was ignored.

Annie was in her element as lady chairman of the
local Licensed Victuallers' Association and enjoyed her
finest moment when the widowed corner shop proprietor
Councillor Alf Roberts invited her to act as his Lady
Mayoress. Mrs Walker duly invested in a second-hand
Rover and pressed the protesting potman Fred Gee into
service as her chauffeur.

Doris Speed described Annie as "always a silly vain
woman", but the character did not lack humanity. She
proved a sympathetic "auntie" to the wayward slut
Lucille Hewitt, for example, and a tolerant mother to
her grasping son Billy, who finally wrested the tenancy
from her in 1983. And with moist eyes she always
cherished the memory of her husband, Jack.

Speed also said that Annie Walker "stood for everything I'm not", and despite playing the acidulous beldam
for more than 20 years she had little in common with
her. Speed admitted to a dislike of pubs and a lack of
patience with Annie Walker's posturing.

Her colleagues on the *Street* used to describe the

actress as "intellectual", "very politically minded" and "a keen socialist". She also developed a reputation for being easily distracted during filming.

"She hated handling props," recalled Jean Alexander (who played Hilda Ogden, Annie's put-upon drudge of a cleaner). "If she had to pour a cup of tea and speak at the same time she often used to 'dry'. Doris's famous stare into the middle distance was only to stop herself being put off by other actors."

In 1983 the tabloid press published details of Doris Speed's real age – she was over 80 but claimed to be still in her sixties. When she had joined the cast in 1960 she was already an old age pensioner, but insisted that she was in her early forties.

When the truth about her age was revealed Speed suffered severe depression. "It broke her spirit completely," recalled a friend, "she would never go back on the *Street* after that."

She eventually left the house she had shared with her mother for most of her life and entered an old people's home at Walshaw, Bury, where she remained until her death.

Doris Speed was born in Manchester on February 3 1899, the daughter of music-hall artistes George and Ada Speed. She made her stage debut at five in *The Royal Divorce*. "I toddled on in a velvet suit as the Infant Prince of Rome," she recalled.

She spent her early childhood touring with her parents: "I was at a different school every Monday, but I thought that was normal."

In 1915 she took a course in shorthand and typing at a local technical college. Soon afer completing it she was offered a post with Guinness in Manchester, where she became a typist to support her parents' continued efforts on the stage.

She worked for Guinness for the next 40-odd years, becoming in her spare time an active member of the local amateur dramatics group, the highly regarded Un-Named Society. "Acting was all I ever wanted to do," she would recall.

After many years she established herself as an accomplished performer, and she began to receive offers of radio work in Manchester. In the late 1950s she appeared in a police series *Shadow Squad*, in an episode written by Tony Warren, and when Warren created *Coronation Street* for Granada he wrote the part of Annie Walker with Doris Speed in mind.

At first Speed twice turned down auditions for the *Street*. "I was in Bristol at the time," she remembered, "and it seemed such a long way to travel. In the end a friend persuaded me, and I took the milk train up to Manchester."

By this time Warren had already auditioned 24 actresses for the part, but had found none suitable. "I knew the part was mine as soon as I did the audition," Speed said. "It was just a feeling."

For the next 23 years she appeared twice weekly as the *doyenne* of pub landladies. "Annie Walker really was a dreadful snob," she admitted. "She used to complain because the corner shop didn't stock game soup."

When not rehearsing or filming, Speed spent her time playing bridge with other cast members and doing the *Guardian* crossword. "She played bridge like a professional," Jean Alexander remembered, "and went through crosswords like a knife through butter."

At home her preferred pastimes were reading theatrical biographies and watching the *Street*. "I study Annie to make sure that no silly mannerisms creep in," she said. "It's her I'm watching, not myself."

In 1977 Speed was appointed MBE and two years later received an award for "Outstanding Services to Television". She collapsed during filming in 1983 and was rushed to hospital suffering from stomach pains.

While recuperating at her home, Speed said that she had every intention of returning to the *Street* after her recovery, but continuing ill-health kept her at home.

During the next three years Speed's illness prevented her from returning to the programme. She became increasingly deaf and, with the loss of her hearing, reclusive.

In 1985 thieves broke into her house as she slept and ransacked the living-room. The shock of the robbery forced her into hospital, and she never returned to her home in Chorlton-cum-Hardy.

Three years later Annie Walker made her final appearance at the Rovers Return. Independent Television had asked Speed to take part in the 1988 Telethon and to pull a pint of beer for charity. She was filmed behind the bar looking frail but happy.

During the 1990 celebrations of *Coronation Street*'s 30th anniversary, Doris Speed appeared on the television spectacular hosted by Cilla Black. When she entered, helped onstage by Miss Black, Speed received a standing ovation from the cast of the *Street*.

Although unsteady on her feet she managed to recount an anecdote about her mother. "She couldn't believe it when I told her they were going to pay me £50 a week," she said.

Miss Black, thinking that the story was over, started

a round of applause, but Speed continued as if uninterrupted. "*'Fifty?'*" my mother said. "'You're never worth that!'"

She never married.

November 18 1994

JAMES WATTS

JAMES WATTS, the American neurosurgeon who has died aged 90, was, with his colleague the neurologist Walter Freeman, responsible for popularising the pre-frontal lobotomy – one of the most contentious and macabre practices in the history of medicine.

The pre-frontal lobotomy was an operation in which the leukos, or white fibres connecting the frontal lobes to the rest of the brain, were severed to relieve symptoms of anxiety in psychiatric patients. At first prescribed as an operation of last resort, it was soon being promoted as a remedy for all human sadness, and even a means for social control.

"Society can accommodate itself to the most humble labourer," observed Freeman, "but justifiably distrusts the thinker . . . lobotomised patients make good citizens."

Ignaz Moniz had developed the leucotomy in Portugal in the early 1930s, and in 1936 Freeman and Watts began practising the operation in Washington, renaming it the lobotomy.

A casual, softly spoken Southerner, Watts was then 32, nine years younger than Freeman, and the more circumspect of the two; he was also the qualified neurosurgeon. Freeman was a Philadelphia-born doctor with a strongly Calvinist background, and a complex mixture of ambition, altruism and showmanship.

He believed in strong intervention for psychiatric disturbance, and later attempted to prove that Freudian analysts were suicidal depressives. Although a brilliant neurologist and neuropathologist, he had never qualified as a surgeon, and ostensibly needed Watts to perform the lobotomy under his guidance.

By the end of the year they had performed 20 lobotomies with Moniz's method, cutting holes in the top of the skull and inserting an instrument modelled on the apple corer. Later they modified the technique, making holes on either side of the head and using a steel probe with its end flattened rather like a butter knife; this was the pre-frontal lobotomy.

After Freeman was caught operating, and reprimanded, he would sit in front of the patient, using his remarkable knowledge of the brain's geography to guide Watts's hands. To measure the brain Watts would insert a thin tube in one hole and feed it through the brain towards the hole on the other side. So accurate was he that he could pass the tube clean through and out the other side. "That's kind of fun," he said. "To be able to do that with that degree of accuracy is very good. And, of course, it always impressed."

Surgery was performed under local anaesthetic, and the pair monitored the progress of the operation by engaging the subject in conversation, reckoning from the response how much matter had yet to be destroyed. The weird transcripts of the patients' failing utterances often pinpointed the moment at which some aspect of personality vanished.

Freeman, Watts recalled, was "a ham actor with a flair for the dramatic", and guests would be invited to watch operations in which Watts fiddled away inside the head while Freeman urged the subject to sing *God Bless America* or *Mary Had a Little Lamb*. He might join in the chorus.

In one exchange, Freeman asked a patient, "What's going through your mind now?", to which came the reply, "A knife."

In 1942 Freeman and Watts used their considerable earnings to publish *Psychosurgery*. On the book's title page was a drawing of a swarm of black butterflies escaping from a trepanned skull, inspired by the French saying, "*J'ai les papillons noirs.*"

"This work", the authors claimed, "reveals how personality can be cut to measure." The book sold out, with some copies reaching Europe.

But despite the growing enthusiasm, results were uneven. Patients often relapsed or became vegetables. Some died, either from bleeding during the operation or subsequent trauma. Others seemed to benefit, and lived long lives, although it was observed that the operation invariably dimmed some spark – that their spiritual lives perished.

One post-operative feature in male patients was an implacable drive for copulation. Freeman and Watts counselled concerned wives thus: "Her husband may have regressed to the caveman level, and she owes it to him to be responsive at the cavewoman level. It may not be agreeable at first, but she will soon find it exhilarating, if unconventional."

The majority of those lobotomised were women, and the operation perpetuated such 19th-century practices as ovariectomy and clitoridectomy, which were carried out on women diagnosed as hysterics.

By late 1945 traumatised war veterans were causing the asylums of America to overflow; nearly half the 1.5 million beds in public hospitals were occupied by psychiatric patients. Freeman wanted to work faster, and believed that if he developed a sufficiently simple technique he might operate independently of Watts.

Secretly he carried out a transorbital lobotomy. For this the patient was anaesthetised by ECT shocks; the eyelids were lifted and a sharp stiletto-like leuctome was hammered through the orbital bone to a depth of 2.5 inches, one incision through each eye socket.

The leucotome was then vigorously flexed. Freeman limited his post-operative advice to, "Wear a pair of sunglasses." The operation took 10 minutes and was first performed with an icepick taken from Freeman's kitchen drawer.

Watts thought the technique degrading and too freely administered. In 1946 he threatened to break off their association, and Freeman promised not to perform the operation in Washington. But in 1948 Watts caught Freeman performing transorbital lobotomies at their joint practice in the city.

"He asked me to hold the icepick," Watts recalled, "while he photographed the patient and the angle of the instrument. I said 'I'd rather not', and pointed out the risks of transorbital lobotomy as an office procedure." They could not be reconciled, and Watts walked out.

Freeman repeatedly traversed America promoting his technique. Between 1945 and 1955, the peak years, at least 40,000 Americans were lobotomised, many by psychiatrists using the icepick. On occasion Freeman himself would perform more than 20 in a day, developing a conveyor belt system, the sight of which caused hardened soldiers to faint. One of his patients was the actress Frances Farmer.

In the early 1960s the arrival of anti-depressants and growing public suspicion brought about a rapid decline in the use of the lobotomy. Before Freeman and Watts split they performed at least 700 pre-frontal lobotomies, on patients as young as four. Watts had ethical doubts about only one, a young female schizophrenic who loved to play the harp.

"As I look back," he said, "I think I did it more to help the mother than I did the patient, because the patient was happy. Usually the voices call you bad names, call you a pervert. They accuse you of all kinds of bad deeds . . . every once in a while I used to think about it and say, my gosh, did I do that for her comfort or for the mother's? Maybe I did it for her mother's."

James Winston Watts was born at Lynchburg, Virginia, on January 19 1904, and educated at Virginia Military Institute and Virginia University, where he studied medicine. By 1930 he was a resident in neurosurgery at Chicago University, and two years later he became a research fellow at Yale.

He published an influential paper in which he argued that the large frontal lobes in humans were more concerned with basic animal urges and functions than previously thought, and that the mind did not function independently of the body – the frontal lobes could affect cardiac rate and kidney function. This brought him to the attention of Freeman.

The first patient they lobotomised was a 63-year-old woman who Freeman described as a "typically rigid, emotional, claustrophobic individual . . . a past master at bitching who really led her husband a dog's life". At the last minute she backed down, fearful that her head would have to be shaved. She was promised that her curls would be spared; this was a lie, but after the operation she no longer cared.

Patient 10 sued the duo for paralysis; patient 18, an alcoholic lawyer suffering from paranoia, absconded from his bed after the operation, and was found drunk in a bar, the lobotomy having cured his paranoia but having left his addiction intact. Patient 20 had 18 cores made in her brain, and became the first fatality. Freeman remarked that he and Watts learned much more from their failures than their successes, because failures could be subjected to autopsy.

Freeman and Watts never lost their mutual respect. After their split Watts continued to live and work in Washington, practising privately and at the George Washington University hospital. He briefly experimented with the transorbital lobotomy, later forsaking it for more orthodox forms of neurosurgery. He retired in 1969.

Walter Freeman's personal life was always troubled. He once suffered from deep depression and a nervous breakdown, which left him with a lasting animosity towards the brain, and was later afflicted by diabetes and cancer. He died in 1972.

James Watts married, in 1931, Julia Harrison; they had two sons.

November 19 1994

THE RIGHT REVEREND MERVYN STOCKWOOD

THE RIGHT REVEREND MERVYN STOCKWOOD, who has died aged 81, was one of the century's most controversial Church of England bishops.

He was Bishop of Southwark from 1959 to 1980 and before that a notable vicar of the university church at Cambridge. An avowed Socialist, he enjoyed the friendship of Clement Attlee, Sir Stafford Cripps and Aneurin Bevan during the years of the postwar Labour government.

Stockwood was a reformer in moral and ecclesiastical matters and often expressed his opinions in vivid language (Enoch Powell's 1968 speech on immigration, for instance, was described as "an evil fart") which brought widespread publicity. He seemed to enjoy this.

At his final service in Southwark Cathedral he was presented with a jeroboam of champagne, which he acknowledged to be an appropriate gift: "I have attempted to bring a little fizz into the diocese."

He had a complex personality. He craved affection, but could be a demanding, even ruthless friend. He made much of his egalitarian ideals, but kept a liveried servant and would tolerate only a *cordon bleu* cook. He had a genuine concern for the poor, but was more often in the company of the titled rich, among whom he was pleased to number at one time the Duke and Duchess of Windsor. He hated fascism but was a close friend of the late Sir Oswald Mosley.

In Church matters he was the *enfant terrible* of the

Establishment, but in his personal faith he was traditional and sometimes exhibited the less attractive aspects of prelacy.

A solicitor's son, Arthur Mervyn Stockwood was born on May 27 1913 at Bridgend. After the death of his father on the Somme in 1916 the family moved to Bristol. Young Mervyn was educated at Kelly College, Tavistock.

Much influenced by the Anglo-Catholicism of All Saints, Clifton, he decided to seek ordination. Some indication of Stockwood's character may be gained from a story he told of being rebuked as a little boy at All Saints by a "ferocious looking man called a sacristan" for failing to remove his cap. Fifty years later he returned to the church as a bishop, declaring triumphantly that "that little boy is now standing in this pulpit, and today he is allowed to wear a hat in church".

Before ordination, however, he had to finance a university education, so he taught at Shrewsbury for two years before going up to Christ's College, Cambridge, and thence to Westcott House.

In 1936 he was ordained as a curate of St Matthew's, Moorfields – a large parish in the east end of Bristol – where he remained for 19 years, becoming its vicar in 1941. He exercised a remarkable ministry there, not least during wartime, when the parish was heavily bombed and the church damaged by fire.

The local MP was then Sir Stafford Cripps, later to become Chancellor of the Exchequer, and it was through him that Stockwood joined the Labour Party. He used to say that his Lenten penance was to wear the tie of the Cambridge University Conservative Association, to which he had belonged in his sinful youth.

In 1946 Stockwood was elected to Bristol City Council and became chairman of its health committee, causing some controversy by setting up a birth control clinic in one of the poorer areas of the city.

During his Bristol years he was elected to the Convocation of Canterbury and also served on the British Council of Churches and the Central Religious Advisory Committee of the BBC, often staying when in London at No 11 Downing Street with Cripps. He became an honorary canon of Bristol Cathedral in 1952.

Three years later he became vicar of Great St Mary's, the university church in Cambridge. It proved an inspired appointment, and although Stockwood held the post for only four years he made a great impact on both the university and the town. Average Sunday congregations rose from 200 to 1,000 and famous, and sometimes infamous, preachers and speakers occupied the pulpit.

In 1960 he became Bishop of Southwark, on the nomination of Harold Macmillan, and began an episcopal ministry of considerable style and vigour. Soon after his consecration he fiercely attacked a magistrate for sending a young mother to prison; a few days later the magistrate died of a heart attack.

After Stockwood spoke on the radio in favour of birth control clinics, the Roman Catholic Apostolic Delegate refused to sit next to him at a charity lunch at the Savoy Hotel. A priest of the diocese who declined to use the *Book of Common Prayer* was forced to resign.

"You are doing a great job," Geoffrey Fisher, the Archbishop of Canterbury, wrote to him, "though very often in the wrong way." Much later Stockwood fell out with Fisher after refusing Freemasons the use of a church.

In an attempt to revive the Christian mission in south London, Stockwood brought into the diocese a number of able young priests, many of whom he had known at Cambridge and most of whom were enthusiastic supporters of the reforming movement of the 1960s. The most prominent of these was John Robinson, the Dean of Clare College, who had been Stockwood's curate in Bristol and became Bishop of Woolwich.

The publication of Robinson's book *Honest To God* in 1963, combined with the activities of the other reformers, led to the coining of the phrase "South Bank Religion". In fact, Stockwood was no theologian, and felt no personal need of Robinson's questioning approach, but he was ready for one of his suffragan bishops to break new ground and supported him strongly in the face of a storm of public criticism.

One project on which the two bishops collaborated and which was to have lasting significance was the Southwark Ordination Course – a scheme designed for men (and later women) who could not undertake full-time study.

Stockwood was often in the House of Lords and spoke frequently about housing, unemployment, Rhodesia, apartheid and homosexuality. In one debate on Rhodesia, held shortly before Christmas, he suggested that those peers who supported the Smith regime should take tins of whitewash and change the colour of the black and yellow kings at the Christmas crib.

He generally voted with Labour, whether in government or opposition, though in the 1970s he became disenchanted with the Wilson administration.

During his time at Southwark he made a number of

overseas tours, visiting the Pope on two occasions and accompanying a Parliamentary delegation to the Soviet Union. In 1978 he wrote an article praising the achievements of Nicolae Ceausescu in Romania, particularly maintaining churches and building new ones.

Stockwood's last five years at Southwark were spent, as he put it, "immersed in depths of despairing gloom", plagued by boils and eczema, with "less and less interest in organised religion". He had a special antipathy to the development of a synodical government in the Church of England.

Twenty-one years in a demanding and often discouraging diocese had been too long for a man of his temperament, and he might well have benefited from translation to another See, although it would not have been easy to place him elsewhere.

After his retirement to Bath in 1980 he recovered some of his earlier zest and took part in the ordination of an Englishwoman to the priesthood in the United States. He also wrote an autobiography, *Chanctonbury Ring*.

He was unmarried.

January 14 1995

ROSE FITZGERALD KENNEDY

ROSE FITZGERALD KENNEDY, President John F. Kennedy's mother, who has died aged 104, knew the extremes of triumph and disaster but neither ever broke her stoic Catholic will.

She married for love, and soon had every cause to repent. Instead, she supported her brutal husband in the creation of a great political dynasty, only to see her achievement destroyed by the assassination of President Kennedy in 1963 and of his brother Robert five years later.

These were the culminating horrors in a long litany of grief. Of her other seven children, her eldest boy, Joseph Jr, a naval lieutenant and pilot, was killed in 1944 when his aircraft exploded over East Anglia; her eldest daughter, Rosemary, was mentally retarded; the second daughter, Kathleen, died in an air crash in 1948 (her husband, the Marquess of Hartington, had been killed in action four years before).

In this context, it seemed only a minor misfortune that Rose Kennedy's youngest boy, Edward ("Ted"), should have blighted his presidential prospects by failing immediately to report his having driven off the side of a bridge at Chappaquiddick in 1969; his passenger, Mary Jo Kopechne, was killed.

"Kennedys don't cry," was Mrs Kennedy's reaction to misfortune. She insisted that she would encourage her grandchildren too to go into politics. "When all three of our surviving sons", she once wrote, "were in positions of leadership and responsibility in the nation's government, then, looking back over all the years to when they had been children . . . those impressionable years when the 'twig is bent', I thought to myself that I must have done something right."

Her husband, Joseph ("Joe") Kennedy, made a fortune through crooked share-dealing and liquor distributorships acquired during the Prohibition years. For the rest, his energies were concentrated on political ambition, dynastic dreams and rabid womanising.

On the surface Mrs Kennedy reacted to the void at the heart of her life as she met all other difficulties and embarrassments – by pretending it was not there. But the price was paid: duty usurped the place of love; religiosity overlaid humanity; and sentiment dwindled into prudery. Social convention became the centre of Rose Kennedy's moral universe. She even took elocution lessons to disguise her Boston-Irish origins.

The only indulgences she allowed herself were jewellery and *haute couture*. She regularly went to Paris for the shows: "Every time Mrs Kennedy had another baby," one of Jack Kennedy's teachers observed, "she hired another nurse and took another trip abroad." She submitted her small frame – she was 5ft 3in – to rigorous dieting.

The same iron will guided her maternal obligations. "I would much rather be known as the mother of a great son," she declared in her memoirs, *Times to Remember* (1974), "than the author of a great book or the painter of a great masterpiece."

In fact she had had no temperamental affinity with the witty, irreverent, profligate charmer who became President of the United States. But her boast was justified in one sense: even Jack Kennedy, who generally, had little time for her, admitted that his mother was the glue that held the family together.

She was born Rose Fitzgerald in Boston on July 22 1890, the eldest of six children of John "Honey Fitz" Fitzgerald, himself one of 20 children born to an Irish immigrant who had arrived penniless in Boston in the

1840s. Honey Fitz was the driving force in his huge family, a fine sportsman and a dynamic operator in the shady world of Irish Democratic politics. In 1905 he was elected mayor of Boston, despite the hostile manoeuvrings of a rival Irish Democrat, Pat Kennedy. But both Fitzgeralds and Kennedys were socially far removed from such "Boston Brahmins" as the Lowells, Cabots and Adamses.

Rose was educated at Dorchester High School and the Manhattanville College of the Sacred Heart at Purchase, New York. Her mother, a shy woman, encouraged her to accompany Honey Fitz on his mayoral rounds.

Young Rose took after her father. Voted the prettiest high-school senior in Boston, she had inherited his flair for political campaigning and soon developed social confidence to match. While she was a teenager, her father introduced her to Presidents Cleveland and McKinley and Taft, as well as to other prominent friends including the English tea merchant Sir Thomas Lipton, who allegedly became one of her suitors.

Rose met Joe Kennedy during a summer vacation at Old Orchard Beach, Maine, when the two were still at high school. Her father strongly disapproved of the young man, the son of an old political enemy, and committed Rose to the Sacred Heart Convent on Commonwealth Avenue.

When the adolescent crush persisted Fitzgerald sent Rose to a nunnery at Blumenthal, Holland, for two years. There she polished her French and German, but failed to rid herself of her romantic fancy.

On her return to Boston she founded the Ace of Clubs, for the study and discussion of national and international affairs, and taught catechism classes in the North End slums.

In the spring of 1914 Joe Kennedy, by now the youngest bank president in America, felt confident enough to give Rose a two-carat engagement ring, bought at a special discount from a Harvard classmate. They were married in October 1914, in the private chapel of the Archbishop of Boston.

Rose's husband, however, was not the man to deliver her from the inhibitions of her Catholic education. The couple set up home in what was then the last house in Beals Street: beyond No 83 was nothing but empty building lots. Joe Kennedy spent most of his time at work, and was as likely to spend his spare moments with his mistresses as with his wife.

Rose Kennedy's first child, Joseph Jr, was born in 1915; Jack, the future President, in 1917; and Rosemary in 1918. But the next year, when she was pregnant with her fourth child, Rose Kennedy could take no more, and walked out on her children and husband to return to her parents at Dorchester.

Joe simply ignored her absence; Honey Fitz was unsympathetic. "You've made your commitment, Rosie," he told her, "and you must honour it now." And so, for the rest of her life, she did.

As Joe Kennedy always had another woman with him, Rose Kennedy tended to avoid him. "She would find out if he was going east," one observer recalled, "and if he was, she took a trip west."

Nevertheless Kathleen was born in 1920; Eunice in 1921; Patricia in 1924; Robert in 1925; Jean in 1928 and Edward in 1932.

Rose Kennedy approached motherhood as an exercise

in management efficiency. She kept a card-index system in which she noted her children's progress, and carried out daily inspections for missing buttons. She also oversaw her children's religious education, taking care to discuss the sermon with them after Mass. And at least she agreed with her husband on the virtues of Catholic boarding schools.

Joe Kennedy set the competitive pace – "We don't want any *losers* around here," he would tell his offspring. "In this family we want *winners*." Mrs Kennedy never dissented from this philosophy.

She encouraged intellectual curiosity by posting a daily bulletin board of news items for the children to read on their way to meals. There would be two sittings at dinner, so that conversation could be conducted according to age.

"If any child was stupid," she explained, "he was just left in the corner." When lesser sanctions failed she would whack her offspring with a ruler or a wooden coat-hanger.

She set up competitive programmes in skiing, tennis, swimming, golf and other games, and took the children on visits to local historical sites. Apparently in an attempt to develop their conversational powers they were urged to study such topics as the city's public transport service. Yet Rose Kennedy also found time to spend with her retarded daughter, Rosemary.

In 1927 Joe Kennedy transferred his entire family to New York, where they lived first in the affluent suburb of Riverdale and then at Bronxville. Partly he wanted them closer to Wall Street, partly he hoped to spare them the odium which Irish Catholics incurred in Boston. Although he also acquired holiday estates at

Hyannis Port and Palm Beach, Rose Kennedy felt the move from her native town as "a blow in the stomach".

As his fortune increased Joe Kennedy invested in films, which necessitated further long absences. It also led to an affair with Gloria Swanson, which Rose Kennedy assiduously failed to notice. "Was she a fool . . . or a saint?" Swanson later wondered. "Or just a better actress than I was?"

Husband, wife and mistress visited Paris together in 1929. The press, Rose Kennedy bemoaned, "mistakenly decided that something was going between the two of them. I knew I never had a thing to worry about and I only felt sorry for poor little Gloria."

In 1937 Joe Kennedy's cultivation of Franklin D. Roosevelt was rewarded when he became American Ambassador to the Court of St James's. In this post his endorsement of appeasement, his defeatist views and his cowardly behaviour during the Blitz covered his name in shame.

But Rose Kennedy looked back on her time in London as the high point of her life. Her Boston-Irish background was no longer a drawback; as the Ambassador's wife she was an automatic guest at all the grandest functions.

To her presentation at Buckingham Palace in 1938 she wore a luminous Molyneux gown of embroidered silver and gold lace over white satin. The gown was much admired then, and again 23 years later, when she wore it, without any alterations, at the inaugural ball of President Kennedy.

In 1941 Joe Kennedy, now back in America with his public career ruined, decided that a lobotomy should be performed on Rosemary, whose sexual drive had been creating embarrassment. Whether Rose Kennedy was privy to this decision is unclear; certainly she came bitterly to regret it.

The Kennedy ambitions were now invested in the next generation, and during the 1960 presidential campaign Jack exploited to the full the image of family solidarity that his mother had created. Rose Kennedy was 70 when her son entered the White House, and still in her prime. She would substitute as hostess when Jacqueline Kennedy (with whom she had her differences) was away, and was heard briskly telling her son to keep his hands out of his pockets, or to wear a striped tie on television because, "it's *chic*."

Joe Kennedy was laid low by a stroke in 1961, but Rose seemed immune to decline. In that year she campaigned enthusiastically for her youngest son, Edward, who ran for the Senate seat which his brother John had vacated. Three years later she went out on the hustings for Robert when he stood for the Senate in New York, and was equally supportive when, in 1968, he decided to seek the Democratic Presidential nomination.

Mrs Kennedy had no time for hostile remarks about the Kennedys using their fortune on "Bobby's" behalf: "It's our money," she said, "and we're free to spend it any way we please . . . If you have money you spend it, and win." "Teddy must stand," she is alleged to have remarked on first hearing that Bobby had been shot.

When he died she found religious consolation. "This is a good life," she insisted, "God does not send us a cross any heavier than we can bear." In 1970 she ensured that the family was solidly behind Teddy's campaign for re-election to the Senate.

Three years later *Teddy Bare*, which exposed Teddy's

equivocal role in the Chappaquiddick affair, was published. Mrs Kennedy announced that the book would be a best-seller without anyone having read it: within hours of publication she had bought up all the copies.

She retained an extraordinary vitality into extreme old age. Besides retaining her enthusiasm for travel, she kept fit by playing golf, swimming and taking long walks. She continued to attend Mass every day, and maintained that she pitied rather than hated the assassins of her sons.

All through her life she had been involved in charitable work. After the death of her eldest son she played a leading role in establishing the Joseph P. Kennedy Jr Foundation to help the mentally handicapped.

Mrs Kennedy was also active in the launch of the J. F. Kennedy Center for the Performing Arts, built in Washington in 1971 as a tribute to the former president.

Rose Kennedy concluded her memoirs on an upbeat note. "I find it interesting to reflect", she wrote, "on what has made my life, even with its moments of pain, such an essentially happy one. I have come to the conclusion that the most important element in human life is faith."

Only in her very last years did she finally seem to lose her spirit, withdrawing into virtual solitude in a house overlooking the sea on Nantucket Sound.

Jack Kennedy was survived by two children, a son and a daughter. Joe Jr and Kathleen both died childless. Rosemary, also childless, is living in a home in Wisconsin.

Eunice married Sargent Shriver in 1953; they have four sons and a daughter. Patricia married the film actor Peter Lawford in 1954; they had a son and three daughters. The marriage was dissolved in 1966.

Robert Kennedy had seven sons and four daughters. Jean, who became American Ambassador to Ireland, married Stephen Smith in 1956; they have two sons. Ted is still the Senator for Massachusetts; he has a daughter and two sons.

January 24 1995

GEORGE ABBOTT

GEORGE ABBOTT, the American theatre producer, director and writer who has died aged 107, created the original productions of *On Your Toes*, *The Boys From Syracuse*, *Pal Joey*, *On The Town*, *Call Me Madam* and *A Funny Thing Happened On The Way To The Forum*.

Lean and impatient, "Mister Abbott" – as he was reverentially termed – confronted New York's sweltering heat in jacket and tie for more than 50 years and showed the same obduracy in arid artistic climes. "I'm an enthusiast," said Abbott. "There's no point in doing anything badly." A relentless worker, he thrived on difficulty and was by his own admission easily bored.

Until middle age he was variously an actor, a Broadway "show-doctor" and a prolific director of melodrama and farce. In 1935, aged 48, he turned his hand to musical comedy, a genre that he was attracted to because of the structural problems it posed.

"When I started," Abbott recalled, "the typical musical just stuck a song in with a cue like, 'Isn't it a nice day?' Then they'd have a song about the nice day."

Abbott habitually began rehearsals for a musical with a bare outline of the plot and a few pages of script. He was adept at securing billing as a co-writer of many of the shows he directed, though some averred that his function was less to originate than to introduce into the work of tyros the commercial disciplines of pace, humour and a steady level of action.

Such canny populism had its drawbacks – "Anything partly written, and entirely directed, by George Abbott is unlikely to score high marks for either subtlety or coherence," noted *The Sunday Telegraph*. Nevertheless, he revolutionised a hitherto static form.

He made hits of the first musicals of Leonard Bernstein, Kander and Ebb, Jule Styne, Frank Loesser and Stephen Sondheim, and trained the three most influential directors of musicals in recent times: Harold Prince (*Cabaret, Phantom of the Opera*), Jerome Robbins (*Fiddler On The Roof*) and Bob Fosse (*Sweet Charity*).

"Actors trust me," said Abbott, "because they know I can make them better." He virtually invented the process of auditions. Previously, actors had been invited for a chat in the producer's office; now their skills were judged in a formal atmosphere, and they were advised not to smoke or drink when they met Abbott.

He saw comedy as a strict discipline – "I prevent the actors from making jokes" – in which there was no place for the emotional contortions of method acting. A celebrated actor of that school once asked the director his motivation for crossing the stage. "To pick up your pay-check," Abbott snapped.

In 27 years Abbott staged 26 musicals, 22 of them financial successes; the longest runner was *Never Too Late* (1,007 performances). In 1934 and again in 1939 he was billed as director of five different Broadway productions.

Between 1948 and 1962 Abbott's shows won 40 Tony awards, including five for himself.

He never dwelt on failures, dismissing them as "wasted time", and disliked staging further productions of successful shows; when he did he would always seek to improve on the original.

In 1993 Abbott rewrote his 1955 hit *Damn Yankees* – a Faustian tale about an aspiring baseball player who sells his soul – for a new Broadway production. He was asked how the new script was progressing. "Hard to say," he replied, "but it's better than most 106-year-old writers are doing."

George Francis Abbott was born at Forestville, New York, on June 25 1887. ("Always remember," said "Hal" Prince, "that George was too old for the First World War.") His father was an unsuccessful businessman, and George's parents were in constant conflict. "It was many years later," Abbott recalled, "that I came to realise that a home could be a place where there was no nagging, no fault-finding, no grim silences."

Although he read voraciously, Abbott was a poor student with a bellicose streak. On being expelled from school he entered a military academy, from which he emerged "a much better individual". Previously he had been reluctant to admit his shortcomings, but when the English headmaster described him as "the boy who never does anything wrong", he stopped creating alibis for himself, and never again excused his failures.

Abbott went on to Rochester University, intending to become a journalist. But he developed an interest in the theatre, and at Harvard studied the practicalities of playwriting, learning that "if it was good, a farce or a melodrama was just as important as a tragedy".

Abbott made his professional acting debut in 1913, as Babe Merrill in the New York production of *The Misleading Lady*. During the next two decades he played a dozen roles, and began writing. His first produced work was *The Fall Guy*, written in collaboration with James Gleason. He was also much in demand as a "show-doctor" tuning up Broadway-bound productions.

He directed a number of films for Paramount, including *Manslaughter* (1930), and the same year collaborated on the screenplay of *All Quiet On the Western Front*.

In the theatre Abbott specialised in "screwball comedy", and directed the original productions of *Three Men and a Horse* and *Room Service*. By the mid-1930s Abbott had evolved a routine: he cast the plays, supervised the read-through and basic blocking, then delegated rehearsals to an assistant, returning only to tighten up the production.

Looking for new problems, he experimented with musical comedy. *On Your Toes* (1935), a collaboration with Rodgers and Hart about an American jazz dancer eager to join the Russian ballet, was notable for its use of songs to advance the narrative. A long-running success on Broadway, it received a somewhat frostier reception in the West End. In contrast, *The Boys from Syracuse* (1938; based on Shakespeare's *Comedy of Errors*) was a great success in London, where it was hailed as "the most satisfying musical comedy that has been presented for many seasons".

From then on there was hardly a major musical production in which Abbott was not involved. His taste proved sound, and perhaps the only piece to survive his rejection was *West Side Story*. "I thought it was silly," he said. "They talked like a lot of kids and sounded nothing like tough guys. When I saw it, I loved it."

He turned around the most unpromising storylines, as when he collaborated on *The Pyjama Game* (1955), a comedy-romance set against the background of a strike in a small-town pyjama factory (the Broadway production saw Bob Fosse's debut as choreographer). Abbott shared the Pulitzer Prize for *Fiorello* (1960), a musical based on the life of Fiorello La Guardia, the colourful mayor of New York.

In 1968, aged 81, Abbott visited Britain to direct the West End premiere of his Broadway triumph *A Funny Thing Happened On The Way To The Forum*. Adapted from the Roman comedies of Plautus and Terence, with a score by the young Stephen Sondheim, it featured Frankie Howerd as the slave Pseudolus.

Abbott continued to work into his ninth, then into his 10th decade. "Why should I retire?" he asked. "Work is fun."

He denied that he was obsessed by the theatre, and in his defence cited his interest in golf. But the auditorium was a home to him, "somewhere you can go at night; a place where you can meet friends backstage, and talk".

Abbott married first, in 1914, Ednah Levis, who died in 1930. They had a daughter. He married secondly, in 1946, Mary Sinclair, an actress. The marriage was dissolved in 1951 and he announced, "I've had it." But in 1983, aged 96, he married thirdly Joy Moana Valderrama, a furrier, who was 44 years his junior.

February 2 1995

ODETTE HALLOWES, GC

ODETTE HALLOWES, who has died aged 82, was tortured by the Germans while working for Special Operations Executive (SOE) during the Second World War, and was subsequently awarded the George Cross.

In November 1942 Odette Sansom (as she then was) landed by boat in the South of France, with instructions to help to establish a Resistance circuit at Auxerre. When that plan was abandoned she acted for several months as a courier for the Resistance circuit based at Cannes, which was operated by Captain Peter Churchill. In February 1943 the group was forced to relocate to the mountains surrounding Annecy, where they arranged arms drops for the *Maquis*.

After a brief spell in London, Churchill parachuted back into France on April 15; the next night the Resistance circuit was betrayed, and Churchill and Sansom were captured. The traitor was believed to be a young French double agent, who, it is thought, was killed in a gunfight with members of the Resistance in the rue de Rivoli, Paris.

On the way to a prison at Fresnes, Churchill and Sansom were able to confer, and in order to protect each other agreed to pretend to be married. Sansom also pretended that Churchill was a relation of the Prime Minister, a claim which probably helped to ensure their survival. She stuck to her story through some 14 subsequent interrogations.

Her citation for the George Cross read: "She drew Gestapo attention from her commanding officer and on to herself, saying that he had only come to France on her insistence. She took full responsibility and agreed that it should be herself and not her commanding officer who should be shot. By this action she caused the Gestapo to cease paying attention to her commanding officer after only two interrogations."

The Gestapo were determined to locate a wireless operator and another British officer, whose whereabouts they were (correctly) convinced were known to Sansom. "The Gestapo tortured her most brutally to make her give away this information," continued the citation. "They seared her back with a red hot iron and when that failed pulled out all her toe nails ... [she] refused to speak and by her bravery and determination she not only saved the lives of the two officers but also enabled them to carry out their most valuable work."

She was condemned to death and in May 1944 was taken to Germany, along with six other women agents; three were executed at Dachau concentration camp and three at Natzweiler.

Sansom was held at Ravensbrück, where she was first placed in a cell 10ft by 6ft, with no light, only straw for bedding and water for sustenance. Later she was moved to a cell overlooking the camp crematorium. She saw women being dragged to their deaths behind the crematorium's iron doors and heard the screams of victims of the beatings constantly administered in the adjacent cell. Her evidence was later used in the trial of 16 of the camp's guards.

In April 1945 she was unexpectedly released, and found her way to the advancing Allies.

The daughter of a French bank manager who was killed in the First World War, Odette Marie Celine

Brailly was born at Amiens, France, on April 26 1912. She was educated privately and at the Convent of Ste Therese, Amiens.

She was a quiet, withdrawn child, who cared for horses and for music. At eight she went almost blind, and it took several years for her to regain her sight completely. She later said that the experience helped her to cope with her incarceration in Ravensbrück.

In 1931 she married Roy Sansom, an Englishman and old friend of her family, and the next year they moved to Britain.

In the spring of 1942 Mrs Sansom heard a BBC broadcast in which the War Office requested photographs and postcards showing the European coastline. She sent off some family snapshots of her brother playing on the beach at Boulogne. It turned out that the War Office had arranged the broadcast to contact potential agents, and she was soon recruited to SOE.

At the end of her training she was assessed as enthusiastic, though "impulsive and hasty in her judgements . . . Her main asset is her patriotism. Her main weakness is her complete unwillingness to admit she could ever be wrong."

Though Colonel Maurice Buckmaster, the head of SOE's "F" Section, was not impressed by this assessment, he saw Sansom's stubbornness as a potential asset. In September 1942 she said goodbye to her children, and handed over to SOE a great bundle of letters to be posted to her family at intervals. Buckmaster gave her two farewell presents – a silver powder compact and a poison pill.

On her return to England in 1945 Sansom was

deeply traumatised. She was presented with the George Cross by King George VI in November 1946.

The next year she married Captain Peter Churchill. The marriage was dissolved in 1953 and 1956 she married Geoffey Hallowes.

She was the subject of a biography, and of a film, *Odette* (1950), directed by Herbert Wilcox and starring Anna Neagle in the title role.

In the 1960s there was a certain amount of controversy aroused by the official history *SOE in France*, which questioned the effectiveness of the organisation's operations. But Hallowes's reputation remained unsullied.

She was appointed MBE in 1945 and awarded the *Légion d'Honneur* in 1950. She was vice-president of the Women's Transport Services (FANY), a regular attender at FANY reunions and a stalwart of Forces charities.

On one occasion her medals were stolen by a burglar; but such was her popularity that they were soon returned, along with an abject letter of apology.

She and Roy Sansom had three daughters.

March 17 1995

DAME LUCIE RIE

DAME LUCIE RIE, who has died aged 93, was one of the most admired potters of the century. Her work had an austere elegance, combining formality with delicacy, strength with subtlety, and attracted comparison with the art of Henry Moore and Pablo Picasso.

Impeccably modern in her approach, Rie was also

influenced by the pottery of prehistoric Europe, Ancient Rome, the Far East and medieval Islam. Her pots were remarkable for the sober richness of their surface texture and the thinness of their walls. Her work was once-fired and raw-glazed – which is to say that the pot was thrown and slip and glaze applied to the unbaked clay before it entered the kiln.

Other potters have never mastered her complex glaze recipes, which piled bronze on purple, bled manganese into charcoal or created a lively Chinese yellow with a poisonous uranium (now illegal). The results were of surpassing beauty, in such shades as peacock, emerald, gold and conch pink.

The precision of Rie's forms was achieved by the use of a razor or a steel tool known as a kidney. She then decorated the eggshell-like membrane with a brush. Because clay, slip and glaze were all fired at the same time, elaborate and often unpredictable interactions could take place.

Sometimes oxides in the body of the pot would melt into the outer layers to produce a speckled or streaked effect. For other pieces Rie favoured a rough, pitted surface, a bronze sheen or areas of strong colour.

Frequently she would score lines into the clay (an idea she borrowed from the Celtic pottery of Wiltshire), but in every case the decoration seemed an integral part of the object.

She was born Lucie Gomperez in Vienna on March 16 1902. She first came into contact with Modernist design in the study of her father, a doctor and colleague of Sigmund Freud; she encountered Roman pottery (another source of her mature style) in her uncle's museum at Eisenstadt near the Austro-Hungarian border.

Throughout her life she employed the clean, clear lines of Modernism, which in the early part of the century were the essence of Viennese good taste. In a cooler vein, Rie's pottery also owed something to the luxuriant refinement of Viennese Art Nouveau.

From 1922 to 1926 she studied pottery at the Kunstgewerbeschule in Vienna, under Michael Powolny; by the 1930s she had developed a repertoire of clear and forceful shapes with discreetly complex textures. At the Paris Exposition Nationale of 1937 an entire section of the Austrian pavilion was devoted to Rie's work.

But as she and her husband Hans Rie were Jews they found themselves increasingly ostracised, as well as deprived of most of their property. After the *Anschluss* of 1938 the couple borrowed money from a non-Jewish aunt of Hans Rie's to move to London, where they soon separated; in 1940 he went to America to manage a felt-hat factory, and she to a tiny mews house near Marble Arch, with an interior designed for her by Freud's son Ernst.

Lucie Rie had hardly any money and subsisted mainly on cabbage (she recalled her early London years as her "cabbage days"). But she was glad to have escaped Austria: "I had never liked the Viennese people. They were jealous, not good-hearted, and most of them were Nazis." The British, by contrast, had "fine minds".

The world of British pottery was then dominated by the charismatic Bernard Leach, who believed passionately in the robust ideals of the Arts and Crafts movement.

Leach and his followers found Lucie Rie's work lacking in the virtues they admired, and criticised her severely. Leach described her pots as "too thickly glazed, thinly potted, too much like stoneware . . . [with] no humanity".

Rie tried to adapt to Leach's aesthetic – "he educated me and I owe him a tremendous lot," she later said – but she was insistently unpretentious and dismissed Leach's evocation of "life flowing for a few moments perfectly through the hands of a potter."

"I just throw", she said, "until I like the shape."

But for a time she lost confidence in her own style. During the Second World War she gave up pottery altogether, and for a while worked in an optical factory; she was also briefly an ARP warden.

It was not until 1945 that she began to make a comeback, by agreeing to make ceramic buttons for an enterprise run by a Viennese compatriot. Soon she was making not only buttons but also ceramic jewellery, mirrors and pots.

In 1946 she took as her assistant Hans Coper, a German refugee 18 years her junior: "I knew somebody fantastic had come," she later said. "I am a potter, but he was an artist."

Coper's encouragement helped her to regain confidence, and over the next 12 years the two produced work that was starker and chunkier than her Viennese pottery, matt in finish and often marked with incised (sgraffito) lines.

Rie and Coper had an immense influence on the postwar generation of potters; indeed, they succeeded Leach as the dominant forces in British studio pottery. Leach admitted he had been wrong about Rie's work, and became a firm friend and supporter.

Rie came to wider attention in 1967 with a one-woman show for the Arts Council, but her prices did not rocket until by 1992, when her bowls were selling for more than £5,000 and a vase fetched £14,500. She continued to insist that her pieces were designed for everyday use.

Even in her late eighties she rose for work at five in the morning – "sometimes 5.15" – and produced more than 300 pieces a year. A tiny woman with a formal manner and a ready smile, she tied weights round her feet when she was alone to make sure that she did not fall into the kiln.

She lived for 50 years in her mews house, where she received a constant stream of visitors. "Some I like," she said, "some I don't. But mostly I like them. People who like pots are usually nice."

She would ply visitors with home-made cakes and coffee, served in her own vessels. "Her chocolate and rock cake recipes," said her friend Cyril Frankel, a ceramics expert at Bonham's, "with a touch of marmalade here, a sliver of ginger there, are as varied as her glazes."

Rie usually dressed in white, and though she produced beautifully coloured glazes confessed that she liked white pots best.

The fashion designer Issey Miyake came across Rie's work in the 1980s and used the ceramic buttons she had created during the war in his 1989 collection. He then organised an exhibition of her pots in Japan. Rie's work, he said, "embodies a world view that is unique to western culture. It is also very modest, very human and, most of all, humane."

In 1987 some of her work was featured in a series of Post Office stamps. In 1992 the Crafts Council staged a retrospective of her work. Having suffered a stroke the previous year, she was no longer producing pots.

"She is still working in her mind," said Frankel, "but she has always sought a standard of excellence – and she's still intelligent enough to grasp that she might not now maintain that excellence."

An exhibition of pottery by Rie and Coper opened at New York's Metropolitan Museum of Art a few weeks before her death.

She was appointed OBE in 1968, CBE in 1981 and DBE in 1990.

April 3 1995.

KENNY EVERETT

KENNY EVERETT, who has died aged 50, was a disc jockey and television comedian with a disconcerting line in coarsely satiric comic sketches in what one of his characters, Cupid Stunt, would have insisted were "all in the best *pahssible* taste!"

"Cuddly Ken", as he liked to be known, first came to public attention in the 1960s, when his manic broadcasts for pirate radio won him a large following among adolescents. Snapped up by BBC Radio 1, Everett pioneered the role of disc jockey as popular entertainer, with nonsensical jingles, scatological extemporisations and wild lunges at figures of authority.

Nervous and unconfident in company, he found that the seclusion of the radio studio allowed him to escape from his own neuroses into a world of fantastic invention.

"Radio is a good place to work," he said, "if you are not really a jolly person, but want to appear to be one."

Among Everett's favourite creations was the Captain Kremmen series – a cross between *Dan Dare* and *The Goons*, which began life on Capital Radio. Everett as the skinny hero did battle with the Enemies of the Universe (the Krells, a species of man-eating blancmange).

From the late 1970s Everett was much in evidence on television. Diminutive and bearded, with receding hair and wildly rotating eyes, he presided over an hysterical melange of music and fustian lampoon, laden with innuendo. His zenith in this line came with *The Kenny Everett Video Show* and *The Kenny Everett Television Show*.

Everett created a gallery of memorable grotesques, the foremost of which were Sid Snot (a filthy Hell's Angel), Mr Angry of Mayfair, Marcel Wave (a fastidious French hairdresser), the Thora Hird-inspired Verity Treacle and the pneumatic American starlet Cupid Stunt, for whom Everett coined the celebrated catchphrase about taste, as "she" crossed her legs with an extravagant lack of discretion. There was also a bearded baby, who used to say: "When I grow up I'm going to be Kenny Everett – pathetic isn't it?"

Everett introduced to television the dance group Hot Gossip, who writhed athletically in scanty leather; he indulged his fascination for lavatories; addressed royalty as "Your Royal Aubergineness"; and terrified his producers when he offered viewers Ferraris as prizes, failing to mention that they were Dinky toys.

In 1970 Everett was sacked by the BBC for making a jibe about Mary Peyton, the wife of the then Minister of Transport, after she had taken her driving test – "She only passed because she slipped him a fiver – I know these people."

The BBC took him back, but in 1984 he made another unfortunate joke, albeit one handed him on a piece of paper by his producer. "When England was an empire," he gurgled, "we had an emperor, when we were a kingdom, we had a king, and now we are a country, we've got Margaret Thatcher."

This was characteristically inconsistent of Everett, as in the previous year he had "come out" as a Tory at a Young Conservatives' rally attended by the Prime Minister, at which he jovially yelled (to the embarrassment of the assembled faithful): "Let's bomb Russia! Let's kick away Michael Foot's stick!"

In 1985 Everett came out as a homosexual, declaring that since his sexual predilection had twice led him to attempt drug overdoses he found it impossible to accept the label "gay". He was upset by the hostile reaction of his fans.

By the late 1980s Everett's critics were arguing that his insinuating humour failed to conceal a dwindling comic inspiration. Everett was hurt: "I'm so thin-skinned, I'm completely raw."

In 1989 Everett vowed never again to dress up as Sid Snot or Marcel Wave, and returned to the isolation of the radio studio. It was announced that he was suffering from an Aids-related illness, but he maintained his sense of humour.

"I see death in my own philosophical way," he remarked. "I can't imagine I was nowhere before this. I'd like to come back living in Italy or Spain or somewhere. As long as I don't come back bald or in Bosnia, I don't mind."

The son of a tugboatman, Kenny Everett was born Maurice Cole into a working-class family of Liverpool Roman Catholics on Christmas Day 1944; he was educated at St Bede's Secondary Modern and St Peter Claver College. A spindly, sensitive child, he recalled his schooldays with distaste: "Most kids thought the best way to get on top was to punch someone in the mouth – usually me."

After leaving school, he had a brief flirtation with the priesthood and spent a year at a missionary college. "I'm no longer Catholic," he later said. "I'm freelance." His first job was "scraping gunk off sausage-roll trays" in a Liverpool bakery, before moving on to an advertising agency and to the advertising department of the *Journal of Commerce*.

Having acquired an ability to impersonate everything from the Goons to the opening of the airlocks in *Journey into Space*, he bought two tape-recorders and began to make his own programmes, interspersing music with bouts of silliness.

He changed his name to Kenny Everett, and in 1964 became a disc jockey for Radio Luxembourg; before long he moved to the pirate ship Radio London, where he teamed up with Dave Cash for *Kenny and Cash on London*.

When the Government cracked down on the pirate stations Everett switched to Radio 1. Sacked from the BBC for the second time, he joined the new Capital Radio, where he was reunited with Cash.

In 1968 Granada Television teamed him up with the practical joker Jonathan Routh and the Australian academic Germaine Greer for *Nice Time*, on which massed ventriloquists' dummies sang *Congratulations*. Subsequent television successes included *The Kenny Everett Explosion*, *Making Whoopee*, *Ev*, *The Kenny Everett Video Show* and *The Kenny Everett Television Show*. He even hosted a religious quiz show – one of his many attempts to create a more orthodox act.

In 1991 he played the "wacky" Billiard Marker in his first West End musical, *The Hunting of the Snark*, a short-lived show by Mike Batt (best known for his songs for *The Wombles of Wimbledon*) based on Lewis Carroll's epic nonsense poem.

For 12 years Everett was married to a spiritualist known as Crystal Clear. When they parted his wife revealed that the main obstacle to nuptial bliss had not been Everett's homosexuality but his profound depressions. "Even the plumber would leave our house feeling depressed after talking to Ev," she wrote. She further described him as "a little boy whose hobby is polishing the bathroom taps"; when they split up she found him a flat with three bathrooms.

After his divorce Everett moved in with his friend Nikolai Grishanovich (a computer analyst and former Red Army soldier) and Grishanovich's wife. "I'm not a homosexual," he would say, planting a kiss on Grishanovich's cheek, "just helping out."

The menage was later augmented by the arrival of a Spanish waiter: "There's nothing worse than only having one husband," explained Everett.

Grishanovich died in 1993. Latterly Everett lived alone in a flat he kept obsessively tidy, even vacuuming the plastic grass on the balcony.

Everett was fond of animals, and at one stage had a chihuahua–Yorkshire terrier cross, two cats, a parrot and several horses. His companion in his last years was a cat called Pussy Cat.

By way of recreation, Everett enjoyed needlework.

April 5 1995

THE EARL OF CLANCARTY

THE 8TH EARL OF CLANCARTY, who has died aged 83, devoted his life to propagating belief in flying saucers.

Brinsley Clancarty, a tall, amiable figure with a rather haunted expression and elegant braces, claimed that he could trace his descent from 63,000 BC, when beings from other planets had landed on Earth in spaceships. Most humans, he said, were descended from these aliens: "This accounts for all the different colour skins we've got here," he said in 1981.

A few of these early aliens did not come from space, he explained, but emerged through tunnels from a civilisation which still existed beneath the Earth's crust. There were seven or eight of these tunnels altogether, one at the North Pole, another at the South Pole, and others in such places as Tibet. "I haven't been down there myself," Clancarty said, "but from what I gather [these beings] are very advanced."

He once produced a satellite photograph showing a large circular blob in the North Polar ice which, he said, was the entrance to one of the tunnels. He remained adamant even when it was pointed out to him that he was looking at part of the camera.

When he addressed a 1981 meeting of the British Unidentified Flying Objects Research Association, its chairman rebuked reporters for laughing at Lord Clancarty's views: "We are tired of people treating us as a joke. We are serious people and this is a serious subject."

Clancarty said that most of the aliens who were still arriving from space (and from the centre of the Earth) were friendly. But then he pointed to the sky and added: "I'm told there is one hostile lot."

For years he was frustrated in his desire to see a flying saucer. He installed a UFO detector in the bedroom wall at his flat in South Kensington, but with disappointing results.

"It did buzz one Saturday afternoon," he said, "but when I rushed out I found that the sky was cloudy and completely overcast. Presumably it was above the cloud."

At last he spotted his first (and last) UFO: "It was an eerie white light zigzagging over South Kensington," he recalled. "I had to climb into the kitchen sink to get a good look at it through the window."

The fifth son of the 5th Earl of Clancarty, William Francis Brinsley Le Poer Trench was born on September 18 1911 and educated at the Nautical College, Pangbourne.

In the 1950s he edited the *Flying Saucer Review* and founded the International Unidentified Object Observer Corps. He also found employment selling advertising space for a gardening magazine housed opposite Waterloo Station; office wags pointed out that Trench earned his renown by gazing at space and his living by selling it.

When he succeeded to the Earldom (created in 1803) on the death of his half-brother in 1975, the new Lord Clancarty founded a UFO Study Group at the House of Lords, and introduced *Flying Saucer Review* to its library.

Four years later he organised a celebrated debate on UFOs which attracted many speeches on both sides of the question. Lord Strabolgi, speaking on behalf of the Government, declared that there was nothing to convince him that any alien spacecraft had ever visited the Earth.

Lord Clancarty's books, written under the name Brinsley Le Poer Trench, included *The Sky People*, *Men Among Mankind*, *Forgotten Heritage*, *The Flying Saucer Story*, *Operation Earth*, *The Eternal Subject* and *Secret of the Ages*.

He married first, in 1940 (dissolved 1947), Diana, daughter of Sir William Younger, 2nd Bt. He married secondly, in 1961 (dissolved 1969), Mrs Wilma Belknap. He married thirdly, in 1974, Mrs Mildred Spong, who died in 1975. He married fourthly, in 1976, Mrs May Beasley. The heir to the Earldom is his nephew, Nicholas Power Richard Le Poer Trench, born 1952.

May 22 1995

LANA TURNER

LANA TURNER, the film actress who has died in Los Angeles aged 75, packed as much melodrama into her life off-screen as into her sizzling appearances before the camera.

"My life has been a series of emergencies," Turner once observed, and indeed her career would have done credit to a Hollywood scriptwriter. Her father was murdered when she was nine, and she was partly brought up by unloving foster parents before she wooed and won the American public.

It was in fact Turner's tight-fitting sweaters which first suggested her dramatic potential – it was as "The Sweater Girl" that she became a pin-up in the Second World War. Though she was said to change her costumes more often than the expression on her face, the young Turner always had a compelling mixture of sexiness and ordinariness.

Cheap showgirls, sleazy adulteresses, murderous wives, alcoholic actresses and neurotic mothers were her stock in trade. The most enduring of her films is perhaps *The Postman Always Rings Twice* (1946), in which she and John Garfield whip up an overpowering sexual chemistry as she incites him to murder her husband.

"You won't find anything cheap around here," Turner told Garfield.

"The harder the wind blows, the hotter it gets", Garfield returned. Still tighter than the dialogue was the white "hot pants" suit Turner wore.

Turner was also striking in *The Bad and the Beautiful* (1952), playing an alcoholic film star opposite Kirk Douglas's megalomaniac producer. And in 1957 she was nominated for an Oscar when she took on the role of a neurotic mother in *Peyton Place*.

Off the screen, she worked her way through seven marriages, as well as engaging in widely publicised affairs with Frank Sinatra, Tyrone Power and Howard Hawkes. "When I was a playgirl, honey," Turner remembered at the end of her life, "I played."

In 1958 there was a sensation when Turner's current

lover, a gangster called Johnny Stompanato, was stabbed to death with a carving knife by her 15-year-old daughter Cheryl.

Cynics observed that mother and daughter had previously communicated chiefly through the pages of fan magazines; it seemed that Turner had been unaware that her fourth husband, Lex Barker (Johnny Weissmuller's successor as Tarzan) was regularly raping Cheryl, then barely a teenager.

At the coroner's inquest Turner explained how Stompanato had been killed. "We had a violent argument," she told the court, "and he went to the closet where he had a jacket and a shirt on a hanger. He came to me like he was going to strangle me with the jacket. I said 'Don't ever touch me again. I want you to get out.' I went to the door, and, as I opened it my daughter was standing there. She came in, and everything happened so fast I thought she had hit him in the stomach. I never saw a blade."

The court found that the killing was a justifiable homicide, in that Cheryl had acted to protect her mother's life. Years later mother and daughter came to refer to this episode as "the paragraph", since neither of their names was ever mentioned without a reference to the case.

Turner's ardent love letters to Stompanato, read out in court, did her image no harm. In 1959 she made a fortune from her percentage of the profits of Douglas Sirke's *Imitation of Life*, the plot of which centred on an actress's troubles with her daughter.

By this time the ordinariness which she projected in her earlier films had long since been exchanged for contrived sophistication and glamour. The actress and her legend had achieved a perfect symbiosis.

A mine foreman's daughter, Julia Jean Mildred Frances Turner was born at Wallace, Idaho, on February 8 1920. Her parents moved to California, where they separated, and her father was killed by thieves. Years of poverty followed, though there was some attempt to educate the girl at a convent in San Francisco and at Hollywood High School.

According to the legend, at the age of 15 Turner was playing truant from school and sipping soda at Schwab's drugstore on Sunset Boulevard when she was observed by the editor of the *Hollywood Reporter*, who passed on his discovery to the director Mervyn LeRoy.

In no time Turner was under contract to Warner Brothers, and after a bit part in *A Star Is Born* (1937) made a distinct impression with her provocative walk in *They Won't Forget Her*. Later she would pass on the secrets of this perambulation to her daughter: "Pretend there's a nickel stuck between your buttocks and you have to hold it there for dear life so it won't fall out."

Moving on to MGM with LeRoy – Jack Warner held she would never amount to anything and willingly let her go – Turner appeared in several more minor roles before making a breakthrough in *Ziegfeld Girl* (1941) with Judy Garland, Hedy Lamarr and James Stewart. In the part of an ill-fated showgirl, she lightened her hair to a golden blonde, sat in a bubble bath wearing diamond and emerald jewellery and walked on a mink coat flung on to the floor.

Turner's next success was in a western, *Honky Tonk*. "Clark Gable kisses Lana Turner and It's Screen History," announced the posters, and certainly when Gable knocked down her door on their wedding night, she did not look displeased.

Her subsequent ventures with Gable – in *Somewhere I'll Find You*, *Homecoming* and *Betrayed* – were less memorable. Back in 1942 *Johnny Eager* featured another much touted pairing, with Turner as a society girl being pursued by Robert Taylor's gangster. The publicists hit upon the formula "T-N-T" – for Taylor and Turner.

By now Turner was the GIs' favourite, a popularity relentlessly exploited in such vehicles as *Slightly Dangerous*, *Marriage is a Private Affair*, *Keep Your Powder Dry* and a remake of *Grand Hotel*.

In the box office hit *Green Dolphin Street* Turner braved an earthquake, a tidal wave, a native uprising and childbirth; in *Cass Timberlane* she lured Spencer Tracy's judge into marriage against his better judgement; and in *The Three Musketeers* she essayed Milady de Winter, sounding according to the *New Yorker*, "like a drive-in waitress exchanging quips with hotrodders."

In 1960 in league with Anthony Quinn she killed another husband in *Portrait in Black*. The next year she had a less fulfilling role opposite Bob Hope in *Bachelor in Paradise*. Her performance in *Madame X* (1966) pleased her fans more than the critics. Latterly film roles became scarce, and Turner herself described *Persecution* (1974), a British horror film, as "a bomb".

She turned to television and in 1969 appeared with George Hamilton in a series called *The Survivors*. She bravely took to the stage, touring in *Forty Carats* in 1971 and four years later performing in a production of *The Pleasure of His Company* in Chicago. In 1981 she briefly returned to television in *Falcon's Crest*. Her last films were *Bittersweet Love* (1976) and *Witches' Brew* (1978, released 1985).

In latter years Turner developed a horror of explicit

sex on screen. "Thank God I was never asked to do nude scenes," she said in 1983. "I watch some of the things they do today and even when they kiss – the mouths opening before they get together, the tongues lashing in and out, the bodies grinding – it's all so different from the beautiful kisses we had from our lovely leading men. It offends me, it's ugly. I turn my eyes away."

In 1981 the National Film Society presented Turner with an Artistry in Cinema award. Her autobiography, *Lana . . . The Truth*, was published in 1982.

Lana Turner married first in 1940 (dissolved 1941), the bandleader Artie Shaw; secondly, in 1942, Steven Crane. It was subsequently discovered that Crane was already married, and another, legal, wedding took place in 1943, prior to the divorce in 1944. Cheryl, Turner's only child, was born of this union.

Turner married thirdly, in 1948 (dissolved 1952) Henry "Bob" Topping; fourthly in 1953 (dissolved 1957) Lex Barker; fifthly, in 1962 (dissolved 1962) Fred May; sixthly, in 1965 (dissolved 1969) Robert Eaton; and seventhly in 1969 (dissolved 1972) Ronald Dante.

"I used to lean on men," Turner reflected after the end of her last marriage. "But whenever a crisis happened, they fell apart, and suddenly I became the strong one. I am not ashamed to say that I have no desire to marry again."

July 1 1995

SIR STEPHEN SPENDER

SIR STEPHEN SPENDER, who has died aged 86, was a poet, critic, novelist, short-story writer and anthologist.

"The Rupert Brooke of the Slump", as a contemporary called him, Spender was the last of the group of poets who found fame in the 1930s under the half-affectionate, half-contemptuous sobriquet "MacSpauday" – an amalgam of the names of Louis MacNeice, Spender, W. H. Auden and Cecil Day-Lewis.

As a poet Spender was never in the same class as Auden or MacNeice but he built himself a place as a man of letters on both sides of the Atlantic. His output, in both verse and prose, was considerable, though only a handful of his poems are likely to endure.

"Being a minor poet is like being minor royalty," he once complained. "And no one, as a former lady-in-waiting to Princess Margaret once explained to me, is happy as that."

Philip Larkin, no great admirer of "MacSpauday", included five of Spender's poems in *The Oxford Book of Twentieth-Century English Verse* (as against 15 from Auden and eight from MacNeice). Other judges were less kind. "To see him fumbling with our rich and delicate language," wrote Evelyn Waugh, "is to experience all the horror of seeing a Sèvres vase in the hands of a chimpanzee."

"That was a horrible remark," Spender said. "But then the truth is that I do write with great difficulty and have absolutely no confidence that I write well."

Like the rest of his circle, Spender was deeply

involved in the Left-wing causes of the 1930s – he even joined the Communist Party for a few months before being expelled for writing critically of party policy in the *Daily Worker*.

At its best his socially aware verse retained a vivid, personal quality that lifted it out of the common rut. "The Pylons", a poem celebrating the spread of electricity ("There runs the quick perspective of the future"), includes the verse:

> *Now over these small hills*
> *they have built the concrete*
> *That trails black wire:*
> *Pylons, those pillars*
> *Bare like nude, giant girls*
> *   that have no secret.*

The son of Harold Spender, a Liberal journalist and biographer of Lloyd George, Stephen Harold Spender was born at Hampstead on February 28 1909. His mother, who died when he was 12, was from a German-Jewish banking family, a bloodline belied by young Stephen's Nordic appearance – wild, flying fair hair, penetrating blue eyes and great height (6ft 3ins), much admired when he lived in Germany in the 1930s.

Spender was sent to school at Gresham's, Holt, where Auden was a pupil, but on the death of his mother he was called home to keep his father company, and attended University College School, Hampstead. He went on to University College, Oxford.

The great days of Acton (*qv*) and Waugh were over, and the new star in the literary firmament was Auden, who held court in his darkened rooms at Christ Church. Spender took his poems there, and was grilled and lectured by the master (who was little more than a year older than him). He was accepted into the group of Oxford Poets, though his gawkiness and lack of sophistication were much mocked by the others, particularly the Cambridge incomer, Christopher Isherwood, who put his version of Spender into his novel *Lions and Shadows* (1938): "He burst in upon us, blushing, sniggering loudly, contriving to trip over the edge of the carpet – an immensely tall, shambling boy of 19 with a great scarlet poppy-face, wild frizzy hair, and eyes the violent colour of bluebells."

Spender hoped to become an artist or graphic designer, and at 17, after his father's death, he bought a hand printing-press on which he printed Auden's first published poems. Spender's first work appeared alongside that of Auden and MacNeice in the two volumes of *Oxford Poetry* he helped to edit.

By the end of Spender's second year the group was dispersing, and he decided to leave Oxford without finishing his degree. His modest private income enabled him to follow Auden and Isherwood to Germany in 1929, though he went to Hamburg rather than Berlin.

He was fascinated by the male prostitutes. "The boys were unemployed," he recalled, "and technically I suppose they were prostituting themselves, but they were always looking for a great romantic friendship."

His experiences of the Rieperbahn, and an idyllic love affair with a young man on a walking tour down the Rhine, provided the material for his novel *The Temple*. Despite a recommendation from T. S. Eliot the novel was refused by Faber & Faber on the grounds of indecency and libel, and did not see the light of day until 1988.

Spender's first solo volume, *Poems*, was published in 1930, and soon – particularly after his inclusion in the anthology *New Signals* (1932) – his work was widely reviewed. *The Burning Cactus* (a volume of short stories), *Trial of a Judge* (a verse play) and several political pamphlets appeared before Spender briefly joined the Republican side in the Spanish Civil War, as an observer.

His time there increased his horror of war and shook his allegiance to the Left, as he explained in one of the most emotional essays in *The God That Failed* (1949), an anthology produced by those, like Arthur Koestler, who had been Communists but had lost their faith.

Soon after the outbreak of the Second World War he joined the Auxiliary Fire Service in London and saw out the Blitz. In his autobiography, *World within World* (1951), he made no great claims for his effectiveness as a fire-fighter, and others have said that he was more in demand as chairman of discussion groups than as a handler of a hose.

In the early months of the war he joined Cyril Connolly in founding the monthly magazine *Horizon*. He did much to shape its attitude to poetry, though two years later he quarrelled with Connolly and withdrew from the board.

Connolly described Spender as really two people: "one an inspired simpleton, a great big silly goose, a holy Russian idiot"; the other "shrewd and ambitious, aggressive and ruthless, a publicity-seeking intellectual full of administrative energy and *rentier* asperity".

In 1953 he helped found *Encounter*, and for the next 14 years ran the literary half of the magazine. When it became known that the magazine had once received financial backing from the CIA, Spender resigned.

He was showered with requests to lecture, and later with honorary degrees, from American universities. In 1966 he was the first foreigner to become Consultant in Poetry in English to the Library of Congress, Washington. Because of his brief Communist Party membership he had to be granted a special "waiver" by the State Department to obtain a visa.

Throughout the 1960s and 1970s he produced a steady stream of poetry, essays, translations and textbooks on such figures as D. H. Lawrence and T. S. Eliot. For seven years from 1970 he was Professor of English at University College, London.

Spender was a sort of shop steward of the poets' union. In 1971, after Cecil Day-Lewis had been appointed Poet Laureate, Spender was awarded the Queen's Gold Medal for Poetry, and became very much a member of the literary establishment.

He was a stalwart of Foyle's literary lunches, and in 1955 he stormed out of one in protest at a speech by Lord Samuel about the obscurity of modern poetry. Sad to say, his dramatic exit was somewhat spoilt by his walking into the kitchen rather than out of the hall and, "poppy-faced", he had to make a second exit.

Old age did not diminish his literary activity. Reworked poems, written decades earlier, were published. He produced *China Diary* after touring the Far East with David Hockney, and edited his journals, published in 1985.

Spender was appointed CBE in 1962. His emergence as a senior statesman of the arts world was recognised by a knighthood in 1983 for services to literature; it reflected the happiness and solidity of his home life, both in London and at his house in Provence. The homosexuality of youth "just withered away", as he put it.

His reminiscences of the 1930s continued to attract readers. As *The Sunday Telegraph* observed of a book of these, *The Thirties and After* (1978), Spender could not at the time have imagined "that most of his choices would prove to be wrong, many of his actions absurd, and nearly all his arguments incorrect" – but he was, at least, "brave enough to reprint his early blunders in their original form".

Spender's first marriage, in 1936, to Inez Pearn broke down within three years. In 1941 he married the pianist Natasha Litvin, by whom he had two children: Matthew, a sculptor, and Lizzie, an actress and playwright married to the Australian writer and entertainer Barry Humphries.

Spender never claimed "greatness" for himself – though "even today," he admitted in the late 1980s, "it often disgusts me to read a newspaper in which there is no mention of my name".

He once wrote a poem, the first line of which runs, "I think continually of those who were truly great." The second verse expresses well his attitude to life:

What is precious is never to forget
The essential delight of the blood drawn from ageless springs
Breaking through rocks in worlds before our earth.
Never to deny its pleasure in the morning simple light
Nor its grave demanding for love.
Never to allow gradually the traffic to smother
With noise and fog, the flowering of the Spirit.

July 18 1995

LADY ALEXANDRA
METCALFE

LADY ALEXANDRA METCALFE, the former chairman and vice-president of Save the Children, who has died aged 91, was a daughter of the 1st (and last) Marquess Curzon of Kedleston, a god-daughter of Queen Alexandra, and a close friend of King Edward VIII.

She was born Alexandra Naldera Curzon on March 20 1904, the third and youngest daughter of Lord Curzon by his first wife, the American heiress Mary Leiter. Her father was then Viceroy of India, and named his daughter Naldera after the beautiful weekend camp he had set up in the Himalayan foothills beyond Simla.

A special cow was shipped from England to provide the infant with milk, and her Indian nurses called her "*Baba sahib*". The nickname "Baba" stuck, and in later life she complained that it was used even by people she heartily disliked, such as Lloyd George and Lord Beaverbrook.

When Baba was two her mother died. Her mother's complicated will later sparked off a series of furious family rows.

Alexandra inherited her father's strong personality and common sense, and if her intellect was not as profound as his it was as quick. She became a fixed star in the social firmament of the 1920s, an adornment to parties, receptions, nightclubs and balls.

The aesthete and politician Sir Philip Sassoon proposed to her, as did a plethora of eligible aristocrats. At one time it was thought that she might make a candidate for the hand of the Prince of Wales or the Duke of Kent. So it caused a mild sensation when she announced her engagement to Captain Edward "Fruity" Metcalfe, the son of an Irish prison inspector, some 17 years her senior.

This, however, was an affair of the heart. Metcalfe was handsome, debonair and a superb horseman who had won an MC in the First World War. Moreover, he was firm friends with the Prince of Wales, who had visited India when Fruity was stationed there with the 3rd Skinner's Horse in 1921. They became inseparable, and the Prince promptly appointed him an ADC. The many stories of Fruity's adventures – such as when he lost his trousers in a Canadian brothel in 1924 – shocked the Court but amused the Prince.

Lord Curzon died a matter of weeks before his daughter's wedding took place in the Queen's Chapel, St James's, in 1925. Lord Louis Mountbatten was best man and four crowned heads of Europe attended. A throng of 6,000 watched the bride and groom depart for India where Fruity served on the staff of Field Marshal Sir William Birdwood. He rose to the rank of Major and retired from the Army in 1927.

The couple had a son and twin daughters, but Fruity proved an incurable eccentric. Lady Alexandra's sense of social obligation did not then allow her to countenance divorce, and the couple separated amicably.

A great friend of Nancy Astor's, Lady Alexandra was a frequent guest at Cliveden in the 1920s and 1930s. She adored the conversation of the Marquess of Lothian, Bob Brand and the rest of the "Milner Kindergarten".

Lady Alexandra was a member of the house party at Cliveden in October 1937 which Claud Cockburn's journal *The Week* denounced as a pro-Nazi plot designed to send Lord Halifax to Berlin against the will of the Foreign Secretary, Anthony Eden. *The Week* focused on Lady Alexandra's Cliveden connections, and her close friendship with her sister Cimmie's husband, Sir Oswald Mosley, Bt, the British Fascist leader, and accused her of pro-Nazism. The nickname "Baba Blackshirt" was coined.

In fact there was no "Cliveden plot" (Eden himself had been staying in the house) and Lady Alexandra had often advised "Tom" Mosley – on whom she had a sentimental schoolgirl crush – to drop his anti-Semitism. When Mosley was arrested in 1940, Lady Alexandra strove to ameliorate his conditions in Wormwood Scrubs; she later pulled every political string she could to try to obtain his release on compassionate grounds.

Lady Alexandra was a spectator rather than a major participant in the Abdication crisis, as Edward VIII had dropped Fruity in rather the same way that Prince Hal dropped Falstaff. After the Abdication, though, when Mountbatten found himself unable to be the Duke's best man, Fruity came to the rescue as a witness at the civil ceremony, and as best man at the Church of England ceremony. Lady Alexandra attended both occasions.

Lady Alexandra was present at the tea party at the British Embassy in Berlin in November 1937 when Joseph Goebbels attempted to persuade Lord Halifax to compel the cartoonist Low to tone down his anti-Hitler stance. On their return to London she introduced Halifax to Michael Wardell, Low's employer.

When the Second World War broke out Lady Alexandra volunteered for the St John Ambulance and during the Blitz worked at London Bridge Underground station. On free nights she slept in the old Turkish baths in the bowels of the Dorchester Hotel, where she joined Duff and Lady Diana Cooper, Sir George Clerk and the Halifaxes.

Her friendship with Lord Halifax dated back to his Viceroyalty of India. She was with Halifax on the night of the Norway Debate and advised him not to form a government. When Halifax returned to the Dorchester after the interview in which he ceded his position to Churchill, it was to Lady Alexandra that he first wrote. He in turn advised her, in his High Church way, not to divorce Fruity.

During the war Victor Cazalet and the hostesses Lady Colefax and Lady Cunard invited her to lunches and dinners where she collected gossip to send to Halifax in weekly letters. She also used to stay with Mr and Mrs Ronald Tree and Winston Churchill at Ditchley Park in Oxfordshire. She threw open her own beautiful manor house at Little Compton to American officers; by the end of the war some 1,500 had passed through.

In 1950 she was a guest of Sir Charles Peake at the Athens Embassy during the Ionian earthquake; this prompted her to join the Save the Children Fund. She poured her energy, organisational ability and powers of persuasion into the charity and helped to make it an international organisation.

India remained her first love. In the 1950s she helped the Indian government to cope with the children of the 80,000 refugees who fled Tibet when the Dalai Lama was expelled.

She was appointed CBE in 1975.

In 1955 her marriage to Fruity Metcalfe was dissolved. When he began to ail, Lady Alexandra dropped everything in order to nurse him. He died in 1957.

She retained in old age her incisive intelligence, which, combined with her charm and generosity, made her a delightful companion. She was always formidable, though (with a deep, authoritative voice), and the soul of discretion in the protection of the reputations of her own and other grand dynasties.

She drove her motorcar, which she referred to as "the motor", with disdain for the Highway Code and other motorists. Never coy about her age, she refused to bow to the passing years, and well into her eighth decade she was sighted para-sailing off Corfu. She retained both her looks and her patrician ways until her death.

August 9 1995

KATHLEEN HARRISON

KATHLEEN HARRISON, the actress who has died aged 103, was a superb exponent of comic Cockney roles.

A small, bright-eyed woman with a mischievous smile, she had the knack of putting life into stereotype parts, and could be moving as well as funny. George Bernard Shaw coached her as Eliza in *Pygmalion* in the 1920s, and having perfected her Cockney accent, Harrison went on during the next 50 years to play a string of maidservants, cooks, charwomen, nannies, working-class mothers and grandmothers. Her "Lawks" and "Lummes" and tendency to "mug" were memorably guyed by the brilliant television comedian Stanley Baxter.

"I've never played an ingenue in my life," she

observed in the 1960s, "or anything with a really romantic interest."

Her favourite writer was Dickens, and it showed in the tremendous relish with which she performed, and in her meticulous attention to detail: she prepared for her roles by keeping notes on encounters with landladies and other characters. Her performances were always fresh and inventive.

She won the nation's heart in the 1950s radio series *The Huggetts* as the humble, loving and uncomplaining Ma Huggett, wife to the no less admirable Joe (Jack Warner). When Ma Huggett announced "bacon and sausages" her husband would salivate noisily, and then aver that this was his favourite fare.

Kathleen Harrison found her widest audience in 1966, with *Mrs Thursday*, Ted Willis's television comedy about a charlady who inherited £10 million and a controlling interest in a huge company. In its first week the programme knocked *Coronation Street* off the top of the ratings.

Harrison was as surprised as anyone by this success: "With all those sex and violence plays on television," she said, "I didn't think there would be parts for people like me."

A shy person, she never cared for publicity. Nor did she seek to mingle with the celebrities with whom she played. "I like to come out of nowhere," she said, "act, and go back to nowhere."

Kathleen Harrison was born on February 23 1892 in Blackburn. Her father became borough engineer at Southwark, south London, and young Kathleen was educated at St Saviour's, St Olave's and Clapham High School.

From the moment she was taken to a music-hall as a small girl Kathleen wanted to go on stage. She enrolled at ADA (as RADA then was), and duly won the Du Maurier bronze medal. On leaving she immediately found work with professional touring companies.

In 1916 she abandoned acting to marry John Back, an instructor with the Western Telegraph cable company in Buenos Aries, and for nine years lived with him in Argentina, Madeira and Las Palmas. But her longing for the stage grew rather than diminished, and in 1925 she took a refresher course at RADA, where she was taught by George Bernard Shaw and Claude Rains. Shaw sent her to Covent Garden and Lisson Grove to hone her Cockney accent.

She acted in *The Constant Flirt* at Eastbourne in 1926, and the next year played a maidservant given to eavesdropping in *The Cage* at the Savoy – she ran away with the honours, supposedly the prerogative of Gwen Ffrangçon-Davies. The *Sunday Times* described Harrison's performance as "a gem of naturalistic humour".

During the next decade she won consistently good notices. In 1935 she landed her first notable part, as Mrs Terence in Emlyn Williams's *Night Must Fall* (Duchess). She then went to Hollywood to play the role in the film, which starred Robert Montgomery.

In 1942 she was Mrs Miller in Terence Rattigan's *Flare Path*, about Polish airmen in the RAF. She reprised the part on an ENSA tour to Africa and the Middle East in 1944.

"I can look and listen at and to Kathleen Harrison till the cows come home," Joyce Grenfell noted in her diary after seeing Harrison act in Cairo. "She is a joy. Her hands – full of washing and chores and kindnesses, hanging over her stomach with the elbows pressed to her side. And the bird movements of her incredible Cockney head."

At one stop on their tour, Harrison and the other women in the party found themselves regarded with more than ordinary curiosity by a long queue of servicemen outside the entrance. It transpired that they had been delivered to a brothel which bore the same name as their hotel.

Back in England, Harrison played Violet, the maid, in Terence Rattigan's *The Winslow Boy* (Lyric, 1946), a role she repeated two years later in the film, which starred Robert Donat and Margaret Leighton.

The Daily Telegraph described Harrison's portrait of a harassed mother with a drunken husband in *Flowers for the Living* (Duchess, 1950) as "tender, moving and extraordinarily faithful to the character". In John Galsworthy's *The Silver Box* (Lyric, Hammersmith, 1951) she brought great pathos to the part of a charwoman accused of theft in a Liberal MP's household. A few months later she began a two-year run as the kind-hearted Cockney Mrs Ashworth in the production of N. C. Hunter's *Waters of the Moon* at the Haymarket, starring Dame Edith Evans and Dame Sybil Thorndike.

In *All for Mary* (Duke of York's, 1954) she scored one of her greatest theatrical triumphs as Nanny Cartwright, dragged out of retirement to nurse two British men struck down with chickenpox in a French ski resort; the values of the nursery soon reassert themselves. "She gives the performance of her life," wrote W. A. Darlington in *The Daily Telegraph*, "and those who have admired the work of this superb comic actress will know how high a compliment that is." Once more she repeated the role for a film which came out in 1955.

In Noël Coward's *Nude With Violin* (Globe, 1957) Harrison for once played a fallen woman, as the Cockney ex-chorus girl opposite John Gielgud's rascally valet. In 1962 she appeared under Sir Laurence Olivier's direction at the Chichester Festival in the 17th-century comedy *The Chances*. She continued to perform on the stage into the 1970s.

The Huggetts first appeared in the film *Holiday Camp* (1947). Harrison's other films included *Hobson's Choice*, *The Ghoul*, *I Killed the Count*, *The Ghost Train*, *In Which We Serve*, *Oliver Twist*, *The Pickwick Papers* and *Cast A Dark Shadow*. Her television parts included Betsy Prig in *Martin Chuzzlewit* and Mrs Boffin in *Our Mutual Friend*.

John Back died in 1960; they had two sons (one of whom predeceased her) and a daughter.

December 8 1995

EVELYN LAYE

EVELYN LAYE, the actress and singer, who has died aged 95, was billed as the "Queen of Musical Comedy" between the two World Wars.

"Boo" Laye delighted audiences with her singing voice and with what the leading critic of the day, James Agate, called her "inventory of beauty". The affection she inspired endured all her life; and she was nearly always in work throughout a career that lasted well into her ninth decade.

In her heyday Evelyn Laye won rather more compliments for her acting than leading ladies in musical comedy generally receive. She could not help wondering whether she should not descend from the world of prettified musical romance to the sterner stuff of straight dramatic comedy. A decade or so later in plays by Sheridan, Maugham, Coward or Daphne du Maurier she had plenty of chances to show what a good actress she was.

Any critic who dared to utter a word against the former darling of Daly's when she turned "legitimate" risked lynching by her fans. She was never less than competent, but those who had seen her in *Helen* or *Bitter Sweet* (in which she sang "I'll See You Again" so memorably) could hardly consider her talent as a straight actress worthy of comparison.

For "Boo" had been born, so to speak, in a musical comedy trunk; it was her destiny to express to perfection the British ideal of feminine beauty in her blonde, blue-eyed, porcelain frailty, with a naughty smile at the corner of her lips.

Elsie Evelyn Lay (she added the "e" later) was born in London into a theatrical family on July 10 1900 and educated at Brighton and Folkestone. Her father, Gilbert, was an actor-manager and her mother, Evelyn Stuart, a popular principal boy in pantomime. It was in her arms that young Evelyn made her first public appearance during a tour of *Charley's Aunt*. Neither parent wanted her to make the stage her career; nevertheless at 15 she persuaded them to let her leave school.

After such openings as film crowd work at Twickenham, she made a minor breakthrough with the non-speaking part of Nang-Ping in *Mr Wu* at the Brighton

Royal. *Mr Wu* was not a musical but it led to work in a succession of revues, such as *Honi Soit* at the East Ham Palace, and *Oh, Caesar* at the Edinburgh Lyceum. When she turned up in *Goody Two-Shoes* at Portsmouth in 1917, a West End talent scout booked her for the Gaiety, then enjoying an Indian summer after its Edwardian heyday of aristocratic stage-door-johnnies.

At the Gaiety, Evelyn Laye was launched in *The Beauty Spot*, *Going Up*, *The Kiss Call*, *The Shop Girl*, *Nighty-Night* and *Phi-Phi*. In the Twenties she became the toast of the West End in hits like *The Merry Widow*, *Madame Pompadour*, *The Dollar Princess*, *Merely Molly*, *Lilac Time*, *Blue Eyes* and *The New Moon*.

For her those were days of orchids and Lagondas, of a grand piano and dining table in her dressing room – and of publicity. In 1930 the popular newspapers gave front-page coverage to Evelyn Laye's divorce from her husband, Sonnie Hale, whom she had married in 1926. She cited Jessie Matthews, the young entertainer, who had just divorced her own husband, the actor Henry Lytton. In the meantime, Evelyn Laye had taken up with the actor Frank Lawton, whom she married in 1934. Her ill feelings towards Jessie Matthews endured for many years.

During the turmoil of her personal life, Evelyn Laye's professional triumphs continued, with a debut on Broadway in Coward's charming operetta *Bitter Sweet* at the Ziegfeld Theater. Her success in the role was repeated in London in 1930–31.

She was tempted over to Hollywood with a record offer of £1,000 a week to be the apple of a dull count's eye in *One Heavenly Night*. Sam Goldwyn, who produced it, said of its leading lady, "sometimes she worked all night, and yet would not give in. Everybody loves her in Hollywood."

It was the same in London and New York. Of her performance in the title role of A. P. Herbert's *Helen*, Agate said that she brought "competence to the hard business of acting" – high praise from a critic who notoriously detested musical comedy.

When she returned to England from another tour of America in 1938 she expressed herself weary of sugar-and-spice heroines and turned to the variety halls. She played the Palladium for the first time.

Evelyn Laye wanted to prove she could be funny in her own right after having so many scripts tailored for her. Although she was not actually all that funny (it was her innocent charm that counted), she knew by now how to hold her own.

During the Second World War Evelyn Laye was almost as busy as she had been in the First. In Cochran's revue, *Lights Up*, and *The Belle of New York* she remained, as a critic had once put it, "the only English musical comedy actress who can sing, dance, act and still be a lady".

After the war, however, her career slowed down. Going straight seemed a natural thing to do. She toured as Lady Teazle in *The School for Scandal* and in the title role of Coward's mock-18th-century comedy, *The Marquise*.

Things became difficult after she was turned down for the part of Anna in *The King and I*. It was back to provincial variety halls. She was even booed at Belfast, but she never gave in.

At last, in 1954, she made her musical comeback at the Hippodrome, opposite Anton Walbrook, in *Wedding in Paris*. On the first night her fans excitedly chanted her nickname: "Boo, Boo, Boo", as they had 30 years before.

In 1965 she played Lady Catherine in *The Circle*, with Frank Lawton. Lady Catherine in Maugham's comedy is a raddled old hag without trace of the beauty which had made her famous in her day. Evelyn Laye at 65 did what she could to look raddled.

In cheerful 1960s musicals such as *Strike A Light* and *Charlie Girl* (in which she temporarily replaced Anna Neagle) the natural gaiety of the former Gaiety Girl seemed more at home, and she enjoyed another long run as the corrosive mother-in-law in *No Sex Please, We're British*.

In 1992 she appeared on stage at the London Palladium, when Sir John Mills led more than 100 stars in a salute to her career. She also took part in a star-studded tribute to mark the 40th anniversary of the Queen's accession.

She was appointed CBE in 1973. She published an autobiography, *Boo to My Friends*.

Her second husband died in 1969.

February 19 1996

WILLIAM BULWER-LONG

WILLIAM BULWER-LONG, who has died aged 58, was one of the greatest countrymen of his generation and a quintessential Englishman.

He stood and fought for what was at the heart of country life – landscape, farm, village, country house, country church and country sport – and his deep love of archetypal England was infectious. Through the uncompromising example he set at his village and estate of Heydon in north Norfolk – as near to the pastoral idyll as anywhere in the land – he influenced politicians, landowners, farmers and local people in an understanding of the country and how it was possible to combine the best conservation practices with profitable farming.

A few days before he died he heard that he had won the Royal Agricultural Society's 1996 Bledisloe Gold Medal for Estate Management.

William Hanslip Bulwer-Long was born on May 9 1937, the son of Brigadier "Boy" Long and Molly Bulwer, heiress to the Heydon estate, which had come into her family's hands through a marriage in 1780.

Young William was educated at Wellington and Sandhurst. In 1957 he was commissioned into the 9th Queen's Royal Lancers; he served with them for nearly 10 years and was an extremely popular officer.

He was a man of great physical prowess, representing his regiment at athletics, boxing, swimming, hockey and rugby, and the Army on the Cresta Run. He also read and wrote poetry and could quote, unerringly, long passages from Siegfried Sassoon, Wilfred Owen and Whyte Melville.

Always most at home in the saddle, when Bulwer-Long was ADC to General Mike West in York in the early 1960s he rode for the trainer Mick Easterby. "William was my chief nagsman," Easterby recalled. "I could put him up on anything – he rode every bad horse in the yard. 'You'll kill me Mick,' he said, but he kept on coming back for more."

Bulwer-Long went on to beat the great Major Guy

Cunard on more than one occasion in the tightest of finishes, and in the end won 35 races (33 point-to-points and two under National Hunt Rules), including the Grand Military Hunter Chase in 1963.

Bulwer-Long's Army career equipped him with an extraordinary efficiency which, combined with his philosophy, enabled him to carry out what most would only have dreamed of.

In 1962 he married Sarah Jane Rawlinson, who had been brought up in the beautiful but crumbling Elizabethan mansion, Heydon Hall. Her father, Sir Frederick Rawlinson, had rented it from Bulwer-Long's parents, who lived in the village. For a long time the vast Heydon Hall had stood empty and derelict, the surrounding park and estate lying tattered at the edges. William and Sarah Jane Bulwer-Long determined to rescue her childhood home and his family seat, and to resurrect the estate.

From the outset – "with 10 quid in the bank" – Bulwer-Long stuck to his principles. He hung on to his hedges when all over Norfolk others were ripping them out; he hung on to his water-meadows when others were reclaiming them for cereal. He restored the houses and cottages in the village with a gentle approach; it became the first conservation area in Norfolk. He let none of his estate houses to weekenders but to young married locals. He restored farm buildings for no immediate financial gain, but because he believed it was in the long-term interests of the estate and those who depended on it.

Bulwer-Long considered himself a guardian more than an owner. The interior designer David Mlinaric recalls: "When dealing with the large-scale restoration of the hall he never compromised; it was his own and Sarah's vision of how to have the house for their stage in its story. For them it was not a burden, but a pleasure, individual and loved."

Bulwer-Long's philanthropic approach not only won him conservation awards but also led to many appointments. He was appointed Deputy Lieutenant of Norfolk in 1992 and served as High Sheriff, chairman of the Norfolk Country Landowners Association and a council member of the Royal Norfolk Agricultural Association.

He also contributed to the good management of racing. He was a Steward of the Jockey Club from 1991 to 1993 and simultaneously chairman of the Point to Point Liaison Committee. He insisted that all aspiring trainers produce a business plan, a concept alien to some of them, but very much in their own interest.

His concern with the welfare of riders was paramount. He was both a director and steward of his local racecourse, Fakenham, as well as of both courses at Newmarket. He was also a steward at Great Yarmouth and Aintree.

The Marquess of Hartington, chairman of the British Horseracing Board, said: "William held two ideals in all his work for racing and point-to-pointing. It must be straight and it must be fun. That was the man."

Bulwer-Long was unassuming and modest, with a delightful grin. He was a fearless and legendary rider across Leicestershire and hunted regularly with the Cottesmore and Quorn. His regular articles on country lore in the *Eastern Daily Press* were widely appreciated. He was the most loyal of friends and generous of hosts.

He is survived by his wife. They had two sons and a daughter.

March 1 1996

GEORGE BURNS

GEORGE BURNS, the comedian who has died aged 100, was the diminutive, cigar-smoking straight-man to his wife Gracie Allen in the long-running *Burns and Allen Show* on television.

Determinedly modest about his own role in the series – that of a patient husband trying to cope with his scatter-brained wife – Burns claimed that Gracie Allen was solely responsible for their enduring success. "Without Gracie I would never have stayed in showbusiness," he once claimed, "I would have got out and become a cutter of ladies' dresses."

After Gracie Allen's death in 1964, Burns continued as a solo comic, his impeccable timing and delivery making him perennially popular as a raconteur, and much in demand on television spectaculars. Having outlived contemporaries such as Jack Benny and Groucho Marx, he became a Great American Institution, often referred to as "the Dean of Comedy".

In 1975, after Jack Benny's death, Burns took over his friend's role as a broken-down old comic in Neil Simon's film *The Sunshine Boys*. "My last film was in 1939," he recalled, "my agent didn't want me to suffer from over-exposure." Starring opposite Walter Matthau, he proved a triumphant success, and at the age of 80 became the oldest winner of an Oscar, as best supporting actor.

One of nine children of an impoverished Jewish family, he was born Nathan Birnbaum on January 20 1896 in New York's lower East Side. His father was cantor in the synagogue, and at the age of six young Nathan sought to exploit his own vocal potential by forming the Pee Wee Quartet, a group of child performers who sang and told jokes on street corners. "I wasn't too successful," he remembered. "My mother used to wear this second-hand wig, and she got more laughs than I did."

Birnbaum changed his name to Willy Delight, and in 1916 began working as a trick roller-skater on the Keith Vaudeville Circuit. He later left the theatre and, as Pedro Lopez, set up as a teacher of ballroom dancing.

He tried several other names – Captain Betts, Jed Jackson, Buddy Lanks – before appearing at the Union Theater in 1923 as George Burns, comedian. Under this guise he worked with a series of partners and gained a reputation for being "difficult" and "a perfectionist".

Later in 1923 he met Gracie Allen, who was then working as a singer, billed as "The Irish Colleen". When it was suggested that they should get together friends warned her off: "Burns is murder." But Burns and Allen made their debut in 1924. In the original act Burns told the jokes. "It was a disaster," he admitted. "I got no laughs and Gracie got laughs for doing nothing at all."

So he decided to let Allen have the punchlines. "I just asked Gracie a question," he explained, "and she kept talking for the next 37 years." The couple were married in 1926 and rapidly became one of the most

George Burns

popular double acts in the country. "It was a perfect act," Burns reminisced, "a perfect marriage, a perfect everything."

In 1932 Burns and Allen arrived in Britain to make their radio debut with the BBC. Initially signed to do one show for £15, they proved popular enough to be retained for the rest of the week.

Eddie Cantor heard the broadcast and offered them a contract with his touring variety show in the United States. After this, they were offered their own radio show, and continued to broadcast with CBS for the next 18 years. With programmes regularly attracting 45 million listeners, they were among the best-paid entertainers in America, earning $4,000 a week.

The couple made their film debut in 1932 in *The Big Broadcast* and subsequently appeared, on average, in two films a year for Paramount. These included *College Humour*, *We're Not Dressing* and *A Damsel in Distress*. Their last film for Paramount was *Honolulu*, which starred Eleanor Powell and Robert Young.

At 45 Burns was too old for active service in the Second World War, and continued his radio broadcasts with Gracie Allen. Then in 1950, without in any way altering the format which they had established on the wireless, they made their first television show. As successful in the new medium as the old, they continued until Gracie retired in 1958.

Later that year Burns made his first solo appearance since 1916 in *The George Burns Show*. "I had to start learning to be a comic in 1958", he observed. "Before that all I did was stand next to Gracie smoking a cigar."

Gracie Allen died in 1964. Burns never married

325

again, and made almost daily visits to his wife's grave. "I don't think it's morbid," he explained. "I miss her so I go visit and tell her what I've been doing."

Later in 1964 Burns began producing television programmes, including *No Time for Sergeants* and *Wendy and Me*, in which he starred with Connie Stevens.

He also featured as a guest in various television "specials", including *Jack Benny's New Look* (1969). He enjoyed appearing with Jack Benny. "Jack always listened when I sang," he explained, "and I always listened to him play the violin. That's how we stayed friends."

Having re-established his film career at the age of 79 with *The Sunshine Boys*, Burns went on to play the title role (clad in a football cap) in the comedy *Oh God!*, attempting to send His message to the world via an inept supermarket manager (John Denver).

There were two sequels and he also appeared in *Sergeant Pepper's Lonely Hearts Club Band* (1978). None of these films did very well, but Burns was undisturbed: "I just like to be working," he said.

Burns was still much in demand on television in the 1980s, and published various books, culminating in *A Hundred Years, A Hundred Stories*, issued to celebrate his centennial.

In his 80s and 90s Burns developed an enthusiasm for taking out young girls. "They sit with me in a quiet corner of a restaurant doing their homework. My tuxedo is older than they are. After the date I go home, take off my *toupée* and put it on its block. The block looks great; I look lousy."

Burns was still appearing live on stage in 1993, at the age of 97, and was so confident of reaching his 100th birthday that he accepted a booking at the London

Palladium for January 20 1996. "I'm taking care of myself," he said, "I can't afford to lose a booking. Every day I get up early and work until 10, I have lunch with friends, play a little bridge and then usually go to a party or a restaurant in the evening and I'm in bed by 10." As for the secret of his longevity: "I dance close to young girls and smoke 15 cheap cigars a day."

A bad fall at 98 forced him to slow down, and he had to cancel his date at the London Palladium. "The Brits wouldn't give me a three-year deal," he complained. But he still enjoyed his bridge. "As long as I can smoke a cigar, my soup is hot, and my Martini is cold, I'm fine," he said.

George Burns and Gracie Allen adopted a son and a daughter.

March 11 1996

JOHN SNAGGE

JOHN SNAGGE, the broadcaster who has died aged 91, was one of the best-loved voices of the BBC, most familiar for his annual commentaries on the Boat Race, which he covered from 1931 to 1980. He would time the strokes with a throaty chant of "in, out".

In 1935 the *Manchester Guardian* commented that the lead which Cambridge soon established in that year's race allowed small chance for an exciting commentary. However, Snagge was an Oxford man and his "scrupulous determination not to give Oxford more than their share of his attention or praise adds a pleasant and amusing note to his broadcast".

In 1938 his sound commentary accompanied the first televising of the race. In 1949 he was heard to say: "Oxford are ahead. No Cambridge are ahead. I don't know who's ahead – it's either Oxford or Cambridge." At the end of his last Boat Race commentary on Easter Saturday 1980 he presented the trophy.

It had been Snagge's idea to present a sovereign minted in 1829, the year of the first race, for the presidents to toss. "Someone had the brilliant idea that it should be kept by the losing president," he recalled, "so that the race was being run to *lose* money – you can't get more amateur than that."

In a career lasting from 1924 to 1965, Snagge's imperturbable tones were broadcast from almost every kind of public event. In 1938 he made the first broadcast from within a diver's suit. In the same year he also spoke to the nation from a bucket 120 feet down a shaft in the Derwent hills, from a bareback circus ride and from mid-air as he jumped through a window into a sheet in a firefighting exercise.

During the Second World War he announced the attack on Pearl Harbor, the capture of Rome and D-Day. He prepared for months for VE Day. "When it finally happened," he recollected, "May 7 and 8 almost merged into one. Churchill was expected to speak at 6 p.m. then cancelled it. Great anticlimax; except that at midnight the chap in charge of the various transmitters came into the duty room and said: 'I wouldn't bother sleeping much if I were you.'

"Word of VE Day came early from No 10. I just thought, thank God it's over. At nine I announced the King. Then we did messages from Eisenhower, Alexander, Mountbatten and Montgomery. At 10.45 p.m., when broadcasting ended, I was summoned by Sir William Haley, the Director-General, to his office for a glass of sherry." He suddenly remembered it was his 41st birthday.

When working with outside broadcast in the 1930s he had to circumvent a ban by the Football Association on transmission of the Cup Final at Wembley."We had to pay our way through the turnstiles, and then leave at intervals to report on the match by microphone at a house rented nearby."

In 1936 he made successful broadcasts from the *Queen Mary* during her maiden voyage, speaking on air from 28 microphones set up in the first-class dining-room, the swimming pool and the crow's nest.

After the Coronation in 1953 he received an apology from the Archbishop of Canterbury. "He said he turned over two pages at once," Snagge remembered, "and that I must have had a heart attack when, instead of introducing 'All people who on Earth do dwell', he said: 'Let us pray.' I told him that nobody in the Abbey was praying half as hard as I was."

Snagge's voice was once described as rumbling up "from lungs surely bred on inhaling only the best of tobacco or having sniffed the best of port". Snagge himself recalled that his own "Voice of Doom" was reserved for especially portentous announcements.

John Merrick Mordaunt Snagge was born on May 8 1904, the second son of Judge Sir Mordaunt Snagge. He was educated at Winchester and Pembroke College, Oxford, where by his own admission he did not excel academically. Nor did he row for the university.

He joined the BBC in 1924 straight from Oxford as assistant station director at Stoke-on-Trent. His voice and aptitude led in 1928 to promotion as announcer at Savoy Hill.

The Corporation was not always an easy place in which to work. As a young announcer Snagge was paid £350 a year. One day Sir John Reith, the director-general, summoned him and his colleagues to tell them that a maximum of £500 would in future be fixed for an announcer's salary.

"I told him I could not accept a fixed ceiling and the meeting ended frigidly," Snagge recalled. "Half an hour later he sent for me again and asked what I had meant. I told him I could not accept a ceiling for a job in which I might remain for life. He agreed, but he warned me never again to argue with him in public."

Snagge was, however, intensely loyal to the BBC and applied his public school code of honour to all he did. He was a good mixer in the pubs and clubs around Savoy Hill (and, later, Broadcasting House) but made no secret of his preference for integrity above personal gain.

Although more at home at the microphone than at a desk, he filled a succession of administrative jobs, eventually becoming Head of Presentation (Sound).

In retirement Snagge bought a small lake near his home at Stoke Poges, Buckinghamshire, in which to row as exercise. An early member of the Lord's Taverners, the cricketing charity, he was thrice chairman, and president in 1952 and 1964.

He was appointed OBE in 1944.

He married first, in 1936, Eileen Joscelyne, who died in 1980. He married secondly, in 1983, Joan Wilson, who died in 1992.

When Snagge commented on his last Boat Race, the *Radio Times* carried some verses by Roger Woddis:

Yours is the kind of soldier-scholar face
That seems designed for a saluting-base.
Youth goes; the voice has mercifully remained,
God's gift, you say, and Corporation-trained.

March 27 1996

SIR FITZROY MACLEAN, BT

SIR FITZROY MACLEAN, 1st Bt and 15th Captain and Hereditary Keeper of Dunconnel in the Isles of the Sea, who has died aged 85, led an extraordinarily glamorous career as diplomat, soldier, politician, writer and traveller.

The most crucial period of his life began in July 1943, when Winston Churchill chose him for a secret mission to Tito, leader of the Partisans in Yugoslavia. What was required, Churchill had informed General Alexander, was "a daring ambassador-leader with these hardy and hunted guerrillas".

At that time there was already fierce rivalry between Mihailovic's Royalist Cetniks and Tito's Communist Partisans for the leadership of the resistance to the German occupation forces. Tito accused the Cetniks of attacking Partisans instead of Germans, and of co-operating with the Germans instead of fighting them.

The Foreign Office, anxious to prevent the emergence of a Communist regime after the war, was wary of the Partisans. At the same time the Special Operations Executive wanted to bring all resistance operations under its own control. When Maclean was finally able to read the SOE files, he discovered that the enemy was referred to by the initials PX. He assumed, at first, that this was code for the Abwehr. But he was corrected: "PX? Oh, that's the Foreign Office."

Fortunately, Churchill, at least, had a single, clear aim in view. "My task", wrote Maclean after seeking the Prime Minister's instructions, "was simply to find out who was killing the most Germans and suggest means by which we could help them to kill more."

On the ground in occupied Yugoslavia, Maclean became a firm friend and passionate admirer of Tito. The Partisan leader, he believed, was "probably the greatest guerrilla/resistance fighter of all time", and was operating in country which maximised opportunities for harassing the enemy.

Furthermore, Maclean observed, the Partisans were sustained by a creed. "Few ideas", he wrote, "equal revolutionary Communism in its strength, its persistence and its power over the individual."

Maclean urged that, if Britain wanted to prevent Tito from becoming a Soviet puppet, she would have to abandon Mihailovic. His report to this effect in November 1943 carried weight, not merely because it was powerfully argued, but also because it sorted well with Churchill's preconceptions.

After the liberation of Yugoslavia in the winter of 1944 to 1945, Mihailovic, who by this stage had also been abandoned by King Peter, tried to hide from the now-dominant Partisans. He was captured and, in 1946, hanged for treason. When Tito established a Communist state, doubts grew whether Maclean should have accepted Tito's version of Cetnik activities quite so uncritically.

Against this, it was argued that, had Tito not been

in such a powerful position at the end of the war, Russian armies might well have swept through Yugoslavia and established themselves on the Adriatic. Maclean's intervention seemed further justified in 1948, when Tito defied Russia and was expelled from the Comintern.

It is possible that, without Maclean's friendship, Tito might never have gained the confidence to open up this first major crack in the Communist bloc. "What is happening today in the USSR", Maclean observed in 1992, "was made possible by Tito."

As for his own role, Maclean insisted that he was merely riding the course of history, not changing it. "People who glibly talk about the British 'creating' Tito have no idea of the complexity of events in the 1940s, of the ferocious passions, the bloodshed and the chaos. Part of Tito's greatness was imposing order on all this."

Maclean, too, had to impose himself, on the disparate elements under his own command. "Fitzroy was immensely physically fit," remembered Mike Parker, who was in charge of supplies in Yugoslavia. "He had immense confidence, was charismatic, knew the Establishment inside out. Extraordinarily nice man. Although he was firm and clear in his aims, he never raised his voice. When he asked you to do something, it was quite clear that he meant *now*. He loved peers of the realm and famous people and liked to collect them, but of course he had to have a few people like . . . me to do the work. We regarded ourselves as second-class citizens – not that he gave that impression."

Even so, there were those who resented Maclean's speedy elevation from lieutenant to brigadier through his contacts in high places. Maclean gave himself more trouble by recruiting Randolph Churchill, the Prime Minister's son, for his mission to Yugoslavia. Not only was the younger Churchill extraordinarily difficult and quarrelsome on his own account; he in his turn recruited Evelyn Waugh.

With his commitment to Roman Catholicism and his horror of Bolshevism, Waugh took an instant dislike to his commander, referring with a sneer to "the Maclean youth centre at Stalingrad". In his diary he wrote: "Maclean dour, unprincipled, ambitious, probably very wicked; shaved head and devil's ears."

Waugh also propagated the notion that Tito was a woman. On that issue, however, Maclean was able to score heavily. When Waugh was introduced to the Partisan leader he was for once left speechless by Tito's question: "And why do you think I am a woman?"

Later, after the Foreign Office and the War Office had been provoked by Waugh's leaking of official secrets to English Catholics, Maclean helped to save him from a court martial. In truth, Maclean was tough and ruthless enough to handle even the most brilliant dissident. His willpower was scarcely less evident in the making of his own career.

Fitzroy Hew Maclean was born on March 11 1911 in Egypt, where his father was serving with the Cameron Highlanders. "Thank God I am a Maclean," runs the family motto, and this pride in ancestry has gone with a consistently martial strain.

The name indicates "the sons of Gillean" – that is Gillean the Battle-Axe, a 13th-century warrior who commanded the territories of Duart, Lochbuie and Ardgour. In the 17th and 18th centuries the Macleans fought bravely for the Jacobite cause.

"Gentlemen," exhorted Sir John Maclean of Duart at the battle of Sheriffmuir in 1715, "this is a day we have long wished to see. Yonder stand MacChailein Mor for King George. Here stands Maclean for King James. Gentlemen, charge!"

Charles Maclean, Fitzroy's father, had passed out of Sandhurst in the same group as Winston Churchill. Both were near the bottom of the list. "Many congratulations on becoming an officer and a gentleman," wrote Churchill when Charles Maclean was commissioned into the Cameron Highlanders, "don't let the double promotion go to your head." Maclean went on to win the DSO in the First World War. He married the daughter of Lt-Cdr Royle, RN.

Young Fitzroy was brought up in Scotland, India and Italy, so that a life of adventure became as natural to him as his roots in the Maclean clan. From his mother he gained a love and facility for languages.

Maclean was educated at Eton and King's College, Cambridge. Afterwards, in 1933, he passed into the Foreign Office, where he became known as "Fitzwhiskers", to distinguish him from his contemporary Donald, or "Fancy Pants", Maclean (the Stalinist spy).

He spent three years in the embassy in Paris before going to Moscow, where he learned to speak Russian fluently. He also travelled by himself through the Central Asian provinces of the Soviet Union, and wrote such an enthralling account of his adventures that the Foreign Secretary had it circulated through Whitehall. In 1949 an expanded version was included in *Eastern Approaches*, the story of Maclean's life from 1937 to 1945.

On the outbreak of the Second World War Maclean was not allowed to join the Army because his post in the

Diplomatic Service was a reserved occupation. But in 1941 he discovered that if he declared his wish to stand as a parliamentary candidate he would be obliged to resign from the Foreign Service.

Having stated this intention and handed in his letter of resignation to the Permanent Under-Secretary, he took a cab to the nearest recruiting office and enlisted as a private in the Cameron Highlanders.

"At meal times we threw ourselves on our food like a pack of wolves," he remembered of his early days in the Army; "and wherever we were given a chance we slept, indoors, out of doors, in broad daylight, in the middle of a room full of men shouting, singing and swearing." But Maclean was unconcerned: "At Eton, you know, there is a tougher ambience."

After several months he was given a commission, but, on learning that the Foreign Office was now trying to get him back from the Army, he renewed his efforts to get into Parliament. At that time there was a fortuitous by-election in Lancaster, and Maclean, having obtained a few days leave, won the Conservative nomination.

After a frenzied month of electioneering, Maclean was astonished to find himself elected. Before he took his seat, however, the Army sent him on a mission to Cairo, where he bumped into Colonel David Stirling, who had just formed the Special Air Service for raiding enemy installations deep in the Western Desert. Maclean joined, and was soon engaged in hazardous operations.

On one occasion he and a few others, including Randolph Churchill, made their way with a truck-load of explosives to Benghazi, which was in enemy hands, with the intention of blowing up installations in the harbour. When they were challenged by an Italian sentry, Maclean informed him they were staff officers and demanded to see the guard commander.

When the latter appeared, Maclean upbraided him in fluent Italian for dereliction of duty, saying that they had been walking around all night in the area for which the guard was responsible without once before being challenged or asked to produce identity cards.

"For all you know," added Maclean, "we might have been British saboteurs carrying explosives." When the guard commander tittered incredulously, Maclean said he would be let off this time but he had better not be caught napping again.

At the end of the desert campaign Maclean was sent to Persia, where he frustrated a coup by the pro-German General Zahidi. Soon afterwards he was summoned to London to be briefed about his mission to Yugoslavia.

At the end of the Second World War Maclean was given the local rank of Major-General and entrusted with the controversial assignment of heading the Special Refugees Commissions in Austria, Germany and Italy.

On the completion of these duties he returned to take up his parliamentary seat. He represented Lancaster from 1941 to 1959, and Bute and North Ayrshire from 1959 to 1974.

Maclean was a poor speaker, and though he was a member of the Conservative Group in the Council of Europe Assembly from 1951 to 1952, his career in the Commons languished.

"I've always wanted to give you a job," Churchill told Maclean in 1954, not long before he resigned as Prime Minister, "but they [the Whips] wouldn't let me. Now I'm old and finished and I'm going to give it to you whatever they say. How would you like to be Under-Secretary of State for War?" Maclean liked it very much, and before long he was caught up in the drama of the Suez.

However, he did not survive Eden's fall. "I was sorry to lose Fitzroy Maclean," noted Harold Macmillan in 1957, "but he really is so hopeless in the House that he is a passenger in office . . . a great pity since he is so able."

Maclean was created a Baronet, and retired to the estate he had purchased at Strachur, in Argyllshire by the shores of Loch Fyne. He and his wife ran an inn in the neighbourhood, and Maclean turned out a succession of books, although none of them received the acclaim of *Eastern Approaches*.

In the 1960s Maclean carved out a new career for himself on television, but he never developed a relaxed manner on screen. He travelled frequently to Russia, whether to make films, explore unknown areas, enjoy his beloved Georgia, or to carry out investigations on behalf of the British Government. In 1985 he advised Mrs Thatcher to cultivate close relations with Mikhail Gorbachev.

Previously, as chairman of the Great Britain–USSR Association during the Brezhnev era, Maclean had sometimes been accused of being soft on Russia. But he strongly criticised the invasion of Czechoslovakia and the imprisonment of dissidents, and on numerous occasions warned the Russians of the damage they were doing to their own interests by antagonising those who were willing to be well disposed.

From 1962 to 1974 Maclean was with the Conservative Group in the Council of Europe and Western European Assemblies, and during the same period a member of the Conservative Group in the North Atlantic Assembly, where he was chairman of the military committee from 1964 to 1974.

As a schoolboy Maclean had been rather small and unathletic, but later grew tall, though somewhat lanky and stooping. His charm was as legendary as his ability to endure hardship.

He would have liked, as his friend Lord Henniker observed, to have been "a Lothario in a kilt, but he wasn't. He's a very good old thing in most ways – a very moral old thing. He talked a lot about women but it didn't come naturally."

Maclean was appointed CBE in 1944, and a Knight of the Thistle in 1993. His many foreign decorations included the Croix de Guerre, the Order of Kutusov, and the Yugoslav Partisan Star (1st Class).

Fitzroy Maclean married, in 1946, Veronica Phipps, a celebrated cookery writer, the widow of Alan Phipps and the second daughter of the 16th Lord Lovat. They had two sons, the elder of whom, Charles, born in 1946, succeeds to the baronetcy.

June 18 1996

MOLLY KEANE

MOLLY KEANE, who has died aged 91, will have a place among the immortals of literature as the last of the great novelists of Ascendancy Ireland; the last of a line which begins with Maria Edgeworth and includes Charles Lever, George Moore, Somerville and Ross, and Elizabeth Bowen.

No future novelist will be able to follow Molly Keane into this exalted company – in which the women very much outnumber the men, a sign of how far the world of the Ascendancy was from being an all-male preserve. No writer of her stature is old enough to have known that now-vanished Ascendancy world at first hand.

She was born Mary Nesta Skrine on July 20 1904, the younger daughter of Walter Clarmont Skrine, then living near the Curragh Army camp in Co. Kildare with his wife, the former Agnes Shakespear Higginson. Her father came of a long-established Somerset family, which has been seated at Warleigh Manor, near Bath, since 1634. Her mother's family has been established in Ulster since the early 17th century, when an ancestor, John Higginson, was described as "a gentleman that kept high company".

Agnes Skrine wrote poetry under the name "Moira O'Neill" and was a woman of all-round brilliance, liked and admired by a large circle of friends but uneasy in her relationship with her younger daughter. One can recognise in her the irresistible Cynthia in *The Rising Tide*, one of the best of her daughter's pre-war novels, as well as in the mothers of Aroon in *Good Behaviour* and of April, May and June in *Time after Time*; the mother–daughter relationship being a major theme in both novels.

Molly Keane's father appears to have been an amiable if not very positive figure, judging from the father of Nicandra in her last novel, *Loving and Giving*, who, on her own admission, is partly based on him.

When Molly was about three, her father bought Ballyrankin, a spacious early Victorian country house situated above the River Slaney in Co. Wexford. There she grew up in a typical Ascendancy ambience of horses and hunting, receiving (according to her account) no education and believing that there was "no pleasure to compare with hunt balls and race meetings".

The burning of Ballyrankin during the "Troubles" of the early 1920s, which caused her father to declare that he would rather be "shot in Ireland than die in England", made surprisingly little impact on the young Molly. In *Good Behaviour* the upheavals of those years do not impinge on her narrative, while in *Loving and Giving* they are referred to only casually.

In *The Rising Tide* Cynthia turns the civil war to her advantage: the fact that "it was not possible to be out late at night, where neighbours dined, there they must sleep" meant that her lover could "lie five nights out of the seven" at her house without anyone thinking very much of it.

Molly Keane's view of Ireland during the Troubles is in contrast to that of Elizabeth Bowen, who, although *her* home, Bowen's Court, escaped burning, burned it in her imagination in *The Last September*. Both views are historically true, depending on which part of Ireland the novelist had in mind.

In Molly Keane's own words, "It was my crying need for money (dress allowance £30) that sent me to writing." Because she felt that young men would not want to dance with a girl known to be "brainy", she wrote under a pseudonym.

First she used the *nom de plume* of Jane Fairyhouse (after the racecourse), but then she spotted a name over a cross-roads pub near Ballyrankin on her way back from hunting – "M. J. Farrell".

This was the name that appeared on her first novel, the suitably named *Young Entry* (1920). Altogether she published 11 novels under this pseudonym between then and the early 1950s.

She achieved her first success with *Conversation Piece* (1928) and was no less successful with *Devoted Ladies* (1934); with *Full House* (1935), which was chosen as *Evening Standard* Book of the Month; and with *The Rising Tide* (1937).

She won the admiration of her fellow writers. Compton Mackenzie thought *Devoted Ladies* "infernally good". Hugh Walpole ranked her among "the best half-dozen younger women novelists". Barbara Pym recorded in her diary in 1943: "Afternoon in the garden reading an excellent novel *Two Days in Aragon* by M. J. Farrell. Very penetrating – about sorrow going to the stomach too!"

In her acute observation of character, particularly of feminine character, and in her evocation of atmosphere and place, Molly Keane, as a writer, resembled her close friend and long-distance neighbour in Ireland, Elizabeth Bowen. But in other respects she comes nearer to Somerville and Ross, notably in her feeling for Irish country life and her sense of comedy.

"Black comedy, perhaps, but with some of the truth in it," was how she later summed up her own literary achievements. "And the pity I feel for the kind of people I lived with and laughed with in the happy maligned '30s."

In 1933 she collaborated with Snaffles, the sporting artist, on *Red Letter Days* (a collection of essays), in which she told many good stories. One concerned a dispute following a "farmers' race", when the rider who came second objected to the winner on the grounds that he was more of a gentleman than a farmer because he owned "a lake with a swan on it".

Molly Keane followed up her success as a novelist by writing for the stage. When she showed the script of her play *Spring Meeting* to the actor John Perry – another scion of the Ascendancy – he suggested various changes and "added his name to the title page" before submitting it to his close friend and partner Hugh "Binkie" Beaumont of H. M. Tennent Productions.

Spring Meeting, directed by John Gielgud, had a good run at the Ambassadors Theatre and went to New York in 1938. Molly Keane and John Perry collaborated a second time in *Treasure Hunt*, performed at the Apollo in 1949. Her other plays included *Ducks and Drakes* (Apollo, 1941) and *Guardian Angel* (Gate Theatre, Dublin, 1944).

James Agate said of her plays: "I would back this impish writer to hold her own against Noël Coward himself." Molly Keane numbered Coward among her friends, along with Dame Peggy Ashcroft and Sir John Gielgud, who directed all her plays.

In 1938 Molly married Robert Lumley Keane, a nephew of Sir John Keane, a Co. Waterford baronet who had the distinction of serving not only in the original Senate of the Irish Free State (in which the Ascendancy was well represented), but also as one of the few Ascendancy figures in de Valera's reconstituted Senate.

Although her husband was six years her junior, her marriage – unlike the marriages of many of her characters

– was blissfully happy; but it came to an untimely end in 1946 when "Bobby" Keane died unexpectedly at the age of 35 after an operation.

Molly's creative energy was gravely affected by this blow, and the responsibility of bringing up two young daughters on not much money left her no time for writing. Her literary output had virtually dried up by the beginning of the 1950s, although she attempted to make a comeback in the early 1960s.

This, however, was not a period sympathetic to Molly Keane's wit and style. Collins, the publishers, turned down her novel, *Good Behaviour*; and in 1961 her play *Dazzling Prospect* enjoyed only a brief run at the Globe.

For the next 20 years Molly Keane wrote nothing at all. She concentrated on gardening, cooking delicious food and entertaining her friends. Theatre friends, writers and painters came to stay, and country neighbours were enchanted to meet them all.

Peggy Ashcroft's visit was extended when she caught 'flu, and books were in such demand in the sickroom that eventually Molly produced the manuscript of the novel Collins had turned down. When she returned to London, Dame Peggy took the book to her friend, André Deutsch, who agreed to publish it.

And so, in 1981, aged 77, Molly Keane burst upon the novel-reading public once again, but no longer as M. J. Farrell. *Good Behaviour* became a bestseller and was shortlisted – many felt it deserved to win – the Booker Prize. It was also filmed for television with Daniel Massey and Joanna McCallum.

As Molly Keane, M. J. Farrell was not just alive and well but on top form; her talent, after being laid down for 30 years, had matured well, although it can hardly be said to have mellowed. Her wit was sharper than ever, her comedy blacker, her powers of observation more disturbingly acute.

To her older readers, the saga of Aroon St Charles in *Good Behaviour* may have seemed like a nostalgic return to the M. J. Farrell Ascendancy world of the 1920s and 1930s; but to the far more numerous younger people who read the book, it was a fascinating and horrifying satire that was entirely contemporary.

Good Behaviour was followed up in 1983 with *Time After Time* in which the three sisters, April, May and June, their one-eyed, domesticated, cat-loving brother Jasper, and their terrible cousin Leda are some of the most memorable characters in 20th-century fiction.

Time After Time was as great a success as *Good Behaviour*, and was also filmed for television, with her old friend Johnny Gielgud as Jasper. Her last novel, *Loving and Giving* (entitled *Queen Lear* in America), was written when she was severely ill with heart trouble; but she finished it and was well enough to travel from Ireland for its launch in London in the autumn of 1988.

It was as widely acclaimed as its two predecessors and followed them on to the best-seller list; it is perhaps the best of all her novels in that it combines the unmistakable Farrell/Keane black comedy with a more sympathetic treatment of her characters. The unfortunate Nicandra and the unforgettable Aunt Tossie evoke our sympathy in a way that few others of her characters do; perhaps at 83, their creator was mellowing at last.

In Ireland, however, Molly Keane's new sharper style made some a little uneasy. The Crowhurst twins in *Good*

Behaviour, for example, were easily identified; it was said that their only sin was that their garden was better than Molly's.

But however hard Molly Keane may have been on her fictional characters, to her wide circle of friends and acquaintances she was one of the kindest and most understanding of people. After the long years when her books were out of print and largely forgotten, she became famous and comparatively rich as an octogenarian. She enjoyed the change in her fortunes and was glad it was no longer necessary to let her house by the sea for summer holidays.

She was much in demand for television, radio and newspaper interviews; almost all the M. J. Farrell novels were reissued in paperback under the name of Molly Keane. She was full of praise for the people who adapted her work for television – though stoutly refused to own a set.

Instead she set herself the mental exercise of reading French, happy in the knowledge that she had become a celebrity in France. Honorary doctorates of literature came her way, and at last she felt her work had won a place alongside that of Elizabeth Bowen, for whom she had the greatest admiration.

Molly Keane became something of a cult figure, particularly to the young, and she remained a mischievous, girlish presence, slim, dark-haired, remarkably good looking and dressed with *chic*. When she reminded people that she was in her mid-eighties it seemed like one of her more preposterous jokes.

A journalist once asked her to define "good behaviour" and she gave a considered reply: "Never telling all, keeping a smiling face when things were going against you, consideration, good manners, punctuality, never boasting."

Molly Keane is survived by her two daughters.

April 23 1996

SIR FRANK WHITTLE

AIR COMMODORE SIR FRANK WHITTLE, who has died in America aged 89, was the greatest aero-engineer of the century.

Whittle ensured that Britain was the first to enter the jet age when, on May 15 1941, the jet-propelled Gloster-Whittle E 28/39 flew successfully from Cranwell. During 10 hours of flying over the next few days, the experimental aircraft – flown by the test pilot Gerry Sayer – achieved a top speed of 370 mph at 25,000 ft. This was faster than the Spitfire, or any other conventional propeller-driven machine.

Although this was a moment of triumph for Whittle, it was tinged with some bitterness, for he had had to overcome years of obstruction from the authorities. He felt, with justification, that if he had been taken seriously earlier, Britain would have been able to develop jets before the Second World War broke out.

He had been granted a patent for the first turbo-jet engine in October 1932, but the Air Ministry's indifference had caused a long delay in realising his ideas. Thus it gave Whittle particular satisfaction when, days after the E 28/39's maiden flight, Sir Archibald Sinclair, the Air Minister, and a gathering of officials stood stunned as Sayer put it through its paces over Cranwell.

347

As John Golley noted in his biography: "Whittle – who had been the first man to get a turbo-jet running – had thrust Britain forward into the Jet Age and stood the aviation industry on its head."

Whittle's engineering genius led to the creation of several other aircraft: the RAF's Gloster Meteor, which saw action during the latter stages of the Second World War; the de Havilland Comet, the world's first passenger jet, and Concorde.

Frank Whittle was born on June 1 1907, in the Earlsdon district of Coventry, the son of a foreman in a machine tool factory.

When Frank was four his father, a skilful mechanic who spent Sundays at a drawing board, gave him a toy aeroplane with a clockwork propeller and suspended it from a gas mantle. During the First World War Frank's interest in aeroplanes grew when he saw aircraft being built at the local Standard works, and was excited when an aeroplane force-landed near his home.

In 1916 the family moved to Leamington Spa, where Frank's father had bought the Leamington Valve and Piston Ring Company, which comprised a few lathes and other tools, and a single cylinder gas engine. Frank became familiar with machine tools and did piece work for his father.

Frank won a scholarship to Leamington College, but had to leave when his father's business faltered. Instead he spent hours in the local library, learning about steam and gas turbines.

In January 1923, having passed the entrance examination, Whittle reported at RAF Halton as an aircraft apprentice. He lasted two days: 5ft tall and with a small chest measurement, he failed the medical.

Six months later, after subjecting himself to an intense physical training programme supported by a special diet, he was rejected again. Undeterred, he applied using a different first name, passed the written examination again and was ordered to Cranwell where he was accepted.

In 1926, strongly recommended by his commanding officer, he passed a flying medical and was awarded one of five coveted cadetships at the RAF College. The cadetship meant that he would now train as a pilot. In his second term he went solo in an Avro 504N biplane after eight hours' instruction.

Whittle graduated to Bristol fighters and, after a temporary loss of confidence due to blacking out in a tight loop, developed into something of a daredevil. He was punished for hedge-hopping. But he shone in science subjects and in 1928 wrote a revolutionary thesis entitled *Future Developments in Aircraft Design*.

The paper discussed the possibilities of rocket propulsion and of gas turbines driving propellers, stopping short of proposing the use of the gas turbine for jet propulsion. However, Whittle launched his quest for a power plant capable of providing high speed at very high altitude.

In the summer of 1928 he passed out second and received the Andy Fellowes Memorial Prize for Aeronautical Sciences. He was rated "Exceptional to Above Average" as a pilot on Siskin operational fighters – but red-inked into his logbook were warnings about over confidence, an inclination to perform to the gallery and low flying.

At the end of August 1928, Pilot Officer Whittle joined No 111, an operational fighter squadron equipped with Siskins and based at Hornchurch, and was then posted to the Central Flying School, Wittering, for a flying instructor's course. In his spare time he conceived a gas turbine to produce a propelling jet, rather than driving a propeller. A sympathetic instructor, Flying Officer Pat Johnson, who had been a patent agent in civilian life, arranged an interview with the commandant.

This led to a call from the Air Ministry and an introduction to Dr A. A. Griffith at the ministry's South Kensington laboratory. Griffith was interested in gas turbines for driving propellers, and scorned Whittle's proposals. The Air Ministry told Whittle that successful development of his scheme was considered impracticable. Whittle nevertheless took out his jet patent, and qualified as a flying instructor.

Johnson, still convinced by Whittle's ideas, set up a meeting at British Thomson-Houston, near Rugby, with the company's chief turbine engineer. While not questioning the validity of Whittle's invention, BTH baulked at the prospect of spending £60,000 on development.

At the end of 1930 Whittle was posted to test float-planes at the Marine Aircraft Experimental Establishment at Felixstowe. On leave he publicised his jet engine proposal, unsuccessfully. But a friend from Cranwell days, Rolf Dudley-Williams, was based at Felixstowe with a flying-boat squadron, and his efforts on Whittle's behalf soon bore fruit.

In the summer of 1932 Whittle was sent on an engineering course at RAF Henlow. He did so well that he was permitted to take a two-year engineering course as a member of Peterhouse, Cambridge, where in 1936 he took first-class honours in the Mechanical Sciences Tripos.

While he was at Cambridge his jet engine patent lapsed; the Air Ministry refused to pay the £5 renewal fee. But he had an inquiry from Dudley-Williams, who was by then a partner with another former RAF pilot, named Tinling, in General Enterprises Ltd.

The two men undertook to cover the expenses of further patents, to raise money, and to act as Whittle's agents. In the New Year of 1936 an agreement was signed between Dudley-Williams and Tinling, Whittle, the president of the Air Council, and O. T. Falk & Partners, a firm of City bankers.

A company, Power Jets, was incorporated and Whittle received permission from the Air Ministry to serve as honorary chief engineer and technical consultant for five years, providing there was no conflict with his official duties. It was as well, because in July, turbo-jet experiments began at Junkers and Heinkel in Germany; at this stage, Whittle's ideas were not subject to the Official Secrets Act. It was a relief when the He 178, after some promise, was scrapped.

Whittle, seeking somewhere to develop his design on modest Power Jets capital, returned to BTH at Rugby and the company contracted to build a "WU" (Whittle Unit), his first experimental jet engine. He tried to persuade companies to develop the specialised materials he needed.

First attempts to run Whittle's jet at Rugby in April 1937 caused alarm as it raced out of control and BTH hands bolted for cover. Money was needed for further development, but this was scarce. An Air Ministry contract provided a paltry £1,900.

In 1938 BTH moved the test-bed to its Ladywood

works at Lutterworth where, in September, the engine, reconstructed for the third time, was assembled. A further £6,000 was pledged by the Air Ministry and engine tests resumed in December.

With the outbreak of war in September 1939, the project gained a further lease of life. The Air Ministry commissioned a more powerful W 2 from Power Jets, and asked the Gloster Aircraft Company for an experimental aeroplane, specified as E 28/39.

With finances more secure, Whittle faced a new threat. Relations with BTH, never easy, deteriorated as the company took the view that the jet engine would not compare favourably with conventional power plants. Whittle was further bedevilled by the politics of possible participation by the Rover motor-car company.

In the event, the Government cut the ground from under Whittle's feet in early 1940, bypassing Power Jets and offering shared production and development contracts direct to BTH and Rover. Power Jets was demoted to the level of a research organisation.

Then the Air Ministry, eager to obtain an operational jet fighter, sidestepped Whittle, ignoring the E 28/39 and authorising Gloster to press ahead with a twin-engined jet interceptor specified as F 9/40. This was to become the Meteor. In 1941 the ministry's director of engine production was to agree to Rover alterations to Whittle's design behind his back.

But fortunately, on July 9, Lord Beaverbrook, the Minister of Aircraft Production, personally assured Whittle that the jet fighter would go ahead. Whittle was relieved by the reprieve, but agonised over the difficulties of, literally, getting his engine off the ground.

He smoked and drank heavily, and the elbowing-out by BTH and Rover further depressed him.

But the events of April and May 1941, when he saw his E 28 test-bed aeroplane flying successfully at Cranwell, lifted his gloom. When Johnson, who had long encouraged Whittle, patted him on the back and said, "Frank, it flies," he replied: "Well, that was what it was bloody well designed to do, wasn't it?"

Details of Whittle's inventions were made available both in Britain and America. Rolls-Royce, de Havilland and Metropolitan-Vickers became involved. In June 1942, Whittle was flown to Boston to help General Electric to overcome problems. It built the engine under licence in America with the astonishing result that Bell Aircraft's experimental Airacomet flew in the autumn of 1942, beating the Meteor into the skies by five months.

On his return home, Whittle arrived at Power Jets' new factory at Whetstone and was astonished by its size after so many years of parsimony, although in practice it could not provide the capacity that would be needed.

Rolls-Royce stepped in and took over work on the W 2B engine, which in 1943 cleared the way for Whittle to plan improvements which would evolve as later mark numbers. Then, with Rolls-Royce in almost total control of Power Jets, Whittle lost touch for three months while attending the RAF Staff College.

Fearing that private industry would harvest the pioneering work of Power Jets for nothing, he suggested it should be nationalised. By the time Whittle had come to regret this proposal, he was taken up on it by Sir Stafford Cripps, the Minister of Aircraft Production. Cripps imposed a price of £135,563.10s, and renamed the company Power Jets (Research & Development). Whittle received nothing, having earlier handed over his shares worth £47,000 to the ministry.

But six months later Whittle was promoted Air Commodore and had the satisfaction of knowing that Meteors of No 616 squadron were shooting down V1 flying bombs.

In 1946 Whittle accepted a post as technical adviser on Engine Production and Design (Air) to the Controller (Air) at the Ministry of Supply. In 1948 he retired from the RAF on medical grounds.

Soon after, he was awarded an ex-gratia sum of £100,000 by the Royal Commission on Awards to Inventors, and he was knighted. In 1986 he was appointed a member of the Order of Merit.

Whittle settled in America in 1976, and was a member of the Faculty of the Naval Academy, Annapolis, Maryland. He published *Jet* (1953) and *Gas Turbine Aero-Thermodynamics* (1981).

Frank Whittle married in 1930, Dorothy Mary Lee; they had two sons. The marriage was dissolved in 1976 and that year he married Hazel Hall.

August 10 1996

GEOFFREY DEARMER

GEOFFREY DEARMER, who has died aged 103, was the last surviving poet of the First World War and, until a selection of his work was republished in celebration of his 100th birthday in 1993, the most overlooked.

Dearmer was modest to a rare degree, and since 1923, when he had last published a volume, *The Day's Delight*, he had resisted the idea of a further collection, seldom even keeping copies of his work. It was not until Dearmer was well into his 100th year that his admirers, stumbling belatedly on the fact of his continued existence, received his permission for the compilation of a representative collection, *A Pilgrim's Song*.

Three days younger than Wilfred Owen, Dearmer served at Gallipoli and, like Owen, on the Western Front. Yet despite the terrible human suffering he witnessed, his war poetry – in marked contrast to the brilliant bitterness of Owen or Sassoon – reflected his unshakeable religious belief and optimism.

Reviewing Dearmer's first book *Poems* for the *New York Times* in 1918, Robert McBride noted that "Mr Dearmer is, *par excellence*, a poet of the war; not that he glorifies bloodshed in any way, but because in each of the poems the vision of battle holds the foreground. His work is characterised by an extreme simplicity of form that seems almost austere, but there is no lack of feeling in it or in the author. Even in the most unassuming of his verses, such as 'The Turkish Trench Dog' there is dignity that approaches grandeur."

A review by John Harvey of *The Day's Delight* (a collection of "peace-time" poems) for the *Fortnightly Review* in 1923, noted: "This little collection of poems is the essence of Mr Dearmer's continuous work during the last five years. His verse is familiar to literary lovers of flowers and animals. Certain of his songs have been set to music, and his long poem, 'The Death of Pan' caused quite a sensation on its original appearance."

Many years later, Dearmer's poem "The Blue Whale", written originally for children, was performed by Hoagy Carmichael all over the world.

Geoffrey Dearmer was born at Lambeth on March 21 1893. His father was the Revd Percy Dearmer, the Vicar of St Mary's, Primrose Hill, who compiled *The English Hymnal*. His mother, Mabel, was an author of children's books, novels and plays, and an illustrator for *The Yellow Book*.

Young Geoffrey was educated at Westminster, from where he went up to Christ Church, Oxford. But he left without taking a degree – "I liked the life of pleasure too much," he recalled – and worked briefly as a journalist.

When war broke out in August 1914, he rushed to the nearest drill hall, in Hampstead, to enlist in the Royal Fusiliers, into which he was promptly commissioned. He remembered the feeling of elation felt by so many young men of his age.

His mother, who was a pacifist, volunteered to serve as a nurse, and was sent with an ambulance unit to Serbia. In 1915 she died of enteric fever at Kragujevatz, and the posthumous publication of her *Letters from a Field Hospital* created intense interest.

His younger brother, Christopher, was killed at Gallipoli, a few days before Dearmer landed there himself. Dearmer's recollection of Gallipoli was that "the Turks didn't want to fight, and we never advanced more than five miles". In his poem "The Sentinel", about the evacuation of troops from Gallipoli, a shell crashes into the sea. "It was almost the only shell I saw," he used to say.

After evacuation to Egypt, Dearmer was posted with

the Fusiliers to France, but there he transferred his commission to the Royal Army Service Corps, and was posted on to the battlefields of Flanders. The RASC had the extremely hazardous task of transporting ammunition and stores up to the front line, often under intense enemy bombardment, sometimes for months without a break. His poem "The Somme" was one of those included in *A Pilgrim's Song*.

After the war Dearmer continued to write, and read play scripts for Maurice Browne, a noted impresario of the 1920s. He also joined the Stage Society, which produced new plays, and in 1928, as a member of the society's six-man committee, was responsible for getting R. C. Sherriff's Great War play *Journey's End* produced for the first time. The play was staged by the society in December 1928, with Laurence Olivier in the lead. Maurice Browne snapped it up, and transferred the production to the Savoy.

Sherriff inscribed a copy of the script to Dearmer: "The production of this play is due so entirely to your determination that it should be produced that your name is the only one I shall always couple with *Journey's End*."

Dearmer also worked as an examiner of plays for the Lord Chamberlain. The least censorious of men, Dearmer did not remember having ever recommended that a play be banned, and looked back on his role with amusement.

After his marriage, in 1936, to Margaret "Mardi" Proctor, Dearmer went to work for the BBC, to begin with assessing church choirs and preachers for their broadcasting potential.

In 1939 he became editor of BBC *Children's Hour*, which probably had as many adult as juvenile listeners.

This was his main source of income for the next 20 years, during which he not only edited the programme but also made his own contributions.

After the death of his wife, Dearmer moved to a small flat at Birchington on the Kent coast, where he received a constant procession of visitors. He was always ready with a story of some encounter at the Garrick or the Poetry Society. Sharp as a needle and full of humour, Dearmer would quickly correct any misquotation with the utmost diffidence and good nature.

The centenary of Owen's birth provided an opportunity to publish a volume of Dearmer's poetry in time for his 100th birthday, March 21 1993. John "Jock" Murray was approached, and agreed to publish the compilation without profit.

One of the most recent poems in the collection has the old poet speaking with characteristic wit as an old soldier:

> LORD, when I stand in Thy celestial court
> And render Thee a poet's last report;
> From my worn, working body, dearly prized,
> Discharged or, at the best, demobilised;
> Curse me if so Thou must, Thou art divine,
> And say that little verse is worse than mine;
> Blue-pencil all, but give me not, I pray,
> Upon that (Oh, I hope long-distant) day
> My poems back complete, corrected, clean—
> Lord, show me not how good they should have been.

Besides poetry, Dearmer wrote novels, pageant scripts and several hymns. The best known of his hymns, also called "A Pilgrim's Song" and included in *100*

Hymns for Today, begins with the line, "And didst Thou travel light Dear Lord".

Dearmer was a member of the Garrick Club for more than 70 years, and the longest-standing member of the Society of Authors.

He was appointed MVO in 1958.

Geoffrey Dearmer's wife died in 1980. Their only daughter, the Revd Juliet Woollcombe, is married to Bishop Kenneth Woollcombe, a former Bishop of Oxford.

August 20 1996

WILLIAM RUSHTON

WILLIAM RUSHTON, one of the founding fathers of *Private Eye*, who has died aged 59, was an exceptionally gifted illustrator with a firm line and a wild humour; on television and the wireless he was by turns satirical and warm.

His drawings were distinguished by their clean line and bold use of black and white. His caricatures were always recognisable as the politician or star chosen for dissection.

His secret seriousness was heavily disguised by a bluff jokiness that prevented him from discussing anything other than in humorous terms lest he be thought pretentious. "In the main," he said, "my basic defence is Blitz humour." He was a complete master of the one-liner and cheered friends.

There was no doubt of "Willie" Rushton's seriousness; some friends thought him truly unhappy. He was both affable and solitary, a lover of beer, chatting in pubs, cricket and Australia. He liked to recount how he brought the ashes of Tony Hancock back from Australia in an Air France bag.

It was through his association with *Private Eye* that Rushton's work first became widely known. He had been at Shrewsbury with Richard Ingrams with whom he was co-editor of *The Salopian*. Rushton also supplied it with cartoons, for which he was already attracting attention.

Rushton and Ingrams became firm friends; their birthdays were one day apart. Ingrams's mother always called Rushton "Sir Harry", for reasons he never understood. Their principal satirical target at school was the "Pseud", short for pseudo-intellectual, a word later to be perpetuated by *Private Eye*.

Rushton himself claimed to remember little of his time at school: "I understand why the Sixties should be a blur, we'd discovered drink by then, but why the Fifties should be a blur I don't know. I just remember it was Blandings country. The sort of place you go to die, not to be educated."

In the holidays in London Rushton and Ingrams spent hours at the Classic Cinema in the King's Road, at the Gaumont and at the Essoldo, later fictionally relocated to Neasden in the pages of the *Eye*. Their favourite Tati film was *Monsieur Hulot's Holiday*, which once they watched three times in a row.

When Ingrams and Paul Foot were at Oxford together, contributing to *Mesopotamia*, Rushton, who was living in London, used to go up at weekends to draw cartoons for it. He was the one who persuaded his Oxford friends that their hobby could make them a living.

When, in October 1961, the first issue of *Private Eye*

came out, it had been put together largely in Rushton's room at the top of his much-loved widowed mother's house in Scarsdale Villas, South Kensington. His room was as neat as a new pin, and he remained highly organised throughout his life.

He was responsible for *Private Eye*'s fashionably scruffy, home-made look. But he was also the only one of the team to master the technology needed. In the early days of the *Eye* he always wore a hat when drawing, a rather shapeless soft tweed trilby. He also proved a crucial ally to Ingrams in many disputes.

The satire boom of the 1960s, focused on Peter Cook's Establishment Club, caught up Rushton too. By 1962 he was performing on *That Was The Week That Was* with David Frost, Roy Kinnear, Millicent Martin, Lance Percival, David Kernan and so on. Rushton regularly impersonated the Prime Minister, Harold Macmillan. His Colonel Buffie Cohen was also much admired.

In 1963 Rushton, egged on by his *Eye* cronies, stood against Sir Alec Douglas-Home in the Kinross by-election. He got 45 votes, having urged the electorate to vote Liberal.

Willie Rushton retained a loose but loyal connection with *Private Eye*. When Ingrams was still editor, the staff would lunch at Norman Balon's Coach and Horses pub in Greek Street, Soho, where Ingrams drank water, Peter Cook spirits and Rushton beer, until diabetes was diagnosed in 1985 and he decided to follow Ingrams's example on the wagon.

After the death of Nicolas Bentley, Rushton illustrated Auberon Waugh's fantasy diary in *Private Eye*. In *The Daily Telegraph* his drawings for Auberon Waugh's "Way of the World" column sometimes went into flights of fancy even beyond the text. He showed a mastery of colour with his covers for the *Literary Review*, in which he took great delight ("The only job I do without looking at my watch," he used to say). His colour illustrations for his book *Great Moments in History* are now in the V&A.

On the wireless he became well loved for his part in *I'm Sorry I Haven't a Clue*, the anti-quiz-show quiz, for which he completed 27 series. His oddly drawling and stuffy tones were eagerly used by radio advertisers. When he became more avuncular, he was a favoured story-reader on *Jackanory*. Nor was he afraid to earn money by taking part in television shows such as *Celebrity Squares*, where he relished the opportunity of meeting showbusiness figures. He was shrewd about money.

Talking about his likes and dislikes he said not long before his death from heart trouble: "I don't much like Sky TV. I also hate anything to do with computers. But my permanent hatred is for cordless phones. As for the things I like, there aren't many. Though it's now fashionable to say you hate them, I quite liked the Sixties."

William George Rushton was born on August 18 1937, the son of a publisher (who had worked with his friend Auberon Waugh's grandfather, Arthur Waugh, at Chapman & Hall). At Shrewsbury, he claimed to have failed Maths O-level seven times.

He emerged from public school detesting the system. In later life he refused to speechify at any public school function. During National Service, he refused to apply for a commission, and his anti-Establishmentarianism was much fortified by his Army days, when he first encountered, as he put it, "the native wit of his fellow man".

He did, though, always enjoy cricket; his father had sent him for coaching at Lord's in preparation for public school, and in his first year at Shrewsbury his mother sent each week cuttings of E. W. Swanton's reports of the MCC tour of Australia. Later he played for the Lord's Taverners. He was proud of scoring 62 in his 50th year, "all in ones and fours of course – 22 yards at one time is enough".

After abandoning his articles as a trainee solicitor, Rushton found acting a natural pastime. He had a part in *The Bed-Sitting Room* by Spike Milligan (at the Marlowe Theatre, Canterbury) and wanted his gravestone to carry the words of Kenneth Tynan's review – "brilliant, bespectacled". Subsequently he played the robust Squire opposite Michael d'Abo in *Gulliver's Travels* at the Mermaid and starred in Eric Idle's *Pass the Butler* and Peter Tinniswood's *Tales from the Long Room*.

If cricket seemed amusing to him, butlers seemed inherently risible. On his telephone answering machine he left the message: "Bollocks the Butler here."

Of his films, the most memorable was *Those Magnificent Men in their Flying Machines* (1964). Latterly he toured with Barry Cryer in a show entitled *Two Old Farts in the Night*.

Among the books he wrote and illustrated were *William Rushton's Dirty Book*; *The Day of the Grocer* (a spoof of *The Day of the Jackal*); *Superpig* (a spoof of Shirley Conran's *Superwoman*); *Pigsticking: A Joy for Life*; *W. G. Grace's Last Case*; and *Willie Rushton's Great Moments of History*.

Willie Rushton married, in 1968, Arlene Dorgan; they had three sons.

December 12 1996

TONY PARKER

TONY PARKER, who has died aged 73, made himself into a *tabula rasa* on to which the misfits and outcasts of society recorded their mournful histories.

When Parker talked, it was with a gentle Lancashire accent. But his real gift was for creating sympathetic silences into which murderers, thugs, child molesters, rapists and baby-batterers could pour their confidences without inhibition.

Parker took immense trouble to get to know his subjects, and some of his interviews were the fruit of lengthy acquaintance. He reported faithfully and without comment everything he was told, and worked the material into narratives that brought out the quirky humanity of the pariahs he was interviewing.

But he was unsentimental; he held that for the most part the convicted deserved to be locked up. Having quoted William Penn about God being in everyone, he was at pains to point out that he did not intend to imply God was good. "I meant that if there is a God, he is in the murderousness as well as in the goodness."

His first book, *The Courage of His Convictions* (1962), presented a portrait of irreducible criminality. "I'd willingly gamble away a third of my life in prison," declared Robert Allerton after committing robbery with violence, "so long as I can live the way I want for the other two-thirds."

Convinced of his own superiority, Allerton could hardly contain his contempt for chaplains, psychiatrists and welfare workers. He professed moral revulsion, though, at the atom bomb, apartheid, anti-Semitism and capital punishment, and declared that he could not go on reading Hemingway after discovering that the American writer liked bullfighting.

Parker's next book, *The Plough Boy* (1965), though deliberately calm in tone, was rather more partial than most of his writing, being a defence of Michael Davies, who was sentenced to death for a murder on Clapham Common. He spent 92 days alone, awaiting execution, before the sentence was commuted to life imprisonment.

Five Women (1965) showed that, for some, prison was a deliberate choice. "Being free, it just means being lonely, that's all," said one of the women.

The Unknown Citizen (1968) uncovered a similar case. "Send me to Parkhurst, send me where you like," says Charlie Smith, quite incapable of making a life for himself as a free man. "I want to be behind a wall." After recording Smith's stumbling address to the court, Parker himself makes an eloquent appeal on his behalf in the final chapter.

He next turned his attention to sex offenders, in *The Twisting Lane* (1969). Though he was as careful as ever not to preach, his transcriptions of eight case histories not only evoked sympathy, but demonstrated the uselessness (and worse) of prison as remedial treatment.

Parker did not deal with criminals in all his 22

books. *The Lighthouse* (1975) is an account of how personalities are affected by lonely months of duty. *The People of Providence* (1983) is about a London housing estate; *Soldier, Soldier* (1985) tells of life in the Army; and *A Place Called Bird* (1989) describes the pressures of conformity in a small town in Kansas. "In all my life I've never met a black person, and I wouldn't want to," opines one inhabitant, "not because I'm prejudiced or anything, because I'm not; it's just I don't like black men, that's all."

In the 1960s and 1970s Parker wrote a number of television plays, but he was far less gifted as a dramatist than as a plain recorder. Of his later books, *Life After Life* (1990) is a record of conversations with 12 murderers, and *The Violence of Our Lives* (1995) is a series of interviews with lifers in American jails.

Many of Parker's subjects appear as victims of moments of madness which they are at a loss to explain, and Parker, sharing their puzzlement, eschews simple prescriptions. Of psychiatry, he expresses some hope; of religion, none. "I don't understand anything in *this* world," he once said, "never mind any other world."

Anthony Parker was born in Manchester on June 25 1923, the son of a bookseller. His mother died when he was four, and he was brought up by an elder sister who attempted, unsuccessfully, to instil in him Low Church piety. He became an agnostic, and later, after attending a Roman Catholic funeral, adopted atheism.

He was educated at Stockport Grammar School. Afterwards he determined to be a poet and a playwright, and entered into correspondence with Edith Sitwell. Literary ambition, however, had to be set aside during the Second World War.

Parker registered as a conscientious objector – "I'd been reading Aldous Huxley and Wilfred Owen," he recalled – and went to work in the coal mines, an experience which sharpened both his social conscience and his socialist convictions.

At the end of the war – by this time married with a daughter – Parker took a job as a publisher's representative with Odham's Press.

At some stage in the 1950s he came across *Ask the Fellows Who Cut the Hay*, a book of interviews with agricultural labourers, tape-recorded by George Ewart Evans. "Life and my way of thinking about it and looking at it were never the same again," Parker said.

Already a prison visitor, he began to interview the more difficult inmates. The result was a radio programme which was published in the *Listener*, and then his first book, *The Courage of His Convictions*.

Once established as a writer Parker lived in a village near Southwold, Suffolk, where his manuscripts were typed by the vicar's wife.

He was twice married, and had five children.

October 10 1996

RONNIE SCOTT

RONNIE SCOTT, the tenor saxophonist who has died aged 69, gave his name to one of the world's great jazz clubs.

He was a sardonic master of ceremonies at Ronnie Scott's, habitually affecting to regard the audience as completely inert or worse. A typical welcome would be: "You're a great crowd tonight. Stone dead, but great. You should have been here last Tuesday. Somebody should have been here last Tuesday. A fellow rang up and asked, 'When does the show start?' and we said, 'When can you get here?'"

Though it induced groans, Scott's patter became an essential part of a night at Ronnie Scott's. Sometimes there would even be requests for particular jokes.

The club in Frith Street, with its whitewashed walls, gingham-covered tables, slow service and indifferent food, hardly changed over the years. But it continued to feature the best jazz. Scott was proud of presenting Sonny Rollins and Count Basie, Sarah Vaughan, Ella Fitzgerald and Carmen McCrae.

What Scott expected from jazz was "melody, I like to hear a guy make up tunes as he plays. To me that is the whole idea, the instant composition, with all the things that go with it, like warmth and feeling and time."

Ronnie Scott's was opened in 1959, in partnership with a fellow saxophone-player, Pete King, in a cellar in Gerrard Street, Soho. Scott had visited New York in the 1940s, been bowled over by bebop, and wanted to emulate the jazz clubs of 52nd Street, in particular the Three Deuces. But he always claimed that he started a club "so that I could guarantee myself somewhere to play".

At first the club promised to provide four nights of British jazz a week. Pete King soon gave up playing to concentrate on managing the club. It was through his tenacity, according to Scott, that Zoot Sims agreed to play for four weeks in 1961. This booking set the club's tone and established its reputation.

Since they were musicians themselves, Scott and King knew how to maintain good relations with other jazz-men, even the more temperamental. Within three years they had brought to the club a top-class roll, who "through no coincidence at all," Scott said, "all happened to be tenor saxophonists". These included Dexter Gordon, Al Cohn, Stan Getz and Sonny Rollins.

The club moved to its present site in Frith Street in 1965. It now had to attract twice as many customers to cover overheads, but Scott did not compromise its standards. In 1967 he booked the Buddy Rich band and the innovative tenor saxophonist Coleman Hawkins. Though he might sign up novelty acts such as Cheech and Chong or The Scaffold, Scott's ideas were usually imaginative. He once paired the classical guitarist John Williams and the jazz guitarist Barney Kessel; he even persuaded Jimi Hendrix to play, in the last week of his life.

In the late 1960s financial success did not come easily. Scott and King would regularly meet on Sunday mornings to decide whether they could afford to open on Monday.

Scott always regarded himself in the first place as a performer: "I think of myself as a saxophone player. Having a club is very nice but it is really incidental to what I want to do."

Ronnie Scott was born on January 28 1927 in Aldgate, east London. His father, Joseph Schatt, was a Russian immigrant and as Jock Scott played the saxophone in Jack Hylton's dance band. When Ronnie was four his parents divorced; his mother remarried when he was eight. In the meantime Ronnie went to the Jews' Infant School, Aldgate, then to an elementary school in Stamford Hill.

Though the boy had had little contact with his father he was determined to follow in his footsteps and become a musician. He bought himself a cornet for five shillings, and then a soprano saxophone. He was given lessons by Jack Lewis, a dance-band player.

On leaving school aged 15, Ronnie Scott found a job in the Keith Prowse music shop. He would spend his spare time playing informally with other musicians in wartime bottle clubs. In 1944 he joined the Johnny Claes band and 18 months later found a place for a time with Ted Heath's band.

By taking a series of jobs on trans-Atlantic liners Scott was able to experience American jazz at first hand. He was highly impressed by the bebop of Gillespie, Parker and Powell.

In 1948 Scott joined Club Eleven, Britain's first jazz club, which began in Great Windmill Street and moved to Carnaby Street. In 1950 the premises were raided for drugs. At the ensuing trial the magistrate asked in passing "What is bebop?" A helpful constable supplied the answer: "A queer form of modern dancing – a negro jive."

In the 1950s Scott played with a number of ensembles including the Jack Parnell band, with Pete King, and a nine-piece co-operative with Benny Green, Jimmy Deuchars and Victor Feldman. They would often try out their latest ideas on surprised audiences at dance halls who were expecting easy listening.

After a failed attempt to form a big band, Scott joined Tubby Hayes in 1957 to form the Jazz Couriers.

Scott, exhibiting the influence of Coleman Hawkins, was able to produce a large tone with an aggressive attack to it. The Couriers split up in 1959. During the years that he was running his own club, Scott would usually play with a quartet.

Among the albums that Scott recorded were *The Night is Scott and You're so Swingable* (1965), *Great Scott* (1979) and *Never Pat a Burning Dog* (1990).

Scott's autobiography, *Some of My Best Friends are Blues*, written with Michael Hennessy, was published in 1979. A biography by John Fordham (1989) took its title from one of Scott's customary exhortations to his audience: *Let's Join Hands and Contact the Living*.

Scott was appointed OBE in 1981.

Ronnie Scott never married; he had two children.

December 26 1996

SIR JAMES COMYN

SIR JAMES COMYN, the former High Court judge who has died aged 75, had been one of the Bar's outstanding jury trial advocates, with a string of unexpected verdicts to his credit.

This genial Irishman's remarkable run of courtroom successes began with the Alfie Hinds libel case in 1964, for which he was only third choice as leading counsel. Put simply, Hinds's case was that Detective Sparks had framed him for the robbery of Maples, the London store, a conviction that had resulted in 11 years' prison for Hinds.

Comyn, typically, opened the case forcefully and in

ringing tones: "This man Hinds is innocent, and Sparks knows it." In his decidedly hostile summing-up, Mr Justice Edmund Davies described Comyn's remarks as "one of the most terrible things I have heard in the law". But the jury thought otherwise, and awarded Hinds damages. (The case led to a change in the law, preventing libel writs based on alleged wrong convictions.)

Hinds had previously performed several daring escapes and continually protested his innocence. He wrote a book about his experiences called *Contempt of Court* – meaning his contempt for courts generally – in which he lavished praise on his counsel, whom he called "Sir Jimmy". (Jimmy was how Comyn was known at the Bar.)

The publicity of the Hinds case brought Comyn well-known clients as diverse as April Ashley – the sex-change model on whose behalf he unsuccessfully contested a divorce petition – Brian Jones of the Rolling Stones, Lord Lucan, and the journalist Harold Evans.

James Comyn was born on March 8 1921, the son of an Irish barrister and nephew of Eamon de Valera's principal legal adviser. It was at the uncle's request that his parents hid de Valera and his secretary in their remote, rambling house in Co Dublin for six months in 1921 during the Irish civil war.

Although de Valera lost both the civil war and subsequent parliamentary elections, he went on to win power in 1932, and his Fianna Fail party has dominated Irish politics ever since. Hence it was something of a family misfortune that Comyn's uncle and de Valera should fall out irreparably just when the latter gained power.

Comyn's uncle and father were both subsequently passed over for legal promotion, and although Comyn

was called to the Irish Bar in 1947, his two applications
to be admitted to the Inner Bar were turned down by
the Irish government. (He was welcomed at the Gibraltar
Bar, however, and also practised in Hong Kong, which
he christened the Far Eastern Circuit.)

His father's disenchantment with Irish law and
politics led him to send young James to the Oratory
School in Berkshire, which he adored. (He later became
a governor.) From there, after six months on the *Irish
Times*, Comyn went up to New College, Oxford. He
became President of the Union, defeating Roy Jenkins
by four votes.

In 1939, Comyn was summoned by de Valera, by
then Taoiseach, and all but invited to join the Irish
diplomatic service. But Comyn was by then set on the
English Bar. His fascination with advocacy stretched
back to childhood: at the age of eight he was found in a
silk dressing gown and his father's wig, addressing a 12
Guinness-bottle jury on behalf of a soda syphon. He had
passed his Bar exams while still at Oxford and was called
by Inner Temple in 1942.

Throughout his life Comyn suffered from recurrent
bouts of depression, or "Black Dog", and he spent time
in hospital before taking up his first proper job with the
BBC's Empire Service. In 1944, when he had daylight
hours off duty, Comyn began pupillage at Fountain
Court in the Temple.

One of Comyn's qualities was rarely to get bogged
down in detail. From his pupil master he had learned
the trick of dividing documents into the "Balls Bundle"
(to be tied up and never referred to again) and the "Real
Bundle".

Comyn also coupled an affable courtroom manner

with a knack of tailoring his submissions to his audience. Opening one case before Lord Denning, Comyn began: "I appear for a poor widow of 87 who has been ejected from her little flat by order of the county council." Denning sighed: "Come, now, Mr Comyn, we are a court of law, you know, not a court of sympathy." There was a moment's pause, then he asked: "What age did you say this poor old widow was?"

Following the Hinds case, Comyn's briefs included the defence of Will Owen MP (1970), cleared of selling secrets to the Czechs; the *Crossman Diaries* case (1974), in which Comyn successfully appeared for the *Sunday Times*; and *The Sunday Telegraph* secrets trial (1971), in which Comyn's client Colonel Cairns was cleared of breaching the Official Secrets Act. In the latter case, Comyn admitted to being helped along the way by the irrepressible Mr Justice Caulfield, who at one point interjected: "Throw your shoulders back, Colonel, and tell the jury who you are."

In 1975 began the three-year battle between Sir James Goldsmith and *Private Eye*, which involved Comyn – acting for the *Eye* – in a torrent of litigation arising from an article written by Patrick Marnham which Goldsmith claimed suggested that he had aided Lord Lucan's disappearance.

By pure coincidence, Comyn had acted for Lucan in his prolonged contest with his wife over custody of their children. Indeed, he had had a conference with Lucan two days before his disappearance. He was later to write: "Instinct makes me feel very strongly that Lucan was not – is not – a murderer."

Goldsmith v Private Eye was eventually settled, helped, Comyn later wrote, by the plaintiff's ambitions to enter

Fleet Street. The case led to Comyn's becoming a friend of Richard Ingrams, Patrick Marnham and Auberon Waugh, and a lifelong reader of the magazine, whose schoolboy humour he never tired of.

Before agreeing to act for the *Eye*, Comyn had stipulated that he reserved the right to continue acting for Harold Evans, a regular client (and friend) of his and a periodic target of the magazine, which dubbed him "Dame Harold Evans".

Having represented one of the last men to be hanged in England – a pathetic semi-literate Cornish lad named Pascoe – Comyn welcomed the abolition of the death penalty. This reform "removed nearly all the strain and all the unhealthy drama and unhealthy public interest in a murder trial".

Comyn's election as chairman of the Bar for 1973–74 was proof of his high standing among his peers. But he later admitted that he was neither a born administrator nor a committee man.

Comyn had gained some judicial experience as Recorder of Andover (1964–71) and of the Crown Court (1972–77), but he was by nature an advocate. He turned down the first offer of a High Court judgeship, before accepting Lord Chancellor Elwyn-Jones's invitation in 1979 to join the Family Division.

Comyn admitted that he found the bench a "lonely and responsible life", far less enjoyable than being a QC. He also disliked the Family Division, where cases involving children particularly worried him. He was greatly relieved to be accepted for transfer to the Queen's Bench Division after just a year.

He didn't much care for the judicial circuit life either, with all the panoply of police escorts and outriders. He was happiest at the Old Bailey, especially No 1 Court, which he liked to call Centre Court. Sir John Mortimer QC, has said that Comyn was the only judge he had encountered who summed up fairly.

As counsel, Comyn had appeared in the longest divorce case in England, in 1962. During 1980–81, as a judge, he was to hear the long defamation action in which the Unification Church (the "Moonies") unsuccessfully sued the *Daily Mail* over an article headed "The Church that breaks up families". After more than six months of evidence, Comyn's summing-up was a model of compression and clarity, lasting just a day.

Three years later Comyn presided over Derek Jameson's action for defamation against the BBC over a Radio 4 *Week Ending* programme. The programme had described Jameson as an "East End boy made bad". Comyn forgot to mention at the outset that he had once worked for the BBC, but he was as impartial as ever. He later confessed that he expected a verdict for Jameson, which was not what the jury decided. Comyn had sympathy for Jameson, and was delighted when the quarrel was patched up and Jameson became a disc jockey on Radio 2.

For much of his life Comyn lived at Belvin, a lovely Georgian house in Co Meath, to which he retreated most weekends from London. He bred the prize-winning Clareville pedigree herd of Aberdeen Angus, and planted countless trees. The house was attacked by an arsonist, thought to be acting for the IRA, in 1981, but Comyn rebuilt it.

Comyn retired from the bench due to ill health in 1985.

He wrote several volumes of light verse, legal anecdote and unusual cases, in some of which he tapped the rich source of courtoom drama provided by the wit and turbulent history of Ireland. He also wrote three volumes of memoirs: *Summing It Up*, *Watching Brief* and *Leave to Appeal*. He was a frequent writer of letters to *The Daily Telegraph*, pleading on one occasion for Irish barristers to retain their wigs.

He married, in 1967, Anne Chaundler, a solicitor; they had a son and a daughter.

January 7 1997

THE REVEREND
W. AWDRY

THE REVEREND W. AWDRY, who has died aged 85, was the creator of Thomas the Tank Engine, Gordon the Grumpy Express, the Fat Controller and the whole group of human-faced rolling stock whose adventures celebrated the golden sunset of steam railways.

Their stories – recounted in some 30 books which led to television series and numerous commercial spin-offs – began in 1944, when Awdry's three-year-old son Christopher was ill with measles. Nursery rhymes had palled with repetition. So Awdry, although no artist, drew some engines with faces to illustrate the lines, "*Early in the morning, down at the station,/ All the little engines standing in a row.*" To go with them he wove a few tales which the child, long after he had recovered, insisted be repeated word for word.

The first engine Awdry named Edward ("it was the

first name that came into my head"), and he jotted the stories down on the backs of old circulars. He saw little value in the stories, but at his wife's suggestion they were sent to Edmund Ward, a fine art printer in Birmingham, who paid £40 for the copyright and commissioned an indifferent illustrator.

The Three Railway Engines was published in 1945; it sold remarkably well, and over the next year was reprinted four times. *Thomas the Tank Engine* appeared in 1946, and a steady flow of additions appeared every autumn for the next 24 years. By then Awdry found the task of coming up with new stories too onerous, and handed over to Christopher.

One part of the Awdry books' success was that they came out in small, easy to handle volumes; another was the fine work of the later illustrators whose bright, brochure-style pictures showed a world of well-kept stations, neatly dressed passengers and overalled workmen.

They also appealed for the way the narrative was crafted to trip off parental lips with the rhythm of rolling stock. James the Red Engine puffs, "Come along, come along," as he struggles up a steep hill, while his coaches say encouragingly, "You're pulling us well, you're pulling us well." As Gordon is made to haul some trucks, he complains, "A goods train, a goods train" in disgust.

For all their simplicity, each of the stories was based on a real incident, such as the loss of some trucks, a derailment, or a fish found in an engine's boiler.

Sometimes Awdry's readers questioned the likelihood of such events. In one story, Percy is forced down a gradient by his loaded trucks and collides with the rear of a stationary train at the bottom, ending up perched precariously on top of a wagon.

Railway enthusiasts by the score wrote to Awdry claiming that such an event or anything like it was quite impossible. "My reply", said Awdry, "is that it actually did happen on April 13 1876, on the London, Chatham & Dover Railway, and that a photograph of the accident is to be found on page 31 of Volume XXXIV of *Model Railway News*."

Wilbert Vere Awdry was born on June 15 1911 at Ampfield, Hampshire, where his father, a railway enthusiast, was Vicar. Every Wednesday afternoon, young Wilbert went for a walk with his father which ended with them climbing an embankment to see the engines of the London & South East Railway pass on the way from Romsey to Eastleigh. If it was raining they were admitted to the platelayers' cabin, where there was always talk of steam-engines and their ways.

Awdry was educated at Dauntsey's School, Devizes, and St Peter's Hall, Oxford, and Wycliffe Hall, Oxford. He spent three years teaching at St George's School, Jerusalem, before being ordained at Winchester Cathedral in 1936.

He first took a curacy at Odiham, Hampshire, and then moved to West Lavington in Wiltshire. During the Second World War his pacificism led him to take charge of the large parish of King's Norton, Birmingham.

He next became Vicar of Elsworth with Knapwell in Cambridgeshire, where he proved a diligent pastor in the moderate Evangelical tradition, and was a great favourite with the children of the parish. In 1951 Awdry became Rural Dean of Bourn. Two years later he moved to the larger parish of Emneth, near Wisbech, where he ministered faithfully for another 12 years before retiring to Stroud, Gloucestershire, to give part-time assistance in local parishes.

Inevitably problems ensued as the stories became international bestsellers. Pressing enquiries from eager children were fielded by placing his railway on the mythical island of Sodor, located somewhere between the Isle of Man and Barrow-in-Furness. For Sodor Awdry designed, with the help of his children, an entire fictional landscape criss-crossed by a network of railway lines.

Awdry halted the first television series in 1959 because the BBC wrote in a scene that he believed inauthentic. Thirty years later he was pleased by a new animated production put out by Central Television, using the voice of Ringo Starr, but he was exasperated when Central started to write their own story-lines.

In 1951, Awdry published *Our Child Begins to Pray*. Besides his children's books, he edited *Industrial Archaeology in Gloucestershire* (1973), which ran to three editions, and was joint editor of *A Guide to Steam Railways in Great Britain* (1979). In 1987 he was joint author of a history of the Birmingham and Gloucester Railway.

In his last years, Awdry looked back philosophically on his two callings. "Railways and the Church have their critics," he would say. "But both are the best ways of getting man to his ultimate destination."

He married, in 1938, Margaret Wale, who died in 1989; they had a son and two daughters.

March 22 1997

'BUNNY' ROGER

NEIL ROGER, who has died aged 86, was universally known as "Bunny" because, so he claimed, when his nurse first set eyes upon him she exclaimed that he looked like "a dear little rabbit".

The rabbit turned into a bird of exceedingly rare plumage. Couturier, art collector, *flâneur*, wit and exotic, Roger's creation was himself. In the years after the Second World War his delicately perambulating figure became one of the minor sights of London. For passers-by he seemed something between a reincarnation of Beau Brummell and a *fin-de-siècle* apparition from the pen of Aubrey Beardsley.

This consummately dandified image would appear round the corner of a Mayfair street dressed from head to toe in flared, pinch-waisted Edwardian apparel of exquisite cut and of the palest shades – cerulean blue, lilac, shell pink, lavender – the whole ensemble topped by a curly-brimmed bowler and a high, stiff collar with jewelled tie-pin. The effect was to draw admiring glances or perhaps mutterings of disapproval.

In his passion for dressing-up he expressed a streak of bravado. But he had invented for himself a style which fitted him as perfectly as his wasp-waisted jackets. He wore it defiantly, a challenge to all comers.

Roger was also one of the most inventive party-givers of his age. To this he devoted the same fastidious sense of style and dedication as he brought to his own appearance.

His series of New Year's fancy dress parties, given

from the 1950s in his house in Knightsbridge, had themes such as *Sunset Boulevard* and *Quo Vadis* (when two Christians were rather unsuccessfully put to the torch in a damp London garden). They attracted many of the more adventurous spirits of the Bohemian *beau monde*, as well as providing copy for rapt write-ups in society glossies and scandalised disapproval in the popular Sunday press.

Roger's final sequence of parties, given at his last house in Addison Road, near Holland Park, had the themes of Diamond, Amethyst and Flame to celebrate his 60th, 70th and 80th birthdays. They were included in *Harper's & Queen*'s list of the most memorable balls of the half century. The Amethyst Ball had Roger at 70 still dancing in the early morning summer sunshine.

His last great party, on the theme of Hades, saw him appearing through flame and smoke in a sparkling creation of scarlet sequins to preside over 400 variously demonised guests. Characteristically at the time of his death he was planning the next party to celebrate his 90th. It was to be called the Haunted Ballroom.

Neil Munroe Roger was born on June 9 1911 in London, the second of three sons of a self-made Aberdonian industrial magnate, Alexander Roger, whose chief business was in cable and telephones. Alexander Roger was knighted in 1916 for his war work, and returned to public service in the Second World War as a government adviser.

It would be hard to conceive a starker contrast between father and son. When his father asked him what he would like as a present if he was chosen for his school's first XV, Roger replied: "A *doll's house*, please, Father."

He was educated at Loretto, Edinburgh, where he

was miserable, and at Balliol College, Oxford, where he read history under the sharp eye of F. F. ("Sligger") Urquhart but mostly devoted himself to the pastimes of the late Twenties: popular music, dancing and developing his stock in trade as a winningly exotic personality.

After leaving Balliol without a degree, Roger attended the Ruskin with a view to becoming a dress designer. In 1937 he inaugurated his first London showroom in Great Newport Street with a grand Society opening.

One quality he did inherit from his father was fortitude, and it was this which saw him through a strenuous war in the Rifle Brigade in which, during the Italian campaign, he saw much active service. Typically, he claimed to have advanced through enemy lines with a chiffon scarf flying as he brandished a copy of *Vogue*. He also said that being in no man's land at least gave him a chance to repair his make-up.

After the war he again set up as a designer, in Bruton Street. From there he moved to create his own *couture* department at Fortnum & Mason's. There he sold pretty, much-pleated dresses in filmy materials for women of a certain age, most of them his friends.

After leaving Fortnum's Roger established himself at the fashion house of his friend Hardy Amies, in which he was an investor. He continued for nearly two decades to make charmingly suitable outfits for his well-bred, well-heeled customers.

For his friends, Roger's party-giving was not only a demonstration of his love for dressing-up and the diversions of make-believe, but also of his generosity. Whether he was holding house parties on a grand scale at his Highland estate or giving dinners and small summer garden parties in Addison Road, each entertainment was brought to a fine edge of perfection.

Beneath the cultivated epicene exterior lay a stalwart friend, a man with no illusions or false sentiment, who was possessed by a stoic tough-mindedness. Few who knew him well failed to recognise that the gossip and gossamer of the surface disguised a character of formidable strength.

Erudite and formidably well read (he had latterly developed a passion for ecclesiastical history), Roger could also name every small-part actor of an MGM comedy of the 1930s.

In his last years he had begun to live a somewhat Proustian existence, largely alone in his London house of 26 rooms filled with paintings by Delvaux, Burra, Derain and Sutherland and his eclectic and ornate collection of old furniture.

He still, however, punctuated his routine with Christmas and summer visits to Dundonnell, his romantic seat in the north-west of Ross and Cromarty. Here was a place for roaring log fires and the dancing of Scottish reels in which, well into his ninth decade, he was an indefatigable participant.

May 1 1997

PRINCESS PAUL OF YUGOSLAVIA

PRINCESS PAUL OF YUGOSLAVIA, the former Princess Olga of Greece, who has died in Paris aged 94, was the widow of Prince Paul, Regent of Yugoslavia from 1934 to 1941.

"Chips" Channon, admittedly impressionable in the matter of royalty, considered Princess Paul and her sister Princess Marina, Duchess of Kent, "surely two of the most beautiful Princesses, if not women, in the world". Fate, though, plunged Princess Paul into the quagmire of Balkan politics, from which Machiavelli himself might have been hard put to emerge unscathed.

She was born Princess Olga of Greece at Tatoi, near Athens, on June 11 1903, the eldest of the three daughters of Prince Nicholas, the artistic second son of King George I of Greece and the Grand Duchess Helen of Russia, a niece of Tsar Alexander III.

Princess Olga was therefore the first cousin of the last Tsar, Nicholas II, with whose children she played. Not only was she about as royal as it is possible to be; her otherwise gentle character was shot through with hints of Russian autocracy.

In 1917 she received an early lesson in the vicissitudes of royalty when her uncle, King Constantine of Greece, abdicated, and her family was obliged to take refuge for four years in Switzerland. When King Constantine was restored by plebiscite she was able to resume her life at Tatoi.

In 1922 Princess Olga became engaged to Crown Prince Frederick of Denmark, whom she had met at Cannes, and who declared himself much taken with her beauty. Later that year, however, he called on her in Paris, to declare that his love for her had died. "It couldn't have been very strong while it was there," Princess Olga observed in her diary.

In that same month, September 1922, King

Constantine was again forced to abdicate. Princess Olga's family was condemned to years of poverty and restless travelling, beginning with a dismal sojourn in a hotel at San Remo. But things looked up for Princess Olga herself when the expert eye of the Duke of Connaught, the third son of Queen Victoria, lit upon her.

It was speedily arranged that she should visit London for the season of 1923. Princess Olga was seen at balls, polo matches and on the tennis court; and went more than once to see Fred and Adele Astaire in *Stop Flirting*. And though she failed to fulfil her parents' hope that she might catch the attention of the Prince of Wales, she succeeded in wholly enslaving Prince Paul of Serbia.

They were married that October, and settled in Belgrade, where they lived in the gloomy palace of King Alexander and Queen Marie of Yugoslavia. Relations between the two families were strained. Prince Paul was artistic, which may have appealed to the daughter of Prince Nicholas, but cut little ice with King Alexander; indeed after Prince Paul had founded a gallery of modern art in Belgrade the King was driven to suggest they should look for a new residence.

Matters were smoothed over, but in October 1934 King Alexander was shot dead by an assassin at Marseilles. Prince Paul became Regent until the majority of King Peter in September 1941. It was a task for which he was – as he himself recognised – wholly unsuited.

He detested politics at the best of times; and, in the years leading up to the Second World War, politics in Yugoslavia were more than usually taxing. "I lead a hard, difficult life with hardly any leisure," he complained to Mary Berenson. "I have had to give up all I cared for and must now lead the existence of a galley slave."

Princess Paul did her best to support her husband, not least in his disapproval of Edward VIII's liaison with Mrs Simpson. In the summer of 1936, when the King and his mistress cruised in the Mediterranean in the *Nahlin*, she refused to receive Mrs Simpson as his consort. A few months later, Edward's Abdication left her aghast at the breach of royal duty and taste. "So awful to see their names on posters in the street," she noted.

In foreign affairs Prince Paul strove to remain disengaged from the Fascist dictatorships which were now dominating central Europe. In April 1939 he and Princess Olga visited Mussolini in Rome, but were careful to avoid making any firm commitments on Yugoslavia's behalf.

Two months later they went to Berlin. Hitler put on a big show for them, spending much time with the Regent, while consigning Princess Olga to the care of Frau Goering. At a parade of German military might Princess Paul was shrewd enough to notice that a seemingly endless line of tanks was in fact the same unit coming round twice. Once again the Prince managed to escape without signing any pacts.

In July 1939 George VI invited them to Buckingham Palace and appointed Prince Paul a Knight of the Garter. Cecil Beaton took some striking pictures of the Princess bedecked in fine jewellery at the Palace.

Her position was difficult on the personal as well as the political level, what with one sister living in England and another – Elizabeth, Countess Toerring-Jettenbach – in Germany. Though Prince Paul's sympathies lay with the British, the shadow of the Axis powers increasingly lay upon Yugoslavia. By the end of 1940 he was contemplating resignation; and he made no secret of his longing to hand over to King Peter in September 1941.

In January 1941 Prince Paul was horrified to learn that Winston Churchill intended to send a mechanised force to Greece in order to form a united Balkan front. He saw the plan as doomed from the start; Churchill, for his part, regarded him as "an unfortunate man in a cage with a tiger, hoping not to provoke him while steadily dinner time approaches".

In March 1941 Prince Paul had a five-hour meeting with Hitler, from which he returned to Belgrade determined on resistance. But he gave way when his Council voted for Yugoslavia's alignment with the Axis.

The next day there was an uprising in Belgrade. On March 27 1941 the Regency was overthrown, King Peter (still only 17) was proclaimed ruler, and Prince Paul and his family went into exile, leaving the young King to the mercy of the new government. In April the Germans bombed Belgrade, killing 17,000 people, and after 12 days occupied Yugoslavia.

Princess Olga loyally defended her husband to her family in Greece. They began a humiliating exile, first in Cairo, and later in Kenya, where they settled at Osserian, near Lake Naivasha, the house of the recently murdered Lord Erroll.

Prince Paul was treated as "a political prisoner allowed the liberty of a normal visitor to the colony". Their isolation was made harder by lack of funds. "Olga is wonderful," Prince Paul reported, "so brave and so efficient doing things you wouldn't expect servants to do."

In August 1942 George VI made it possible for Princess Olga to come to England for a few months to comfort her sister Marina after the death of her husband the Duke of Kent. But her visit was marred by vindictive attacks in the press and the Commons, in particular by Captain Alec Cunningham-Reid MP, who harped on about her pre-war visit to Germany.

When she returned to Kenya in January 1943 she found Prince Paul in a state of nervous collapse. "It would be extremely unfortunate," reflected Anthony Eden, "if he became permanently insane while in our custody."

Soon afterwards the Prince and Princess were transferred to South Africa, where the Prince's health improved – notwithstanding fears that he might be tried at Nuremberg. But they became close to General Smuts, and were comforted when King George VI and Queen Elizabeth visited the Dominion in 1947 and extended the hand of friendship.

Later Prince and Princess Paul settled in Paris, where the Prince was able to indulge his artistic bent. They lived there for the rest of their lives, spending summers at Pratolino, near Florence, until 1970.

They often visited Britain, and attended the reburial of King George VI at St George's Chapel in 1969. Princess Marina died in 1968, and Prince Paul in 1976.

Princess Paul continued to come to London in her widowhood, staying either at Kensington Palace with Princess Alice, Countess of Athlone (who died in 1981), or at Clarence House with Queen Elizabeth The Queen Mother.

Those who were held in her stern gaze were not always convinced by the suggestion that she might be more frightened of them. Her conversation, too, could be grand. "Quite nice, my niece-in-law, sometimes," she remarked of Princess Michael of Kent. "But I can't bear seeing darling Marina's tiara wrapped up in those *dreadful* sausage rolls."

During her last years her memory faded and she was moved from her home in Paris to a nursing home in the suburbs, where her door bore the simple title: "Princesse de Yougoslavie".

Princess Paul had two sons: Prince Alexander, a pilot with British Airways and later a businessman; and Prince Nicholas, who died after a car crash near Datchet in 1954. Her daughter Princess Elizabeth's first husband was Howard Oxenberg; and her second Neil Balfour (who wrote a life of Prince Paul for which Princess Paul made her diaries available). Princess Paul was therefore the grandmother of Catherine Oxenberg, the star of *Dynasty*, who somewhat embarrassed her by playing the Princess of Wales in a television film.

October 29 1997

MICHAEL WARD

MICHAEL WARD, who has died aged 88, was a finely cut gem in the array of British cameo players to have shone fleetingly but regularly in films from the 1940s to the 1970s.

Those who have seen Norman Wisdom's first and funniest film *Trouble in Store* (1953) will probably recall Wisdom's disastrous foray into window-dressing. If so they will doubtless remember his reluctant supervisor: a tall, epicene, ultra-precious wisp of a man with wavy hair, prominent features and a lightly brittle patrician voice. On first sighting his new assistant he exclaims with infinite scorn: "How *utterly* grotesque!"

The actor was Michael Ward; his solitary line one of many with which he convulsed cinema audiences through four decades. He grandly minced his way through more than 100 movies and television programmes: as a fashion photographer ("Samantha – do stand *still*!"); an obsequious jeweller ("Madam has such *excellent* taste"); a City gent revolted by Hancock's cafeteria manners ("I'm feeling a *little sick*"); and, in a rare leading part, as a touchingly soft aristocrat uncle – all embroidery and silk pyjamas – in *Up in the World* (1956).

Although his name was not widely known, his appearances always caused a flutter of pleasurable recognition. British audiences – women in particular – always loved a "cissy": though Ward's aloof, ethereal persona was far removed from the wrist-flapping music hall stereotype.

For this reason his *Carry On* vignettes made his camp colleagues look somewhat crass. Like his polar opposite, the stoutly plebeian Arthur Mullard, he was a genuine oddity rather than a manufactured one.

Ward's natural drollery – despite impeccable timing and professionalism – disconcerted some egotistic star comics, but with a quiet firmness at once disarming and alarming he always stood his ground. Perhaps only Morecambe and Wise – not long before Ward's retirement in the 1970s – appreciated his true value as a super-refined foil.

George Michael Ward was born at Redruth, Cornwall, on April 8 1909, the son of a Rural Dean. From childhood he enjoyed dressing-up and make-believe – once fooling numerous villagers when disguised as an old woman.

An accomplished pianist, he studied music and drama in Paris and won a scholarship to the Central School of Acting in London. In the theatre he played such roles as Beverley Carlton in *The Man Who Came to Dinner* and Roland Maule in *Present Laughter*. He appeared in the London Coliseum revue *The Night and the Music* (1945), also understudying Vic Oliver.

His screen debut was in *An Ideal Husband* (1947); afterwards he acted with some distinction a near straight role in *Sleeping Car to Trieste* (1948), directed by John Paddy Carstairs, who cast him in such 1950s comedy hits as *Man of the Moment*, *Jumping for Joy*, and *Just My Luck*. He also appeared in several Boulting Brothers, *Doctor* and *Carry On* films: notably *Carry on Cabby*, *Carry on Cleo* and *Don't Lose Your Head*.

Ward played an assortment of fops in period pictures and was an unusual member of the Rank Charm School. On television he had some more serious roles, such as a homosexual son in *The Richest Man in the World* (1960), and was a guest in nearly every popular sitcom and sketch show.

In the late 1970s ill health forced him to retire and he became semi-bedridden during the past 12 years. A devout Roman Catholic convert and something of a recluse, he had always lived a monkish existence like the late Kenneth Williams, though quite without the latter's tortured psyche.

During the last sad years he unfailingly captivated those who cared for him with his childlike charm and an unforced but quite startlingly flamboyant old world courtesy. His zest for gossip and laughter never left him: in his final enfeebled months he could still raise an affectionate smile from the devoted staff of the Princess Louise Hospital in west London.

Jonathan Cecil writes: I last saw Michael Ward very recently – now white-haired and elegantly bearded, blue eyes as candidly clear as ever. I felt a certain regret that no Visconti or Eisenstein ever discovered him. Indeed he could have played a fascinating medieval or renaissance princeling; one of a wilting breed, part regally cunning, part Holy Fool.

Instead Michael Ward will be gratefully remembered as a unique link with another vanished era: when British comedy films were plentiful and even the feeblest ones could be momentarily transformed by a colourful supporting actor. His friends will miss the delightful company of a sweet-natured, sometimes comically unworldly gentleman eccentric.

November 11 1997

LADY HEATHCOAT AMORY

LADY HEATHCOAT AMORY, formerly Joyce Wethered, who has died aged 96, was arguably the greatest woman golfer of all time.

Indeed, when Bobby Jones was asked if there had ever been a better woman player, he replied: "I am very doubtful if there has ever been a better player, man or woman." He had come to this conclusion after playing Joyce Wethered at St Andrews in 1931, the year after he had won the professional and amateur Opens of both Britain and the United States.

They drove from the same tees, and Joyce Wethered was two up with three to play. Though she lost the last three holes she was still round in 71. But for his greater strength, Jones acknowledged, he was "utterly outclassed".

Joyce Wethered was born at Brook, Surrey, on November 17 1901, and educated privately, having been adjudged too frail to go to school. She first hit a golf ball at the seaside town of Bude, in Cornwall; 80 years later she still remembered the outrage she felt when a small boy scuttled his ball along the ground past her shot.

She received only one lesson, from Tom Lyle, the professional at Bude, though she occasionally caught glimpses of such great champions as Harry Vardon and J. H. Taylor. In the holidays she played at Dornoch with her brother Roger, who won the British Amateur championship in 1923.

Her swing was a model of balance and grace. Ideally, she used to say, nothing on earth could dislodge her from her right foot at the top of the back swing, or from her left at the finish of her follow-through. The most remarkable feature of her game was her accuracy with iron shots.

Yet Joyce Wethered never thought of playing championship golf until 1920, when Molly Griffith, a leading Surrey player, suggested she should come with her to the English Ladies' Golf Championship at Sheringham, in Norfolk.

Joyce Wethered proceeded to play her way to the final, in which she encountered the formidable "Cecil" Leitch. She found herself six down with only 16 holes to play. Wrapping herself into a cocoon of concentration – she always played the course rather than the opponent – she managed to retrieve the situation and win 2 and 1 on the 17th green.

Had she not been disturbed, she was asked afterwards, by the train that whistled as she was bending over her winning putt? "What train?" she replied. The victory was the more remarkable as she was coming down with whooping cough which kept her in bed for weeks afterwards.

Not only did she hold on to the English Ladies' Golf Championship for the next four years: in 1922, 1924 and 1925 she also won the Ladies' Open Amateur Championship. Her defeat in the semi-final in 1923 seemed like a departure from the natural order of things.

In 1925 Joyce Wethered retired from competition, but was tempted back to play in the Ladies' Open of 1929, on the Old Course at St Andrews, her favourite. The final, in which she took on the American champion Glenna Collett, was a memorable contest. Joyce Wethered was five down after nine holes (her opponent going out in 34), but clawed her way back to win 2 and 1.

Once more Joyce Wethered retired from championship play, though in 1931 she captained the British women's team to conclusive victory against the French. They lost to the Americans the next year, but Joyce Wethered inflicted another defeat on Glenna Collett.

Her family was now on its uppers, and the next year she took a job advising customers about golf equipment at Fortnum & Mason. In 1935 she undertook a tour of America, to publicise Wanamaker's golf supplies with a series of exhibition matches.

At first things did not go well, at least by her standards. "The change from amateur to professional has affected my game in a way I really cannot describe," she mused. "Perhaps it is a feeling of obligation to the public instead of the old idea of simply hitting the ball." But, she told reporters, she would do better when she became acquainted with American greens and with the coarser sand in the bunkers ("I fancy a heavier niblick might help").

Five months later, she had played 53 matches in all parts of America, and established 36 new records, notwithstanding the vast distances travelled and her lack of knowledge of local conditions. She also made herself a tidy £4,000 – perhaps £100,000 in today's money.

In 1931 Joyce Wethered had been engaged to the Scottish golfer Major Cecil Hutchinson, though the match never came off. In 1937 she married Sir John Heathcoat Amory, 3rd Bt. He was the elder brother of Derick Heathcoat Amory, who was Chancellor of the Exchequer from 1958 to 1960 and created Viscount Amory.

It is said that Sir John had refused to propose to Joyce Wethered until he had beaten her at golf – a rash undertaking even for a fine games player, with a handicap of two.

From 1921 Joyce Wethered had invariably been the star of the annual mixed foursomes at Worplesdon. Even in 1930, when she was partnered by Lord Charles Hope, who fired the ball in all directions and into every obstacle, she only lost 2 and 1.

In the next three years she was partnered successively by Michael Scott, R. H. Oppenheimer and Bernard Darwin, and won every time. "Why bother to hold the meeting?" asked Darwin in 1933, after Joyce Wethered had announced her intention of playing with Oppenheimer again the next year.

She triumphed eight times in the tournament between 1922 and 1936, with seven different partners. But she never managed to win at Worplesdon with her husband, despite reaching the final in 1948. As a pair, they seemed less happy on the golf course than off it, and in the 1950s they abandoned the event.

With Sir John Heathcoat Amory suffering from arthritis, they increasingly concentrated their energies on their garden at Knightshayes House, near Tiverton. It became celebrated for its alpines, rhododendrons and azaleas; and Lady Heathcoat Amory was awarded the Royal Horticultural Society's Victoria Medal of Honour.

Sir John Heathcoat Amory died in 1972. His widow continued to live at Knightshayes House, which was now run by the National Trust. The remarkable collection of pictures which her husband and she had acquired (including Poussin's *The Mystic Marriage of St Catherine*) went to various national galleries, subject to Lady Heathcoat Amory's life interest.

Joyce Heathcoat Amory took a detached view of the Gothic glories of Knightshayes, built in the 1870s in a queasy mixture of red Hensley and yellowish Ham stone. "Perhaps it would be as well to admit at once that the Amorys were unable, from early days, to appreciate Victorian architecture," she told a visitor. "Each generation has played its part in dismantling the house's most eccentric features." Nevertheless she looked on with fortitude as the National Trust restored the lost workmanship of William Burges and John Crace.

She retained her interest in golf, though no longer as a player. In 1951 she had become the first president of the English Ladies' Golf Association. She was admitted into America's Hall of Fame.

Always a perfect sportswoman herself, and never given to complaints about bad luck, she did not like everything about the modern game. She considered that Nick Faldo would do well to stop fiddling with his swing and practising morning, noon and night. Her preference was for more romantic players such as Seve Ballesteros, or chivalrous competitors such as Nick Price.

In 1994, under the auspices of *The Daily Telegraph*, the Joyce Wethered Award was established, to be presented annually to an outstanding and upstanding woman golfer under the age of 25.

November 20 1997

'BIG DADDY'

"BIG DADDY", the fighting name of Shirley Crabtree, who has died aged 64, was the star attraction of the professional wrestling circuit during its televised heyday in the 1960s and 1970s.

Weighing in at 28 stone and clad in spangled top hat and overburdened leotard, Big Daddy was a portly avenging angel in a comic-book world of heroes in white trunks and villains in black masks.

At its peak, wrestling drew Saturday afternoon audiences of 10 million, attracted not so much by the finer points of the hammerlock and Boston Crab as by its unvarying rituals. These began with the commentator Kent Walton's Transatlantic tones of welcome – "Greetings, grapple fans", – and climaxed with the entry of Big Daddy into the ring, usually to save a small wrestler from the attentions of his *bête noir*, Giant Haystacks.

His arrival was accompanied by chants of "*Ea-sy, easy*" from stout matrons in the crowd, in manner the spiritual descendants of the *tricoteuses* who sat by the guillotine.

For Big Daddy's vast belly easily held opponents at bay before he despatched them with his speciality – the "splashdown". This was a manoeuvre in which he mounted the ropes, leapt on top of his stupefied opponent, and squashed him flat to the canvas.

These antics brought Big Daddy notable fans, among them The Queen, whose interest in the sport was first recorded in Richard Crossman's *Diaries*, and Margaret Thatcher, who found the wrestler a useful topic of conversation in Africa, where he was a household name.

The *persona* of Big Daddy was the creation of Shirley Crabtree's brother, Max, and only came relatively late in the wrestler's career. The name was taken from that of the character played by Burl Ives in the film of *Cat On A Hot Tin Roof.*

Max Crabtree was one of the sport's main promoters, and the revelation in the mid-1980s that the result of many of the bouts was predetermined, while no surprise to those who had seen the unathletic carriage of Big Daddy, dented its popularity.

Some in the profession blamed the Crabtree brothers for making the sport too predictable, and its image was further damaged when Mal Kirk, a similarly large wrestler, died of a heart attack in 1987 while fighting Big Daddy.

A year later ITV stopped showing wrestling deeming audience taste to have changed. The sport has never recovered its lustre.

Shirley Crabtree was born in Halifax in 1933, though as he strove to prolong his career his real age became as uncertain as the true colour of the blond hair he sported. He was named after his father, who had in turn been called after the eponymous heroine of Charlotte Brontë's novel by his mother, a 22-stone music-hall actress. She admired the character so much that she chose her baby's name before knowing its sex.

Shirley senior became a rugby league player for Halifax and later worked as a circus strongman. He believed that poverty could only be resisted by the tough, and taught his three boys to wrestle from an early age. This came in useful in the playground of Battinson Road Primary School where such skills were needed to fend off jokes about Shirley Temple.

When young Shirley was seven, his father left their mother, who subsequently brought up the boys, working in a brickyard for the half wages paid to women. Shirley particularly disliked Christmas, as the presents dispensed to him by well-meaning charities were invariably dolls and girls' annuals.

He left school at 14 and worked as a doffer in a cotton mill, replacing empty bobbins with full ones. Two years later he left to join Bradford Northern rugby league club, but his aggressiveness led to numerous suspensions for foul play and he became a lifeguard at Blackpool instead.

Crabtree began his wrestling career as a middle-weight, weighing in at a mere 16 stone and fighting as "The Blond Adonis" and "Mr Universe". His two brothers often appeared on the same bill, until Max, who had the best technique, became a promoter, and Brian after breaking his leg turned to refereeing.

By the early 1960s Shirley Crabtree had realised that it was the larger wrestlers who gained the biggest following, and he began to boost his weight with a concentrated diet of steak, eggs and cream cakes. His size made him a considerable attraction on the circuit, but he was still cast in the mould of villain, most notably as "The Battling Guardsman", a role created for him by his brother.

Crabtree had briefly served in the Coldstream Guards, and would enter the ring wearing a bearskin, to the sound of Joseph Locke singing "The Soldier's Dream". It was not until 1975 that the Big Daddy character was created, with his first leotard being made from the chintz covers of his wife's sofa.

He was twice married and had six children.

December 3 1997

JAMES LEES-MILNE

JAMES LEES-MILNE, who has died aged 89, was a prolific, witty and elegant writer of architectural and social history, biography and fiction; as a passionate conservationist, he played an important role in the National Trust's "Country House Scheme" from its inception in 1936.

The success of the scheme owed almost everything to "Jim" Lees-Milne. It is unlikely that so many owners would have given their houses to the Trust had it not been for his combination of knowledge, enthusiasm, efficiency and understanding. As the scheme's first secretary, Lees-Milne lent a kindly ear to the woes of the private owners, and battled against the bureaucrats in order to preserve many places of historic interest.

His brilliantly observed diaries of the 1940s – published under titles culled from Coleridge's "Kubla Khan" such as *Ancestral Voices* (1975), *Prophesying Peace* (1977), *Caves of Ice* (1983) and *Midway on the Waves* (1985) – capture the exhilaration of rescuing endangered buildings in those inauspicious years, as he combed the country on a series of rickety bicycles and temperamental old motor cars. Two further volumes spanning the 1950s and 1970s, *A Mingled Measure* (1994) and *Ancient as the Hills* (1997), appeared, and a seventh volume, *Through Wood and Dale*, was in the press at the time of his death.

Though they offered a unique record of the early days of the Country House Scheme – and of the Georgian Group, of which he was a founder member – the diaries contain much more than purely architectural material. His eye for detail and ear for gossip made them one of the funniest and most enjoyable social documents of the 20th century.

What set him apart from other leading diarists – such as "Chips" Channon and Harold Nicolson (a close friend of Lees-Milne and the subject of his prize-winning two-volume biography) – was his lack of interest in the ersatz excitement of the House of Commons. Instead the reader can relish a beautifully written mixture of salty character sketches, anecdotes, philosophical and religious ruminations, and constant self-deprecating irony.

There is nothing finer in the diaries than his powerfully romantic vision of the "true county squirearchy" struggling to survive. He celebrated the eccentricity of the English with an engaging sympathy – Lady Etheldreda Wickham, for example, was described as "very broad-minded when one discounts the fact that she hates all foreigners".

He did not spare the unworthy (Godfrey Winn "minces like a harlot"), though he was seldom less than understanding of his subjects – and relentlessly hard on what he saw as his own querulous, prickly and shy persona. Although his tall, dandified figure was a familiar sight at Brooks's and in the *beau monde*, he never lost his air of anxiety (it was observed that he shivered like one of his beloved whippets) or the sense of being an "outsider".

The diaries revealed a striking independence of mind and a breathtaking disdain for fashionable opinion. Lees-Milne was, for instance, one of the few to have expressed in print regret for not having gone to Spain to fight on Franco's side in the Civil War – a "life-and-death struggle with the forces of world disruption".

His views on the Second World War were equally forthright: "The Midsummer Day [1941] on which while lying in bed in hospital I listened to Churchill on the radio magnifying the virtues of our new ally Soviet Russia, marks without question the nadir of my whole life."

Perhaps equally disconcerting to liberal sensibilities was the remark that he loved class distinctions (which he differentiated from detestable class *barriers*) and hoped they would last for ever; talk of egalitarianism he saw as hypocritical cant. The benevolent squirearchical system, he maintained, was the best form of government ever invented.

James Lees-Milne was born on August 6 1908, into a family of Lancashire landed gentry that had settled in Worcestershire at Wickhamford Manor. He recalled that when his father announced the outbreak of the First World War over the breakfast table after dropping his copy of the *Morning Post*, he piped up: "Does that mean I shan't get enough to eat?"

Rather frightened of his family, the young Jim used to spend "many happy hours in the servants' hall as a small boy; I can still hear the screams of laughter."

He was at private school with Tom Mitford and used to visit him and his subsequently celebrated sisters at Swinbrook, where he raised the blood pressure of their fiery father Lord Redesdale (the "Uncle Matthew" of Nancy Mitford's novels) through such solecisms as carrying a comb in his pocket and even, on one notorious occasion, suggesting that "we ought to make friends with the Germans".

After leaving Eton – where, according to one of the Munchausen-like escapades which illuminate his autobiographical comic masterpiece, *Another Self* (1970), he danced *en travestie* at a Bray roadhouse with a "po-faced bachelor beak" called Hartington-Jones – Lees-Milne spent a year at Miss Blakeney's Stenography School for Young Ladies in Chelsea. His difficult father had dumped him at this establishment – the only male in a class of 20 girls – in the hope that the course might prepare him for employment in the City, so he could "stand on his own two feet".

It was only through the determination of his mother – who arranged matters while his father was shooting in Scotland – that he went up to Magdalen College, Oxford, in 1928. *Another Self* also relates how young Jim helped his mother to elope in a balloon from the top of Broadway Hill "vaguely scattering sand and pound notes into the air" as she drifted skywards.

It was while up at Oxford that Lees-Milne had a vision on the road to Damascus. One evening he was invited to Rousham by the tenant, "a capricious alcoholic . . . rich, clever and slightly mad" – unnamed in the book but in fact Maurice Hastings.

After dinner the drunken Hastings proceeded to attack the 18th-century Dormer family portraits with a horsewhip and then to take pot shots at the classical statues in William Kent's landscape garden with a gun. He was egged on by most of those present – including such supposed champions of civilisation as, Lees-Milne later disclosed, Maurice Bowra.

"The experience was a turning point in my life," Lees-Milne recalled. "It brought home to me how passionately I cared for architecture and the continuity of history, of which it was the mouthpiece . . . Those Rococo rooms at Rousham and the man-fashioned landscape outside were the England that mattered. I suddenly saw them as infinitely fragile and precious. They meant to me then, and have meant ever since, far more than human lives. They represent the things of the spirit. And the ghastly truth is that like humans they are not perdurable."

On coming down from Oxford, Lees-Milne worked as private secretary to the empire-builder, Lord Lloyd, whom he liked, and then for Sir Roderick Jones of Reuters, whom he detested.

In 1936, with the sack hanging over him, he confided to a fellow "Saturday to Monday" guest about his predicament. Acting on the advice he had received, Lees-Milne managed to give notice before the ogre could administer the *coup-de-grâce*. "And who, I would like to know, has advised you to do this foolish thing?" sneered the Reuter's boss.

Lees-Milne had an unbeatable reply: "The Prime Minister, Sir Roderick." For the fellow guest had been Stanley Baldwin, who shared Lees-Milne's love of Worcestershire.

Now fate took a hand. Suddenly the job of which he dreamed when at Oxford and did not believe existed, presented itself. The National Trust, founded in the 1890s to preserve landscape, was launching a scheme to save some of the historic houses of England, and needed a secretary. Recommended by Vita Sackville-West, Lees-Milne landed the job; he had found his vocation.

During the Second World War Lees-Milne served in the Irish Guards but was invalided out in 1941 after a bomb explosion in London broke the base of his spine and initiated intermittent attacks of epilepsy.

He gave up the secretaryship of the National Trust Country House Scheme in 1951 but served the Trust for another 15 years as an adviser on historic buildings.

The original intention of the Country House Scheme had been to retain the houses where possible as family seats but with some public access, on the model of the French *Demeures Historiques*. Lees-Milne came to view with some reservations the more recent development of the National Trust: families mainly departed and the houses run as standardised museums with excessive numbers of visitors and obtrusive bric-à-brac shops.

While editing his first book, *The National Trust* (1945), Lees-Milne urged G. M. Trevelyan to stress in the introduction that the organisation was opposed to "museumisation" but wished to preserve the face of England as it was under private ownership.

Nearly half a century later, on revisiting Hanbury Hall in his beloved Worcestershire, the author noted in his book *People and Places* (1992) that the rooms had been "submitted to that suave good taste expertise which it may be difficult to criticise and yet is easy to lament. Can an ancient squirearchical house be quite the same after such tremendously drastic treatment? Is it not bound to look glossy and almost new? And just very faintly suburban?"

Lees-Milne's loyalties "were to the houses, the families and the National Trust (which I regard as the instrument of the others' preservation) in that order". But, as he concluded, while "fewer and fewer families live in their old homes . . . posterity is at least lucky to have and be able to visit, even as museums, the domains of the defunct regime".

Lees-Milne's other books included *The Age of Adam* (1947), *Tudor Renaissance* (1951), *The Age of Inigo Jones* (1953), *Roman Mornings* (Heinemann Award, 1956), *Baroque in Italy* (1959), *Baroque in Spain and Portugal* (1960), *Earls of Creation* (1962), *The Shell Guide to Worcestershire* (1964), *St Peter's* (1967), *English Country Houses: Baroque 1685–1714* (1970), *William Beckford* (1976), *The Last Stuarts* (1983), *The Enigmatic Edwardian*, a biography of Lord Esher (1986), *Venetian Evenings* (1988) and *The Bachelor Duke* (1991). *Fourteen Friends* (1996), which he was mischievously tempted to entitle "Bent and Straight", contained sketches of such fellow aesthetes as Robert Byron, James Pope-Hennessy and Osbert Lancaster.

He also published three novels: *Heretics in Love* (1973), a heady Gothic story highly charged with Roman Catholicism and incest; *Round the Clock* (1978), a deft little account of a chain of unreciprocated loves, not excluding the dog, in a Cotswold country house; and *The Fool of Love* (1990), again set in an authentically realised country house and also dealing with the dangers of searching for affection. "So long as one is madly in love", observes the squirearchical *paterfamilias*, "one is living in a fool's paradise."

His ambition for many years was to be a poet, but he never published any verse. "I did show some sonnets of mine to Vita Sackville-West," he said. "She told me they reminded her of Tennyson's younger brother."

The Lees-Milne muse was stirred by love, nature, religion (after converting to Catholicism in the early 1930s he returned to the Church of England in the wake of Vatican II) and, of course, country houses – "the dimmer the better".

Lees-Milne's special quality as a writer was that he could not only reveal the spirit of a building in poetic terms but also portray the follies of human beings with the art of the novelist.

Lees-Milne married in 1951, Alvilde, formerly wife of the 3rd Viscount Chaplin and daughter of Lieutenant-General Sir Tom Bridges. After a spell in France they restored a fine Georgian house – Mrs Lees-Milne, a noted garden writer, created a beautiful garden – at Alderley in Gloucestershire where they lived until the 1970s.

Subsequently they acquired a smaller house on the Badminton estate, from where he commuted regularly to write in William Beckford's old library at Lansdown Crescent, Bath. Lees-Milne was a leading member of the Bath Preservation Trust and author (with David Ford) of *Images of Bath* (1982). "Bath is to Britain", he pointed out, "what Venice is to the world."

Alvide Lees-Milne died in 1994. Although plagued by recurring bouts of cancer, Jim Lees-Milne remained extraordinarily alert and active into his 90th year, with an insatiable appetite for sightseeing at home and abroad. His unfailingly sympathetic curiosity about people never flagged.

Modestly unaware of his legendary status in the literary and heritage worlds, he always managed – through his exquisite courtesy and charming good manners – to give the impression that his interlocutor's concerns were of paramount importance.

He was a Fellow of the Royal Society of Literature and a Fellow of the Society of Antiquaries. Though Lees-Milne saved much of what we now take for granted as the "national heritage", he – quite inexplicably – never received any official recognition or honour.

Dubbed "the Worcestershire Grumbler" by his friend John Betjeman, Jim Lees-Milne channelled his energies into striving to uphold what remains in England of the long tradition of European civilisation.

December 29 1997

SIR FRANK ROBERTS

SIR FRANK ROBERTS, who has died aged 90, was known as "the pocket Hercules of the Foreign Office"; he advised Churchill and Attlee at Yalta, negotiated face to face with Stalin over the Berlin blockade and was Ambassador in Moscow during the Cuban missile crisis.

Small, dynamic and immensely hard-working, Roberts shot up through the ranks of the Service. His juniors found themselves dealing with a ceaseless flow of minutes, observations and instructions; his seniors were deluged with dispatches.

As a head of mission abroad – he served as Ambassador in Belgrade, Moscow and Bonn – Roberts was noted for sending telegrams of great length and prolixity containing a wealth of circumstantial detail. It was a style much imitated in parlour games by irreverent juniors with time on their hands.

But Roberts's reports were also a reflection of his remarkable tenacity in the task at hand, and of his insatiable curiosity. The series of comprehensive dispatches on the Soviet scene which he sent to London from the Moscow Embassy after the war have seldom been rivalled in scope, or length.

Once Roberts had made up his mind about a problem, he did not hesitate to express a firm view. Perhaps as a result he never climbed to the very top of his profession, the post of Permanent Under-Secretary for Foreign Affairs. Too many people resented his energy, acuity and self-confidence.

Field Marshal Montgomery once said that Roberts had

a "constipated mentality", and considered him to be "a menace to the country". Colleagues were said to appreciate Roberts most of all when he was abroad; and although Ernest Bevin, when Foreign Secretary, recognised Roberts's brilliance and appointed him his private secretary, he was said to find Roberts's manner irritating and bossy.

There were questions raised, too, over Roberts's reluctance to recognise the particular plight of the Jews in Nazi-occupied Europe. His eirenic attitude after the war to a Soviet Union in oppressive possession of a new empire also exasperated idealists.

None the less, by the time Roberts retired from the Service in 1968, there was no more widely experienced or knowledgeable British diplomatist.

Frank Kenyon Roberts was born in Buenos Aires on October 27 1907. His father was the representative of Lever Brothers (later Unilever) in South America. Young Frank was educated at Bedales, Rugby and Trinity College, Cambridge, where he was a scholar. He was a useful scrum-half and wicket-keeper.

He joined the Diplomatic Service in 1930, having come top in the entrance examination. His first posting was to Paris, where Lord Tyrrell was Ambassador. As Roberts played golf and bridge he got to know Tyrrell well.

When it came to official paperwork, Lord Tyrrell generally confined himself to initialling the papers submitted to him. On one occasion, when a file he had initialled was returned to him marked "This requires a decision", he wrote on it "Yes it does" and sent it back.

After Paris, Roberts was posted to Cairo, where in 1937 he met and married Celeste Leila Shoucair, daughter of

Sir Said Shoucair Pasha, one-time Financial Adviser to the Sudan government.

Later that year Roberts returned to the Foreign Office, where he concentrated on German affairs, during the hectic period preceding the outbreak of the Second World War. Between 1937 and 1940 it fell to Roberts to annotate and circulate every file concerning Anglo-German relations. These covered all aspects of the scene, from the Nazi military build-up to Unity Mitford's latest escapade.

As the first to comment upon and make policy recommendations on the cover pages of these files, Roberts was highly influential. It was unusual for his superiors to reject Roberts's interpretation of events or proposals.

Roberts saw the Prime Minister Neville Chamberlain in action at close quarters, and found him tough and obstinate. "His was a genuine quest to keep the peace. But he just didn't understand Hitler or his ruthlessness. We in the Foreign Office kept telling him it was all in *Mein Kampf*, but he wouldn't believe it."

In 1943 Roberts became head of the Central Department, and intimately concerned with all policy relating to the main European theatre of war. The same year he was sent to Lisbon to join Sir Ronald Campbell, the Ambassador in negotiating with the Portuguese dictator, Dr Antonio Salazar, for an Allied airbase in the Azores. The concession obtained for staging and fuelling rights on the islands enabled British aircraft to search for U-boats in the Atlantic, and was crucial to their success.

To some critics it seemed that Roberts remained too cool in his attitude to the plight of the Jews in Nazi-occupied Europe. As late as May 1944 he argued against giving any unnecessary publicity to their suffering. "The Allies resent the suggestion that Jews in particular have been more heroic or long-suffering than the other nationals of occupied countries," he noted.

In 1945 Roberts attended the Yalta conference as an adviser on German and Polish questions to Churchill and Eden, and then to Attlee and Bevin. Later he rejected the view that at Yalta the West "gave away" Eastern Europe to Stalin. "This just was not the case," he said. "By 1944 the Russian Red Army had occupied the whole of Eastern Europe, including Poland. Short of going to war, what could we do?"

After Yalta Roberts spent two years as Minister in the Moscow Embassy. The Cold War had not yet begun, though there was a great deal of British distrust of Soviet intentions; comparisons were drawn with Nazi Germany. Yet Roberts argued that it should be possible to co-exist with the Russians, provided the West stood firm in defending its vital interests.

"Since Europe has been divided by the Soviet Union into two parts," he wrote to the Foreign Office in April 1945, "we had better lose no time in ensuring that ours remains the better and, with the support of the outside world, the stronger half."

Roberts saw Soviet political dogma as only one of a number of critical factors in the Soviet make-up at a time when there was deep fear in Britain of Marxism–Leninism.

In Moscow the British worked closely with the Americans. Ambassador Averell Harriman and his British opposite number Sir Archibald Clark-Kerr (one of whose affectations was to insist on goose-quill pens) were in almost daily contact; and this extended to the two embassy staffs who learned to work together as a team, above all in the impossible task of trying to make the Russians honour their Yalta commitments.

Away from his desk, Roberts played cricket for the Embassy against the Military Mission – on a football ground through which ran a right-of-way. Matches were interrupted to allow the passage of bewildered Russian peasants going about their business.

From 1947 to 1949, Roberts was principal private secretary to the Foreign Secretary Ernest Bevin, whom he both liked and admired. In 1948, when the British Ambassador in Moscow fell ill, Bevin sent Roberts as his personal representative to negotiate with Stalin over the Berlin blockade.

"With Stalin you had to be extremely well briefed," Roberts recalled. "In those days, Soviet leaders delegated very little and tended to conduct the important business themselves. Stalin was very clever. He would get his foreign minister, Molotov, to negotiate the difficult bits and take any flak. Then, once a decision was around the corner, he'd come in all smiles and agree. He appeared the very antithesis of the ruthless dictator he was."

Roberts remembered how Stalin used always to get Molotov to countersign the bundles of death decrees he routinely issued – so as to make things look legal. "He even forced Molotov to sign an order exiling his, Molotov's, own wife to Siberia."

In 1950, again at Bevin's express wish, Roberts was loaned by the Foreign Office to the Commonwealth Relations Office to go as Deputy High Commissioner to India, second-in-command to Sir Archibald Nye.

He returned to London in 1951 to become Deputy Under-Secretary of State for Foreign Affairs. As a member of the Foreign Service he could display no political alignment, but Roberts's personal sympathies were with the Labour Party, and he was not enthusiastic about the return of the Tories that year.

Roberts conducted most of the negotiations over German re-armament, and regularly helped, with his American and French opposite numbers, to draw up the combined Western replies to the series of Russian "Notes" on Germany's future.

In 1953 he was a member of the British delegation at the Bermuda Conference, which was intended to crystallise a positive Allied policy for Western Europe, preparatory to a meeting of the Four Power Foreign Ministers in Berlin.

The next year Roberts became Ambassador to Yugoslavia, in the years when Tito was veering away from the Soviet bloc.

Two years later Roberts became Britain's Permanent Representative on the North Atlantic Council, in Paris, and from 1957 to 1960 he was UK Permanent Representative on the Council of Nato.

In 1961 Roberts succeeded Sir Patrick Reilly as Ambassador to the Soviet Union. During a two-year term he weathered a succession of crises, including the war in Laos, the Cuban Missile crisis and the building of the Berlin Wall.

He got to know Khrushchev well, and at a Kremlin party, when the talk turned to shooting, asked Khrushchev whether there were still bears in Russia. "Bears?" Khrushchev replied. "Of course. I am a bear." And he picked up the 5ft 4in Roberts and gave him a bear-hug.

Roberts left Moscow in November 1962 after a farewell talk with Khrushchev which lasted nearly two and a half hours. A few months later he succeeded Sir Christopher Steel as Ambassador to the Federal Republic of Germany. Typically, upon arriving in Bonn he insisted on going to the Embassy before visiting the Residence, creating a tornado of work while Lady Roberts sat waiting in the car.

After the Queen's successful visit to the Federal Republic in May 1965, Roberts was appointed GCVO. But as a diplomat in Bonn he was saddled with the tricky task of keeping Anglo-German relations on an even keel during the negotiations that accompanied Britain's second application to join the Common Market. It was a measure of Roberts's value that he remained *en poste* six months beyond his 60th birthday.

Few people have been less wearied by age or less anxious to put their feet up in retirement than Roberts. He was recruited by his former Foreign Office colleague Bill Bentinck (later the 9th Duke of Portland) to Unilever, as a foreign affairs adviser; and he performed a similar role at Lloyd's of London. He also joined the board of Dunlop, and, to keep himself occupied outside office hours, he became president of the Atlantic Treaty Association and the European Atlantic Group.

He was also an outspoken but valued member of the three-man review committee on overseas representation set up in 1968 by the Labour Foreign Secretary Michael Stewart to look into the working of the Diplomatic Service. The committee was headed by Sir Val Duncan, chairman of the Rio Tinto Zinc Corporation.

The Report recommended slashing and streamlining Britain's diplomatic effort, to be concentrated on the "towering importance" of the export drive. "Britain is now a major power of the second order," the Report pronounced. It called for special attention to Western Europe and North America, and cuts in most other areas. The old idea that a diplomat should do "a bit of everything" during his career was outdated: "commercial work is the most urgent task of our overseas representatives".

Roberts was president of the German Chamber of Commerce in Britain, and president of the Anglo-German Association. For many years he chaired the annual three-day Anglo-German Society's Königswinter conferences at Cambridge.

As long as Nato existed and continued to provide a minimum of security, Roberts observed at the Conference held in 1975: "There is no real alternative to *détente*, even for Russia."

Roberts was president of the European Atlantic Group and also presided over the British Atlantic Committee, the educational arm of Nato, from 1968 to 1982, and was vice-president of the Britain–Russia Centre.

Roberts was appointed CMG in 1946, KCMG in 1953 and GCMG in 1963.

Lady Roberts died in 1990.

January 9 1998

MARTHA GELLHORN

MARTHA GELLHORN, who has died aged 89, was one of the great war correspondents of the century: brave, fierce and wholly committed to the truth of a situation, she was among the first women to be acknowledged by male journalists as an equal.

She covered the globe in pursuit of conflict, reporting on struggles as geographically and temporally remote as the Spanish Civil War in 1937 and the American invasion of Panama in 1989.

Her interest was not in the politics of war, but in the experience of those most directly affected by it. Instinctively Left-wing but an immaculate detector of slant and cant, on the front line she eschewed briefings and conversation with generals in favour of the company of soldiers and postmen, those asked to fight and those trying to survive.

After her reports from Vietnam led to her ejection by the South Vietnamese, she warned repeatedly of attempts to restrict the freedom of journalists in war-time, of manipulation and selection of what could be reported. This made her unpopular with governments, but the dislike was mutual, and rooted in history. Since witnessing the betrayal of the Czechs in 1938 Martha Gellhorn had followed a stern credo. "Never believe governments," she wrote, "not any of them, not a word they say; keep an untrusting eye on all they do."

Martha Ellis Gellhorn was born in 1908 at St Louis, Missouri. Her father was an eminent gynaecologist, her mother a suffragette and social reformer who opened a pioneering, and controversial, co-educational school at which young Martha was briefly a pupil.

She then attended Bryn Mawr College, Philadelphia, but her emerging social conscience prompted her to leave in her junior year to try to help those suffering in the Depression. Her heroine was Eleanor Roosevelt, and she worked for a time in the White House on a study of unemployment.

She spent the early 1930s in France, enjoying a

lengthy affair with the Marquis de Jouvenel (Colette's stepson), and wrote her first journalism from Paris for *Vogue*. She also wrote a novel, *What Mad Pursuit?* (1934), about three American women in interwar Europe.

Of German stock herself, Martha Gellhorn then went to Bavaria in the summer of 1936, intending to work on a novel that would express her pacifist beliefs. Instead she found herself appalled by the frenzied rhetoric of the Nazis and became an opponent of Fascism. Coupled with her idealism, this led her in 1937 to Spain, then on the verge of civil war, and in Madrid she ran into an acquaintance, Ernest Hemingway.

The pair had met the previous year in Florida, and Hemingway had been entranced by her blonde hair and blue eyes, borrowing those characteristics for Maria, the heroine of *For Whom The Bell Tolls* (1940), which he dedicated to Martha Gellhorn. She already had a brief marriage behind her, and the pair soon became lovers.

At Hemingway's prompting, she sent a piece about the Spanish war to the American magazine *Collier's*, which published it; she had become a war correspondent.

Yet though Hemingway came to exert a powerful influence on her literary style, she had already developed her own rules for reportage. Recollecting a visit to a hospital in 1937, she wrote that she had little time for objectivity in war reporting: "You go into a hospital and it's full of wounded kids. So you write what you see. You don't say there's 37 wounded children in this hospital but maybe there's 38 on the other side. You write what you see."

After Spain, she reported from Prague at the start of the Second World War, and was in Helsinki when it was bombed by the Russians in 1939. Then in 1940 she married Hemingway, becoming his third wife; Robert Capa photographed the wedding.

It was Martha Gellhorn who found the farmhouse outside Havana that was to become Hemingway's base thereafter, but already their natures were taking them in different directions; only reluctantly did Hemingway spend the first months of married life on the front-line of the Sino-Japanese conflict, from where his wife was reporting.

The couple spent most of the Second World War apart. Initially she chided him for staying in Cuba, then began to hate his drinking, jealous rages and resentment of her ambition. An Anglophile, she preferred to endure the bombing of London, and watched from a balcony at the Dorchester Hotel as the first V1 flying bomb flashed along Park Lane.

When her estranged husband did arrive in Europe, it was to replace her as *Collier's* chief correspondent and to strip her of her accreditation to report on the D-Day landings. Undaunted, Martha Gellhorn hid in the lavatory of a hospital ship, emerging on the Normandy beaches to work as a stretcher-bearer. She was the only unauthorised journalist to cover the invasion. Then she accompanied the US 82nd Airborne Division across Europe to Berlin.

She and Hemingway were divorced in 1945. Under Cuban law, he was entitled to all her possessions, and refused even to return her typewriter. He also incorporated a bitter portrait of her in *Across the River and Into the Trees* (1950); she refused to let his name be mentioned in her presence ever again.

Martha Gellhorn continued to work as a war correspondent into her eighties, reporting on Vietnam, the Arab–Israeli conflict and, at the age of 81, as the first correspondent into Panama as Noriega was ousted.

She remained a stern critic of American foreign policy, especially in Central America. Having lived in Mexico, Italy, Kenya and Cuba, she made her home in Wales, later moving to a flat in Chelsea. She remained an unsentimental and curious observer; in the year before her death, partially blind and arthritic, she visited the slums of Brazil.

Her energy was matched by an utter lack of culinary skill and hatred of what she termed "The Kitchen of Life", the dull and necessary business of human existence, such as putting up shelves.

She wrote five more novels, the best being *Liana* (1943) and *The Weather in Africa* (1978), although the virtues which made her so fine a reporter perhaps prevented her (much to her regret) from developing as an imaginative novelist.

Among her non-fiction works, *Travels With Myself and Another* (1978) told of her worst journeys, while *The Face of War* (1959) collected pieces on war from locations as diverse as Madrid and Dachau.

Her final book, *The View from the Ground* (1988), was a selection of her journalism, and proved that she attracted trouble even in peacetime. One piece, from the *Spectator* in 1936, told of an episode in Mississippi after her car had broken down. As two local men were giving her a lift, they made a detour to lynch a black man. Martha Gellhorn described how she was taken to view the victim as he was soaked in kerosene and set alight: "The flames didn't take so well at first. Then they got on to his trousers and went well, shooting up, and there was a hissing sound and I thought a smell. I went away and was sick."

Then the man giving her a lift approached her: "We'll get you to Columbia now. Sorry we had to keep you waiting."

Martha Gellhorn married secondly in 1954 (dissolved 1963), T. S. Matthews, a former editor of *Time*. She also adopted a son, Sandy.

February 17 1998

BENJAMIN SPOCK

BENJAMIN SPOCK, who has died aged 94, wrote what became a bible for a generation of young mothers; his *The Common Sense Book of Baby and Child Care* (1946) long remained the world's best-selling book after Holy Scripture.

The secret of Dr Spock's success was simple; he told parents to react spontaneously to their children, to give them love, cuddles, food and discipline when they felt it was appropriate, and not according to a rigid schedule. The famous opening of his child-care classic lifted the hearts of faltering mothers everywhere: "Trust yourself. You know more than you think you do."

The Spock philosophy, although not entirely original – a pre-war manual called *Babies are Human Beings*, by Charles and Mary Aldrich, foreshadowed the Spock phenomenon – liberated mothers from the previous guru, Dr Truby King.

A New Zealander who admired aspects of Germanic

paediatrics, Truby King had recommended mothers to feed their babies according to a timetable. Spock came along and told mothers to feed their babies when they cried – or when the mother felt like it. From Spock, parents learned there were no absolute laws of child-care.

Later, during the 1960s, Spock threw himself into opposition to America's entanglement in Vietnam. In 1967, he and four others were charged with conspiracy to aid and abet draft-dodging. Four of them, including Spock, were sentenced to two years in prison. Spock and another man were also fined $5,000.

Execution of the sentences was waived, and in 1969 the convictions were quashed on appeal, on the grounds that the 85-year-old trial judge had improperly directed the jury. By then, however, Spock's baby-care philosophy was being denounced by conservatives as the very breeding ground of the Permissive Society.

Spock's belief in demand-feeding babies – giving the baby the breast or the bottle when the baby wanted it – was now seen as the root cause of the self-indulgence associated with the "Me Generation". Spock was blamed for a decline in the Protestant work ethic; the Spock baby was raised, it was said by critics, to "want it now", and grew up to live for instant pleasures, instant responses, with a low capacity for duty, self-sacrifice, and responsibility.

This contrasted sharply with Spock's own background, which was the epitome of upright New England Protestant orthodoxy.

Benjamin McLane Spock was born at New Haven, Connecticut, on May 2 1903, the eldest of two sons and four daughters. The Spocks were descended from Dutch immigrants named Spaak.

Benjamin Spock would remember his father, a lawyer who worked for the Newhaven Railroad, as a remote figure – "grave but just" and "very quiet, like some men are, especially in America". His puritanical mother was "very moralistic, excessively controlling".

Spock recalled that "in the stern family in which I grew up . . . there was no allowance made for psychological or human explanation of naughty or unwise behaviour. Every issue was somehow a matter of morality or health."

Young Benjamin proved to be the model of a diligent, devoted son. He spent his schooldays at Hamden Hall County Day School, Connecticut, and at Phillips Academy, Andover, Massachusetts. He went on to Yale, with aspirations of becoming an architect.

One summer, he worked as a counsellor in a camp run by the Newington Crippled Children's Home, near Hartford. "I watched the orthopaedic surgeon working with the children who had had polio," he recalled. "I realised how much he was helping them and I decided that I wanted to be a doctor."

Consequently, in 1925, Spock enrolled at the Yale Medical School, going on from there to Columbia University College of Physicians and Surgeons. He completed residencies in paediatrics at the New York Nursery and Child's Hospital, and in psychiatry at New York Hospital. In his spare time he also trained for six years at the New York Psychoanalytic Institute.

In 1927, Spock married Jane Davenport Cheney, a silk heiress. In due course, the young couple had two sons, and Jane Spock recalled that her husband was at first "a little stricter than I was" in bringing them up. Later, he became "a little more permissive".

From 1933, Spock practised paediatrics privately in New York, taught at Cornell and acted as a consultant in paediatric psychiatry. "One of my faults as a paediatrician," he later said, "has always been that I whoop it up too much with children." But it was a fault that soon won him a large clientele, who appreciated his gift of putting children at ease.

The first public event that touched Spock was the Spanish Civil War, though his involvement went no further than helping his wife to raise funds for war relief. Although sprung from a Republican family, Spock voted for Roosevelt and the New Deal.

During the Second World War, Spock served in the Medical Corps of the US Naval Reserve. He worked as a psychiatrist in naval hospitals in New York and California, and by 1946 had risen to the rank of lieutenant-commander. It was in his spare time during these years that he prepared the manuscript of *Baby and Child Care*, which his wife helped to research and typed up.

At that period, apart from the works of Truby King and the Aldriches, the most commonly consulted American baby-care book was Dr John B. Watson's severe treatise, *Psychological Care of Infant and Child* (1928). Typical of Watson's many stern admonitions to parents was: "Never, never kiss your child. Never hold it in your lap. Never rock its carriage."

Spock's *Baby and Child Care* was first published in 1946, and was an immediate success. Spock's intention was to counteract the fostering of fear and rigidity in paediatrics typified by Watson's chilling code, particularly in the area of infant feeding. He emphasised the importance of the differences between individual babies, and of the need for flexibility. Parents, he suggested, need not worry constantly about spoiling their offspring.

Spock continued to lead a busy professional life. He was on the staff of the Rochester Child Health Institute, the Mayo Clinic, and the University of Minnesota; he directed teaching programmes in child psychiatry and paediatrics, and regularly published articles on the problems of parents and children.

During the postwar years Spock was conventional in his politics. He approved of the Korean War as a "necessary repelling of aggression" and of Eisenhower's spending on arms. In 1960, he supported Kennedy, which some believed helped to secure JFK "the mothers' vote".

Spock's conversion to peace politics came sometime between 1961 and 1962, when the Soviet Union and America resumed the testing of nuclear bombs. He joined Sane, an organisation opposed to nuclear weapons, and from 1962 threw his energies into protests.

He became a familiar, controversial figure in anti-war protests, and something of a thorn in the side of President Johnson. In 1972, he stood for President, representing the Presidential People's Party, a somewhat eccentric anti-war grouping, and won 75,000 votes.

While his politics on peace remained radical for the rest of his life, on child-care Spock modified his earlier liberal views. He altered sections of the original *Baby and Child Care* book in later editions, gently reminding his readers that discipline also played a part in child-care.

His more recent works, including *A Teenager's Guide to Life and Love*, showed that Spock's roots remained firmly planted in the Protestant family ethic under which he had grown up. The best sex education a teenager could have, he wrote, was the example of two parents who showed love and respect for one another.

Many child-care books would follow in Spock's wake; his very success created a market for ever more tracts in the same vein. But Spock's manual remains remarkably helpful as a practical guide. Child psychology is notoriously vulnerable to fashion, but colic and cradle cap go on for ever.

A lanky 6ft 4in, in his young days at Yale, Spock rowed in the university crew which won a gold medal in the 1924 Paris Olympics.

Benjamin Spock was twice married. After 49 years, he divorced his first wife and married a young businesswoman in her thirties, Mary Morgan Wright.

March 17 1998

MONSIGNOR ALFRED GILBEY

MONSIGNOR ALFRED GILBEY, the former Chaplain to the Roman Catholic undergraduates of Cambridge University who has died aged 96, was an unusual ecclesiastical figure – well known in Cambridge, London clubs and country houses, but very easy to caricature and misunderstand.

For generations of Cambridge men, non-Catholic as well as Catholic, Alfred Gilbey was the University dignitary who had made the most impact on them and for whom they felt the greatest affection and respect. His extraordinary influence as Chaplain, from 1932 to 1965, was due in part to his piety, his rock-like faith and his ability to explain Catholic beliefs in clear and simple terms; and partly to his kindliness and friendliness, his sympathy, his courtesy and charm.

At Fisher House, the Catholic Chaplaincy in Guildhall Street, all comers were given a warm welcome – and also sherry or port if the hour was appropriate. Having some private means (though not nearly as much as was supposed) enabled him to be generous with his hospitality: luncheon parties at the Pitt Club, the Lion or the Bath, dinner parties in his panelled dining-room hung with Stuart portraits, Sunday teas at which any member of his flock could turn up.

At this former inn of 17th-century origin Gilbey created a country-house atmosphere and built up a library which eventually boasted a fine collection of books and pamphlets about Cambridge. He was himself an authority on the history of Cambridge and its lore. To this and to his many other intellectual interests, which included architecture, he had a very scholarly approach; though he would mention his pass degree as evidence that he was no academic.

His anecdotes were entertaining and he would tell them succinctly and with precision, in his distinctive but not always distinct voice; he had an uncanny facility for the *mot juste*. But what, more than anything else, made his company so delightful was the air of serenity which came partly from his religious faith and partly from his intense interest in people and things.

His enjoyment of life was particularly infectious when out with the Trinity Foot Beagles, of which he was a regular and enthusiastic follower, having been a fox-hunter in his youth.

Inevitably myths were woven around Alfred Gilbey. Because as Chaplain he instructed many converts, he was believed to be an active proselytiser; but in truth most of his converts had never met him until they came to him for instruction.

The non-Catholic undergraduates with whom he associated tended to be sporting young men not much given to religious discussion; many of them became his lifelong friends while never having any leanings to Catholicism.

His patrician manner and his sartorial elegance – the frock coat, the broad brimmed or tall hat, the cassock trimmed with the purple of a Domestic Prelate to the Pope, which he became in 1950, and of the superior dignity of Protonotary Apostolic, to which he was elevated in 1963 – caused some people to imagine him to be more socially exalted than he was. He never aspired to move in high society; his friends were drawn from all stations in life. He would say that men are not equal in the sight of God – some saints being greater than others. But he did not pretend to divine powers of discrimination himself.

Yet, when in the 1960s the University became increasingly class-conscious, it began to be felt, in certain quarters, that Gilbey was unsuited to be Chaplain to the new type of undergraduate. It was even suggested that some young men would be intimidated by the sight of the volumes of the *Peerage* on his bookshelves (he was an enthusiastic armorist).

The more immediate cause of his departure from

Cambridge in 1965 was his refusal to open his Chaplaincy to women undergraduates (who up until then had had a separate Chaplaincy of their own). His reason was that he considered it important that his Chaplaincy should retain the quasi-monastic atmosphere of the traditional men's colleges.

This gave rise to the myth that he disliked women; in fact he welcomed women to Fisher House as guests, and numbered many women among his dearest friends. He was delighted to officiate at the weddings of former members of his flock and he would afterwards take the same fatherly interest in the wives as he did in the husbands.

Alfred Newman Gilbey was born on July 13 1901 – he used to say how glad he was not to have been born a day earlier or later, on Orange Day or Bastille Day. His middle name did not derive from Cardinal Newman; he was the youngest of the seven children of Newman Gilbey of Mark Hall, Essex, and Maria Victorina de Ysasi. His grandfather and namesake was one of the founders of the family wine business.

Both his father and his uncle William Gilbey brought back Spanish brides and Catholicism from Jerez as well as sherry; William's grandson, Dom Gabriel Gilbey, who inherited the Barony of Vaux of Harrowden, was the first Benedictine to sit in the House of Lords since the Reformation.

Alfred Gilbey looked Spanish, loved Spain and used to say that Spanish mothers were the best in the world. At the same time he was English to the core, devoted to hunting and to the countryside of East Anglia.

He was a staunch upholder of the Edwardian customs, conventions and traditions of Englishmen of his generation and background. For instance he was always punctilious in doffing his hat when he passed the Cenotaph.

Influenced by the writings of Monsignor R. H. Benson, the brother of A. C. and E. F. Benson, Gilbey decided at an early age that he wanted to be a priest. But his father insisted that he should first enjoy himself in the world, which he proceeded to do with gusto; going from Beaumont to spend four blissful years at Trinity College, Cambridge, ending with only a pass degree but with his priestly vocation stronger than ever.

So he went to study at the Beda College in Rome and was ordained priest in the family chapel at Mark Hall, in the diocese of Brentwood, in 1929. He was ordained in his own patrimony (the last priest to be so); that is, he retained responsibility for his own maintenance, instead of being sponsored by a bishop and incardinated into a diocese.

He served as the Bishop of Brentwood's private secretary until he went to Cambridge as Chaplain three years later.

Alfred Gilbey's retirement was spent mostly in London, at the Travellers' Club, where he had a permanent bedroom and a tiny oratory in the former boot room. He would declare that he felt entirely at home at the Travellers' – more so than at his other clubs, the Athenaeum and Buck's, which he considered to be above him: the one intellectually, the other socially.

As an octogenarian, he felt greatly touched at being unexpectedly invited to become an honorary member of Pratt's; he was no less gratified at being invited to join the Old Brotherhood, a dining club of the Catholic secular clergy. Two other distinctions came to him when he was in his eighties – he was made a Canon of Brentwood and a Grand Cross Conventual Chaplain *ad honorem* in the Order of Malta, of which he had been a member since 1947.

In his retirement his days were almost fuller than they had been in Cambridge; in London he was more accessible to his friends, who could never have enough of his company. He kept all his faculties into his 10th decade and enjoyed amazingly good health, which he attributed to his going about as much as possible on foot.

On his visits to Cambridge, even in his late eighties, he never missed an opportunity of going out with the Trinity Foot Beagles; and he went to Northumberland every September to hunt with them there.

He did become very bent of stature and, when he was 94, he gave up catching the omnibus (as he continued to call it) each morning, after a benefactor insisted on sending a car instead to take him to Brompton Oratory, where he said his Mass – in the Tridentine rite, which, in conformity to Canon Law, his age entitled him to use.

As yet another interest for his youthful old age, his *Commonplace Book* was published and the course of instruction which he gave his converts also appeared in print as *We Believe* (1983). It was widely acclaimed and its sales exceeded all expectations. The volume's underlying theme, that Catholicism entails an acceptance of the teaching authority of the Church, was the bedrock of Alfred Gilbey's own life and ministry. He was resolute in refusing to construct a Church of his own devising, in accordance with personal preferences.

Once, in 1968, at the time of the controversy over the Church's attitude to birth control, a woman sitting next to him at dinner said to him brightly: "Do tell me, Monsignor, what do you think of the Pill?"

"I don't" was his reply.

David Watkin writes: Alfred Gilbey once observed to Monsignor Ronald Knox, "Dear Ronnie, I have the sort of mind that turned the Last Supper into a Pontifical High Mass." This was when they were both staying at Downside Abbey and Knox observed with mild amazement Gilbey's slow and ritualised process of packing a suitcase, gradually building up a three-dimensional mosaic in which every object had its allotted space.

Gilbey's comment well conveys his humour, self-knowledge and unswerving devotion to the forms of pre-Vatican II Catholicism. Packing, moreover, was to play a large role in his life, especially in the years following his retirement as Catholic Chaplain at Cambridge. He constantly travelled about Britain and the Continent to perform weddings, baptisms and requiem Masses for his vast flock which, though centred on his Cambridge undergraduates, continued to expand.

He was also one of the most sought-after spiritual advisers of his time, giving unstintingly of counsel which was rooted in his life of prayer. What gave unique power to his advice to those trying to be Catholics in the modern Church was his own ability to combine spiritual devotion with enjoyment of temporal goods.

He moved between the two with disconcerting rapidity. The Travellers' Club in Pall Mall might seem a surprisingly worldly home for a Catholic prelate, yet he created a chapel at the top of the back staircase where he could retreat from the guests on whom he lavished unceasing hospitality in the public rooms of the club.

Cardinal Heenan gave him a licence to reserve the Blessed Sacrament in this chapel, and also permission to say the Tridentine Mass on all occasions, whether public or private. This privilege made him much in demand from the many Catholics who found the post-Vatican II liturgy intolerable. He contrived to serve them without becoming a renegade like Archbishop Lefebvre.

It would be impossible to exaggerate the influence on Alfred Gilbey of his upbringing at Mark Hall, Essex, where he was born into a world which unusually combined traditional Edwardian country-house life with the Spanish Catholic piety of his mother who had come from Spain to marry his father. As a gilded, amusing, clever, generous and attractive undergraduate at Trinity, he kept from many of his friends his inner life and his ambition to become a priest.

As Catholic chaplain at Cambridge he received an extraordinary number of young men into the Church, though he achieved this without any direct proselytisation. He ran Fisher House, the Catholic chaplaincy, as an open house, like a free London club.

Catholic undergraduates would bring their non-Catholic friends who, falling under Gilbey's magnetic spell, would remain for instruction in the faith. He was persuaded to publish these instructions as a book, *We Believe* based on a tape-recording made by a Peterhouse undergraduate whom he was instructing in his room at the Travellers'.

We Believe was the subject of an admiring article in *The Times* by Roger Scruton, while Auberon Waugh wrote a preface to the American edition, and A. N. Wilson interviewed Gilbey for *Harper's*.

The Beda College, where he had studied, moved to

new and unattractive premises, and Mark Hall had been burned down by landgirls, thus sparing it, as Gilbey wryly observed, from the worse fate of becoming the community centre of Harlow New Town. The external fabric of much of his life was destroyed, but his faith remained so utterly intact that to his thousands of friends and admirers he seemed to embody the notion of sanctity in the modern world.

March 29 1998

DAVID HICKS

DAVID HICKS, who has died aged 69, was a very grand and successful interior decorator – still more grand and successful after his marriage in 1960 to Earl Mountbatten of Burma's daughter, Lady Pamela.

Yet Hicks's first appearance in Mountbatten's diaries was less than auspicious. "Walked with Pammy barefoot on the lawn for one hour hearing about David Hicks," Mountbatten recorded for September 13 1959. "As a result had blood blisters on both feet. Very painful."

Certainly interior decorators did not feature at the peak of Mountbatten's vision of the social hierarchy. But Hicks was not only talented; he was impossible to put down. "I enjoy being me," he once remarked, and no one ever succeeded in undermining that delight.

Such chutzpah appealed to Mountbatten, who supported the marriage wholeheartedly as soon as he was satisfied it would make his daughter happy. And even if he was not always convinced by his son-in-law's work, he knew how to tout for business.

"For an interior decorator like David, it is essential to get the maximum publicity," Mountbatten observed in 1969. "He is absolutely bound to get this," the diary entry went on, "having built the first house on Eleuthera [in the Bahamas] as far from the beach as the plots permit and with practically no view of it. I hope this will help to continue to build up David's international reputation."

A year later, all Mountbatten's doubts had dissolved; the house was absolutely charming, he admitted, "much nicer than I thought it was going to be." Eager to reinforce success, he fell into the habit of suggesting to his more celebrated friends that their residences might profit from redecoration. As it happened, he knew a fellow who might undertake the work . . .

When Mountbatten visited Kosygin in 1975 he pressed upon the Russian prime minister brochures from David Hicks and expressed the hope that the firm might be allowed to tender for the nine new hotels shortly to be built in Moscow. He also employed his son-in-law to redecorate some rooms at his house at Classiebawn in Ireland – though wags observed that the Gothic pile really needed an *external* designer.

Undoubtedly Hicks's marriage increased his prestige, bringing him such clients as the Prince of Wales and Princess Anne. But well before January 1960, when he left Romsey Abbey with Lady Pamela on his arm, he had established himself as a leading designer.

David Nightingale Hicks was born on March 25 1929 and brought up at Coggeshall in Essex. Both his father (very much a Victorian, born in 1863) and his maternal grandfather were stockbrokers. His father's ideal of painting, he remembered, was a series of coloured hunting prints by John Leech.

At Charterhouse young Hicks did not sit his school certificate, because his master considered he would never pass. He was more at home at the Central School of Art, but hated his first job, in an advertising agency.

His breakthrough came after he had redecorated his mother's house in South Eaton Place. *House and Garden* ran a feature on it, and suddenly Hicks found himself in demand as an interior decorator. In 1956 he went into partnership with the antiques dealer Tom Parr, and three years later set up his own business, specialising in the redecoration of houses in both London and the country.

Hicks departed from the chintzy styles in vogue between the wars, and introduced classical ornament mixed with geometric patterns of a bold symmetry. He paid great attention to lighting, and thought not so much in terms of colour as of colour *schemes*.

Similarly he believed that the quality of furniture and objects in a room was less important than the manner in which they were put together. He did not mind mixing styles from different periods, holding that good design always goes with good design.

His ideas caught on because he spoke as one having authority. "This house is a marriage of Inigo Jones, Palladio and myself," he declared of a building he had designed for some Iranians in the Algarve. Such a manner annihilated his clients' indecision, albeit at considerable expense.

"I really *abhor* standard lamps," he declared in 1966. "I *hate* satin, particularly when it has got designs painted on it; I *hate* wrought iron; I *loathe* colour used on modern office buildings." Such themes were developed in his book, *David Hicks on Decoration*, and in many subsequent volumes.

By 1973 David Hicks had two shops in London, and another in Paris. The business expanded further afield, to Germany, Greece, Pakistan and Australia. Unquenchably energetic, he diversified to design carpets, jewellery, gardens, fabrics, furniture, wallpapers, sheets and tiles. His attention to detail extended even to table mats and ashtrays.

At home he worked at Windsor and Buckingham Palace. He stylishly remodelled the interior of Baronscourt in Northern Ireland for the Duke and Duchess of Abercorn. Abroad, he decorated hotel chains in Japan and offices for Aeroflot. His nightclub for the original *QE2* had walls covered with grey flannel edged with silver, and featured bright red screens to be drawn across the windows at night. His flat for Helena Rubinstein was a study in purple.

He designed the library for the British Embassy in Washington, a yacht for King Fahd, and two restaurants for the Barbican. He acted as a consultant on car interiors for BMW. In the 1970s he branched out into fashion accessories for the Japanese market, producing everything from umbrellas to bedroom slippers. In 1982 his collection for women, cool, elegant and very English, was bought by Fortnum & Mason.

Somehow he also found time to be Deputy Director General of the English-Speaking Union of the Commonwealth.

Hicks and Lady Pamela lived at Britwell Salome House, in Oxfordshire. The main house was sold in 1979, and much of the contents auctioned off. The

Hickses then removed to a house on the estate. They also had a set in Albany.

If Hicks's clients were sometimes conscious of a certain hauteur, in private he was excellent company, sharp, witty and irreverent. He courageously made light of the illness which latterly disfigured his clean-cut elegance.

David and Lady Pamela Hicks had a son and two daughters.

April 1 1998

DOROTHY SQUIRES

DOROTHY SQUIRES, the singer who has died aged 83, so relentlessly followed the return journey from riches back to rags that at times her life seemed a ridiculous parody.

It was not that she was without some responsibility for her eventual misery. She had pathologically jealous feelings of love and hatred for her former husband, the film actor Roger Moore. Having tasted fame as a star selling millions of records, she was later made bankrupt, evicted from her home and eventually declared a vexatious litigant. She was repeatedly arrested for offences related to her drinking, including assault and dangerous driving.

Her behaviour became increasingly eccentric. She once placed a full-page advertisement for a concert in *The Stage*; it included several appeals to God ("If vengeance be thine . . .") and enjoined everyone planning to attend the concert to "have bums on seats by seven-thirty sharp, in honour of Her Britannic Majesty Queen Elizabeth II". But none of the Royal Family was attending the concert.

She was born Edna May Squires on March 25 1915 in a travelling van parked in a field at Pontyberem, Carmarthenshire. She always referred to herself as "Nenna". She was brought up at Dafen, near Llanelli, found a job at a local tinplate factory and toyed with nursing, but decided instead to be a singer.

"I was sixteen and a half when I auditioned for Billy Reid," she would recall. Reid was 22 years older, and married "to a dead ringer for Myrna Loy", but neither fact proved an obstacle to Miss Squires's affair with the bandleader. "Extreme youth was my only excuse for breaking up that marriage", she later said. "Besides, his wife had been away on holiday for eight months."

They formed an act called The Composer and His Voice, which toured the variety halls, with Miss Squires singing and Reid at the piano. She moved in with him and they caused a scandal by living "as man and wife". During the years the couple were together, she made her wireless debut on *Variety Bandbox*, singing ballads with The Billy Reid Accordion Band.

The couple scored hits with Reid's songs "Gypsy" and "I'm Walking Behind You". With the proceeds, Miss Squires bought a house and Reid bought the Llanelli Theatre. Despite Dorothy Squires's initial success, it seemed that Reid's songs sold better in the United States if American artists recorded cover versions.

The Ink Spots sold a million with "Gypsy", and Eddie Fisher's version of "I'm Walking Behind You" was a No. 1 in 1953. To her enormous chagrin, Dorothy Squires never made it as big as she expected.

Her break-up with Reid has been described as a "catalogue of tears and fisticuffs". In the seemingly endless court cases that followed, Reid claimed he had contributed a large amount to the cost of her house and Miss Squires claimed that she had invested in his theatre. She also claimed that Reid beat her in public and that he was so jealous he had to follow her.

The couple finally parted after a scene in the Llanelli Theatre bar in 1950. Miss Squires's father tried to separate the arguing pair and was slapped in the face for his pains. During the court case, Dorothy Squires was asked by a barrister if she liked Reid, and answered: "Well, would *you* like him?"

Dorothy Squires met Roger Moore in 1952. Moore was then a struggling actor who made a living as a male model, advertising chunky knitwear, Brylcreem and Macleans toothpaste. He was 25 (12 years younger than she) and married to a skater, Doorn van Steyn. These difficulties had little effect on Miss Squires and she and Moore began an affair. Moore left the Streatham council flat he shared with Doorn, and moved into Squires's mansion. Moore was eventually divorced, and married Miss Squires in 1953.

The Moores entertained regularly at her suburban spread, St Michael's Mount – so regularly that she tried to have it registered as a club. The application was turned down, to the relief of the neighbours, who complained about the noise.

Dorothy Squires often found herself at odds with the press and the BBC. As early as 1953 she was accusing the Corporation of nepotism and claiming the press hounded her.

She and Moore travelled to America in 1954, he to

make his first Hollywood film, and she to seek publicity. However after the film, he became more widely known in America than his wife. "By God!" she exclaimed, "in England I wouldn't be Mrs Roger Bloody-Moore."

In 1956, when Roger Moore was appearing in the television series *Ivanhoe*, the couple wrote a song to go with it. It was intended to be sung by a baritone over each episode's opening titles, but on the day of the recording, it proved impossible to find a male singer. Dorothy Squires volunteered to sing, saying: "I'll give it all the balls I've got!" The song was never used.

Moore became increasingly successful in America, but Miss Squires found that she was no more popular than when she had first arrived. She did manage cabaret bookings but often lost her temper if the audience wanted to dance.

Though Dorothy Squires made it into the British hit parade in 1961 with "Say It With Flowers" (accompanied by the toothy nine-fingered pianist, Russ Conway, late of the Merchant Navy), by then her marriage had started to collapse. Moore occasionally spent the night sleeping outside the house rather than face Miss Squires indoors.

Although Dorothy Squires had always been a "social drinker", her consumption grew rapidly when the press began to concentrate on her marital problems. One night Moore had to stop her "ranting" at an American comedian who was making jokes about the British. "I thought I was drinking fruit cup", she later claimed, "but it had seven different kinds of rum in it."

Moore told the press that they were separating. At first she said that this must be a joke: "His sense of humour is weird," she told reporters, "sometimes I don't understand it myself."

Moore flew to Italy to begin work on *The Rape of the Sabine Women*, and started an affair with Luisa Mattioli. Miss Squires was appearing at the Talk of the Town and later recalled how she discovered the affair. "Roger was in hospital, and there were some letters for him which I opened." When asked how she knew they were love letters she replied, "Oh come on, *Cara mia, tutti tutti*, of course they were love letters. Anyway I got them translated by the *maître d'* at the Astor Club."

Moore went to live with Luisa Mattioli (who changed her name by deed poll to Moore), but Dorothy Squires refused to divorce him. She served Moore with a writ in 1962, "for the restitution of conjugal rights", in an attempt to force him to come home.

In 1968, Dorothy Squires sued Kenneth More for libel. More had been the *compère* of a charity event and introduced Roger Moore and Luisa as "Mr Roger Moore and his wife". Miss Squires was furious and claimed that "people might think I had never been married to Roger at all".

When asked about the case later, Kenneth More answered: "Well, what could I say? 'Here's Mr Roger Moore and his mistress of eight years'?" Moore was adamant that the marriage was over and they finally divorced in 1969.

Miss Squires found it impossible to accept that Moore no longer loved her. Her behaviour became wilder, and on one occasion she smashed the Moores' French windows. She was arrested several times for driving under the influence of drink. When stopped for a breath test she knelt weeping on the pavement and then attacked her arresting officer, "punching and kicking him".

Dorothy Squires's catalogue of court appearances verged on absurdity. In 1971 she assaulted a taxi driver and was fined £50. In 1972, she was in court again, accused of "kicking a taxi driver in the head". The cab driver (who happened to be the *Carry On* star Bernard Bresslaw's brother), suffered injuries to an ear and had a "huge graze on the side of his face". In court, Miss Squires insisted: "I did not kick that man. I was practically barefoot." The judge told her that if she carried on in this way "some court in the future will have no alternative but to commit you to prison".

In 1970 Dorothy Squires planned a grand comeback with a one-woman show, for which she hired the London Palladium. It was a sell-out, but the coach parties did not all find the Squires magic they had hoped for. She hired the Palladium on three other nights, but there was no comeback. She began singing "My Way" with heavily emotional phrasing. Her career was definitely flagging.

She accused the BBC of carrying on a vendetta. "I intend to do something about it," she said. "I am planning a march on Broadcasting House. Thousands of my fans will demonstrate outside the Houses of Parliament."

The following year she hired Carnegie Hall for $20,000, but the venture made a loss. "I'm prepared to invest money," she said, "to prove that I can still fill a venue as large as this."

Miss Squires was in trouble again in 1973, this time in connection with a BBC "payola" scandal. She was accused of bribing Jack Dabb, the producer of *Family Favourites*, to play her records. She admitted paying Dabb's hotel expenses, but said they were a gift. She was cleared of the charge 18 months later.

After the case her popularity plummeted. She tried

to raise interest in a charity show and invited Queen Elizabeth The Queen Mother and other members of the Royal Family to attend. All had "previous engagements".

By the mid-1970s, Dorothy Squires was appearing more often in court than on stage. She continually broke contracts, claiming the fees were too low or conditions were not up to standard.

In 1977 she wrote an autobiography, *Rain, Rain, Go Away*, in which she wanted to publish several of Roger Moore's love letters, "to prove how much he loved me". Moore took out an injunction to prevent this.

Her publisher arranged for the sale of extracts from her book to Sunday newspapers. Dorothy Squires claimed she did not receive her share of the money. An interminable legal battle followed. Squires brought writ after writ against her publisher, but with no success. At one point she staged a sit-in in his office to publicise the case. "It's not the money," she claimed, "it's the principle." By 1979 it had finally been established in court that she had not been cheated.

Miss Squires's finances were by now in a bad way. She tried to promote a musical, *Old Rowley*, about Charles II, but with no success. She accused "theatreland" of a vendetta to stop the show. In 1981 she was declared bankrupt.

In 1982 she tried to make yet another comeback, at the age of 67, at the Theatre Royal, Drury Lane. Her finances did not improve, and in 1987 she was evicted from her 17-room house at Bray, Berkshire, where she claimed Lillie Langtry had once lived. She eventually accepted the loan of a house at Trebanog in South Wales from a fan who kept a fish-and-chip shop nearby.

By then, she had launched 21 High Court actions in

five years. Nine had been dismissed as "vexatious or frivolous". She was prohibited from starting any further actions without High Court consent.

She was declared bankrupt again in 1989 after walking out on a booking in Swansea – her second professional engagement in five years. She had previously been offered £1,500 a week to replace Dolores Grey in *Follies*. She turned the part down, claiming: "I'm worth more than that!"

In 1990 the contents of her house were sold by the Trustees in Bankruptcy. In 1997 she sold her jewellery. At the hospital where she died she was registered as Mrs Edna May Moore. She had no children.

April 15 1998.

PHILIP O'CONNOR

PHILIP O'CONNOR, who has died aged 81, was an eccentric and author of one of the strangest autobiographies of modern times.

Memoirs of a Public Baby, published in 1958, described in startling fresh prose and without a hint of self-pity, O'Connor's ordeals as an abandoned child, his subsequent alcoholism, incarceration in a mental hospital and chaotic early adulthood. The book had an immediate impact on the literary establishment. In a breezy introduction, Stephen Spender (*qv*) hailed the author as "one of the really chosen. He is without pose and affectation. He wears no mask."

"Such lucidity," wrote Cyril Connolly in the *Sunday Times*, "such sincerity, such impatience with all that is irrelevant and extraneous to his demon of self-revelation is proof of an acutely conscious and contemporary sensibility."

One of the few notes of dissent came from the woman novelist E. Arnot Robertson on the BBC programme *The Critics*. Dismissing *Memoirs of a Public Baby* as "a very juvenile picture of a man who seems to be out to shock all the time," Miss Robertson caused a classic clash of opinion among her colleagues, of the sort later parodied by Peter Sellers. When the art critic David Sylvester began to speak of the book's "tremendous maturity", Arnot Robertson reasserted her claim that O'Connor's autobiography could only be of interest to a psychiatrist or nurse.

Philip Marie Constant Bancroft O'Connor was born at Leighton Buzzard, Bedfordshire, on September 8 1916, the son of an Irish surgeon and a mother of English, Dutch and Asiatic blood. He never knew his father but remembered his mother for "her infantile giggle and utter lack of British social seriousness", both of which idiosyncrasies he inherited.

O'Connor's earliest years were spent in Yeovil, Pinner and a hotel in the Cromwell Road, Kensington, which he remembered for its thick carpets and "low, luscious lights". In 1919 the family moved to Wimereux, a French seaside resort near Boulogne, where Philip, then aged three or four, was soon abandoned by his mother in the local patisserie. Here he spent the next two years, sleeping in the bed of the matronly proprietor Mme Tillieux, annoyed by her bottom-pinching but reassured by the great "crash" of her urine into an enamelled pail beside her bed.

Eventually, young Philip was reclaimed from this

"heavy heaven" of sugared almonds and *gâteaux-bateaux* and transported by his mother to a cellar in Dean Street, Soho, where his education began at a nearby convent in Leicester Square.

At the age of 11, Philip was again adopted, this time by a one-legged bachelor civil servant. He went to live with him in a hut, measuring 12ft by 8ft, on Box Hill, in Surrey.

From here he continued his schooling at "a dingily select establishment" called Eton House and thereafter at Dorking High School. "Schoolmasters' flesh looked like old pastry," he wrote of this dismal period of his life. "You could study it until you felt as sleepy as it."

Philip O'Connor left school of his own accord before his education was complete and took the "flashy road of brilliance" to Fitzrovia. During the months that followed, he had tea with Aldous Huxley in Albany, spoke at Hyde Park Corner and then tramped across England and Ireland, living on 10 shillings a week.

At the age of 18, he entered the Maudsley Hospital with schizophrenia. From a verandah there he witnessed the burning of Crystal Palace. He began to produce surrealist poetry which was published in *New Verse* and elsewhere. One of his verses ended with the lines: "*I want money./Editor, print this and send me some when you call it a poem.*"

Even with writing as honest as this, O'Connor was unable to earn a living, but his bright-eyed figure found a place on the fringes of the literary world and in the hearts of its *femmes d'artistes*. His first wife, Jean, was herself the inspiration for fellow bohemian Paul Potts's sad little masterpiece *Dante Called You Beatrice*.

She eventually went mad and tried to murder her

husband with razor blades, cutlery and a wood-chopping axe. In his autobiography, O'Connor describes his state of manic exaltation on leaving his wife in a mental hospital: "My body careered away like an empty removal lorry."

Back in London, O'Connor enhanced his reputation as a madman and a menace by sending a blurred, pencil-written note on dirty paper up to Aldous Huxley's suite at Claridge's requesting £5, and by jumping out from behind a door and saying "Boo!" to T. S. Eliot. A more willing victim was Stephen Spender, who wrote of O'Connor in his *Journals* (1985): "I am a sucker for him."

Memoirs of a Public Baby was followed by *The Lower View* (1960) which described visits by bicycle to literary and artistic people, including Sir Herbert Read, Alan Rawsthorne and Bertrand Russell.

Living in Croesor (1962), which described O'Connor's life in a Welsh village above the Glaswyn Estaury, was less well received. "Croesor has obviously been good for Mr O'Connor," *The Times Literary Supplement* said. "Whether he has been good for Croesor is perhaps for its own people to decide."

Vagrancy, published as a Penguin Special in 1963, with an introduction by Jeremy Sandford, was a study of tramping, and carried O'Connor's interviews with a colourful flotsam of mendicants, including an Old Rugbeian Major addicted to meths.

O'Connor also worked spasmodically as a radio inter-viewer, making a number of Third Programme documentaries produced by David Thomson, in which he chatted to drug addicts, alcoholics and other refugees from society. His highly sympathetic, tentative and offbeat approach often got far closer to the subject than a professional interviewer might. In 1964, he gave the hitherto unknown Soho outsider Quentin Crisp his first broadcast.

In 1967, Philip O'Connor's life was transformed by a meeting with Mrs Panna Grady, an American heiress 20 years his junior and now on the loose in London after playing host for several years to the Beat Movement in New York. "He looked at me over his glasses in the most significant way, even before he had got through the door," Mrs Grady recalled later, and 17 days after this encounter the couple left together for France.

By a deliberate irony, they made their first home together in Wimereux, the resort where O'Connor had been abandoned as a child and which had continued to exercise his imagination. Grady and O'Connor brought up their two children there and later moved to the South of France, occupying various houses near Avignon.

At the age of 60, O'Connor began a long overdue phase of sobriety, but his writing became increasingly convoluted and unpublishable, though a book of poems *Arias of Water* appeared in 1981.

His reputation continued to rest on *Memoirs of a Public Baby*, which was republished in England in 1988 and in New York the following year, attracting further critical controversy. In the *New York Review of Books*, Gabriele Annan wrote that reading this autobiography was like "trying to swallow the contents of a cement mixer a quarter of an hour after it has been switched off". But Joseph Brodsky declared that he would gladly swap his mind and his tongue for O'Connor's.

In old age, O'Connor began to resemble the Ancient Mariner, but remained an inspiration to the younger generation. Told that he was suffering from cancer, he approached the final drama with a giggle, a laugh and a shout. Though he rarely visited London, he was still talked about in the pubs of Soho and sometimes branded "The One Who Got Away".

Philip O'Connor had an untidy private life. He was married at least twice and enjoyed innumerable liaisons. He had at least 10 children.

June 2 1998

CHARLES HORACE JONES

CHARLES HORACE JONES, the South Wales street-corner poet who has died aged 92, stood beside a lamppost in the High Street at Merthyr Tydfil, Glamorgan, for 45 years with a knuckleduster in his pocket as protection against the Welsh whom his poems had attacked.

Jones, perhaps the only poet to have been thrown bodily out of the National Eisteddfod, also caused trouble by refusing to complete a census form. He appeared in court dressed in black and told the Bench he was attending the funeral of man's freedom. He was fined £2.

In 1950 "Horace the Poet", as he was known, earned as much as £138 a week running a crafts business, but he gave it up to write poetry after waking in the middle of the night and feeling compelled by the Muse to scribble down his first verses on the back of a cigarette packet.

In the years that followed, his wife, Delia, became the breadwinner, taking a part-time job in a baker's shop. Her husband would meanwhile spend the entire day at the lamppost, with only an hour's break for lunch. He denounced with increasing violence the Welsh establishment, such as BBC Wales and the Church in Wales, as well as local politicians.

Jones was short and chubby with bushy, crescent-shaped eyebrows. A pencil-line moustache failed to strap down an upper lip that, even when he smiled, would curl towards hairy nostrils in a sneer. His demeanour was suggestive of a paradise lost, perhaps his own, and implied that a tail might fall unnoticed from behind his Chesterfield overcoat. If Satan had been a spiv he would have looked like Jones.

A passion to discredit the corrupt at first endeared him to passers-by. To these he became a champion of Socratic defiance, standing in the market-place each day exposing the incompetences of all who held office: lawyers, policemen, magistrates, baliffs, tax commissioners, civil servants, and members of the Labour-controlled council. An assortment of verses, lampoons and aphorisms would be printed by night and circulate throughout the town the next day.

Over the years, even old friends disappeared, repelled by the hatred he generated, for eventually even ordinary people with whom he found disfavour were castigated in his sour poetry. In time all came to tire of Horace the Poet and avoid the lamppost where he stood.

Charles Horace Jones was born on February 6 1906 and educated at Abermorlais School. When he was five his father, a coal miner, was killed in a mining accident, and he left school at twelve to work in the pits, at his mother's insistence.

His mother, without any reason Jones could explain,

gave away his white cat and pet canary. One of his last poems, "The Exorcist", deals with her cruelty. "I used to wake up at night screaming after having nightmares about those experiences," he once said. "It was only after I wrote the poem that the nightmares stopped. That is why I called it 'The Exorcist'."

In adulthood Jones paid the price of his lamppost lampoonery. He was beaten up in the high street, half-strangled in cafes, knocked unconscious and even set on fire. Asked once why he stood next to the lamppost, he said it was because it left one less side from which he could be attacked.

He did, however, leave the lamppost for seven years between 1976 and 1983 when Plaid Cymru, the Welsh Nationalist Party, gained control of Merthyr Tydfil borough council. It was more than he could bear and he spent the seven years exiled in London until the Labour Party, which he hated marginally less than the nationalists, regained control.

Despite his hatred for socialism, a collection of his work, *The Challenger*, was published by Merthyr Tydfil council in 1966. It cost them £152 10s. Immediately upon publication Jones criticised the council for wasting ratepayers' money. Even so, *The Challenger* was used by local schools in English literature classes.

"Merthyr is a cosmopolitan town. Generations of Jews, Italians, Irish, Spanish and even Chinese have lived here since the Industrial Revolution," Jones would say. "It is they and not just the Welsh who have shaped this town and to a large extent the South Wales Valleys. The Welsh Arts Council give away thousands of pounds each year to people to make walking sticks or fishing rods. But have you ever heard of any great Welsh writer, poet, or playwright who has made his name with the aid of a Welsh Arts Council grant? And yet they're paying out thousands of pounds for this, too."

Jones first came to attention in 1955 when he was ejected by police from the National Eisteddfod at Cardiff at the request of the Gorsedd of Bards. People had been buying booklets from him for a shilling under the impression they were official programmes. Only upon opening them did they find a collection of satirical verses by Jones entitled *A Dose of Salts*. It contained aphorisms such as: "The Eisteddfod is a cultural circus where everything is Welsh except the money."

A poem of his about Welsh rugby that appeared on the sports pages of a national tabloid before an international game in 1956 did little for his reputation in the Valleys. It read:

> *"Ich Dien! I serve."*
> *The motto of a nation*
> *That has lost its nerve.*
> *Lost its nerve and found it all,*
> *In the blown-up bladder*
> *Of an elongated ball.*

After those verses appeared, a gang of thugs closed in on him outside a butcher's shop. He escaped into the shop and got out through a side door without their knowing. An hour later they were still gathered outside the crowded shop waiting for him to come out. "After that," Jones explained, "I carried a knuckleduster wherever I went."

On another occasion a local businessman whom Jones had mocked invited him to his office above a shop in the town. Inside, he brought a chair down over Jones's head, knocking him unconscious. When he came round Jones was horrified to see that this man had lit a gas ring and was pressing it into his side. He managed to get away down the stairs, beat out the flames, and escaped.

When in 1966 he was refusing to complete the census form, the magistrate told him: "When you are living in a state you have to accept the sovereignty of the state." The theme of freedom and state dominance occupied a number of his poems, chief among them "The Jingle" (1971), a complex work of concise phrases that lie almost beyond the fringe of ordinary meaning. It was published at his own expense.

In Jones's poetry, war, materialism, bureaucracy, pollution, technology, sex and religion are treated with expressions taken from the cradle, the pulpit, the trenches, the town hall, bureaucracy and scientific jargon, The Bible and nursery rhymes.

In 1997 a path named Poet's Walk along the River Taff was opened in his honour. One of his poems, "My River", is displayed there.

In 1928 Jones eloped with Delia Griffin, daughter of an Irish immigrant in a neighbouring valley. They married in a register office in Aberdare. Though an atheist he remarried her six months later, at her parents' insistence, at the Catholic Church of Our Lady of the Rosary, Merthyr Tydfil. He is survived by his wife; they had a daughter.

September 16 1998

BRIGADIER MICHAEL CALVERT

BRIGADIER MICHAEL CALVERT, who has died aged 85, earned the nickname of "Mad Mike" during the Second World War for his exploits in the Burma jungle with the Chindits which effectively destroyed the legend of Japanese invincibility.

The epithet "Mad", however, was never used by his friends, who knew that all he did was carefully calculated, even though the odds against success might be dauntingly high.

In March 1944, when commanding 77th Brigade, Calvert established jungle camps by landing men deep in the Japanese lines of communication, thus completely disrupting Japanese planning and at the same time boosting the morale of British Forces in Burma.

Following his exploits in Burma, Calvert played a valuable part in the revival of the SAS, which had been disbanded in 1945. Using his experience of fighting the Japanese, in 1950 Calvert recruited a force in Hong Kong to take on Chinese terrorists in the jungles of Malaya. He named them the Malayan Scouts and they became the nucleus of the regular SAS.

Calvert was an idealist who was chivalrous to the point of folly and would never agree to brutal methods of acquiring information. In training, though, he was ruthlessly efficient: one of his training exercises was to have two men, armed with air guns, stalk each other half-naked through scrub. The impact of a pellet on bare flesh stimulated the recipient's appreciation of skill in fieldcraft.

James Michael Calvert was born on March 6 1913 at Rohtak, India, where his father was a district commissioner. Young Mike was educated at Bradfield, at Woolwich, and at Cambridge University, where he was awarded a half-Blue for swimming and water polo. He also boxed for the university and the Army.

He was commissioned into the Royal Engineers in 1933 and posted to Hong Kong. Having learnt Cantonese, he was allowed to accompany the Chinese Army, then fighting the Japanese near Shanghai. At one point he was taken prisoner by the Japanese, but managed to bluff his way to freedom.

In 1939 Calvert returned to London, but in 1940 resigned his commission to join the Scots Guards Ski Battalion which had been raised to fight the Russians in Finland. However, before it sailed the Finns had been beaten.

Calvert was now sent to Norway, where he was engaged in demolition work to slow the German advance. At the end of the campaign, in which he once nearly froze to death, he was one of the very last to leave.

His next posting was to Lochailort, in Scotland, as instructor in demolitions to the Commando Training Centre. He was then sent to Australia to train instructors for their future Commando units. Here he himself learnt much about explosives from his pupils, who used them in gold mining.

Next he went to the Bush Warfare School at Maymyo, Burma, and when the Japanese invaded he led a counter-attack. He met Orde Wingate and was soon co-operating with him on plans for guerrilla warfare.

In the closing stages of the retreat from Burma, Calvert was ordered to recruit a force for a last-ditch stand, collecting soldiers from convalescent camps and detention barracks. After a few early desertions, the remainder fought like demons.

Just before the end of the retreat, Calvert was involved in a deception plan, "losing" a briefcase where the Japanese would find it. It contained false information about the strength of the forces available to defend India and undoubtedly dissuaded the Japanese from pressing on. After recovering from the retreat, Calvert was sent to Saugor, central India, to train with 77th Brigade, which he would later command.

The first Chindits expedition went into the jungle on foot in 1943 and wreaked havoc behind the Japanese lines, but suffered badly and lost about a third of its number. Calvert later learnt that the force had upset Japanese strategy, causing them to make fresh plans which proved disastrous.

In May 1943 Calvert was awarded the DSO. The following year, six Chindit brigades (a total of 20,000 men) were sent into Burma, this time by air. Although losses were again high, the achievements were impressive.

Calvert established a blocking position at the "White City" airstrip, where he withstood fierce Japanese attacks from April 6 onwards; his brigade had been virtually decimated by the time it advanced to take Mogaung on June 27.

After 77 Brigade had captured Mogaung, Calvert was astonished to hear the BBC announce that it had been taken by General "Vinegar Joe" Stilwell's Chinese–American forces. Calvert sent a signal to Stilwell: "The

Chinese have taken Mogaung. 77 Brigade is proceeding to take umbrage." Stilwell's staff officers spent some time looking for Umbrage on their maps of Burma.

After the second Chindit expedition, and having won a bar to his DSO, Calvert was posted back to Europe in January 1945 to command the Special Air Service Brigade, which took part in the final stages of the campaign in Europe. Then, with 36 men, he flew to Norway, where he had the task of ordering the Germans, numbering many thousands, to lay down their arms.

Calvert ended the war as a temporary Brigadier, aged 33, but he was soon brought down to earth. He was sent as a Major to a Civil Affairs job in Trieste, a post for which he was entirely unsuited. But Calvert's outspoken support for unorthodox ideas had made him unpopular with his seniors.

After returning from Malaya in 1951 he was posted to Germany. There he rapidly went to seed. He was convicted on three charges of gross indecency and his military career ended.

Subsequently Calvert became a lecturer at Manchester University. He also wrote two books, *Prisoners of Hope* (1952) and *Fighting Mad* (1964).

Mike Calvert was a brave and brilliant guerrilla fighter. He sought nothing more than hand-to-hand combat and personal danger. As well as his two DSOs, Calvert was awarded 12 decorations by other countries.

Major-General James Lunt writes: I first met Michael Calvert when I was in hospital in Maymyo during the retreat from Burma in April 1942. He had just returned from preparing the viaduct across the Goteik Gorge on the Mandalay–Lashio railway line for demolition.

The Army Commander, General Alexander, had expressly forbidden him to blow the viaduct without his personal order, which never came. When Calvert returned he was taken to task for not acting on his own initiative, possibly one of the few occasions in his career when he was blamed for not disobeying orders.

Later in the retreat Calvert was nearly captured when he went up to a jungle hut in the dark, knocked on the door and entered. He found several Japanese officers sitting round a table studying a map. Saying, "Excuse me gentlemen, good night!" he hastily closed the door and decamped into the jungle.

He said he could hear laughter as he left. He then had to swim the River Chirdwin, 600 yards wide, before regaining the British lines. This he did disguised as a closely veiled Indian woman, hoodwinking the Japanese.

It was Calvert's misfortune to come to fame too young, and in operations of a kind unpopular with the more orthodox of his seniors. Like his hero Wingate before him, he aroused opposition by his outspoken views and determination to get his own way.

A veritable tiger in battle, but not always wise out of it, Mike Calvert was one of the finest fighting soldiers produced by the British Army in the Second World War.

November 28 1998

LORD GRADE

THE LORD GRADE, universally known as Lew, who has died aged 91, was a founding father of Independent Television and always played the exuberant role of an old-time showbiz mogul. With his nine-inch cigars, his Phantom VI Rolls-Royces, his extravagant self-publicity and his constant readiness to close multi-million-dollar deals over the transatlantic telephone, he became the closest Britain could get to a Sam Goldwyn.

A good day in the life of Lew Grade was one on which he got up (as usual before 6 a.m.) with an idea for a new television series, sold it to an American backer by noon, and informed his partners of the deal over lunch.

In his long career he exploited an unrivalled network of contacts among fellow entrepreneurs and international stars, calling in favours from one when negotiations with another flagged. He lived for his work and was given to joking that he would retire in 2001. His idea of purgatory, he once said, was "sitting on a beach in the South of France, sunning myself, with no phone calls to make."

Grade first made his name as a variety dancer, becoming World Charleston champion at the Albert Hall in December 1926. He then founded, with his younger brother Leslie (who died in 1979), a hugely successful theatrical agency, the Grade Organisation.

In the 1950s, as independent television got off to a shaky start, Grade and his new partner Val Parnell effectively took over an under-financed franchise, newly named Associated Television, from Norman Collins and Sir Robert Renwick. In his late sixties he embarked on a new career as a film producer. Finally, in 1985, already having lost control of ATV and of his own entertainments company, he set up as an independent filmmaker.

The Grade brothers – Lew, Bernie (later Lord Delfont) and Leslie – controlled between them a huge slice of the entertainment world. It was not quite rags-to-riches – Lew's autobiography, *Still Dancing* (1987), revealed that his Jewish-Russian parents had in fact been relatively prosperous. But their progress from East End immigrants to the most powerful showbusiness family in Europe was extraordinary.

Many of the stories about Lew Grade are apocryphal. A true one he told against himself concerned the time he was watching a comedy act in the second half at the old Metropolitan music-hall in the Edgware Road. He thought it was top of the bill material and rushed backstage. "I'm Lew Grade. Your act was amazing. How much are they paying you?" "£25 a week, Mr Grade." "Ridiculous, absurd, outrageous. I could get you £200. Who's your agent?" "You are, Mr Grade."

Many former employees and colleagues, especially those fallen on hard times, could attest to Grade's generosity. But the image of "Lovable Lew" (a phrase coined by one of his long-serving publicity aides) did not fit his ruthlessness in business.

At ATV he was determined to concentrate on high-profile entertainment programmes, preferably those like *Sunday Night at the London Palladium* that employed his own stars, and he was frequently at odds with other leading ITV contractors. Bargaining sessions with Lew and his partner Val Parnell were described by Howard Thomas of Thames Television as "bouts of persuasion, flattery, attack and invective".

Grade's real devotion was to the market-place. Buying and selling, particularly selling, rather than programme production, were his motivation. The creative agony was for others. "The sponsor and the star come first. The scripts are the last thing we do."

Critics might claim that his pursuit of ratings and easy viewing – "All I'm trying to do is to give people

pleasure after a hard day's work" – held ITV back from
the level it was to achieve under different regimes. But
others unhesitatingly proclaimed him the greatest British
showman of the century.

Grade was born Louis Winogradsky in the Ukrainian
town of Tokmak in 1906. Lew delighted in claiming a
birthday in common with the founder of Christianity,
but it was likely that he did not know his true birthday.

His father was a genial jack-of-all-trades with little
business acumen, though he appears once to have owned
a small private cinema. It was Lew's formidable mother,
a matriarch in the richest Jewish tradition, who in 1912
masterminded their emigration to London, where her
brothers were doing well as cabinet makers.

At Rochelle Street School in Bethnal Green, Lew
discovered a talent for figures and a strong memory. He
put these to use in the family embroidery business, but
early visits to the East Ham Palais confirmed that he had
also inherited an aptitude for dancing. By the time he
was 19 he had changed his name to Grad (later Grade)
and become a professional entertainer. His speciality was
doing the Charleston on a tiny table top.

Dancing across Europe, he realised there was more
money to be made as an agent. One of his first bookings
was a juvenile troupe, Beams' Breezy Babes, led by 14-
year-old Kathleen Moody, a prodigy with a Gracie Fields
voice. Seven years later, when the Grade Agency was on
its way to becoming the largest in Europe, she became
Mrs Grade. "The best deal", Lew liked to say, "that I
ever made."

Grade's success was built on flair, an insatiable
appetite for work, and chutzpah. For nearly 25 years he
exploited his ATV franchise, granted to supply the

Midland region, in order to produce populist "action-adventure" series aimed at the American market.

He perfected the art of the television "pre-sale" – upfront finance from American clients. His studios at Elstree made programmes to the 525-line American standard, converting them to 625-line for British consumption.

At the same time he kept a shrewd eye on those in high places who needed placating with judicious doses of "culture". As boss of ATV, he sold Eugene O'Neill's marathon *Long Day's Journey Into Night* to an unconvinced ABC Network. "Think of the prestige," he urged.

Far outweighing such achievements was an unending string of long-running audience-pullers like *The Saint*, *Danger Man*, *The Power Game*, *The Persuaders*, *The Prisoner* and *Robin Hood*. The unpromising puppet-show *Thunderbirds* was later to become a cult favourite.

Grade's ATV gave British viewers the dire motel soap opera *Crossroads*, which ran four evenings a week until the Independent Broadcasting Authority cut it back to three. Yet it also gave the world the enchanting *Muppet Show*, which sold to a record 112 countries.

Grade pulled out the stops with *Jesus of Nazareth* (1977), screened in two three-hour episodes. The title role was given to Robert Powell, who, Grade claimed, had been chosen by his wife Kathie. The choice dismayed the producer Franco Zeffirelli, who had other candidates in mind.

Grade attributed the inspiration for this award-winning film to a remark by Pope Paul VI during a private audience in 1973. Thanks to some exceptionally smart wheeler-dealing, even by Grade standards, among the American networks, the film made $30 million for the Grade organisation.

Grade believed in family values. He wanted no swearing in his shows and disliked showing *Armchair Theatre*, ITV's earliest incursion into contemporary drama – "The viewers don't want plays set in factories."

At the height of his television fame, Grade decided to diversify into feature films, with notably less success. Productions like *The Muppet Movie*, *Sophie's Choice* and *On Golden Pond* did well enough at the box office. But *Raise the Titanic* flopped so badly that Grade was supposed to have quipped: "It would have been cheaper to lower the Atlantic."

Until then he had enjoyed a long run of successful gambles. When in 1955 he put £15,000 into the fledgling ATV, he risked virtually all his capital. Within a few years his stake was worth millions, and he had become chairman and chief executive of the company, and boss of the vast Moss Empire theatre chain.

The Grade theatrical agency, which had on its books such stars as Bob Hope, Jack Benny, Julie Andrews, Shirley MacLaine, Roger Moore, Mario Lanza and Sammy Davis Jr, was sold in 1967 for £12 million to EMI.

Grade's career as a television tycoon ended after the IBA decided that their Midland franchise should go to Central Independent Television. In 1982 he was ousted from his film company Associated Communications Corporation by Robert Holmes à Court, a thrusting Australian whom Grade himself had encouraged.

Undaunted, in 1985 Grade launched The Grade Company, which he ran until his death. Its products – including a series based on novels by Barbara Cartland –

were less than distinguished. But they staved off the lack of occupation that Lew most dreaded. In 1995 he assumed the title of Chairman for Life of his ITC entertainment group.

Grade's energy in selling television to the Americans earned him a knighthood for services to export in 1969, during Harold Wilson's administration. In 1976 he was created a life peer as Baron Grade.

Grade was proud of his relations with the press. Every December for 30 years he invited 40 favoured journalists ("My friends") to a Christmas lunch. In return they played up to the Grade image.

He forged countless personal links with stars and producers around the world. No one could question the energy he brought to every venture.

Lew Grade and his wife Kathie were married for 56 years; she survives him. Their son, Paul, followed Lord Grade into the entertainment business.

December 14 1998

JUDGE MICHAEL ARGYLE

JUDGE MICHAEL ARGYLE, formerly of the Old Bailey, who has died aged 83, was celebrated for his *obiter dicta* from the bench and for imposing sentences that veered between harshness and leniency.

Argyle excited widespread publicity in 1971 when he jailed three young editors for obscenity in the *Oz* magazine "Schoolkids' issue" trial. Two of the convictions were quashed by the Court of Appeal, and although it upheld six-month sentences for sending obscene matter through the post, these were suspended for two years. The Appeal Court found that Argyle had made a "very substantial and serious misdirection" to the jury.

Issue 20 of *Oz* had contained articles on homosexuality and sadism – allegedly written by schoolchildren – and a cartoon depicting Rupert Bear deflowering a character named Gypsy Grannie. Argyle's presence at the trial provoked angry accusations of reactionary bias. "Our case became unrecognisable in your mouth," one of the editors told him. "I don't think you saw the trees for all the naked bears. If you jail us you will damage the already fading optimism of a generation."

Mr John Mortimer, the liberal barrister, acting for the defendants had little difficulty in representing Argyle as absurdly fuddy-duddy. When the trial was later dramatised for television, the *farceur* Leslie Phillips was cast as Judge Argyle.

A succession of defence witnesses made the *Oz* trial irresistibly amusing for many present, though Argyle sought to keep it a sober affair. "Are we going to have *continual* laughter and crosstalk?" he asked. "Are we going to be allowed to smoke and have drinks?" At one stage he even rapped the knuckles of visiting American judges for sniggering. "No doubt these people thought they were in Chicago," he remarked afterwards.

The sentences – ranging from nine to 15 months – were denounced as "disgusting fascism" by John Lennon, who, along with Mick Jagger, offered financial assistance to the convicted men. Effigies of Argyle were burnt, and he was given a police guard at his Nottinghamshire home.

The Daily Telegraph commented that the trial had "brought out all the self-appointed spokesmen of the tear-down-society *demi-monde* which infests our scene."

When Argyle published his memories of the *Oz* trial in *The Spectator* in 1995, 24 years after the event, the magazine was later obliged to print an apology to Mr Felix Dennis, acknowledging that neither he nor his colleagues on *Oz* ever "dealt in drugs or their sale to schoolchildren". Mr Dennis, who went on to become a successful businessman, had not been mollified by Argyle's giving him a lesser sentence on the grounds that he was "very much less intelligent" than his fellow defendants.

But in Argyle's eyes the fight was on a broader issue entirely: a battle for Christian civilisation. During the trial, he recalled, he would fall asleep at night thinking of his war days "fighting the SS alongside the Jewish brigade in the deep Italian snows, advancing across a valley carpeted with the dead, through the Gothic line towards the crossroads in a village called Croce, where hung the figure with the sunken head and the helpless outstretched arms of the Redeemer of mankind".

Argyle, who was a Circuit Judge who sat at the Old Bailey as an Additional Judge, felt that he had been mocked as a newcomer. But in other cases he tended to rule his court with an iron rod, whatever eccentric departures he allowed himself.

He once charged a juror who had talked briefly to a witness with contempt of court, put him in the cells for the afternoon and threatened him with a £2,000 fine. He treated drug traffickers harshly and sentenced the mastermind of a cocaine-smuggling ring to a record 24 years.

Despite his toughness, Michael Argyle became

known for the help he gave to unemployed defendants. He often gave up his lunch break to find work for young offenders. He told a man from his old regiment who had barricaded himself at home with firearms because he was jobless and desperate: "You are lucky to come before me. I led your regiment across the river Po – they are a good lot." He set the man free and sought him help from the Army.

Unemployed offenders would occasionally let him down. When a man given a suspended sentence for a drunken rampage appeared again before Argyle for a string of burglaries, the judge said: "I should not have trusted him, but one does one's best at the time."

Argyle's apparently whimsical leniency sometimes attracted public criticism, as when he handed a suspended sentence to a barman convicted of attempted rape. "You come from Derby," he said, "which is my part of the world. Off you go and don't come back."

Heathrow ground staff reacted bitterly when the press took up a remark of Argyle's renaming the airport "Thief Row" during a case involving dishonest baggage handlers. Other off-the-cuff remarks that attracted attention included a reference to the politician Denis Healey ("I knew him in the war – of course we were both on the same side then") and his tribute to a woman detective ("You are far too attractive to be a policewoman – you should be a film star").

Argyle grew accustomed to his judgments or comments being criticised by MPs, the press and pressure groups. But in 1987 he was publicly reprimanded by the Lord Chancellor, Lord Havers, after a speech to law students at Trent Polytechnic. Argyle had called for hanging for a wide category of serious crimes; he also hazarded that there were more than five million illegal immigrants in Britain. "I don't have the figures, but just go to Bradford," he said. Later that year Argyle told a British-born black defendant convicted of assault: "Get out and go back to Jamaica."

If Argyle's critics were not in short supply, his staff at the Old Bailey – in whom he took a generous personal interest – were fond of him.

He always had a television set in his robing room to keep him abreast of sports, especially those on which money was riding. When a television dispute interrupted coverage of England's 1986 tour of the West Indies, he startled the court with an outburst he was to regret: "Here we are struggling in cold temperatures, while in the Caribbean in glorious sunshine 22 of the best cricketers in the world are playing Test cricket. There is television yet none of us can watch the cricket. It is enough to make an orthodox Jew want to join the Nazi Party."

Michael Victor Argyle was born in Derbyshire on August 31 1915 and educated at Westminster and Trinity College, Cambridge. He read for the Bar and was called by Lincoln's Inn in 1938.

During the Second World War he was commissioned into the 7th Queen's Own Hussars, serving in India, the Middle East and Italy. It was there, in command of A-Squadron, that he won an immediate MC during the final campaign, in which they made opposed crossings of the rivers Po and Adige in amphibious Sherman tanks.

Argyle resumed practice on the Midland Circuit in 1947, took Silk in 1961 and became a Recorder of Northampton in 1962. He had been an unsuccessful

Conservative candidate for Belper in 1950 and Lough-borough in 1955. As a QC he defended the train robber Ronald Biggs in 1964.

In Birmingham, where he was a Recorder for five years from 1965, Argyle was renowned not only for his toughness, but also for his courtesy in court. He was careful and fair in his summing up and seldom interrupted during cross-examination.

He also became known as the reporters' judge, and was not averse to ensuring that the press box was full before speaking. A typical remark from this era was that "a settlement of Gypsies and tinkers is importing a ready-made criminal community".

Argyle's campaign in 1966 to stamp out burglary through deterrent sentencing was as effective as it was controversial. "If you come, boys, we are waiting for you," said Argyle.

Argyle also claimed to have achieved "more or less a 100 per cent telephone service in the city" through stiffer jail terms for vandals of public telephones. He frequently lambasted the authorities for ineptitude or negligence. He called for legislation to combat the menace of replica firearms, and attacked the early release of violent prisoners, once advising a woman who had been brutally attacked by a paroled killer: "Really go for the Establishment."

He also criticised what he termed the irrelevant introduction of racial prejudice into criminal trials. "Justice in this country is even-handed," he said.

He once told a Rastafarian convicted of possessing cannabis that he knew a number of Rastafarians. "I know them socially," he said. "They are totally honest and hardworking. They have their own religion which is fine."

He advocated legalising prostitution, pointing to the "sensible attitude" of the French. "I worked as a legal clerk in Paris in the Thirties," he explained, "so I got to know something about the city's vice system."

In his short farewell speech from the bench in 1988 Argyle said he felt sure that he had made some mistakes, "for which I apologise," but hoped he had also done some good. He confessed to one "bad thing" – arranging for a copy of the *Sporting Life* to be delivered daily to a barrister and two policemen recovering in hospital after the 1973 IRA bomb atrocity at the Old Bailey. "The result", he said, "was that the whole ward became compulsive gamblers."

A keen family man, Argyle once told a woman who had forged a divorce certificate and married bigamously: "You have caught me on a good day. I became a grandfather this morning again." Instead of jailing her, he put her on probation.

Argyle was a keen boxer – as befitted his square-jawed bulldog looks – and a trustee of the Amateur Boxing Association. He was also a resolute defender of the rottweiler and a noted whippet breeder, along with his wife, Ann, *née* Newton, whom he married in 1951. They had three daughters. She died in 1994.

January 6 1999

HENRIETTA MORAES

HENRIETTA MORAES, who has died aged 67, found her home in Soho and was painted by Francis Bacon, Lucian Freud and, much later, Maggi Hambling.

When she arrived in London aged 18, she went under the name of Wendy Welling, her mother's surname. She at once took to the bohemian life of Soho, drinking in the York Minster in Dean Street, known as the French pub, and, in the afternoons when pubs were closed, in the Colony Room Club. She was not unlike other habitués of Soho in her heroic drinking, but she was distinguished by her beauty, wit and surface toughness.

It was the world described by Julian Maclaren Ross in *Soho in the Forties* and by Daniel Farson in *Soho in the Fifties*, of macintoshes, men in hats, cigarette smoke, gangsters, tarts, petty criminals, cold nights, sailors and no money. There was a rough and tumble in conversation, plenty of unconventional sexual liaisons, and a camaraderie between refugees from suburban conventions that sometimes developed into kindness or love. She embraced it all.

At the Gargoyle nightclub she would meet the same crowd night after night: Brian Howard, Cyril Connolly, Philip Toynbee, Francis Bacon, Michael Wishart, Lucian Freud, John Minton, Robert Colquhoun and Robert MacBryde. At the beginning of the 1950s she met and fell in love with another Soho fixture, the film-maker Michael Law. It was he who suggested she find a better name, and for the rest of her life she was known as Henrietta. They married and for a short time lived in a house in Dean Street.

Henrietta now sat for Lucian Freud, whose portrait of her she later put on the dustjacket of her memoirs. Soho life moved fast, from the Coach and Horses to an afternoon drinking club, to the French when it opened again for the evening, to a nightclub. All along the way were strange, witty, unreliable, dangerous and sexually active characters. "In the Fifties, everyone was extremely rude to one another," she remembered. All this time money was short.

Among her friends was John Minton, the painter. He had good looks, talent and friends, but was haunted by a melancholy streak and troubled by his homosexuality.

She also fell in with Norman Bowler, who had been living in Minton's house in Apollo Place, Chelsea. She became pregnant by him and they married; they were to have a boy and a girl.

Some time later, just before his 40th birthday, Minton committed suicide. Henrietta Bowler heard the news when she was in hospital, pregnant, and suffering from typhoid. Many had assumed that Minton would leave his house to Norman Bowler, whom he loved, but he left it to Henrietta.

During her marriage to Norman Bowler she took a job with David Archer, the unpractical patron of literary talents. He had just opened a new bookshop, in Greek Street, and Henrietta worked at the coffee bar inside the shop, making egg and watercress rolls.

"All David Archer really wanted," she recalled, "was a sort of *salon*. Strangers would come in off the street, and he would not *want* them to buy a book. He'd say: 'Hey, don't ask me. I mean, there's a very good bookshop up the road called Foyle's, go there.'"

One of the writers that David Archer tried to help was Dom Moraes. He was a smooth-tongued Indian, a great young hope of Commonwealth poetry who later won the Hawthornden Prize. Henrietta was later to refer to him ambiguously as "that 24-hour poet".

His first volume of poetry, *A Beginning*, was dedicated to her. Quite soon, in 1961, she married him.
Dom Moraes spent three years at Oxford, which Henrietta enjoyed; she made new friends such as Peter Levi,
the poet. But settled back in London, Dom Moraes
went out one day to buy some cigarettes and never
returned.

About this time, Francis Bacon was painting her. He
explained that he would like to paint her from photographs. These were supplied by John Deakin, an impossible friend of Archer's who managed to get sacked as a
photographer by *Vogue* twice. He took a fine series of
images of Henrietta Moraes lying naked on a bed, which
Bacon used. But she was surprised to find that Deakin
was soon offering spare prints for sale to sailors at 10
shillings each.

In the 1960s, as well as drinking hugely, Henrietta
Moraes used drugs more and more. One of Bacon's
paintings of her shows a naked body with a syringe stuck
in one arm. Along with the usual pills, she eventually
took to LSD. Her life became increasingly ramshackle;
the spell of Soho was broken.

Henrietta Moraes was born Audrey Wendy Abbott
in Simla on May 22 1931. Her father, whom she never
knew, was an Indian Air Force officer nicknamed Ginger.
When she was 18 months old her mother returned to
England to work as a nurse; at three Audrey was sent to
board at a convent.

She remembered her childhood as cruelly unhappy.
Her largely absent mother she called "Mummy Judy".
When she was sick over her bed in the school dormitory
she ate up every bit again lest she be detected. When
staying with her grandmother at Bedford, taking dull

walks beside the flooded Ouse, she would hear how her father was an "absolute monster, a really wicked man".

She was shuttled from grandmother (who, she said, beat her with a strap) to schools. Always on the edge of expulsion, she eventually left to take a secretarial course in London, and her life in Soho began.

After the end of her marriage to Dom Moraes, drugs and drink drove her to burglary; she failed and went to prison. Once out she drifted away from Soho, and for four years travelled Britain in a gipsy caravan. She had friends with country houses, many of whom, like her, were captivated by drugs.

She drifted ever westward, via Hay-on-Wye and a job in a bookshop to Ireland. By the end of the 1980s she was back in London, poor and sick from drink. She found a way out of the vicious cycle of drink through Alcoholics Anonymous.

At the end of her life, living in a room in Chelsea with her dachshund, Max, she sat for Maggi Hambling, who became a friend.

Christopher Gibbs writes: Brave, chaotic, heroically self-indulgent, wild yet cosy, Henrietta Moraes, will be mourned by a wide band of friends, whom she terrorised and enchanted over the years.

She made a bridge between the raffish twilight of Muriel Belcher's Colony Room Club with its cynical, hard drinkers, to the hip parade of young Chelsea chancers and their exodus to the hills of the West in the late Sixties.

She was blessed with zest for new experience, thirst for ecstasy and oblivion, a bold eye for a promising encounter (disregarding sex or age), and uncanny antennae for alcohol or drugs that might, unbeknown to her hosts, be lurking in some unlikely corner. Wolf those pills, drain that glass – or jug. She was ever a stranger to moderation.

Transformed by Michael Law's decree into Henrietta, creature of carnival, the tawny voluptuous beauty, she sprawls, legs apart, across the canvases of Francis Bacon.

After Dom Moraes left her for another woman, Henrietta would, after the pubs closed, shy milk bottles at their Chelsea houseboat before moving on to wake a few friends and kill the night.

The gentler, more lyrical atmosphere of the Acid years in the Sixties changed her life. She felt an instant harmony with the new friends she made and soon left London, riding off with Mark Palmer and his rainbow cavalcade, threading the green lanes that led to the wilderness.

Older than most of them (in Soho she had been the younger one), licensed to frolic after years on the road, she found in the Welsh Marches a tiny cottage, The Den, hidden and forgotten, and moved in with her dog, Leaf, and an occasional lover, emerging like a great ripe tomboy to liven the pub.

Friendship with Penny Guinness, forged on the road, led her to Ireland and efforts to live alone. For a year she acted as guardian for the Irish Georgian Society of lonely Roundwood, but her vigour was beginning to succumb to excess and eventually she returned to a council flat in Chelsea, given touches of glamour by her friend David Mlinaric.

She became a jobbing gardener, and could be seen astride her bicycle, festooned with the implements of her calling, dog at wheel, weaving through the traffic.

Francis Wyndham, her old friend and a constant

midwife to good writing, spurred her to a book of memoirs, which after long agonies appeared in 1994. *Henrietta* chronicled her adventures with warmth and generosity – her sharp wit was never unkind.

Her last attachment, to Maggi Hambling, was a fresh outpouring of passion and tenderness, exasperating, delighting, uplifting and completing.

January 9 1999

PHILIP MASON

PHILIP MASON, who has died aged 92, was one of the last of the great figures of the British Raj; his book *The Men Who Ruled India*, which he wrote after an adventurous career in the Indian Civil Service, evokes comparison with Kipling.

It was under the pen-name Philip Woodruff that Mason first published *The Men Who Ruled India*, in two volumes, *The Founders* (1953) and *The Guardians* (1954). As a history of the Raj seen through the lives of the men who ruled India, the book is an undoubted classic of British-Indian literature.

Mason tells of the bad men as well as the good. Thus Frederick Cooper, who unnecessarily caused the death of 282 mutineers who had surrendered to him, is depicted, as well as men like Charles Metcalfe, who abolished slavery in Delhi 50 years before it was abolished in America, and Bartle Frere, who made Bombay into a healthier city than London.

The book is full of brilliant impressionistic portraits of the men themselves; for example, that of Malcolm

Hailey, who once told a junior colleague: "You will have a trying day tomorrow. You will be on the alert all day and will probably have a riot. But I have discussed all your arrangements and I approve of them. One embarrassment at least you shall be spared: I am going fishing."

Mason is as good at describing the installation of a Governor as at recounting the simple outdoor life of the District Officer: "The smell of canvas and smoky fires was in your nostrils, a horse between your knees on a dewy morning, or walking home in the darkness through the wafts of rich scent that eddy slowly round the village".

Better, perhaps, than any other writer on British India, Mason makes one realise what an adventure it all was.

Philip Mason was born at Finchley, north London, on March 19 1906 and grew up in Duffield, near Derby, where his father, a country doctor, had his practice. His forebears had for many generations farmed in Rutland.

Philip was sent to Sedbergh, under W. N. Weech, who considered that young Mason's "zestful admiration" of Kipling "made up for shortcomings in Greek prose and algebra". From Sedbergh, he went up to Balliol, where he was taken under the wing of the celebrated "Sligger" Urquhart.

His numerous Oxford activities, including a tour with the Balliol Players which brought him into contact with the aged Thomas Hardy, did not prevent him taking a First (in PPE) – obligatory for entering the Indian Civil Service.

Mason's first posting, in 1928, was to Saharanpur, in the United Provinces. He later confessed to having been occasionally fooled into paying out bounty on "wolves", which were really hyenas stuffed inside old wolf skins. In 1930 he became Sub-Divisional Officer at Bareilly, after which he was moved to Lucknow, where he discharged various duties and was for a time City Magistrate.

In 1933 he was appointed to the Government of India as Under-Secretary in what was then known as the Army Department, in Delhi. There he met Mary Hayes, who had come out to India for the winter to stay with her uncle General Twiss, the then Military Secretary. They were married in 1935.

The next year, Mason, aged 30, returned to the United Provinces as Deputy Commissioner of Garhwal. This seemed to him to be "the best job in India". He was in charge of a mountain district in which his headquarters was three days' journey from the nearest railway terminus.

The outlying villages were anything up to 18 days' march from his headquarters. Nine months of the year were spent travelling, preceded by his official elephant, whose *mahout* doubled as the local burglar; but Mason and his bride liked walking among mountains better than anything else. "They are like two children, laughing and playing" was how the new Deputy Commissioner and his *memsahib* appeared to the Garhwalis.

Like all the best District Officers before him, Mason managed to be "the father and mother of his people"; he also managed to be on good terms with the Congress ministry which took office in the United Provinces in 1937, something that was not required of his predecessors.

The Second World War put an end to his time in Garhwal and brought him back to Delhi and Simla as

Deputy-Secretary to the Government of India in the newly established Defence Co-Ordination Department.

On Christmas Day 1941, however, Mason lost an eye when he was accidentally shot full in the face while out hunting jungle cock. The injury meant that, despite recovering well, he was less able to cope with heavy paperwork. In 1942 he moved jobs to become Secretary to the Chief of Staffs Committee, India, working closely with Field Marshal Wavell, who won his lasting affection.

Mason accompanied Wavell when, in 1943, he went to London and then on to Washington with Churchill; and it was while they were aboard the *Queen Mary* that Churchill had the idea of setting up a Supreme Allied Command for South-East Asia. Mason and Commodore (later Admiral Sir Ralph) Edwards worked out the original plan for the new structure of command.

When Mountbatten arrived in India as Supreme Allied Commander, Mason joined his staff as Head of the Conference Secretariat and eventually moved with him to Ceylon. He returned to Delhi in the late summer of 1944, as Joint-Secretary to the Government of India in the Defence Department. In 1946, he represented the Defence Department in the Central Legislative Assembly.

In Independence year, 1947, Mason saw something of the old Princely India as Tutor and Governor to the grandsons of the Nizam of Hyderabad. He might have stayed longer in Hyderabad, but, as he afterwards wrote, "I believed it was time for the British to go, time for India to settle her own affairs."

He and his wife were anxious to make a home for themselves and their children in England, and he wished to concentrate on his new career as a writer. His first novel, *Call the Next Witness*, had been accepted by Jonathan Cape just as he was about to leave with Churchill for Washington.

From 1945 to 1962 he was to bring out a book almost every year, both novels and non-fiction, written at first under the pen-name of Philip Woodruff, later under his real name.

From 1952 to 1958, Mason was also Director of Studies in Race Relations at Chatham House. He was a member of the Committee of Enquiry to examine the problems of minorities in Nigeria in 1957, and the next year was appointed Director of the Institute of Race Relations, a post which he held until 1969. A report that he wrote the following year, which advocated support for Southern African guerrillas, shocked many members of the report's sponsor, the British Council of Churches.

He was chairman of the National Committee for Commonwealth Immigrants in 1964–65, and was on the Executive Committee of the United Kingdom Council for Overseas Student Affairs from 1969 to 1975.

After his retirement from the Institute of Race Relations, Mason concentrated again on his writing. His later books include *A Matter of Honour* (1974), a much-applauded history of the Indian Army; a biography, *Kipling: The Glass, the Shadow and the Fire* (1975); *Skinner of Skinner's Horse* (1979) and *The English Gentleman* (1982).

He also wrote a delightful autobiography, *A Shaft of Sunlight* (1978), and in 1985 produced a condensed version of *The Men Who Ruled India*. While the latter has the advantage of combining *The Founders* and *The Guardians* in a single volume, the abridgement necessitated the removal of many good things which someone less modest would have insisted on retaining.

He was appointed OBE in 1942, and CIE in 1946. He was an honorary Fellow of the School of Oriental and African Studies.

He is survived by his wife, and by two sons and two daughters.

January 29 1999

LIEUTENANT-COLONEL THE LORD DUNSANY

LIEUTENANT-COLONEL THE 19TH LORD DUNSANY, who has died aged 92, was memorable on many counts. He was an Irish peer of ancient lineage, one of the last surviving grandees of Ascendancy Ireland. He was a veteran of the Raj, a lieutenant-colonel in the Guides, that *corps d'élite* of the Indian Cavalry, and he had a good war. What was less usual in a son of the Ascendancy who served the Raj, he was also completely at home in sophisticated cosmopolitan society.

Lord Dunsany's sporting prowess was matched by his connoisseurship. He did much to beautify Dunsany Castle in Co Meath, a medieval stronghold with a ravishing Georgian interior, where he and Lady Dunsany lived and entertained in a manner reminiscent of more spacious days.

In his appearance, his dress and his speech, Randal Dunsany was very much a Cavalryman of the old school; but behind this exterior lay an intellect as powerful as it was unconventional. He could hold his own in any company; he could surprise and often shock with his ideas and his dry and devastating wit.

Randal Arthur Henry Plunkett, 19th Baron of Dunsany and also Baron of Killeen (his are the only two surviving Baronies in the Peerage to be styled "of"), was born on August 25 1906 into a dynasty which was in Ireland before Norman times – being of Danish origin, though it is typical of the medieval "Old English" aristocracy of the Pale.

He was the only son of the poet and playwright Lord Dunsany (a famously eccentric bearded figure who was also a sculptor, a champion chess-player and big game hunter) by Lady Beatrice Child-Villiers, daughter of the 7th Earl of Jersey. Sir Horace Plunkett, the agricultural reformer and founder of the co-operative movement in Ireland, was his great-uncle; his maternal grandmother, Margaret, Lady Jersey, was a celebrated Victorian and Edwardian *grande-dame* whose grandchildren also included the present Earl of Longford and his siblings.

One of the latter, Lady Violet Powell, recalls how, while Lady Jersey would dress with eight grandchildren squabbling on the floor of her bedroom (a display of grandmotherly affection that impressed even the motherly Queen Alexandra), she banned the young Randal Plunkett from this "morning *levée*" on account of his wildness.

Randal Plunkett was educated at Eton (where he whipped-in to the beagles) and then joined the 16th/5th Lancers (Supplementary Reserve). Two years later he decided to transfer to the Guides. He attributed this "pull to the Orient", as he called it, to the fact that his

Dunsany grandmother was a Burton, a cousin of Sir Richard Burton.

He saw active service on the North-West Frontier in 1930 and was awarded the Frontier Medal and clasp. He was on the Frontier after the outbreak of the Second World War, and in the summer of 1941 commanded an armoured squadron above the Khojak Pass facing the might of Russia – which then, as during the past century or more, was regarded as the chief potential enemy of British India.

When he heard on the wireless that Hitler's invasion had turned Russia into Britain's ally, he felt that he was at the very watershed of history. He dashed off some Kiplingesque verses which began: "*I was sitting above the Khojak/ Watching the Afghan plain . . .*"

Later that year and in the early months of 1942, he led a reconnaissance expedition into Azerbaijan and elsewhere in Central Asia to ascertain ways of stopping the Germans from invading southwards. He also succeeded in getting a consignment of American trucks to the Russians.

This caused him to claim that he had added a third to Russia's proverbial Generals, General January and General February, namely General Motors. His time in Central Asia was followed by service in the Western Desert, where he took part in a manoeuvre aimed at deceiving Rommel and saw action at El Alamein.

Plunkett retired from the Army at the end of the Raj in 1947 and went to farm at Dunsany, which had been handed over to him by his father, whom he succeeded as Lord Dunsany in 1957. He ran a considerable cattle enterprise in Co Meath.

In 1984, on the death of his cousin, the 12th and

last Earl of Fingall, head of the now extinct senior branch of the Plunketts, he inherited the ancient Barony of Killeen – his 15th-century ancestor, the 1st Baron of Dunsany, having been the second son of the 1st Baron of Killeen. But he continued to use the title of Dunsany on its own.

Until 1953, the Fingalls had lived at Killeen Castle, the demesne of which marches with that of Dunsany; contrary to what is so often the case with kinsmen who are close neighbours, the two families of Plunkett were always the best of friends.

The fact that the Dunsanys had conformed to the Established Church in the 18th century, while the Fingalls had always remained Roman Catholic, made no difference to their friendship: and the Dunsanys did what they could to help their Catholic kinsmen during the years when Catholics suffered disabilities. It was the Dunsanys rather than the Fingalls who possessed the archiepiscopal ring of Saint Oliver Plunkett, the martyred 17th-century Catholic Archbishop of Armagh who came of yet another branch of the family.

Randal Dunsany treasured this relic and if people who were seriously ill asked for it, he would take it to them. He was extremely proud of having a kinsman who was a Saint; he and Lady Dunsany went to Rome for Saint Oliver's canonisation and added to the celebrations by giving a party at the Caccia Club.

Up to the end of his life, Dunsany took a keen interest in what was happening all over the world, and his comments on international affairs were always worth hearing.

During the Falklands War, after General Galtieri had flown to the Falklands to tell his troops there to fight to the last drop of blood, and then withdraw to the safety of the mainland, Dunsany observed laconically in a letter to the *Irish Times* that this kind of order was unpopular and not usually obeyed.

He was Irish Grand Bailiff of the Order of St Lazarus, the leprosy charity. In his younger days he was a crack polo player, and he retained his enthusiasm for shooting well into his eighties. "The Plunketts", he said, "tend to inherit a talent for shooting and chess."

He married first, in 1938, Vera, formerly wife of Ivar Bryce and daughter of Dr Genesio de Sà Sottomaior, of Sao Paulo, Brazil. This marriage was dissolved in 1947 and in the same year he married secondly Sheila, widow of Major John Frederick Foley, Baron de Rutzen, Welsh Guards, and daughter of Sir Henry Erasmus Edward Philipps, 2nd Bt, who survives him with a son of the first marriage and a daughter of the second.

The son, Edward John Carlos Plunkett, born in 1939, succeeds to the peerages.

A widely travelled man, the late Lord Dunsany used to say: "I have ridden a yak in the snows of Central Asia at two miles an hour and flown in Concorde at 1,400 miles an hour."

February 9 1999

KENNETH DE COURCY

KENNETH DE COURCY, *soi disant* Duc de Grantmesnil and a convicted fraud, who has died aged 89, led a life as rich in vicissitude as in the fantasies which sustained him.

In the 1930s, de Courcy was a confidant of Cabinet Ministers and a dining companion of the Duke of Windsor. By the 1960s he was an intimate only of the spy George Blake, with whom he was sharing a table in Wormwood Scrubs.

A champion snob and an accomplished networker, in 1934 the pushy young de Courcy became secretary to the Right-wing Imperial Policy Group, which favoured appeasement as the best means of preserving the Empire. In this capacity he travelled the Continent in the years before Munich, being received by Mussolini and Eduard Benes, president of Czechoslovakia.

Neville Chamberlain regularly asked for de Courcy's reports of these interviews, much to the annoyance of the Foreign Office. In fact, the meetings produced little of value, but they did provide de Courcy with useful contacts – what he called "a spy in every embassy".

Too public-spirited to keep his knowledge of foreign affairs to himself, in 1938 de Courcy began to write and publish *Intelligence Digest*, a private subscription newsletter that served as a platform for his well-informed, if defeatist, analysis of the drift to war. "Mr de Courcy is often right," wrote one civil servant, "but he is a bad influence."

The publication enhanced de Courcy's stock in Downing Street; and his ability to obtain the ear of Chamberlain was increased when William Douglas-Home, the playwright and brother of Lord Dunglass, the Prime Minister's Parliamentary Private Secretary, became his assistant. The high point of de Courcy's brief stay in the back-room of politics came, he would later claim, in June 1940.

With the war going badly, de Courcy concluded that

it would be best for Britain to come to a speedy accommodation with Hitler. The Germans should be offered an armistice and threatened with American intervention if they did not accept. De Courcy alleged that he was asked by R. A. Butler, the Under-Secretary of State at the Foreign Office, to sound out Joseph Kennedy, the American Ambassador in London.

Kennedy liked the proposal, but the scheme was scuppered when Churchill discovered it and threatened, as Butler's PPS "Chips" Channon explained to de Courcy, "to lock up Halifax [the Foreign Secretary], my master and you under 18B [the wartime power of detention]." Butler, perhaps unsurprisingly, had a rather different recollection of the episode.

After the war, de Courcy continued for 30 years to publish *Intelligence Digest* and another periodical, *The Weekly Review*; together, he thought, they afforded "the most vital intellectual defence of the Western world". Their theories of global conspiracy and their firm scrutiny of "The Red Menace" brought de Courcy more than 100,000 readers, most of them in America.

As their subscriptions enriched him, he began to slip into a life of fantasy. He bought a flat in the Empire State Building, had his Rolls-Royce waterproofed for underwater driving, and hired a chauffeur who came complete with a certificate from Lord Mountbatten testifying to his bravery as a Commando.

Now a public figure, de Courcy corresponded with Billy Graham and played generous host to ministers such as Duncan Sandys and Quintin Hogg, as well as to ambassadors and foreign royalty.

Such exalted company flattered de Courcy's vanity; he was at his most content when pontificating at the head of his dining table in Belgravia. Later, he converted the dining room into a chapel and invited in passers-by to pray for "the future of Britain". He led the prayers himself.

This happy state of affairs began to go awry in the early 1960s, when de Courcy's scheme to build a garden city in Rhodesia failed and he was unable to return some £1 million put up by investors. He resorted to fraud and forgery and, though he had made no personal gain, in 1963 he was sentenced to seven years in jail.

A year later, he absconded while visiting his solicitor in Lincoln's Inn to discuss his appeal – he went in through the front door and subsequently escaped from the back of the building. A nationwide hunt ensued, and two days later he was arrested in bed in a hotel at Fareham.

The police had been tipped off by a friend whose help he had sought. The manager of the hotel confessed that his suspicions had been aroused when de Courcy refused ever to take off his sunglasses, despite having difficulty picking the bones out of his poached salmon at dinner.

In prison, de Courcy came to know the Soviet spy George Blake. Blake, in his memoirs, thanked his former cell-mate for not alerting the authorities to his escape plans. For his part, de Courcy remembered how Blake used to practise being dead. "He would lie on the bed with a bandage over his eyes and say 'I'm being dead.' He said it was like black velvet."

Kenneth Hugh de Courcy was born at Oldham, Lancashire, on November 6 1909. His father, a clergyman from Co Galway, founded an evangelising mission which gave magic lantern shows of the Holy Land and was killed while Kenneth was young – when his projector exploded during a Boxing Day show.

The de Courcys liked to believe they were kinsmen of Lord Kingsale, the holder of an Irish Barony dating back to medieval times. After the Second World War, Kenneth de Courcy succeeded in foisting a fictitious pedigree on to the editor of *Burke's Peerage* who obligingly printed it as a cadet branch of the Kingsale genealogy. This was duly removed in subsequent editions.

Kenneth's mother was of Belgian and German descent; her father, she liked to claim, was the genius behind Schafer's unspillable ink-wells, once a feature of every High Street bank. Kenneth de Courcy believed that one of his maternal ancestors had descended from the last Duc de Grantmesnil, a French title extinguished in the Middle Ages.

In later life, de Courcy would style himself Duc de Grantmesnil. No one came forward to dispute his right to the title; equally straightforward was its omission from the *Almanach de Gotha*.

Young Kenneth was educated at King's College School, Wimbledon – he took care to leave out the "Wimbledon" in *Who's Who* – and thereafter, "by travelling abroad". His limited education, however, proved no bar to his social ambitions.

In 1927 he joined the 3rd City of London Regiment, a Territorial force; by 1930 he had procured a transfer to the Coldstream Guards. Meanwhile, he had begun to make money by the simple expedient of buying up village shops in the North and selling them on once he had obtained licences for them to operate more profitably as sub-post offices.

His new-found means, together with his interest in politics, soon brought him to the fringes of the all too gullible Establishment.

After he was released from prison in 1969, de Courcy was reduced to living in a small cottage in Gloucestershire, where he made a nuisance of himself through his over-enthusiastic application of the rights that he believed accrued to him through various manorial titles he had purchased.

In old age de Courcy would crop up occasionally on television programmes, recalling his friendship with the Duke of Windsor. He also voiced his assertion that his conviction for fraud had been a plot by those who wished to silence him.

He continued to write newsletters, latterly drawing the world's attention to Islamic fundamentalism – "The Great Danger" – and produced several books, among them *The Great Marshal Philippe Pétain* (1995). He left a large collection of his private papers to Stanford University.

He married, in 1950 (dissolved 1973) Rosemary Baker; they had two sons and two daughters.

February 18 1999

LADY PANSY LAMB

LADY PANSY LAMB, who has died aged 94, was the sister of the Earl of Longford and the widow of the artist Henry Lamb; she was also witness to the disaster of Evelyn Waugh's first marriage to Evelyn Gardner.

Lady Pansy had moved into a flat with Evelyn Gardner in Ebury Street, Belgravia, in 1927. Such an arrangement was considered quite daringly independent at the time, but Evelyn Gardner had been engaged to a number of unsuitable men, and her mother hoped that Pansy Pakenham would be a steadying influence.

Within a year, however, both girls were married: Pansy to a divorced artist more than twice her age; Evelyn Gardner to Evelyn Waugh. The agony of "He-Evelyn's" and "She-Evelyn's" short-lived marriage is well attested in the number of brittle relationships and desertions described in Waugh's books. Pansy Lamb, who always remained friendly with Waugh, later admitted to feeling slightly guilty that she had encouraged the match.

She had first met Evelyn Gardner when they were debutantes in 1922. Her year, Lady Pansy considered, were "rather a dim lot". "The only glamorous deb was Daphne Bath [then Daphne Vivian] because her mother had run off with someone and she had a stepmother."

All the intelligent young men, Lady Pansy thought, had interesting jobs to go to, whereas the ones who spent their time with the debs were "all rather drab". As girls of her class were not expected to work, she "thought life boring".

Being by nature self-sufficient, she took a job in the office of the architect George Kennedy, through whom she met Henry Lamb, at that time leading a reclusive life in Dorset. In a letter to the artist Dora Carrington he described Pansy Pakenham as a "charming beau monde blonde".

When Pansy Pakenham and Evelyn Gardner both became engaged, they left another flat in Sloane Square and lodged in a boarding house at Wimborne, Dorset, while their respective unofficial fiancés set about arranging their marriages.

Although Lamb had not lived with his wife Euphemia for more than 20 years, he had not obtained a divorce from her, so this had to be accomplished. Evelyn Waugh, meanwhile, moved into a nearby inn, where he wrote much of *Decline and Fall*. Pansy Pakenham also embarked on her first novel, *The Old Expedient*.

When she met Lamb's Bloomsbury friends, she found them "rather gauche", and thought that they "didn't have very nice manners" – though she would always be friends with Frances Partridge.

Lamb, for his part, had an intimidating encounter with his future mother-in-law. According to Anthony Powell, "Lady Longford drew Lamb behind a pillar. 'I have to be father and mother both,' she said. 'It *is* a clean sheet, Mr Lamb?'" For the rest of his life Lamb would wonder what on earth she meant. Nevertheless, he married Pansy Pakenham in 1928.

Lady Margaret Pansy Felicia Pakenham was born on May 18 1904, the second child and eldest daughter of the 5th Earl of Longford; her mother was a daughter of the 7th Earl of Jersey.

Pansy Pakenham's father was killed in action in 1915, and succeeded in the earldom by his eldest son, Edward; he in turn was succeeded after his death in 1961 by Frank, who was born the year after Pansy. Violet, the second of Pansy's three sisters, married the novelist Anthony Powell in 1934.

The Longfords lived at Aston Hall, Oxfordshire, and spent their summers (and the occasional Easter) in Ireland, at Pakenham Hall (now Tullynally), Co Westmeath. Pansy Pakenham retained deeply romantic feelings for the Irish house, which she continued to visit every year, even after moving to Italy in 1981.

Her childhood was spent in the sort of environment in which all laundry from Aston was sent over to Ireland to be washed; and her education was the sheltered and haphazard affair to which girls of her class were then subjected. This now almost surrealistically remote atmosphere was splendidly evoked by her sister Mary Clive in *Brought Up and Brought Out* (1938).

Once, the girls found themselves in a room in Burlington House, Piccadilly, where women were spinning clippings from pet dogs into woollies for the troops in the trenches. "Don't you like this heather mixture?" said one spinning matron. "It's my latest invention – a mixture of red and black chow."

After a series of governesses, Pansy Pakenham was sent for one disastrous term to a domestic economy school. Later in life she instructed her daughters not to bother about cleaning "like a great German Hausfrau"; while "dinner before dust" became one of her mottoes.

Once out of the schoolroom, Pansy Pakenham was allowed to walk around Mayfair and Belgravia by herself – although she was obliged to have a chaperone when she wanted to pass from one district to the other.

After their marriage, she and Henry Lamb lived at Coombe Bissett in Wiltshire, where they remained until Lamb's death in 1960. John Betjeman captured the scene in 1932:

> *Oh, the calm of Coombe Bissett is tranquil and deep*
> *Where Ebble flows soft in her downland asleep*
> *And beauty to me came a-pushing a pram*
> *In the shape of the sweet Pansy Felicia Lamb.*

Other members of the Lambs' circle included Cecil Beaton, Lord David Cecil, Kenneth Clark, L. P. Hartley and Bryan Guinness and his wife Diana (later to be married to Sir Oswald Mosley).

> *I too could be arty, I too could get on*
> *With the Guinnesses, Gertler and Sickert and John*

wrote Betjeman, casting himself in the role of a lovelorn youth at the Lambs' gate.

Sometimes, though, Pansy Lamb may have felt rather isolated at Coombe Bissett, particularly during the Second World War when Lamb (who had kept a studio in London) was an official war artist. She continued to read avidly – and also to write. Her second novel, *August*, was published in 1931, and in 1936 she contributed a biography of Charles I to Duckworth's *Great Lives* series.

During the Second World War, Henry Lamb introduced her to one of his sitters, a Free Frenchman, who had built his own aeroplane in the woods. Thereafter the cause of the Free French appealed strongly to Pansy Lamb, and she organised an exhibition of paintings from Wiltshire houses to help raise money for them.

General de Gaulle became her hero, and she always listened enthusiastically to his broadcasts. Although practical and somewhat unsentimental, she was also an idealist; during the Hungarian uprising of 1956 she did not hesitate to give her exceptionally beautiful best coat to the cause.

After Henry Lamb's death, she moved to London, and lived for 20 years in Notting Hill. Here she helped in a club for the blind, and worked on the *Letters of Charles Dickens* for the Oxford University Press.

In 1981, aged 77, Pansy Lamb decided that Rome would be a more exciting place to live than London. Having been an Anglican all her life, she converted to

Catholicism with a minimum of outward fuss; it was merely, she said, a case of "When in Rome . . .".

Yet she had always, she explained, suspected that Roman Catholics held the stronger position. After all, she had been brought up to regard Protestants as "respectable but dull", Catholics as "dirty but amusing". At school, though, feelings had been more extreme: when the Pope died, Mary Clive recalled, everyone "burst out cheering".

In Rome, Pope John Paul II replaced de Gaulle as the object of Pansy Lamb's hero worship. Her meeting with him — arranged by Benjamin Fraser, the son of her niece Lady Antonia Fraser — was one of the proudest moments of her life.

On three afternoons a week, Pansy Lamb was a familiar sight at the gate of St Peter's, where she would sit on a bench with priests or nuns, ready to act as a voluntary guide for pilgrims to the See of St Peter. Although her eyesight was not good, and she had to wear what she called "special goggles" for reading, she would help to answer people's questions about the Vatican and occasionally show people around.

She considered her work at the Vatican "particularly useful for Americans who so often get lost, but all most people want to know is where the Sistine Chapel is, the roof and the lavatory."

Pansy Lamb seemed to be in a constant state of surprise that she had lived so long, but she managed to look after herself in a modest flat near the centre of Rome, where she cooked English food such as bread and butter pudding, continued to smoke (as she had all her life), and always carried herself very straight.

She and Henry Lamb had a son and two daughters.

Anthony Powell writes: Pansy Lamb was a slightly eccentric, totally unselfconscious figure. I remember, on one occasion, her standing on the beach at Brighton with practically nothing on.

I first really met her through Evelyn Gardner, as she was, and then had no idea that Pansy would become my sister-in-law. But here was an extremely attractive, pretty girl, who at the same time moved both in the social world and in an extremely bohemian one.

Her husband, Henry Lamb, was a remarkable painter, and through Lady Pansy he came to paint a portrait of me; it still hangs in our dining room.

February 20 1999

BOBBY CORBETT

BOBBY CORBETT, who has died aged 58, owes a place in the annals of our time to the great affection in which he was held. He was an Ayrshire institution, a formidable figure on the hunting field in the best 18th-century tradition, and a convivial presence at race meetings all over the kingdom.

As Master of the Eglinton, Corbett would, for want of a horse, travel to the meet on the bus; on arrival, dressed in an ancient red coat, he would alight briskly from the vehicle, leaving a somewhat awed group of passengers, and head straight for the local public house.

A special favourite of Queen Elizabeth The Queen Mother, Corbett developed and spoke in a rapid patois of his own. On more than one occasion, Queen Elizabeth was heard to say: "I adore Bobby, but I shall soon need a simultaneous translator."

His conversational style was based primarily on the staccato use of metaphor, never employing the word "like"; a huge flurry of driven pheasants would be "arrows at Agincourt"; a mildly rough sea would have "white ponies"; when asked for instructions as to the style of flowers to be arranged at the funeral of his friend David McEwen, his reply was "Gangsters".

Although he was frequently asked to put pen to paper, he was never anxious to write. His peculiar gift was for the placing of unusual and highly specialised information into relaxed and undidactic banter.

Part of the difficulty, and the fascination, for Corbett's friends was the speed of his intellect combined with the variety of his reading and a gift of total recall. He seemed an amalgam, improbable yet compelling, of a hard-drinking, hunting squire and the late Sir Isaiah Berlin. "Shape up, shape up," he would say to those trailing behind his quick-fire conversation.

Corbett also had an almost unparalleled knowledge of grand country houses – their architecture, works of art and family history. This knowledge he put to full use as a member, from its inception to his death, of the Curatorial Committee of the National Trust for Scotland. He was also a member of the Trust's Council.

His artistic flair was nowhere more evident than at Stair Castle, his home near Kilmarnock, which he restored. His eye for a painting was unequalled: he bought, for £100, a painting by David Hockney at the first show organised by the dealer John Kasmin. He could claim with some justice that he had put the painter

John Lavery on the map; and he bought his first painting, a Burne-Jones, when he was still a schoolboy, for 10s 6d ("Not so much a song as a *chirrup*").

Robert Cameron Corbett was born on November 29 1940 at Rowallan Castle, near Stewarton, the fifth and youngest son of the 2nd Lord Rowallan. His mother, Gwyn, was an amateur tennis champion and sister of the Liberal leader Jo Grimond.

Gwyn Rowallan's first child was born in 1919, her last in 1942; Bobby never knew one of his brothers, who was killed in the Second World War.

The family seat, Rowallan, at Kilmarnock in Ayrshire, had been built by Bobby's grandfather and designed by Robert Lorimer in the baronial style; its construction was funded by money made from self-raising flour. Bobby's father was a farmer and soldier; he also succeeded Lord Baden-Powell as Chief Scout of the British Commonwealth and Empire in 1945, and later served as Governor of Tasmania.

Bobby respected his father – but teased him mercilessly: "Wouldn't read the *News of the World*, if I were you, this morning Daddy – another naughty scout master."

The first ominous sign that Bobby might not follow precisely in his father's footsteps came when he was kicked out of the Cubs for catching fleas and swearing. But things looked up at Eton, where he was known for his prodigious reading and wide knowledge of the arts.

In 1959 he went up to Christ Church, Oxford, as an exhibitioner – a fact which, in his own words, "went to my head like rich, red wine". With panelled rooms in Peckwater Quad hung with his increasing collection of fine paintings bought for extraordinarily small sums, he embarked with determined anachronism on a Brideshead life.

Lavish entertaining and presents (typically, he made a gift of the best Burne-Jones to a much richer friend) created panic at his bankers, Drummonds. "Any further letters and I shall remove my overdraft," he cabled them.

He and a close friend at that time, Auberon Waugh, were sent down after a year, Waugh in a blaze of first-novel glory. Shortly afterwards, Corbett met the Queen Mother in formal circumstances. They made each other laugh and he asked her to a lunch at the Mirabelle. A long friendship began.

A year or two after his exit from Oxford "the awful moment came when my father thought it a good idea if I worked". He took a job, which lasted 11 months, with the firm of Jardine Matheson.

'Asked why he left, he said: "I was paid so little, I was drained by the end. My piggy bank, my pension book, the whole lot, absolutely stripped to the buff. Cheques were bouncing like confetti. It was also so boring; it was the only time in my life when I did nothing at all."

After that, there was no career to speak of. With the stubborn determination more often associated with very ambitious people, Corbett resolved simply to give pleasure to friends he loved.

He had no difficulty in finding outlets for his boundless energy. In 1975 he became Joint Master of the Eglinton, and he regularly supplemented his sport in Ayrshire with forays to the Quorn, the Beaufort, the Kilkenny and the neighbouring Dumfriesshire, as well as to the Lanark and Renfrew.

He never missed Ascot, where he regularly had a table in White's tent, or the National Hunt festival at Cheltenham, after which he hunted with the Exmoor and the Devon and Somerset. Spring and summer were filled with racing, invariably the Chelsea Flower Show (he was an authority on horticulture), hound shows and, occasionally, a holiday on the Continent.

He was a standing dish at Wimbledon, where once the pronouncedly hirsute armpits of a lady competitor struck him as "two bursts in a sofa". He also had an encyclopaedic knowledge of pop music.

Very good looking in youth, Bobby Corbett resembled a figure drawn by Gillray by the time of his death. A bachelor, he was cared for by his devoted sister Fiona Patterson, the youngest of the Rowallan children.

When his brother, Lord Rowallan, announced his intention to marry the transexual April Ashley, Bobby Corbett's response was, "May I be a bridesmaid?"

March 9 1999

INDEX